Boats Against the Current

American

Culture

Between

LEWIS PERRY

Boats Against the Current

Revolution

and Modernity,

1820–1860

New York   Oxford
OXFORD UNIVERSITY PRESS
1993

Oxford University Press

Oxford   New York   Toronto
Delhi   Bombay   Calcutta   Madras   Karachi
Kuala Lumpur   Singapore   Hong Kong   Tokyo
Nairobi   Dar es Salaam   Cape Town
Melbourne   Auckland   Madrid

and associated companies in
Berlin   Ibadan

Library of Congress Cataloging-in-Publication Data
Perry Lewis, 1938–
Boats against the current : American culture between revolution
and modernity, 1820–1860 / Lewis Perry.
p. cm.   Includes index.
ISBN 0-19-506091-1
1. United States—Civilization—1783–1865.   I. Title.
E165.P47   1993
973.5—dc20   92-11094

Epigraph to Prologue from *Democracy in America* by Alexis de Tocqueville, edited by J. P. Mayer and Max Lerner, translated by George
Lawrence. Reprinted by permission of HarperCollins Publishers.

Epigraph to Part One from "Founding Fathers, Early-Nineteenth-Century
Style, Southeast U.S.A.," by Robert Penn Warren, © 1957, *New and
Selected Poems, 1923–1985* (New York, 1985). Reprinted by permission
of Random House, Inc.

Epigraph to Part Three from *Invisible Cities*, by Italo Calvino, translated
by William Weaver (Harcourt Brace Jovanovich, 1978).

Quotation from "Anecdote of the Jar" from *Collected Poems* by Wallace
Stevens, copyright 1923 and renewed 1951 by Wallace Stevens. Reprinted by permission of the publisher.

9 8 7 6 5 4 3 2 1

Printed in the United States of America
on acid-free paper

For David Brion Davis

So we beat on, boats against the current, borne back ceaselessly into the past.

—FITZGERALD, The Great Gatsby

Acknowledgments

I cannot hope to thank all the scholars whose works have guided or influenced me, though I have tried to mention most of them at appropriate places in the notes. But I am humbled at the thought of the many excellent explorers who have preceded me at every step of this journey and those who are currently blazing trails for the rest of us to follow.

I would like to acknowledge my good fortune in the friends and teachers who have guided me, though here, too, I cannot mention all by name. I must begin by referring to a circle of high school friends in the mid-1950s who read and discussed Sartre and Kafka, Fitzgerald and Camus, passionately and earnestly. Not only were they my first companions on a journey that continues in this book, but thanks to these friends, I can never say with one prominent historian, writing at just about that time, that "I have never read the work of a single existentialist." Heartfelt thanks gʳ to Edwin Sauer, our honors English teacher, who introduced us to a vast body of great modern literature—"The Waste Land," *The Brothers Karamazov*, "Disorder and Early Sorrow"—and to new critical methods that disclosed organic unities and recurrent symbols that a year or two earlier we all would have missed. Dr. Sauer read beautifully: he read to us from *The Crack-up* and gave us "Villonaud for This Yule" as a Christmas present and the closing pages of "The Dead" at the first snowstorm of 1955. He was severe in grading critical essays, friendly in encouraging exercises in creative writing that I would be too inhibited to attempt today. He took a classmate and me to Kenyon

College to meet John Crowe Ransom (who talked, not about poetry, but about the Nashville agrarians). Dr. Sauer gave us all a sense, now rather quaint I suppose, that an intellectual must be, among other things, a writer. He also, with humor and without embarrassment, gave us usable ideas for making sense of our predicament as young people growing up in the modern world. It was from him that I first heard Justice Holmes's aphorism that life consisted of action and passion; that we must take part in the action and passion of our times or else be judged not to have lived at all. It is sometimes said today that only teachers who out of their own vast erudition lead students back beyond the wastes of modernity to the classical past can supply a sense of purpose in an exhausted culture. Maybe so, but I doubt it because my own experience was different. I am grateful to Dr. Sauer.

At Oberlin College I was influenced by many good teachers, including Stan McLaughlin, Thomas Whitaker, John Kneller, William Sellers, and Andrew Bongiorno, but I especially wish to thank Clyde Holbrook, who taught a course on modern religious thought. When I took it, I knew nothing about Holbrook and only in my later career did I discover that he was an authority on Jonathan Edwards, one from whom I might have learned much to my profit. But the course was exhilarating because it took up many of the writers—Kafka, Dostoevsky, Sartre, Camus—familiar from high school and gave them a new context. Weeks were spent on Kierkegaard and Nietzsche; there were at least sideways looks at Heidegger, the Niebuhrs, and many others. My term paper dealt with the theatricality of life as a vexing problem in the quest for commitment and authenticity in all of these writers (and I am sure I brought in Pirandello and other favorite writers on campus in that era). Fortunately, I no longer have the paper, which would surely make me wince with chagrin. But like a good teacher, Holbrook appreciated a student's trying to relate the assigned readings to his own search for identity, and he knew when to praise. "In the life-as-acting theme in Kierkegaard, Sartre, etc., you have grasped something that you should keep all your life," he said: or something like that. Sometimes teachers give assignments that take decades to fulfull.

As a graduate student at Cornell University, I learned much from Walter Simon (who sent me forth to write on the word *modern*), Maurice Neufeld, George Brooks, Paul Gates, and Walter LaFeber. Through sheer good luck, I met an exemplary teacher, David Brion Davis, who became my mentor and remains so to this day. I will not embarrass him with detailed praise. He is a great scholar and demanding teacher, and he was just the guide I needed as I tried to keep the intellectual fire alive, in a troubled time, while disciplining myself to the professional requirements of teaching and writing history in the academy. In those days of the mimeograph, he gave his students long reading lists on American culture, while urging us to read broadly in European philosophers and sociologists. Anyone who has admired the epilogue to *The Problem of Slavery in the Age of Revolution* on Toussaint, Napoleon, and Hegel may appreciate how important the criticism and encouragement of such a teacher were to a young man struggling to find his way from intellectual wandering to scholarly discipline. I dedicate this book to him.

In 1975–76 I was a fellow of the National Humanities Institute in New Haven, Connecticut. So many of the other fellows stimulated my thinking that I hate to single out any of them, but historians Tom Haskell, Kitty Sklar, and Gordon Wood taught me much about subjects that I discuss in these pages; while folklorist Henry Glassie, art historian David Huntington, and literary scholars Catharine Stimpson, Daniel Aaron, and Sacvan Bercovitch set up a crossfire of criticisms of the historians' conceptions of culture that made scholarship seem quite risky for a blessed while. As a follow-up to that experience I received a demonstration grant from the National Endowment for the Humanities to teach a new course at the State University of New York at Buffalo, one that "mixed" history, theatre, and sociology and explored the insight that forms of role-playing change both on stage and in society with major political and economic transformations such as occurred in the post-revolutionary United States. I am grateful to students and faculty colleagues who took part in that experience, which obviously was a step on the way toward this book.

At that time I conducted research in theatre collections of the Lincoln Center Library, the Firestone Library at Princeton University, the University of Pennsylvania Library, the Harvard College Library, and the Edwin Forrest Home, some of which finally sees the light of day in this book. I thank the librarians who gave me assistance at those libraries as well as others where research for this book was undertaken: the Indiana University libraries, the Jean and Alexander Heard Library at Vanderbilt University, the Sterling and Drama School libraries at Yale University, the Houghton and Widener libraries at Harvard University, the Bobst Library at New York University, the Rutgers University libraries, and the Library of Congress.

I am extremely grateful for foundation support, without which this book would have taken even longer to complete. I first saw the outline of this book during a year on fellowship from the John Simon Guggenheim Foundation, when I wrote a general account of intellectual life in America. The book was drafted in 1987 and 1988 when I held a fellowship from the National Endowment for the Humanities under its "American Civilization" initiative. My work has also benefited from a sabbatical and a series of research grants provided by Vanderbilt University in support of the Andrew Jackson Professorship. With one of these grants I was able to employ a dedicated and talented research assistant, Ted Vernon McAllister, at a crucial stage of revising the manuscript.

I have had excellent colleagues, too numerous to mention, who have helped me think through subjects discussed in these pages, at the State University of New York at Buffalo (some of their children now go to college with my son David), Indiana University, and especially at Vanderbilt University. I think of this book as my Andrew Jackson book, my Nashville opus, a modest intellectual repayment for the generous support I have received from Vanderbilt and in Nashville. The earliest draft of one chapter was tried out before colleagues at a seminar on reform and religion, convened by the late Roger Anstey, in Bellagio, Italy, in 1978. Revisions of some of the last chapters were done when I was a visiting professor at the University of Leeds in 1988–89. I have also been fortunate to have chances to present portions of the manuscript at other locations, and I am grateful for searching questions and encouraging comments received at the University of Connecticut– Storrs, Mary Baldwin College, the University of Tennessee–Chattanooga, the Kentucky-Tennessee American Studies Association, and the universities of Kent, East Anglia, Heidelberg, and Göttingen. I would also like to thank the *Gettysburg Review* for permission to include material that first appeared in that journal.

A number of scholars have taken time out from their own important work to read long drafts of portions of this book. Needless to say, they are not responsible for errors of fact or judgment that remain, but they made this a better book. My thanks go to Richard D. Brown, George Cotkin, Mary Kelley, David Lowenthal, Harold D. Moser, and three members of the staff of *The Papers of Andrew Jackson*—David Hoth, George Hoemann, and Mark Mastromarino.

My deepest thanks go to my family. My mother and father, Irene and Albert Perry, have given me love and taken interest in my work every step of the way. My parents-in-law, Irma and Mordecai Bauman, have embraced me in their *mespöke* and demonstrated repeatedly that American culture is vigorous outside academia. My children—Curtis (who argued with me about literature and popular culture in memorable late-night sessions), Susanna (who discussed these chapters and her assignments in honors English every weekday afternoon when she was a high school junior), and David (who cheerfully prodded, whenever my energy flagged, "How's your book going, Dad?")—have enriched my life throughout the years. Words are inadequate to express my appreciation to them and to Elisabeth Israels Perry, my colleague and partner, who has helped me professionally at every stage of this project. She has also helped me keep my eyes on the joys of the present as the past recedes and the stream of time flows on.

Contents

Boats Against the Current

PROLOGUE

Carried away by a rapid current, we obstinately keep
our eyes fixed on the bank, while the stream whirls us
backward—facing toward the abyss.

ALEXIS DE TOCQUEVILLE
Democracy in America

This book, written in Nashville, begins in Nashville. Begin in an airplane
during a storm in June 1935, when air travel is new. Some passengers turn in
to their berths, while others sit up nervously. They talk of the Bonus Army
and revolution: how will you disguise yourself, where will you hide, until it
blows over? The travelers we see are Hollywood people on their way back
from the East Coast. Cecelia Brady, a Bennington student, tells us the story
because she wants us to understand Hollywood—her father is a magnate "in
the picture business as another man might be in cotton or steel"—but she
isn't sure we want to know.

Figuring out who she is, two men, a writer named Wylie and a washed-up
producer named Schwartz, look up: "sidewise," she tells us, "that Hollywood look, that always seems thrown over one shoulder." A third man
brushes past, on his way to the cockpit, engaging briefly in "the kind of
pleasantry that goes on between the powers in Hollywood and their satel-
lites." One of the men has the look of someone who had been beaten up and
"can't even tell you about it." Later we learn that the man who passed down

the aisle is the movie kingpin Monroe Stahr, a man of power and decision, a man of destiny. Cecelia, who has a crush on him, reports that he had once flown on strong wings and looked on the kingdom of the earth, "with the kind of eyes that can stare straight into the sun." And he had just rebuffed Schwartz: "Whatever you're after, the answer is No." That is why Schwartz looked as though a truck had run him over.

The plane lands in Nashville, where the passengers are stuck until the storm blows over. Wylie gets a taxi to take Cecelia to the Hermitage, home of Andrew Jackson. Schwartz, in a state of depression, tags along. They pass isolated shacks, green trees, an occasional farmhouse. They pass a negro driving a few cows, and Wylie gives him a quarter. While Schwartz sleeps, Wylie makes an awkward pass at Cecelia and talks desultorily about what people say about college girls and about sex and power in Hollywood. They wind down a lane in the fragrant night and arrive near the "great grey hulk" of the Hermitage. They get out and sit down and lean against the pillars out in front. He gossips about Hollywood, stops himself—"this isn't anything to talk about on the steps of Andrew Jackson's house"—and rattles on about how hard it is to get anyone to pay attention to you.

Schwartz interrupts them. He has tripped over something lying on the ground and hurt his eye. "Just in time, Mr. Schwartz," says Wylie. "The tour is just starting. Home of Old Hickory—America's tenth [*sic*] president. The victor of New Orleans, opponent of the National Bank, and inventor of the Spoils System."

"There's a writer for you," says Schwartz. "Knows everything and at the same time he knows nothing." Cecelia didn't know Wylie's occupation, and her opinion of him falls when she finds out. Writers, in her experience, "aren't people exactly . . . they're a whole *lot* of people trying so hard to be one person." But Wylie chides Schwartz, "I'm a more practical man than you any day." Schwartz's composure disintegrates. It's time to return to the plane, but he's staying behind. He has made a decision.

"The Hermitage looked like a nice big white box, but a little lonely and vacated still after a hundred years." On the way back to the airport Cecelia keeps thinking of Schwartz. "Manny Schwartz and Andrew Jackson—it was hard to say them in the same sentence. It was doubtful if he knew who Andrew Jackson was as he wandered around, but perhaps he figured that if people had preserved his house Andrew Jackson must have been someone who was large and merciful, able to understand. At both ends of his life man needed nourishment: a breast—a shrine. Something to lay himself beside when no one wanted him further, and shoot a bullet into his head." Actually, it was not until she was back in California that she learned of Schwartz's suicide. He sent a note to Stahr. If the magnate he admired so much had turned against him, he must be no good.

Years later, Cecelia meets one of the plane's pilots and hears about Stahr's visit to the cockpit. Stahr gave this view of flying, of building a railroad, of doing anything: You get all the relevant information, but you still can't be certain what to do. "You can't test the best way—except by doing it. So you just do it." F. Scott Fitzgerald, who related this story in the prologue to his unfinished novel *The Last Tycoon*, had actually had a conversation with a man who said that in building a railroad you had to conceal any uncertainty: "the people under you mustn't ever know or guess that you're in any doubt, because they've all got to have something to look up to and they mustn't ever dream that you're in any doubt about any decision." Fitzgerald visualized Stahr as a "real individualist," increasingly out of place in the corporate world of the movie industry. In a world of fakery, where "Georgie Jessel talks about 'Lincoln's Gettysburg routine,' " the tycoon understood what people wanted. "There is no substitute for will. Sometimes you have to fake will when you don't feel it at all."[1]

The opening scene at the Hermitage, in which the Hollywood people fail to get inside "or even to see the place clearly," establishes a motif of the distance of the present from "the American ideals and tradition." So Edmund Wilson, who salvaged the novel and taught modern readers to admire it, summarized Fitzgerald's intentions.[2] Fitzgerald's characters live in a transformed, modern world, where authentic action is always a problem, and the saddest of them search futilely for a link with a past that will show them understanding and forgiveness.[3] The past hulks beyond recovery, wreathed in sorrow and illusion.

This book offers an interpretation of American culture in which Jackson's epoch will not seem distant or inaccessible. In that era, I believe, lie the origins of enduring tensions in what Americans hoped and believed about themselves and their society. We may detect in the epoch symbolized by the Hermitage much that remains familiar, including the worries that the past is out of reach, conviction is often a sham, and the noblest expressions of ideals are just routines. At one time I considered calling this period the "age of Jackson and Emerson," because Jackson so well epitomized the problem of a pastless, self-made identity, and Emerson so tenaciously analyzed problems of authenticity and self-knowledge. I resisted the temptation because I agree with today's prevailing wisdom that no one, let alone a couple of white men, ever actually stands for everything transpiring in an age. But these pages will pay heed to Jackson's example and Emerson's analyses, and the issue of what constitutes genuine achievement in a culture cut loose from tradition will receive recurrent attention.

The sense that America was being made anew, and not necessarily for the better, has quickened hopes and fears in many eras of our history. The prevalence of such feelings during Jackson's epoch has been shown in many good works of history. We know that after Jackson's victory at New Orleans in 1815 a new generation seemed to recognize that the nation was secure from foreign intervention and free to experiment with its own destiny. The surge of nationalism that briefly united American leaders in this "golden age," as John Quincy Adams described it, soon gave way to hateful charges and countercharges over responsibility for the Panic of 1819, the extension of slavery into Western territories, and the legitimacy of Adams's ascension to the presidency. Accusations that one's opponents were deceiving the public, acting out of "aristocratic" greed, and destroying liberty became rhetorical commonplaces. As political parties used such accusations to create loyalty in their segments of an electorate that rapidly opened to include almost all white men, old notions of disinterested public service seemed to vanish. George Washington, who once congratulated his countrymen that their national history had commenced in an age favorable to human endeavor, died before his century ended, but those of the Founding Fathers who survived into the new epoch appeared and sometimes felt incongruous. Historians have given us memorable portraits of James Monroe, in his old-fashioned pantaloons and white-topped boots, as the last of the Old Republicans, and of James Madison, crippled by rheumatism and struggling against the divisive politics of the 1830s, as the last of the Fathers. Thomas Jefferson and John Adams, former enemies reconciled in old age, inquired whether the nineteenth century was to be "a Contrast to the Eighteenth? Is it to extinguish all the Lights of its Predecessor?"[4] The thought that the virtues of the revolutionary patriarchs were sacrificed to the excesses of democracy has nagged at historical consciousness ever since.

Change always brings feelings of loss—so psychiatrists tell us—and we must face up to these feelings and move on. It may not be surprising, therefore, that our historical consciousness, while haunted by images of loss, for the most part glorifies the great democratic changes of Jackson's epoch. The extension of the franchise and the development of political parties, for example, may have struck some contemporaries as lamentable deviations from early republican virtue, but anyone who has ever tried to teach American history knows that it is generally impossible to get students to entertain the idea that these changes were anything but inevitable and laudable. This was the Age of Jackson, as a succession of historians have portrayed it, when ancient privilege was ripped away; the Age of Common Man, when those who had been shut out from power broke through traditional barriers; the Age of Reform, when every vestige of inequality was subjected to new criticism and tested by new experiments.[5]

Scholars have modified the details of these depictions of the age. In particular, we have learned that Jackson and his supporters opposed many of the reform movements and that many reformers, in turn, detested Jackson and were unenthusiastic about democracy.[6] No revisionist has claimed, however, that change was illusory or that old barriers did not fall (though perhaps new ones were erected in their place). An excellent recent survey of the period points to a "market revolution," facilitated by improvements in transportation but depending also on changes in attitudes and behavior, in which most familiar forms of authority disintegrated. Public leaders responded in many ways—with expressions of nostalgia or condemnations of conspiracy, with appeals to individual self-improvement or programs for guided economic growth—but the reality of change was undoubted.[7] Another outstanding survey speaks of a "revolution in choices" that overthrew traditional hierarchies in government, the economy, religion, and the family and confronted individuals with the prospect that they could aspire to be whatever they wanted.[8] However we conceptualize it, this revolution did not emancipate black slaves, at least not in the short run; nor did it enfranchise white women. It may have impeded sympathy for the poor, who now bore responsibility for their own failures. Nevertheless, this was an age of "egalitarianism," of "psychological equality," in which increasing numbers of people enjoyed the demise of ancient systems of rank and privilege.[9]

One simple way of describing the purpose of this book is to say that it links some key elements in American culture to the fluidity of society in Jackson's epoch. The first two parts explore the changing orientation of Americans toward the past and future: Part One (which foreshadows many themes that run throughout the book) by looking at Jackson's life and the visits of a number of others to Nashville in his time, Part Two by analyzing activities and pronouncements related to history. The third and fourth parts are both concerned with travel, but from contrasting points of view. Part Three seeks to uncover an emerging American attitude toward the endurance and progress of civilization amid all the restless change; to do so, it examines the reports of travelers, including the most famous, Alexis de Tocqueville; the equally acute Swedish writer, Fredrika Bremer; the most searching of all American travelers, Frederick Law Olmsted; and the most incisive critic of civilization's march, Henry David Thoreau. Part Four looks at the hucksering and theatricality that seemed to typify life on the road in a transforming America. I find particularly trenchant analyses of the transformation in writings of Nathaniel Hawthorne and Ralph Waldo Emerson. These reports on travel, whether they emphasize civilization or theatricality, illuminate the consequences of the Revolution. They also help us understand traits in intellectual life that we tend to think of as modern and to associate with experiences in later decades. In Part Five I make this interpretation explicit and look in depth at two figures, Henry Clarke Wright and Theodore Parker, in whose life stories we can most clearly see the transition from revolution to modernity.

A few words may be in order concerning my use of travel writings. Although I benefit from the availability of new editions of writings by Jackson, Tocqueville, Hawthorne, Emerson, and Olmsted, historical writings about the United States for over a century have relied on travelers' reports, and this reliance has been criticized in the cases of Henry Adams's *History of the United States* (1884–1889) and many of his successors. Some of the criticisms have more merit than others. The reports always are secondhand sources of information and often are unsympathetic to behavior they describe. I recognize that their depictions of American life are frequently exaggerated, distorted, or idealized, but the fact that each of them speaks from a point of view about the development of civilization is precisely what makes them valuable to my inquiry into the attitudes and beliefs, the hopes and fears, of those who were trying to make sense of historical change. Furthermore, as I explain below, travel took on the status of a peculiarly important activity, not just for those wishing to write books about the United States, but also for those pursuing professional success or seeking to exert influence in the new nation. So I argue that the conditions of travel became a test of the quality of civilization, and experience on the roads and waterways provided important symbols of intellectual endeavor.

What it means to call someone or something "modern" is discussed extensively in Part Five. It may suffice here to say that the feeling that the past no longer furnishes binding precedents and that we are condemned, or liberated, to make our own way—the feeling that Fitzgerald's characters revealed at Jackson's home—helps define this elusive key word. The dating of the beginnings of "modernity" has recently attracted scholarly attention for several reasons. In art and literature, it is only a few decades since the teaching and study of "modern" masterpieces became a legitimate and exciting enterprise.[10] In the past decade, as critics have discovered, or asserted, that the "modernist" masterpieces are losing their dominion, many books and articles have turned to such questions as when, precisely, modernity set in and whether it is really over. To the extent that answering these questions depends on consideration of formal qualities of art, this book makes no effort to intervene. But if the issues have to do with beliefs and attitudes, then I would say that those who are arguing for the beginnings of modernity in the late nineteenth century could with profit push further back in time.[11]

We are hearing even more about "modernity" from critics of intellectual fashion and public morality. Some writers tell us that, not so long ago, community values were stronger, conviction and commitment came more

readily, selfishness and immorality were more tightly restrained by educational and intellectual values. Probably most of us feel that something of
the sort is true, that it conforms to the experience of our lifetimes.* But
intellectuals have been making similar claims for most of this century,
while also praising, as often as not, the individual release that accompanied the breakdown of community restraints. Perhaps that is the problem
that Fitzgerald's heroine encountered at the Hermitage. In any case, as I
have listened to recent talk about the malady of "modernity," I have
thought that much the same talk might have been heard in the 1830s, '40s,
and '50s. I do *not* argue that no significant changes have occurred in the
recent past. That would be foolish. But I do caution against an idea that
may lurk in some uses of "modernity": the idea that we have lost traditional moorings in some unprecedented way and that current anxieties
about change bear no relation to those of previous generations. It may be
more accurate to see in American history a connected series of debates
about transformation and continuity in which concepts like "modernity"
and "tradition" have always coexisted and competed.

One goal of this book is to challenge some of our certainty about the
periods of American history and about conflicts in our intellectual life. We
cannot understand the emerging intellectual culture[12] of the United States in
the post-revolutionary decades if we search for "lost ideals and tradition" or
for communal bonds we have somehow strayed from. In that period of
transition the oppositions that became clear enough to later generations
awaited formulation. Some leaders clung to memories of revolutionary conflict; others observed a world in the process of remaking. As the new order
took shape, some Americans praised the building of institutions and efforts
at self-improvement in ways that anticipated the later Victorian praise of
"culture"; others, at the same time, described society as a disturbing masquerade in which all the certitudes of common sense were undermined. This
was an opposition that emerged step by step in a period of change that
puzzled even rigorous thinkers and careful observers. For those who journeyed through the era, the ineluctable fact was that nothing was the same as
it once had been. The past became a problem. Although no one could say of

---

*Another visit to Nashville may be relevant here. The city travelers converge on in
Robert Altman's film *Nashville* (1975) is a terrible place, full of showbiz hype, fragile
egos, desperate dreams, oversimplified panaceas, compulsive sex, nasty manipulation,
and traumatic loneliness. The country singers serve up soupy patriotism ("We must be
doing something right to last two hundred years") but also poignant memories of the
sacrifices of their mamas and papas back home. "There is decadence in America,"
Altman said; "I see it all around me." See George Vecsey, "Nashville Has Mixed Feeling
on 'Nashville'," *New York Times*, Aug. 10, 1975, p. 41.

Americans, as Edmund Burke had said of the English, that they always acted "as if in the presence of canonized forefathers," the wish to memorialize colonial and revolutionary ancestors was expressed everywhere, even in the newly settled West. But obeisance to the past could not restore tradition. While in this book we must attend to efforts to rekindle memory, we will discover many presentiments of modernity.

PART ONE

Nashville

They stare from daguerreotype with severe
  reprehension,
Or from genuine oil, and you'd never guess any pain
In those merciless eyes that now remark our own time's
  sad declension.

—ROBERT PENN WARREN,
"Founding Fathers, Early-Nineteenth-Century Style,
Southeast U.S.A."

CHAPTER ONE

Contrasts

Louis Philippe, duc d'Orléans, later the bourgeois king of the French, came to Nashville in 1797 with two brothers, all of them in exile from the Revolution. Along the way they noticed little that would pass muster for civilization in Europe. Even along the seaboard, "whatever is not *field* is *forest*"; and the forest, moreover, was made up of tall, full-grown trees. What the Americans called cities would be no more than villages in France. Dependent on slaves, Americans were lazy; they never walked if they could ride and were generally less "vigorous, active, and enterprising" than men in the Old World. A cobbler irritated the Frenchmen by refusing to repair a boot *"because I'm not in the mood right now."*

Those who had moved out to the Cumberland frontier were especially bad, "crude, lazy, and inhospitable to an extreme." The worst indignity was that visitors were expected to urinate at night through holes broken in the windows. The Americans' egalitarianism was insufferable: "Everywhere they complain, with the same angry acerbity, of government by rich eastern businessmen; everywhere they parrot paltry Jacobin commonplaces, that the poor work hard and the rich get richer, that the rich are not happy merely selling land at exorbitant prices but find various ways to extort what little money the settlers make, etc." The Americans' sense of history was pathetic. On the trip away from Nashville the French exiles saw an Irishman, dressed as Punchinello, parading through a Kentucky town to promote a marionette show. When the event took place that evening, a large hall was

13

jammed, and one woman spoke of taking her children so that "*in their old age* they would be able to say they had seen it."[1]

When Louis Philippe became known as the "bourgeois monarch," a self-proclaimed lover of liberty, his youthful observation of American democracy was supposedly one source of his openmindedness toward change. No doubt he admired the spirit of enterprise he noticed at times in America, but the picture he left was of disturbing breakdown leading to savagery, indolence, and gullibility.

Every visit to Nashville raised one question: how far had the town progressed? When Ann Erwin, a young woman from Georgia, passed through in 1818, she admired the "romantic beautiful" site above the Cumberland River and the cedars covering the hills all around. In New England, Nashville would be considered "quite a village," she thought, but "there is very little taste displayed in the improvements." The brick houses were cramped together and old-fashioned and lacked "plazas or yards in front." Compared to the wide streets and flower gardens she had left behind in Augusta, Nashville was "rude and tasteless."[2]

Others who came to Nashville, and stayed, drew pictures much like Louis Philippe's. This remained true for decades. Philip Lindsley came in 1824 as the new president of Cumberland College, soon to become the University of Nashville, a position that he held for over two decades. Lindsley was a well-educated Presbyterian clergyman and had been a tutor and professor of languages at Princeton since 1807. He had turned down offers of presidencies at Transylvania and Ohio universities before accepting this call to the West. In Nashville he adopted the pseudonym "An Old Field Pedagogue" to ridicule primitive conditions, terrible food, and men spitting everywhere, even at church. Nothing matched the standards of past civilization. Everything "degenerates in Tennessee. Doctors are made by guess . . . lawyers by magic . . . legislators by grog . . . merchants by Mammon . . . farmers by necessity . . . editors and schoolmasters by St. Nicholas." The city was preyed on by jugglers and acrobats, hucksters and frauds. Decent theatre attracted little audience, while the circus was always filled. In a three-year period, Lindsley counted 259 beggars—many of them phony "shipwrecked Germans, Spaniards, and Portuguese," ostensibly devoid of English, with fake credentials, and a few others claiming to be veterans who had fought with Jackson—who sought alms at his door.

For the most part, Lindsley wrote without pseudonym as he sought public funds and private gifts to build a college that, in his view, would benefit the entire state. He set this project in the context of improving the civic landscape: he envisioned a West with cultivated fields, good transportation, a "due sprinkling" of prosperous towns with churches, colleges, and other public edifices. But the resistance was nearly insuperable. Tennesseans, he came to feel, preferred cockfights and horse races to cultural progress. They mistrusted this Easterner, a Presbyterian, an educated man. They clung to the belief that colleges and other cultural institutions aided only the rich.[3] In the contrast between mountebanks and beggars on the one hand, and the builder of a college on the other, and in the conflict between popular suspicion and a project to advance civilization, we may detect tensions that would fundamentally define American culture.

There were, of course, Nashvillians who saluted each sign of advancing civilization: the attainments of the college's president and faculty; the progress of other educational institutions (there was no common school system); the commencement of lecture series at a lyceum and a mechanics' library; performances by flautists, harpists, and pianists, often described as "celebrated" in Europe; a botanical garden; a natural history museum; publishing houses; bookstores; and eventually a comfortable new theatre. A visitor passing through in 1838 found much to praise: a classical courthouse atop a hill, three or four new churches, rows of buildings that were neat if not truly elegant. In contrast to Northern factory towns, there was little "painful and bustling industry," and Nashville also had "none of your care-worn, shy, suspicious-looking faces, so frequent in northern towns." A stranger felt free to speak with anyone in this "sociable, hospitable, orderly and moral population" and could expect a courteous answer to any question.[4]

As early settlers who had prospered moved to the countryside and assumed the lives of gentlemen, a new leadership class took hold. They were mostly professional people who formed an alliance for civic progress with the mechanics of the city. They worked to convert the frontier outpost into their ideal of "the Good Village," an ideal partly adapted from the Eastern past, partly reflecting their knowledge of new currents of reform. Philip Lindsley's son John, a leader in these new circles, even attended a women's rights convention on a visit to New York. Some of their most significant victories, such as the beginnings of public education and the creation of a hospital for the insane, did not come until the 1850s; and the secession movement and Civil War proved to be great obstacles to their labors. But for several decades they kept Nashville a Whig city.[5]

All parties in Nashville cheered the arrival in May 1825 of another French visitor, the Marquis de Lafayette, on his extraordinary, triumphal tour of the nation whose independence he had fought for nearly half a century before. In Nashville, as throughout the land, Lafayette appeared as a relic of the revolutionary past, a reminder that this nation was consecrated to liberty, a source of unified patriotic feeling. To some thoughtful Americans, his visit raised potentially disturbing questions: Was there something exceptional about the American experience that made possible the survival of republican institutions? Would it be possible to keep the torch of liberty aflame in a nation that seemed to have cut itself adrift from tradition? But such questions were not raised, publicly at least, on the Cumberland. Instead, banquets, parades, and florid speeches attested to the joy of the American people in their patriotic heritage and their unexampled current liberty and prosperity.[6]

"The American custom," as Lafayette's secretary, A. Levasseur, noted, was to join great celebrations to partisan purposes.[7] The early stages of Lafayette's tour had coincided with the 1824 presidential campaign and benefited the candidacy of Andrew Jackson, who had fought the British in the Revolution and overcame them at New Orleans. By the time Lafayette reached Nashville, Jackson had lost the election in Congress and was fuming in defeat and suffering from prostatitis. Nevertheless, he escorted "the Nation's Guest" from the steamboat and through the city's streets as banners were unfurled by cheering crowds and artillery hailed the grand occasion. Later he entertained Lafayette at the Hermitage and shared in a grand reception by the Masons, at which portraits of Washington, Lafayette, and Jackson symbolized the virtues of wisdom, generosity, and strength. At a ceremony at Cumberland College, President Lindsley announced the creation of two professorial chairs, one named for Lafayette, in languages, and one named for Jackson, in philosophy. But the occasion belonged equally to all parties. Lafayette had already paid a friendly visit to John Adams at his modest home in Quincy, Massachusetts, and traveled through New Jersey with John Quincy Adams. Levasseur recognized that the general effect of the triumphal tour was to "paralyze" any hostilities left over from the presidential election. The major speech that greeted Lafayette's arrival in Nashville was delivered by Jackson's rival in state politics, Governor William Carroll.

The leitmotif of Lafayette's visit to Nashville, as everywhere, was the memory of the Revolution. This memory was usually reported as "distant," as adorning the pages of history, as something related by ancestors who were now in their graves. The "thirty or forty" veterans of the Revolution, who had come from a hundred miles or more to see Lafayette, were "oppressed with the infirmities of age." One can only wonder at Lafayette's emotions as one speech or toast after another reminded him that all his companions in arms had passed away or could approach him only with "tottering step," and that he himself, "the good old man," was approaching decrepitude and death. This "simple, aged foreigner" was passing through America "in his declining years, like one arisen from the dead." Did he take comfort in the reflection that the brief time allotted to his tour of the West showed that "everything human is transient and fleeting"? That the tears of future generations would "bedew" his remains as they did the noble Washington's?

About five hundred veterans of the Battle of New Orleans convened near Nashville. Though age had not yet destroyed them as it had their fathers, their feats were also relegated to a past, perhaps not as distant as that of "the departed revolutionary heroes," but already separated from present experience. Because they were summoned for the wrong date, many of them had to endure a week's encampment outside the city. These were not feeble geezers with time to spare; they were tempted to "return immediately to their business." But the glory of the occasion "overcame the cold calculations of interest, and almost every individual remained, submitting to rigorous camp discipline, and occasional severe drilling." Lafayette went out to the camp to review their formations and drills. Their virtues as men who had marched long distances to honor the hero and who exhibited unselfishness and good order mirrored those of the French aristocrat who decades before had crossed the Atlantic as "the disinterested friend of our country in the darkest hour of suffering and of peril." There were frequent reminders throughout the visit that it was on virtues like these shown in warfare, or at least the memory of such virtues, that the union of the states and the continued existence of the nation depended.

Veneration of old men was not the only theme. Equally prominent was the "contrast"—a word used repeatedly—between the Nashville of the present and that of revolutionary days. As the French party ascended the Cumberland River toward Nashville, they noted that there were no towns along the shores, but the numerous loaded vessels gave evidence of the richness of the produce of this land. Governor Carroll commented that land that lay in "savage wilderness" during the Revolution was now "filled with a population of hardy and enterprising yeomanry." Mayor Robert B. Currey also pointed out that "this city, now the metropolis of a new and independent state, (the eighth in the union in population,) has since that period sprung up from the wilderness." In replying to each, Lafayette took pleasure in congratulating "the spirited promoters of their own rapid prosperity" for achieving "the blessed results" of the liberty he and his comrades had fought for. Later, Levasseur offered a toast to "Two American sisters, Industry and Prosperity, and their mother Liberty." At the Masonic Hall an orator told Lafayette again of the contrast between "the poor, feeble, and almost desponding confederation of states" he once aided and the "prosperous and powerful nation" to which he returned. Where the roads were formerly impassable, "majestic steamboats" now moved "with a rapidity scarcely to be surpassed in the oldest and most improved countries of Europe." The signs of improvement inspired feelings of satisfaction.

Even in these remote western regions, where, at the time of his [Lafayette's] first arrival on our continent, the voice of civilization had scarcely been

heard; where the Indian warwhoop was then the only music that could greet
the ear; where even the rudest form of agriculture had then scarcely
commenced its inroads upon the native forest, and not a step could be taken
by civilized man, except at the imminent risk of destruction by beasts of prey
or merciless savages of the wilderness—he now finds richly cultivated fields,
thriving villages, and even populous cities, adorned with art, and science,
and taste, and all that can render life comfortable and delightful.

In the transit from warwhoops to taste, colleges and universities were rising,
along with "academies in which the female mind is richly cultivated and
adorned."

Lafayette observed this progress on the second day of his stay. When he
was taken to Cumberland College, President Lindsley reiterated the theme
of contrast: prosperity and knowledge were starting to flourish in what once
was wilderness. Jackson had "driven the murderous savage from our frontiers and then, like Cincinnatus, had "exchanged the sword for the plough."
Now colleges sought to promote learning, traditional and practical, among
the people—and Lafayette was suitably impressed. He was also taken to the
Female Academy, where he learned again that the demise of barbarism was
"a faint emblem" of the liberty he had helped to secure. Nearly a hundred
"young, intelligent, and beautiful females" sang an ode of welcome to "this
retreat of science and the muses." One of the students, Miss Grundy, spoke
of "the lessons of prudence and economy" that young women learned from
Lafayette's family, so often separated from him, while Nashville's men profited from the example of his bravery. The feminine dimensions of progress
were noted regularly during the visit. Nashville was a city second to none in
"female taste, intelligence, and beauty." It was fitting, therefore, that the
visit ended at the Hermitage with about three hundred ladies, "splendidly
dressed," among the guests. Some of them proposed a sentiment in Lafayette's honor, and he replied with this "gallant and pointed toast": "*Tennessee Beauty*—equal to Tennessee valour."[8]

Throughout the days in Nashville there were references to struggles for
liberty in France, in Greece, in Cuba, in the Andes, throughout the world.
But if this age was auspicious for free principles everywhere, the overwhelming emphasis of the ceremonies was on the progress of a particular kind of
civilization, hurried along by steamboats, enhanced by schools, and adorned
by cultivated ladies.

The next day brought a different scene, as Lafayette's steamboat, after
reaching the Ohio, hit a snag and foundered. In the ensuing rescue operations the French party witnessed the exertions of Governor Carroll, "a first
magistrate of a republic, without shoes, stockings or hat, doing the duty of a
boatman as if it had been his real occupation, and that much more for the

benefit of others than for himself, for he had very little on board to lose by the shipwreck." Once it was clear that no one had drowned, it was possible to sit and enjoy smoked meat, biscuits, claret, and madeira that had been salvaged from the wreck and prepare for further acquaintance with the progress of civilization in a land where the past appeared so distant.[9]

CHAPTER TWO

A New Way of Life

In December 1831, two Frenchmen visited Nashville: Alexis de Tocqueville and another young aristocrat, Gustave de Beaumont. Out of favor with Louis Philippe's new regime, they had received permission to tour America and inspect its famous penitentiaries. On this mission, they came down from Louisville and arrived in Nashville during one of the coldest seasons of the nineteenth century. They thought of Tennessee as below the latitude of the Sahara, but they found the Cumberland River frozen over for the first time in almost forty years. Their wagon broke down; they had to trek through snow; Tocqueville got sick; and after leaving Nashville on the eleventh, they were forced to wait through several freezing days in an inn at Sandy Bridge, Tennessee. "If it were not for the vexation we feel in seeing our plans just about failed," Tocqueville wrote to his father (when he finally got to Memphis) ". . . we should not regret the expedition just made through the forests of Kentucky and Tennessee. . . . We made the acquaintance there of a kind of man and a way of life that we had no conception of."[1]

Fever and chill left him with very little good to say about the new man, the Tennessean. The men were "big and strong" and had "an energetic look." Even more than other Americans, they displayed an "instinctive love of country, a love mixed up with exaggeration and prejudices." But they were "indolent," dependent on slaves to do their work, and satisfied with a society that was not "finished" and a way of life "rendered half savage by solitude" and privation. They put up few churches or schools. They lacked

21

the foresight of other Americans. Outside of Nashville itself, one saw few brick homes, only wooden cabins with holes in the walls. They cut firewood and made other provisions—or rather, had their slaves do so—at the spur of the moment instead of planning in advance. Through it all they affected an ease and leisure in the company of strangers.

> As you come in, the master of the house gets up, and receives you with pressing hospitality, but he is careful not to go himself to get what you need; in his mind it would be degrading to serve you. It is a slave who pokes the fire to warm the traveller; it is a slave who gets his clothes dried and brings him the food he needs. The master watches and his gestures direct his servants' work; he does nothing himself. If he opens his mouth, it is to call his dogs or to tell of some of their bold feats. There is no farmer in Kentucky or Tennessee so poor but can represent a fine example of the country gentlemen of old Europe.

The wives looked on "with the tranquil and modest air that distinguishes American women." The men were by no means ignorant rustics. They had the Americans' typical "argumentative spirit," and in comparison with European farmers they were well informed. Tocqueville was astonished by the "circulation of letters and newspapers among these savage woods." The post office, usually an "isolated house in the depths of a wood," was the monument of this civilization. Traveling with the mail, Tocqueville saw the delivery of large parcels "from which no doubt each inhabitant of the neighborhood came to take his share. I do not think that in the most enlightened rural districts of France there is intellectual movement either so rapid or on such a scale as in this wilderness."[2]

Tocqueville saw differences between the residents of the Cumberland region and other Americans. The former had too few slaves to imitate the culture of wealthier parts of the South. They lacked the influence of "the germs of the high civilization of New England."[3] They were not a mixture of racial stocks like people Tocqueville noticed in the Northwest. The Tennesseans had a distinctive appearance. They combined roughness and courtesy, violence and laziness, in a way that was plainly unsettling to him. Yet in the December chill Tocqueville saw in them contradictions that were crystallizing in his general view of America. On one hand, there were lessons to be learned from a society in which so much information passed so freely amid the woods and farms. "I only know of one means of increasing the prosperity of a people. . . . That means is none other than increasing the facility of communication between men."[4] On the other hand, there was no guarantee that roads, canals, and mail service would do anything to create an admirable civilization, one in which anyone who appreciated the religious, artistic, and political traditions of Europe could ever bear to live.

It was disheartening to meet the leaders these people chose. Later in December, Tocqueville found himself traveling with Tennessee's former governor Sam Houston. Here was a man who had, according to rumor, mistreated and left his wife and then married a Cherokee woman. He exemplified the problem of the electorate's making "very bad choices." His leadership could be explained only by the people's wish to honor men like themselves and by the disgusting maneuvers that drove the "fittest men" out of the political field. "One must haunt the taverns, drink and argue with the mob; that is what is called *Electioneering* in America."⁵ In January, Tocqueville and Beaumont were presented to President Andrew Jackson in Washington. They shared madeira and mediocre conversation. By that time Tocqueville's view of American politics was chilly and congealed. He had heard so many disagreeable things about Jackson that he already counted him the prime example of the people's bad choices. Whether or not they conversed about Nashville, there was nothing in Tocqueville's experience in Middle Tennessee to prepare him to warm up to the Old Hero. Jackson remained, in Tocqueville's view, "a man of violent character and middling capacities; nothing in the whole of his career indicated him to have the qualities needed for governing a free people; moreover, a majority of the enlightened classes in the Union have always been against him." Only an exaggerated memory of his victory at New Orleans, "a very commonplace feat of arms" when compared with great moments in Europe's military history, could account for Jackson's great popular following. It was a worrisome feature of a "prosaic" republic in which true distinction was so rare that this kind of military hero could so dominate political life.⁶

This judgment appears in Tocqueville's *Democracy in America* (1835, 1840), one of the most influential works ever written about the United States. In translated and abridged form it achieved immediate fame in the United States itself. Since it frequently disparaged American democracy and since it featured little close observation of American society (the account above rests on his letters and notebooks), its fame is a little hard to explain. We will need to return to this topic at a suitable moment in our own journey. We can see already, however, that the trip to Tennessee and the visit with Jackson suggested a method of evaluating America under separate headings—the way of life of various classes, conditions favoring prosperity, the state of culture, the problem of political stability, the choice of leaders—always in comparison with Europe, always with an eye to American distinctiveness. The method appealed to Americans, especially those who did not think very highly of Jackson, because it seemed at the same time to accord the United

States the status of revolutionary preeminence and to recognize that much lay ahead in the creation of culture. Democracy was irreversible; but what could be preserved, and what created, by those who esteemed an intellectual and cultural life?

What we can see at this point is that Tocqueville belabored themes of contrast between past and present, between Old World and New, between backward indolence and the upward striving of the towns that were commonplace in all efforts to understand America. Though he discounted Americans' contentment with how much they had already achieved, he recognized that even half-savage Americans were seeking to improve their lives. His analysis raised in the clearest possible form the questions of what sort of civilization would be built and what form of culture would embellish it amid the turmoil of democracy. In raising these questions as he did, he showed absolutely no sympathy for what he regarded as American mediocrity: the people wanted leaders like themselves, and leaders in turn must imitate and pander to the people. By emphasizing tyrannous pressures to conform, however, he underestimated the energy with which individuals shaped their own lives and the excitement of the public stage on which new styles of leadership were acted out.

CHAPTER THREE

The Hero and His Roles

Begin over again. In 1788 Andrew Jackson came to Nashville, a town in the Western District of North Carolina, less than ten years old and consisting of a few hundred people clustered in a stockade for protection against the Indians. It had taken a century and a half for white settlement to escape its confinement along the seaboard and to burst past the mountains. The frontier folk on the banks of the Cumberland still had to look to the East to supply many needs.[1] Among the tents, cabins, houses, taverns, and stores was a courthouse, and Jackson had recently been named public prosecutor by his friend John McNairy, the new Superior Court judge. Jackson was all of twenty-one.

Generations of researchers, friendly and hostile, have raked over Jackson's early life without finding very much.[2] His origins were too obscure and too out of keeping with his later life. He was Scotch-Irish, a farmboy, an orphan. He had fought at age fourteen against the British, had been wounded, captured, and released in an exchange of prisoners. He had tried his hand at several trades—saddlery, schoolteaching—before studying for two years with a lawyer in Salisbury, North Carolina. He was licensed to practice in September 1787. Then he drifted for a year, leaving few traces of his activities except that he got arrested for some sort of youthful escapade. For a while he helped two friends run a store.

On their way to Nashville, Jackson and McNairy, together with a third legal chum who had been named court clerk, stopped for about six months in

Jonesboro, in what would shortly become East Tennessee. There Jackson began to acquire some signs of elevated status. He bought a slave, a young woman named Nancy. He fought in a duel. One of the most searching analyses of Jackson's psyche uncovers evidence of a tremendous internal rage accumulating since childhood.[3] Of his rage there is plenty of evidence later on, but this duel was a harmless charade. Jackson's antagonist was forty-seven years old, a lawyer of some prominence (in fact, Jackson had wanted to study with him a few years before), and too sensible to risk his life for no good reason. Jackson evidently took offense at his opponent's sarcasm during a legal proceeding and demanded satisfaction. In the event, both men fired into the air, apparently by previous arrangement, and shook hands; then Jackson declared that his honor was upheld. Without making too much of a brief letter, we may note that in his challenge Jackson referred to his adversary as a "gentleman" and to himself as a "man."[4] These distinctions lost their significance during the nineteenth-century democratic movement of which Jackson eventually became the figurehead. To understand Jackson's career after his youthful wanderings, however, we will need to keep in mind his attachments to such old distinctions and his wish to attain recognition of his own gentility.

His early years in Nashville remain almost as beclouded as his youth in the Carolinas. What is clear is that he became powerful and rich; a century and a half later, in an account some Southerners detested, W. J. Cash took Jackson as representative of the "hard and coarse" men who ascended to the South's ruling class.[5] A succession of offices traces his rise to power. In December 1789, the North Carolina legislature elected him district attorney for the Mero District, renamed (and misspelled—the man's name was actually Miro) to attract favor from the Spanish governor of New Orleans and thus possibly to win commercial access to the Gulf of Mexico. Two years later Jackson kept the same post in the newly organized Southwest Territory of the United States. In 1792, he was appointed judge advocate for the Mero District militia. He served in the constitutional convention in 1796, as Tennessee gained statehood, and represented his state in the U.S. House of Representatives and Senate. In 1798 he was elected to the state Superior Court. In 1802 he was commissioned major general of the state militia. Eventually, as a major general of the United States Army in the War of 1812, he fought Indians, the British, and sometimes, it seemed, his own troops, until he won national fame as the "Hero of New Orleans" and set forth on a new career that led to the nation's presidency.

How did he get rich? Not easily and not without reversals: in 1796 he teetered close to bankruptcy, when a Philadelphia merchant with whom he had extensive dealings failed. Essentially he took chances, used connections, and kept his eye on his goals. While a public prosecutor, he also engaged in a large private legal practice, representing, most notably, influential merchants and creditors who had trouble collecting payments in a frontier outpost. The court was the leading institution of this Western territory with minimal representative government, continual disputes over land, and persistent problems with Indians. Justices and lawyers were men of power in local society and indispensable links to politicians and speculators in the East. They were new men making their own fortunes, and the business that concerned them more than any other was land speculation.[6] Jackson was a trusted lieutenant in the circle of territorial governor William Blount, and like his peers he used his contacts to acquire all the land he could.[7]

In 1795 and 1796 he operated a Nashville store, which he had to sell, along with most of his land, to avoid ruin, but in subsequent years he was a partner in several other stores, which gave him a lucrative role in trade into and out of the growing villages and farms of the Cumberland. He also developed valuable trading connections in Natchez. He traded in a wide range of goods, including furniture, liquor, horses, and slaves. Through a window in one of his stores he sold goods to the Indians. His lifelong interest in Indian fighting fit well with his connections with speculators. Not only did pacification of the Indians make it easier for owners of "uninhabited" land to attract purchasers; but each major treaty with the Indians created bonanza opportunities for speculation. It is not clear that Jackson himself profited from negotiations with defeated nations, though the charge has been made. But his friends and associates did, and Jackson's fortune clearly rose as the Cotton Kingdom took over land wrested from the Creeks.[8]

Jackson followed a pattern observed in other lawyers, store owners, and Indian fighters in early Nashville. After acquiring sufficient wealth, he moved out and turned planter, a role in which he was forever worried about liquid capital and kept close track of changing cotton prices. He always needed the income from his public offices. There were several purchases and sales as he moved into this role, first Poplar Grove on the Cumberland, then a lovely house at Hunter's Hill, thirteen miles west of Nashville, then the Hermitage, slightly to the south. Like many of his associates, he went from wooden house to brick mansion. He accumulated some of the same furnishings from Europe and Philadelphia that, as a merchant, he profited from importing and selling to others.[9] In time, as Nashville acquired a political organization and as opportunities for land speculation in the vicinity diminished, a new generation of merchants and mechanics felt no loyalty to its former resident. His old town almost never voted for Jackson or his party in the years of his national political fame.

Jackson maintained Jeffersonian sympathies. Neither as lawyer-storekeeper nor as planter did he believe that his acquisitive drives and "gentle" aspirations contradicted his belief in revolutionary equality. Early Nashville was a republican town where, as its most recent historian has commented, "to be perceived as a Fed or a Quid meant political death."[10] Jackson was fully at home as he railed against Jay's Treaty or exulted in popular uprising against British rule in Ireland. His enemies, in Nashville, Washington, and Europe, were the "aristos"; his allies spoke for the people.[11] He never relinquished the partisan rhetoric of the 1790s. That is one reason why a populist, anti-aristocratic outlook has appeared to define him politically in most of the best-known accounts of him that have ever been written. His own attacks on "aristos" have merged with others' images of him as a kind of Natty Bumpo or Nick of the Woods,[12] as a backwoods gunfighter, as an unlettered man with utter contempt for social niceties. The triumph over the British in 1815 was immediately, and erroneously, attributed to sharp-shooting frontiersmen's superiority to the blundering, formal warfare of the British.[13] Reports of an unwashed mob thronging into the White House in celebration of his inauguration—reports that began with more than a tinge of genteel disapproval—are still repeated as evidence that his election was the great turning point in America's overthrow of past aristocratic pretensions.[14]

So much mythology, some of it repeated as history, surrounds him that it may be hopeless to try to extricate a "real" Jackson from the morass of distortion and inaccuracy.[15] But the point deserves emphasis that the Jackson who came to Nashville was a man without much more secure identity than his hatred of England and a few memories of the Revolution imparted to him. He was as free as any person has ever been to alter his own image and turn it to uses of his own choosing. When we try to find out who he really was, there are moments when he does not seem so distant as Fitzgerald believed from the world of Manny Schwartz and Georgie Jessel. But on reflection we rediscover the distance: it was a different past that lay behind him (infrequently as he referred to it); his concern for his honor and his aspirations to "gentle" status flowed from visions of hierarchy that his own revolutionary rhetoric undermined.

Jackson will probably stand forever in American history texts as the first modern president, the leader of a party, the champion of "the people" against entrenched elites, a hero of democracy, an agent in the degradation of an office once reserved for intellectual statesmen. There may be truth in these images; certainly they reflect the portraits given by friends and antagonists alike in the political campaigns of the 1820s and 1830s. Yet it deserves notice that Jackson himself disowned some aspects of the Old Hickory persona. In his letters he repeatedly praised attributes of gentility and took pride in his success in achieving them. His political opponents, he noted with indignation, depicted him as a ruffian with "a savage disposition; who allways carried a scalping knife in one hand, and a tomahawk in the other, allways ready to knock down, and scalp any and every person who differed with me in opinion." Those who were honest found instead "a man of even temper, firm in his opinions advanced, and allways allowing others to enjoy theirs, untill reason convinced them that they were in error." He conducted himself "with the determination of a philosopher," with a stoic conviction that he could defend his "private character" and that fairminded associates would appreciate his public character."[16] The nation's capital, he wrote, was a den of intrigue that he had entered as "a perfect philosopher," detached from the scenes of corruption surrounding him, resolute in his concern for the liberties of the people.[17] It might be possible to dismiss this pose as politically concocted or insincere. But Jackson had struggled too hard to master his rage for him to adopt or discard poses casually; they were maintained with great fixity. His image of himself as a man of philosophical calm is not that of a demagogic good old boy. It is an image of patrician leadership.

The value of education, refinement, and polite manners was a constant theme of his letters to young men whom he raised as sons. He offered no praise of rudeness or rusticity in his instructions on what "young gentlemen" ought to know; instead, he recommended frequent writing ("nothing tends more to expand the mind, and improve the intellect"), acquiring a good library, associating with learned teachers and "the better class of society," and learning the principles of government without reference to politics. In all the actions of their lives he was anxious for his wards to be gentlemanly, proper, above reproach.[18] Even if we allow for a measure of political calculation in his entreaties—he wanted his family to avoid unbecoming behavior that might embarrass him—it is clear that the code of conduct that he upheld was anything but vulgar.

So frequently have historians pointed out that Jackson's presidency marked a new departure in American political leadership that his attachment to gentlemanly ideals seems a puzzling anachronism. Richard Hofstadter, in a famous book on American anti-intellectualism, contrasted the impulsive, crude seventh president with his cultivated and philosophical predecessors. In a study of the American political tradition he took Jackson's aristocratic pretensions as a sign of acquisitive, parvenu aspirations at the core of the egalitarian rhetoric of the new democracy.[19] Students of the election of 1840 have shown how Jackson's opponents imitated the highly successful campaign strategy of stressing frontier origins, battle experience, and folksy sentiments and thereby eliminated high intellectual attainments from the presidential office.[20] One of the most thoughtful surveys of the early presidencies argues that the first six were based on republican values of independent virtue: these presidents were "above party." The great watershed was the election in 1828 of a partisan president employing anti-elitist rhetoric to raise formerly disgruntled interests to presidential power.[21]

Certainly national politics was changing, and it is no mistake to view

1828 as a turning point. Jackson the Nashvillian was less well educated than his predecessors. He was the symbolic head of a party that raised the view of politics as a contest between social classes to a height that it had not reached in the United States during the French Revolution or the 1800 campaign. His opponents initially charged that the ascension of a military hero endangered republican liberty. They vilified his hotheadedness and called him mediocre. Eventually they had to organize a party resembling the one that managed his election, but they never ceased to believe that the transformation of national politics was a saga of degradation. His first major biographer traced this history with a cultivated irony: "Columbus had sailed; Raleigh and the Puritans had planted; Franklin had lived; Washington fought; Jefferson written; fifty years of democratic government had passed; free schools, a free press, a voluntary church had done what they could to instruct the people; the population of the country had been quadrupled and its resources increased ten fold; and the result of all was, that the people of the United States had arrived at the capacity of honoring Andrew Jackson before all other living men." James Parton knew that Jackson's life was important enough to merit three careful volumes. But the fact was incontrovertible: Jackson was not qualified for the nation's highest office, and "his elevation to power was a mistake on the part of the people of the United States."[22]

But the past did not belong exclusively to Jackson's enemies. His party had its own historians, especially George Bancroft, who rose to Secretary of the Navy under Jackson's protégé James Knox Polk. Bancroft's monumental survey of the growth of American liberty, the first great American history, stopped at the Revolution. It has been said, with exaggeration, that it voted for Jackson on every page; more accurately, it celebrated the wisdom of the people as an agent in history.[23] What is most important here, however, is that Jackson did not view his own candidacy as a break with tradition. Instead, he viewed it in terms that have been characterized as belonging to traditional republican theory.

From this perspective, he was a virtuous and independent citizen who accepted office against his innermost desires and at the behest of the people, a disinterested pursuer of the public good, not an intriguer, not an office seeker, not the puppet of a party. He always depicted himself as "a plain cultivator of the soil," weary of public life and eager to return home. He never engaged in "electioneering," or so he postured; he declined to answer political letters and turned down invitations to visit friends if there was a chance that his motives could be interpreted as campaigning for office. He skillfully distinguished himself from secretaries John C. Calhoun, William H. Crawford, and others whose ambitions for high office were too obvious. He was a Cincinnatus, a role that George Washington had burnished to perfection. Like the Roman general who relinquished his sword, refused a crown, and went back to his farm, Washington had set the model for the American citizen-patriot by professing his love of his home and his reluctance to accept office at every step on his way to temporary political power.[24] Like all the early presidents, like Jefferson yearning to return to Monticello but also like John Adams longing for his fields in Quincy, Jackson was a responsible patriot, not a politician.[25]

If Jackson in his pre-Nashville days had any special feeling about George Washington, there is no recorded trace of it. As a frontier republican in the 1790s he showed no love for the father of his country. He called for Washington's impeachment at the time of Jay's Treaty, and he was one of twelve representatives who voted against a congressional encomium to Washington after the Farewell Address. Such antipathy dwindled as Jackson's aspirations grew and his image of himself changed. By 1824 when he was presented with a telescope and a pair of pistols that Lafayette once had given Washington, he was deeply honored to be "thought worthy" of these relics of the great protector of American liberty. When he received a medal commemorating Washington's relinquishment of military command and later retirement from governmental office, he praised these events as "imperishable monuments of self-conquest."[26] As a presidential candidate fulminating against the corruption of Henry Clay and other enemies, he attached himself to the warnings against party animosity in Washington's Farewell Address.[27] As president, he came to relish comparisons with his most illustrious predecessor and even issued a Farewell Address (written by Chief Justice Roger Taney) of his own.

There are many explanations for Jackson's changing estimate of Washington. It may have had elements of insincerity, and it surely was affected by the mounting veneration of the Founding Fathers as emblems of bygone nonpartisanship and patriotism that no political aspirant could afford to ignore. For Jackson, so often assailed as a military chieftain unfit for and dangerous in civil office, the image of Washington was undeniably useful. But veneration of Washington was not merely a means to achieving his goals; it was a sign of the direction of those goals. Though in fact he participated avidly in the formation of a kind of party politics that Washington never witnessed, there was no way for Jackson to regard himself in politics except as a gentleman carried from his beloved mansion by the people's call when they needed a protector for their liberties.

The Hermitage was the most impressive symbol of his public standing. It would be nice to show that he named his retreat of virtue after Rousseau's, but he did not. Stories survive that he adopted the name from Jeremy Bentham's country dwelling, but that is not true either. The name came with the property. In part, building an imposing residence simply reflected a pattern followed by other self-made Nashvillians who became planters in the countryside. He may also have been influenced by a visit he took with his wife to Mount Vernon in November 1815 on a journey to Washington that was frequently interrupted by adoring crowds. At such a moment it would have been difficult for the Hero of New Orleans not to nourish comparisons between himself and Washington. And he must have admired this example of the way a stately home and formal garden ("laid out and trim[m]ed with the utmost exactness"[28]) could express and memorialize a great man's public worth. In 1815, however, he still had not recovered fully from the financial losses of 1796, and he and his wife resided in a small blockhouse they had moved into after being forced to sell an earlier home. He built a statelier brick house in 1819 and hired an English gardener to lay out an arrangement of flower beds, hedges, and public paths with brick edging. In 1831 there were extensive renovations to what was now a presidential widower's house: two new wings, including a large dining room and library; two porticos; ten Doric columns. According to Jackson's most authoritative biographer, what had been a plain but commodious dwelling "began to look like an imposing mansion fit for a grand seignior." He was more and more impressed by the colonnade at Mount Vernon, to which he returned many times, and as president he added a colossal portico to the White House. After a fire in 1834, the Hermitage was redesigned and enlarged again, with a false front to enhance the feeling of majesty, and sustained by six monumental Corinthian pillars.[29]

Jackson never boasted openly of the grandeur of his mansion. He always spoke of it as a domestic retreat. For if the roles of gentleman and public hero were models for shaping his identity, he was able to embrace them only with the aid of another set of roles, those of husband and widower. Jackson met his future wife, Rachel, immediately upon his first arrival in Nashville. She was his landlady's daughter, vivacious and flirtatious, recently reunited with a jealous and irascible husband. Her deepening involvement with the gallant young prosecutor provoked her husband's rage, impetuous departure to Kentucky, and threats to come back and get her. She took flight to Natchez with Jackson, and at some point—the chronology will forever be disputed—they began to live together as husband and wife. Meanwhile, her first husband initiated divorce proceedings with a charge of adultery. This charge was legally validated a couple of years later, when a divorce was officially granted, and shortly thereafter the Jacksons were legally married. One can say "without risk of sentimentality," comments a discerning scholar, that this was "one of the great love stories in American history."[30] It has been romanticized in fiction, film, and music. Unfortunately, these events gave Jackson's opponents ammunition from the moment he entered national politics, and in 1827–1828 they supplied a scurrilous dimension to the nastiest presidential contest in American history. Rachel was accused of promiscuity, adultery, and bigamy; Jackson, of seduction and marriage-wrecking. At her death on the eve of Jackson's departure for the White House, the great love story turned into profound tragedy. In Jacksonian hagiography, this benevolent and beloved woman's death in the midst of slander is the single most pitiful moment in the long story of Jackson's battles against enemies who would stop at nothing to hurt him and the nation.

The blows to Rachel's equilibrium in this foul contest must have been unbearable. There is evidence that the breakdown before her death was mental was well as physical. But there is also evidence that Rachel's vivacity had long before given way to melancholy. While Jackson's biographers usually stress her goodness and charity, these qualities were accompanied by bouts of depression, especially when warfare or politics took her second husband away from home. One source of the alteration of character that marriage brought to Jackson was the need to care for a wife whose troubles appealed to the gentlest and most protective recesses of his personality. "Could I only know you were contented and enjoyed Peace of Mind, what satisfaction it would afford me while travelling the loanly and tiresome road." This in 1796 from Knoxville. "I beg of you to amuse Mrs. Jackson let her not fret if possible." This from Philadelphia later the same year. Another year passes, and again in Knoxville, he asks a friend to try to cheer her up. He had left her *"Bathed in Tears."*[31] Concern for her health and mood characterizes his affectionate letters throughout the decades of their marriage. "How my heart bleeds when I read the pain that our seperation has cost you," he wrote from Washington in 1824.[32] There is no doubting the intensity of his loving attachment, no question of his unforgiving anger toward the vile "invaders of Female Character" who assailed her virtue.[33] If one meaning of the Hermitage was as a conventional sign of his gentlemanly status, in another sense the house was Rachel's refuge of domesticity in a heartless, corrupt world.

Cold world, warm hearth. Itinerant male, secluded female. Competitive politics and business, protective and benevolent domicile. In the love story at the Hermitage we are spectators at the emergence of the sharply divided gender roles and the bifurcated values of work and family of the nineteenth century. Furthermore, we might observe the battle against old reports of scandal as a drama recapitulating changes in "Female Character"; that is, here was a personal instance of the transition from associations of the female with frivolity and lust to new associations with superior refinement and morality. This observation was not available at the time, when no one foresaw the transformed meaning of home and marriage in the nineteenth century. But everything in the Jackson story had a grand representative scale. Rachel did not bear children of her own; so to that extent she was deprived of the role of "republican motherhood"—of the extension of moral influence through maternal, apolitical functions—that historians have delineated in interpreting the post-revolutionary transition. Although she and her husband took responsibility for more wards than anyone has ever counted, there is scant record of her activity as moral instructress. They did raise her nephew Andrew Jackson, Jr., as a son, and Jackson spoke of him as having been "reared in the paths of virtue and morality by his pious and amiable Mother."[34] And her goodness, sanctified by suffering and death, converted the Hermitage into a shrine. While he was President, Jackson pleaded constantly in psalmlike refrain: "Could I but withdraw from the scenes that surround me, to the private walks of the Hermitage, how soon would I be found in the solitary shades of my garden, at the tomb of my wife, there to spend my days in silent sorrow and in peace from the toils and strife of this world, with which I have been long since surfeited. but this is denied to me."[35]

Rachel was well liked by most people who met her, but she was emphatically not a grande dame. Some New Orleans socialites ridiculed the sight of this plain, overweight woman dancing at a victory celebration with her hero mate: "to see these two figures, the General, a long, haggard man with his limbs like a skeleton, and Madame la Generale, a short, fat dumpling, bobbing opposite each other like half-drunken Indians, to the wild melody of *'Possum up de Gum Tree*,' and endeavoring to make a spring into the air"— how droll. No one who has visited the present-day Hermitage and looked at the mannequins of the couple wearing their New Orleans finery can fail to sympathize with her discomfort in the world into which her husband's fame transported her. Privately, she returned as good as she got. To her, New Orleans was "Great Babylon. . . . Oh, the wickedness, the idolatry of the place! unspeakable the riches and splendor." The praise showered on her husband was one instance of the idol worship. "The Lord has promised his humble followers a crown that fadeth not away," she admonished. Remarks like these convince modern biographers that Rachel's religious convictions approached fanaticism.[36]

We do not know when or how Rachel experienced conversion. But there is no mistaking the importance of religious devotion in transforming this spirited young woman of the frontier into a benevolent and rather somber lady. Frequently left at home by the public man who was her husband, subjected to calumnious gossip by his enemies, prone to moods of depression and despair, she was still characterized by all who knew her as a paragon of pious attitudes and charitable actions. "She thanked her Creator for being permitted to do good," reads her epitaph in the garden. Nor is there a shred of evidence that her husband resented the transformation or considered her faith fanatical. The church he built near the Hermitage in

1823, where neighbors joined family in Presbyterian worship, signified his admiration of the religious focus she gave to mansion life. In letters he reassured her of his regular church attendance. After her death he read daily the favorite passages she had marked in her Bible.[37] Later on, republican men were supposed to reverence memories of the piety of their mothers. Jackson became a Christian in the sad glow of the memory of his deceased wife.

Before dying in 1845, he summoned around him his house servants "and in a strain of pious eloquence"—according to a newspaper report— "exhorted them to fidelity in all their duties, impressing upon them the all-important subject of Christianity, and upon taking an affectionate leave of them, he expressed the sincere hope that he might meet them all in Heaven." He turned next to his family and urged them to give more attention to religion. "Amongst the last things he said, was, that his suffering was nothing in comparison with his dying Saviour, through whose death and suffering he looked for everlasting happiness." At his burial a Nashville divine, the Reverend John Todd Edgar, spoke of his conversion "six or seven years ago" and affirmed the Christian character of his "life and walk."[38] Thus we come to the final metamorphosis in this protean life. Born again, Jackson had died to glorify the religion of Christ among both the lowly and the superb.

In fact, this transformation was more complicated than the public learned. Early biographers followed Edgar's account, which alluded to a conversion experience following a "protracted meeting" at the church near the Hermitage. In an ad hominem sermon, Edgar had asked how a man who had passed through scenes of peril and conflict could ignore the hand of God in his deliverance. The General, deeply moved, asked the preacher to come home with him, but Edgar could not; so Jackson was left to suffer through a night of anxiety, repentance, and emancipation. By the time Edgar returned the next morning, Jackson was ready to join the elect, even at the price, though paid reluctantly, of agreeing to forgive his enemies. The result was an emotional scene at the church, where even the windows were darkened by the faces of slaves who came to observe.[39] This is the only report of Jackson's conversion experience, and it is dubious. According to the account of the Reverend James Smith, who served the Hermitage church, Jackson "knew nothing of regeneration." Since his mother and wife had been Presbyterians he "felt more satisfied" with that denomination than any other, but he did not accept all its doctrines. He objected to Edgar's preaching on "the depravity of the human heart." He also resented the fact that one elder— perhaps one of Rachel's slanderers—was a public liar. His membership was somehow tied to that of his adopted son's wife, who joined the church the same day. This convenient arrangement was Edgar's responsibility. The scene was "affecting," according to Smith, but there was much to regret: "I would not have accepted General Jackson into our church."[40]

In his youth, so far as we can tell, Jackson held rather liberal, Enlightened views. Like Jefferson, he spoke broadly of "Providence," but seldom of God.[41] He certainly did not obey his mother's reported wish to see him a Presbyterian minister, and he was never a sectarian. He attended churches of several denominations and scoffed at the idea that the Savior cared whether souls that approached him belonged to the Presbyterians, Methodists, Episcopalians, Baptists, or Roman Catholics. "A true Christian" was above such distinctions.[42] He believed that Providence watched over war and politics; mostly, his mind turned to religion when it was necessary to face the loss of loved ones or, in later years, his own mortality. But fatalism and tolerance were elastic attitudes, especially in Jackson's time and place. If we are right to suspect a Jeffersonian antisectarianism in his early years and a rejection of orthodox views of depravity down to the end, we may notice, too, that eighteenth-century liberal notions dissolved in the nineteenth-century republic. For there were many, in the West and elsewhere, who thought God's work could be democratized, that good deeds could be carried out without respect to denominational differences, even that a new nondenominational Christianity would be the outcome of free American institutions.[43] A prominent Philadelphia minister, whom Jackson was closely associated with, Ezra Stiles Ely, proposed in 1827 that all evangelical Christians ought to act as an informal *"Christian party in politics,"* promising never to "vote for any one . . . who does not profess to receive the Bible as the rule of his faith." The reference to the Unitarian Adams was not overlooked.[44]

In any case, it is clear that Jackson's Christianity strengthened under his wife's influence. After losing her he was reassured by Ely that he "was a different being in relation to spiritual and eternal matters" from what he once had been. He had "begun to be one of the humble followers of Christ," and this was a greater distinction than the presidency.[45] Scruples similar to those discouraging political electioneering made him reluctant to join the religious elect until he returned to private life; otherwise, he might be charged with hypocrisy, as the wicked world would say, *"he has joined the church for political effect."*[46] But he had promised his wife to join the church, and once he had satisfied Edgar of his regeneration and doctrinal soundness, this promise was kept. By the time he kept it, there is no reason to think that he disliked the publicity. Nearing its end, his life took on new meaning as a drama of Christian inspiration to slaves, neighbors, countrymen. "He had passed through a life of most eventful scenes—he had returned to his own hermitage—to the tomb of his beloved consort, . . . and . . . was about to pledge himself, to become a soldier in a new army, and to engage in the performance of duties, of higher importance, than ever commanded the attention of earthly thrones or confederated states. To see this aged veteran, . . . while tears of penitence and joy, trickled down his careworn cheeks, was indeed a spectacle of most intense moral interest."[47]

His entire life was spectacle and transformation. Even the most steady-handed biographer will never get a bead on the real Andrew Jackson. If we could catch a long glimpse of him in the 1770s or 1780s, we would see a man and society in process. In his attitudes toward chivalry we might see remnants of a European past; in his cursory preparation for professional life, modifications from the colonial past; in his journey to Nashville, a recognition of new chances ready to be seized. The better-documented years from the 1790s onward reveal a historical actor able to contrive his own identities: planter-gentleman, political protector of liberty, tender husband, great soul brought to God. Even the settings of these identities—his mansion, his party, his church—he supervised in the making. We notice glimmerings of the past in these roles, these settings—the Grecian columns, Washington's weapons and the patrician sense of leadership, his mother's sect. There were new sheens too—cotton prices on a world market, the people's democracy, protracted meetings. Even the love he shared with Rachel, in which he honored feminine characteristics he deemed eternal, we see in historicist terms as constructed of gender roles in transition.

It was characteristic of Jackson to grasp each role he played with all the fixity and earnestness he could muster (a vast amount); yet it is impossible for us not to see in him the contradictions of an era of post-revolutionary transformation. See W. J. Cash's Southern aristocrat, who lacked genuine cavalier lineage and remembered all too well the simplicity and privation of his youth. Or see the great hero of a Democratic party that cried finis to the aristocratic privilege of the past and yet was managed by men of wealth and privilege. Or look again and see the champion of historic Christianity in a world of sectarian competition and cooperation that amazed observers from the Old World. Or see the Indian fighter teaching the gospel of the savior to slaves on land once covered with forest and nourishing complex memories of a love commenced in a stockade, made controversial in an unprecedented political campaign, memorialized in a shrine in an English garden. There was no real past in such a world and no real identity. Soon this past, too, must pass away.

He had no conception of anything that might be called "American culture." As patrician leader in a republican society he was concerned mainly for the taste and manners of his wards and other young gentlemen. He acquired a good library and pleasant gardens as signs of his own standing in that society. As champion of the liberties of an agrarian people he had little use for programs to improve popular intellect or improve cultural institutions. He did not build public libraries or civic gardens. Yet the career that began with his journey to the Cumberland settlements gives us an initial look at several contradictory elements of the culture that took shape in America's post-revolutionary years: the democratic restraints on aristocratic pretensions; changing definitions of family roles and religious professions that were held to be eternally true; the facile adoption of new social roles amid protests of unimpeachable integrity. He was, as Parton once summarized, "the most candid of men, and was capable of the profoundest dissimulation."[48] Jackson was a symbol for his age, a representative man, in an age so transitory and contradictory that sometimes nothing seemed real except symbolic transformations.

CHAPTER FOUR

A Vagabond's Vision
of Civilization

Still another visitor. Frederick Law Olmsted, accompanied by his brother John, arrived by steamboat in November 1853. Slowed down by fog, the trip from Louisville took a week, time that Olmsted used to clarify his thoughts about the South. From reading Ralph Waldo Emerson's essays he had acquired a belief in historical "compensation": the evil qualities of individuals and societies had their corresponding good aspects. He expected to find that the horrors of slavery supported a cultivated, responsible class of gentlemen. But he was beginning to think otherwise. Even though he had used his brother's Yale contacts to gain access to several plantations, he had not found an admirable slavocracy. The non-slaveholders disturbed him even more; they were "unambitious, indolent, degraded and illiterate . . . a dead peasantry so far as they affect the industrial position of the South." They seldom were "observed to work, but are often seen, like young Rip Van Winkle, lounging at the door of a grocery, or sauntering, with a gun and a dog, in the woods." Both classes opposed the "improvement and education of the negroes." Opposition to any form of improvement was not a failing that Olmsted could take lightly.[1]

Thirty-one years old, he was spottily educated but ambitious and had lived, in his own words, a "decently restrained vagabond life." Connecticut-born, Olmsted had studied with a topographical engineer in Massachusetts, clerked in an importing house in New York City, sailed as a seaman to Canton, spent a semester at Yale (where he was converted in a revival), **39** apprenticed on a model farm in upstate New York, and tried scientific agriculture on his own for several years in his home state and on Staten Island. Farming had not brought much profit—"his head is much fuller of Carlyle than it is of farming," his brother reported—but he epitomized the spirit of civic reform and improvement by serving on school boards and agricultural fair committees. He won prizes for his crops and introduced an advanced drainage system. The improvement of farming, in his view, had an aesthetic dimension: "With the Farmer must rise the Man. . . . With increased knowledge of the operations of nature . . . our sensibility to the Beautiful will be awakened."[2] In this spirit he traveled to Britain to study agricultural methods and rural scenery. By 1852 he had published *Walks and Talks of an American Farmer in England* and begun a promising career in the New York literary world.

Later that year he accepted an assignment from New York's new daily *Times* to traverse the South and send back first-hand observations. Fifty letters, entitled "The South" and signed "Yeoman," appeared in 1853 and 1854. A second trip yielded fifteen more reports, entitled "A Tour of the Southwest," later in 1854, and ten more, entitled "The Southerner at Home," in the daily *Tribune* during the same year. He used much of this material in *A Journey in the Seaboard Slave States* (1856), *A Journey through Texas* (1857), and the compilation *The Cotton Kingdom* (1861). Clearly, he had learned how to turn travel into a literary vocation. Between 1855 and 1857 he was partner in a publishing house, a publisher's agent in England, and editor of *Putnam's Monthly Magazine*. Then he landed a position as superintendent of the projected Central Park—his predecessor Andrew Jackson Downing had drowned in a steamboat disaster on the Hudson—and moved on to the vocation in which he is best remembered, landscape architect.[3]

He never disguised his Yankee perspective. "You've no sort of sectional feeling," he wrote during the Mexican War to a Connecticut friend who had moved to Virginia; "I have the strongest in the world."[4] But in *Walks and Talks* he had observed that the laws of God and the principles of the Constitution flourished neither in slavery nor among its Northern foes, and he regarded himself as a paragon of sensible, balanced Northern opinion.[5] He was not an abolitionist; in fact, he had argued sharply with Theodore Parker, William Lloyd Garrison, and other antislavery radicals his abolitionist friend Charles Loring Brace had brought him into contact with. He deplored the denunciatory tenor of many reformers, as he wrote Brace in 1846. "I believe we can do a great deal more for deluded men—Catholics—or Unitarians, drunkards & slaveholders—by praying *for* them than by blackguarding them through the newspapers, and exasperating them—acting as if we hated them as much as their doctrines. . . . Men are oftener drawn to truth and Christ—I believe than driven." He had much greater respect for cautious, therapeutic reforms such as the work among the city poor that occupied Brace as head of the Children's Aid Society.[6]

Olmsted's Southern travels followed the extraordinary success of Harriet Beecher Stowe's *Uncle Tom's Cabin,* which had let loose a torrent of antislavery and proslavery works. Both he and the *Times* intended his reports to supply facts that would endure "after the deluge of spoony fancy pictures now at its height shall be spent."[7] His evenhandedness was displayed in some of the early reports, written before he reached Nashville. In the April 8, 1853, *Times,* for example, he repeated what had become a standard defense of slavery: "No slave is forced to eat of corruption, as are Irish tenants. No slave freezes to death for want of habitation and fuel, as have men in Boston. No slave reels off into the abyss of God, from want to work that shall bring it food, as do men and women in New-York. Remember that, Mrs. Stowe. Remember that, indignant sympathizers."[8] Such reflections were much less common in reports written after his visit to Nashville; nearly all were excised when he compiled his books on the South. No class, white or black, in the North lived more poorly than "the majority of whites" in the South.[9]

What was the "pivotal experience" that occurred in Nashville?[10] It consisted simply of two days of walking and talking with one of his brother's Yale classmates, a lawyer from a large slaveholding family, Samuel Perkins Allison. Olmsted described the encounter in an excited and, as he said, "damnedly drawn out" letter to his friend Brace.[11] Allison was a Democrat who had recently run for Congress and thus could regale the Yankees with stories about Southern electioneering. He also had tales about chivalry and weapons. Curiously, in spite of "all his hodge podge of honor & morality," Allison admitted to a secret penchant for avant-garde texts like David Friedrich Strauss's *Life of Jesus* and Theodore Parker's speculations on religion. This bright, if opinionated, conversationalist forced the Olmsteds to admit that some of their convictions were assailable.

Mostly, they talked about slavery—for example, about Allison's hatred of antislavery politicians and his belief in the necessity of expanding slave territory. California, Mexico, Cuba, even the Amazon: all seemed promising fields for expansion. He and his friends simply could not empathize with the plight of the slaves, and they failed to appreciate the existence of moral conviction in the North—any opposition to slavery, in their view, must be self-interested. Olmsted found these opinions narrowminded and contemptible. But Allison, like Olmsted, placed his opinions in a context of concern for civilization. There were no gentlemen, in his view, in the Northwest and "very few, and they but poorly developed, anywhere at the North." Allison's Yale background had convinced him of the prevailing lack of genteel manners throughout the non-slaveholding sections of the United States; and

Olmsted was forced to concede "a great deal of truth in his view." When Olmsted countered "that there were compensations in the *general* elevation of all classes at the North"—a standard retort to European or Southern criticism of Yankee civilization—Allison scoffed. "He is, in fact, a thorough Aristocrat. And altogether, the conversation making me acknowledge the rowdyism, ruffianism, want of high honorable sentiment & chivalry of the common farming & laboring people of the North, as I was obliged to, made me very melancholy." What did the success of American democracy matter if the quality of the people was so low?

It is hard to tell from Olmsted's letter just why these conversations were so upsetting; he admitted that he was unable to relate much of what was said, perhaps because his emotional reaction was so intense. In part at least, it may be that even thoughtful and well-traveled Americans had little acquaintance with anyone who took a frankly aristocratic position, in spite of the venom with which politicians attacked "aristos." Other slaveowners whom Olmsted met were content to argue, unconvincingly, the benefits of slavery in Christianizing and civilizing the Africans. It was disconcerting to pass time with an amiable, privileged man who cared nothing about the refinement of the lower classes in his region and who criticized, pointedly, the level of civility among ordinary people in Olmsted's region. What small satisfaction the Olmsteds enjoyed came from proving to Allison that he was not really a "Democrat" in spite of his Jeffersonian strict constructionism (which did not, in any case, rule out territorial expansion or transcontinental railroads). For his part, Olmsted expressed his loyalty to an international democratic movement. Admiring as he did, reluctantly, this Southern gentleman, "I must be either an Aristocrat or more of a Democrat that I have been—A Socialist Democrat."

"Hurrah for the Reds," he exclaimed as he tried to collect his thoughts; "I am a Democrat of the European school." But even in these heated reactions, his democracy possessed what today would be called an elitist slant. What were needed were institutions to educate and uplift "the poor and degraded." Brace should redouble his efforts among New York's poor children. Common schools must be multiplied and improved. We see the course toward Olmsted's career in landscape architecture in his call for "parks, gardens, music, dancing schools, reunions which will be so attractive as to force into contact the good & bad, the gentlemanly and the rowdy." All these programs required state assistance; the result would be a kind of subsidized campaign to uplift minds and manners, with lots of work to do for young men like Olmsted and his friends. Finally, he reminded Brace of his hope for a new magazine to promote "a higher Democracy and a higher religion than the popular." This should appear weekly in order to "give it variety & scope enough for this great country & this cursedly little people."

Charities, parks, schools, cultural refinements, and a magazine—this was the program Olmsted outlined on the steamboat that carried him from Nashville to his next venue.[12] This program was reiterated in the *Times*, in *Journey in the Back Country*, and in the *Cotton Kingdom*. In criticizing slavery, Olmsted highlighted a vision of civilization that his early vagabond-age had led him to. Perhaps the South had more "high-toned" gentlemen than the North, but their numbers were few, and many slaveholders displayed the violent, rowdy manners that in the North were restricted to the lower orders. In general, signs of civilization were sparse in the South. Only occasionally had a day's wandering ended in a private room, with comfortable furnishings and decent food, with the sounds of opera or the presence of great books. What was taken for granted among the middle classes in a Northern state—literacy, a regular post, newspapers—appeared infrequently in his Southern journeys. Churches, schools, lectures, libraries, literary societies, theatres, scientific institutions were uncommon; contact with "highly educated professional men" unusual. In short, "the system which is apologized for on the grounds that it favors good breeding" impeded the progress of civilization. A child born on the Northern frontier would probably be surrounded by age ten with "a well organized and tolerably well provided community" with all the familiar signs of ready information, technical improvement, and good taste. The South remained a wilderness.[13]

Other visitors to Nashville knew differently. They might have questioned Olmsted's sweeping contrasts and concluded from his accounts of traveling hundreds of miles through unimproved land that he saw what he wanted to see and told Northern readers what they wished to hear. Olmsted himself conceded that communities in some parts of the South showed evidence of improvement, however feeble.[14] He failed to notice that Southern townspeople often upheld a vision similar to his own. Some of them might even have agreed that a good community needed to be encircled by a well-ordered countryside and well connected with other progressive towns. The escalating conflict over slavery was in some ways a distortion that concealed shared cultural visions, deprived men like Olmsted of their evenhandedness, and permitted men like Allison to speak for all the South.

As we conclude these multiple, repetitive visits to Nashville, where Jackson constructed his own identity, where Lafayette paraded as a relic of antiquity, where Tocqueville encountered new breeds of men, it is easier to see the conflicts of the future than the pull of the past. As we proceed, we will see that for some post-revolutionary observers America was not only disturbingly cut off from history but it had turned intellectual careers into a form of vagabondage and moral assertions into a masquerade. The woman who brought her kids to a marionette show so that in old age they could say they had seen it may serve as a premonition of recurrent feelings about the insubstantiality of American life.

But remember that we have witnessed another kind of reaction to America. We may think back on Professor Lindsley, beset with dissembling beggars, trying to establish respect for educational institutions in the West. Or think of Olmsted returning from Nashville with a grand, if slightly ambitious, vision of civilization. For many leading citizens, American culture was something to be planned and constructed against great odds. That was the vantage point from which the insubstantiality of American life seemed most deplorable. This tense, critical, yet optimistic outlook enabled some Americans to overcome worries about the lack of tradition and to set forth to create culture in America.

PART TWO

The Dead Past

We are, whether we acknowledge it or not, what the past has made us and we cannot eradicate from ourselves, even in America, those parts of ourselves which are formed by our relationship to each formative stage in our history.

—ALASDAIR MACINTYRE, *After Virtue*

CHAPTER FIVE

Looking for Connections

"Who are we? and for what are we going to fight?" Andrew Jackson asked his volunteer troops in 1812. "[A]re we the titled Slaves of George the third? the military conscripts of Napoleon the great? or the frozen peasants of the Russian Czar? No, we are the free born sons of america; the citizens of the only republick now existing in the world; and the only people on Earth who possess rights, liberties, and property which the[y] dare call their own." The principle that motivated America's soldiers was that *"a free people [was] compelled to reclaim by the power of their arms the rights which god has bestowed upon them."*[1] During the second war with England, historical memories were still vital; they were, however, attenuated by insistence on America's disconnection from the remainder of the world and by emphasis on liberty as divine gift rather than historical evolution.

When the wars were over, as all parties embraced popular sovereignty and material progress in ways that were previously unimaginable, the meaning of the past became uncertain. The great revolutions of the eighteenth century, in Europe as well as America, had damaged the claims of the past but had supplied a new store of memories to define allegiances and fortify sense of purpose. Time undercut even those memories. Although nearly everyone paid homage to revolutionary forebears, their heritage meant different things to different speakers. No one could successfully link new issues with old, any more than Jackson could link the party he built with his antique contempt for electioneering. "We still know aged men . . . who firmly believe that all the federal party were identical with the Tories of the [American] revolution, and others who associate their democratic opponents with the Jacobins of France."[2] These words of an observer of American politics in 1840 suggest the totality of the erosion except among some of the "aged." "Overturn, overturn, overturn!" was the maxim of the day, according to one old conservative in 1849. "The very bones of our ancestors are not permitted to lie quiet a quarter of a century and one generation of men seem anxious to remove all relics of those which preceded them."[3]

The continuing consequence of the revolutions turned out to be a feeling of "pastlessness," sometimes linked with the thrilling expectation of boundless improvement in the future. There were too many people for whom the Revolution was not even a memory. The era belonged, or so many remarked, to the young. Ralph Waldo Emerson quoted "a witty physician who remembered the hardships of his own youth." "It was a misfortune," he said, "to have been born when children were nothing, and to live till men were nothing."[4] Observers of the American scene agreed that the discipline of youth became less severe in the years after the Revolution; the common justification was the need to bring up children who could manage themselves responsibly in a world of change.[5] Attention to youth nearly always signified a diminished sense of rootedness in the past and heightened consciousness of the possibilities of the future. Only a few voices inveighed against this shift. Orestes Brownson, once an enthusiastic reformer but disillusioned and newly converted to Catholicism, told a college audience that theirs was "the age of quackery" in which reverence and veneration had been lost. Public life was ruined by an intemperate attack on "old institutions which have come down to us"; in the home "our children hold it to be gross tyranny that they should respect their parents."[6] As he probably recognized, Brownson was shouting into the wind. The forces he hated were irresistible.

My goal is to delineate the patterns of historical consciousness in a time rapidly drifting away from the beliefs and purposes of the revolutionary era, a time when traditions seemed under fire and youth seemed to take precedence over age.[7] I start from this assumption: No matter how tumultuous the times, everyone must carry some sense of the past, as good or bad, as distant or closely related to the choices we make, as warm and friendly or cold and unnerving. The necessity springs from feeling more than intellect. It is, after all, feeling that sustains the primary connection between the individual and society. The motives we acknowledge and the choices we make point toward the future, but we cling to them as portions of narratives that originate in a past we are trying to maintain, to reclaim, or perhaps to alter or disown. Even when the past looks remote, threatening, or irrelevant, those impressions serve to define the sense of bearings or lack of bearings that gives the person an orientation in life. Many questions about affect and knowledge might enter into characterizing and assessing the sense of the past held by individuals or groups, past or present. Here I am especially interested in the stance from which Americans "observed" the past, the strength of their cathexis with previous generations, the choices they made about which periods of the past mattered or did not matter, the connections they drew between truth and the histories of human communities, and the tactics they used to learn about the past, to change it, or escape it.[8] These are elusive issues, demanding an effort to infer tones and feelings from intellectual statements and artistic compositions from the past and about the past. But without the effort, an essential component of America's emerging national culture is certain to vanish from our view.

Severance from the past did not entail a lack of curiosity about history. According to one scholar, "never before or since has history occupied such a vital place in the thinking of the American people as during the first half of the nineteenth century." This judgment echoes what Americans at the time believed about themselves. "No department of literature amongst us is cultivated with more assiduity than history," said one. "There never has been a period in which Antiquities were so intensively and actively cultivated," said another; and a third reported, "historical studies receive more attention than ever before."[9] Before accepting any generalizations about the vital place of history in American culture in that half-century, let us note that by some measures historical activity ebbed after 1830. Measured by the percentage of best-sellers devoted to historical subjects, popular interest climbed steadily until the 1820s when 88 percent (twenty out of twenty-four books) were historical; after that its decline was steady. The quantity of historical material in leading periodicals increased until the 1840s and decreased thereafter. In contrast, the requirement of history in schools and the publication of nonfictional works of history continued to rise for several decades. "Public interest," concludes one analyst of these trends, "was ahead of educators and scholars both in acclaiming the past and in tiring of it."[10]

Historical societies were one expression of an absorption in the past that seemed to grow with time. A few were founded in the 1790s, and at least 111 existed in 1860. Half of these started out in the 1840s and 1850s. They ranked among the signs of urban culture, and in some ways represented less a feeling of attachment to the past than a comfortable sense of civilized attainment in the present. Furthermore, their membership came out of only one segment of the population—male, prosperous, and professional. Members were doctors, lawyers, teachers, merchants, and clergymen. The societies "have excited a spirit of inquiry among educated men generally," said the *Southern Quarterly Review* in 1844.[11] The vitality and excitement of their activities will be questioned by anyone who looks at the published "collections" and "transactions" that they churned out. The societies usually listed among their purposes both "the discussion of original historical papers and the fostering of public interest in historical subjects by the occasional delivery of a public lecture."[12] But the focus was largely internal; the societies existed for the edification of the men who belonged. And for them, the past was inert and buried, its specimens available to be dug up and collected. The study of history and natural history fit well together, since both viewed their subjects from a spectatorial distance and encouraged the acquisition of souvenirs and relics to be catalogued and displayed. When the Essex Institute met at North Andover, Massachusetts, in August 1850, for example, the gentlemen present catalogued plants from the shores of the Merrimack River and received two Indian skulls for "the cabinets."[13] The Institute's *Historical Collections* froze the same attitude in print. Reprints of wills, deeds, and town records; selections from old reports; genealogical sketches; papers read at meetings; narratives of events; biographical entries—these break up the past into hundreds of desiccated objects.[14]

Town histories had the same freeze-drying effect. Even when a local historian eschewed documents and preferred to write on the basis of visiting historical sites and setting down living memory, as was the case with Essex County's James R. Newhall, the result tended to be dismembered geography and chronology. In his "memorial" of his county's past, one searches in vain for the emotional conflicts that had divided the churches into Unitarian and "orthodox" branches, for the rise and fall of Federalism, for the dramatic extension of commerce throughout the world, for the dispersal of youthful population to the West, for the rise of the temperance movement and changes in public standards of sobriety, for dissension during the War of 1812 and heroism during the Revolution, for encounters with Indians or the beliefs of the Puritans, for a dozen subjects of major historical importance, as we think of them today, in which Essex County's role was substantial. Instead, beneath the flimsiest of narratives, Newhall furnished lists of men and institutions.[15] Henry David Thoreau on his travels lampooned the town histories' matter-of-fact reporting and dry mention of past worthies. Here had resided "a classical scholar, a good lawyer, a wit, and a poet"; there, a doctor "distinguished for his urbanity, his talents and professional skill." Every town had housed "some great man," but the traveler "could not find that there were any now living."[16]

In public lectures and magazine articles the past became a source of useful knowledge. History contained an inexhaustible supply of facts and reflections democratically available to all men and women, not just to the rich who could acquire libraries and travel in Europe, but to the self-improving mechanic who attended a lecture series and the forward-looking farmer who subscribed to a periodical. Like travel, literature, or science, history contained miscellaneous information that generous-minded speakers and writers could organize and embellish in a manner that was accessible and reassuring. The connection of the audience to the past came, not through close emotional ties, nor through well-understood sequences of time running backward from the present, but instead through appreciation that in the here-and-now all forms of knowledge existed to be sampled by the public. Morality and piety went hand in hand with curiosity and love of eloquence; no one needed to be excluded from the good, the true, and the beautiful. If history was useful, it was also harmless—so much so that controversial, but eloquent, orators like the abolitionist Wendell Phillips or Whig leader Daniel Webster could lecture without offense on historical subjects, but not on public issues that divided the populace.[17] The distinction between sources of knowledge that were accessible to all and divisive issues of public controversy worked to assign to history a status of honored irrelevance.

To some Americans history retained a personal urgency that time did not weaken. The highly successful writer James Fenimore Cooper was embroiled for years in lawsuits in which historical issues merged with feelings of injured reputation and violated honor. His *History of the Navy of the United States of America* sold well until defenders of Commodore Oliver Hazard Perry denounced its account of the Battle of Lake Erie. Cooper not only attacked his critics in the press but sued for libel, commencing a series of lawsuits that went on for years. A more complicated series of suits centered on his family's ownership of lakeside property that the public was accustomed to using for picnics and swimming. The bitter dispute seeped into several novels and into interminable argument in newspapers and magazines. Vindicated in court, as he usually was, he could never again shake a reputation for crotchety defense of landed privilege in an egalitarian age.[18]

In other instances the historical identity of groups of Americans was at stake. William C. Nell used oral sources to record examples of blacks' patriotism in the Revolution and thus to justify claims to American citizenship. Elizabeth Ellet attempted to recover the collective biography of American women during the Revolution. She sent letters to numerous informants and culled a variety of records and manuscripts to fashion a series of portraits of brave women, widowed, robbed, and raped during the dangers of war. "Political history" had slighted "the influence of woman," she said, in a work clearly intended not only to preserve memories of the fleeting past but also to help make sense of a present in which women's role in countryside and town was changing.[19] Religious groups, in an era of proliferating sects and new departures, felt a special interest in their origins. The Universalists, rapidly expanding but dispersed and faction-ridden, created a historical society to promote knowledge of their ancient teachings and recent successes.[20] On the day the Mormon Church was organized in 1830, a divine revelation ordered them to keep their records, and a subsequent revelation instructed the church historian to "write and keep a regular history." Evangelical sects joined in recording in books and articles what amounted to the social memory of the "Great Awakening" of the previous century.[21] For adherents of older and now-orthodox movements, William Bradford's history of the Pilgrims at Plymouth was published for the first time in 1856, and Cotton Mather's celebration of the heroic first generation of Puritans, *Magnalia Christi Americana*, appeared in a new edition in 1820, sold steadily, and then appeared again in 1853.[22]

As the Revolution receded, leading Americans gave evidence of acute self-consciousness about living in a "post-heroic" era as successors to those who battled for freedom and founded a nation.[23] Although some scholars detect strains of guilt in the psyches of the children and grandchildren of revolutionaries, the evidence is conjectural. Those who participated most avidly in the life of the new era were often most articulate about the lives left behind. They do not at all conform to the image of the melancholy child of the century born too late for heroic action. Certainly that is true of the most famous expression of filiopietism, Abraham Lincoln's 1838 address before the Young Men's Lyceum of Springfield, which praised American institutions as gifts from "a *once* hardy, brave and patriotic but *now* lamented and departed race of ancestors." The message was conventionally patriotic and conservative: the revolutionary heritage obliged the young to oppose all threats to the republic. "Let every American . . . swear by the blood of the Revolution, never to violate in the least particular, the laws of the country. . . . let reverence for the laws . . . become the *political religion* of the nation . . . ; and let the old and young, the rich and the poor, the grave and the gay, of all sexes and tongues, and colors and conditions, sacrifice unceasingly upon its altars."[24] Obeisance to patriotic memories was no deterrent to energetic lives in the world of overflowing opportunity that the fathers bequeathed to their descendants. In an 1842 speech on temperance, Lincoln actually praised this new reform as a greater liberation than "our political revolution of '76" because it broke a "stronger bondage" and deposed "a greater tyrant."[25]

John Greenleaf Whittier, a poet who won fame and fortune in the expanding literary marketplace and an antislavery leader who joined in agitation that shook American politics, recalled in the mid-1840s "the intense childish eagerness with which I listened to the stories of the old campaigners [of the Revolution] who sometimes fought their battles over again in my hearing." These bloody tales raised greater difficulties for Whittier, a Quaker and a pacifist, than for most young people, but it was hard to suppress his fascination. He concluded: "It is only when a great thought incarnates itself in action, desperately striving to find utterance even in the sabre-clash and gun-fire, or, when Truth and Freedom, in their mistaken zeal, and distrustful of their own power, put on battle-harness, that I feel any sympathy with merely physical daring." What he had done in his own life, as he recognized, was to transfer the emotions of childhood to "new and better objects" by turning the revolutionary legacy into a call for principled reform.[26] Urgent personal memories were consistent with lives that promoted change in the dynamic present.

Whittier's concern with noble thoughts and selfless purposes was typical of those men and women who sought to retain some feeling of connection with the lives of their forebears. The great appeal of the historian George Bancroft was his discovery in history of the majestic theme of the progressive unfolding of truth. "The generations that hand the torch of truth along the lines of time themselves become dust and ashes; but the light still increases its ever burning flame, and is fed more and more plenteously with consecrated oil." The American Revolution promoted the inspiring truths of "the establishment of personal freedom" and the emancipation of "the nations from all authority not flowing from themselves." Long ripening in popular intelligence, these truths gained new energy in the struggles of America for independence. Thus the Revolution was "most radical in its character," yet also pleasing to conservatives in its respect for the consecrated memory of past generations, its "fidelity to principle" even among plebeians, and its "spontaneous patriotism."[27] Others generalized that the task of the historian went beyond getting the facts straight. Good history was a moral narrative featuring conflict between good men and villains, great purposes and evil opposition, always with the implication that the story was unending and there were more chapters for new generations to write.

When historians illuminated great thoughts connecting present to past, they fulfilled a need for readers aware of a transformation in their lives that threatened to make the past more distant. The connection, nevertheless, was not of the kind felt in communities marked by strong continuities in custom and belief from one generation to the next. Nor was it always certain that the historian was restricted to meanings actually embedded in the past. Later historians (with smaller audiences) accused Bancroft and his colleagues of straying too freely from what could be documented. More to the point, the writer and reader of history in the second quarter of the nineteenth century would not have denied the charge if it had been expressed in their presence. To go beyond the documents and point out the timeless moral bearings of history was the genius of the historian, as they understood it. This conception of the historian's task concedes the ebbing relevance of the past unless some abstract and presently inspired meaning is breathed into it. No one put the issue in quite these terms, but there is reason to take the popularity of history as itself a sign of the recession of the past.

To some Americans, a past informed by abstractions and rational
choices, real or imputed, was uninspiring. Such was the burden of twenty-
one-year-old Francis Parkman's 1844 commencement oration at Harvard.
"Cool reason, not passion, or the love of war, sent the American to the
battlefield." While "philanthropists may rejoice over the calm deliberation"
of America's revolutionaries, "the poet has deep reason to lament." The
closer historians look at "our fathers' wars," the more "we find the same
cool-blooded, reasoning, unyielding men who dwell among us this day—the
very antipodes of the hero of romance." Parkman was not entirely clear
whether the fault inhered in America's past or in the limitations of those who
wrote about it "in an enlightened age" and the prosaic, business-minded
population who read their books. It was still possible to visit dark woods and
mountain peaks and imagine passionate battles between races and empires.
These were the subjects of Parkman's subsequent volumes of *England and
France in America*. But to the young man of 1844, the past that was most
familiar to Americans was a bore.[28]

Parkman was not alone in this feeling. Washington Irving had registered
the best-known complaint of a paucity of historical associations that made it
difficult for writers to find emotionally affecting allusions. The editor and
writer Sara Josepha Hale spoke of the "barrenness" of American scenes:
"the want of intellectual and poetical associations" rendered America difficult terrain as a setting for art. The literary historian Stephen Fender concludes after examining a series of similar statements that "the deficiency of
usable history in the early republic was not just thought to be a problem: it
was a problem—if only because so widely perceived as such."[29]

CHAPTER SIX

Choosing a Past

When Americans turned their eyes toward the past, which past did they wish to know about? One that was close and comfortable? One remote and filled with passion? It was certainly not a comprehensive past taking in the experiences of people everywhere on the globe. Despite increasing commerce between coastal New England and Asia, few if any Americans showed curiosity about the history of that part of the world or even recognized that it possessed a history. Nor was there much more curiosity about Africa or South America. American Indians entered a bit more often in thinking about the past, but only in pre-Columbian times or as they came into contact with white Europeans. Americans could scarcely imagine a universal history. There was no sense that all peoples have their histories and no interest in a human history that searched out patterns of influence and competition connecting these separate histories over time.

Few Americans devoted attention to the classical past, far away and yet supremely apposite, that eighteenth-century gentlemen had studied and applauded. As the educated population expanded, the importance of the classical world waned. The history of Greece and Rome lingered in exclusive academies and colleges without finding its way into the new public schools or state-prescribed curricula.[1] Nor was it made attractive through historical romances. In one of the great shifts in public taste in America's cultural history, classical models fell into disuse after the mid-1820s in architecture, sculpture, and painting. Jokes about Andrew Jackson's ignorance of anything but the barest rudiments of lawyer's Latin—supposedly he declared upon receiving an honorary degree at Harvard, "E pluribus unum, my friends, sine qua non"—signified his unfitness for public office, according to old standards of leadership. But the public relish for such stories about Jackson, which did nothing to hurt him or his party politically, signaled instead the submergence of the classical world in a democratic era.[2]

In popular artistic taste, the decline of the classical was matched by enthusiasm for anything medieval or gothic. The success of Walter Scott's romances and the new architectural style promoted by Andrew Jackson Downing were cases in point. But in some ways the "Middle" Ages lost their meaning wherever there was no sharply defined understanding of the classical period which they supposedly differed from. Americans, moreover, were too generally Protestant to favor anything more than fanciful literary interest in the "dark" Catholic past. The European history taught in schools was mostly of the recent centuries, with preponderant emphasis on England. Within English history what mattered most were the growth of liberty and the triumph of Protestantism. England was simultaneously the Old World tyranny from which Americans had migrated and wrested their independence and the motherland in whose struggles American institutions found their antecedents.

Yet it is not clear that English history meant anything more than textbook learning to most Americans, even to the thousands of families whose migration from Britain had occurred in the previous half-century. American liberties were, by the end of the War of 1812, celebrated as an American birthright, not as an inheritance from someplace else. In the second quarter of the century, vast numbers of Americans cared little about England. Mounting numbers of Catholic Irish were hostile, and Germans, Scandinavians, and other immigrants from the Continent had no emotional investment in it. Americans also lacked a single folk past to be recovered from an official or imperial history of the Old World. Instead, they favored a highly fractured and inexact sense of history made up of scenes of struggles for liberation culminating in the present.

The miscellany of history was exemplified in the favorite roles played by America's first great tragedian, Edwin Forrest.[3] Born of an artisan family in Philadelphia, Forrest was a self-made hero whose muscular, vehement performances were cherished by working-class audiences. Refined critics disliked him. He "revolted against culture," said one; "he had knowledge enough to know that there is such a thing as learning, and he resented, with fierce irritation, the nevertheless irrefutable fact that this was possessed by others and was not possessed by him."[4] His partisans insisted that he was well read even if self-educated; they praised his courtesy and admired the Gothic mansion he built. A democrat who made Fourth-of-July appearances for

Jackson's party, he gave theatrical form to the motives and resentments of all those who felt a new day was coming in which cruel and effete rulers would no longer lord it over society. Forrest's non-Shakespearean roles, usually written for him and often played in sequence in a week's visit to a single city, were these: Spartacus the gladiator in rebellion against the Romans, Oraloosa the Inca in rebellion against the conquistadores, Jack Cade the peasant in rebellion against London's rulers, and Metamora the Wampanoag in rebellion against the Puritans of New England. Those were not performances that demanded historical verisimilitude. In fact, the sets were interchangeable, and every gesture, every motive, was instantly recognizable.

These plays reflected a great reversal of values. Shakespeare's Jack Cade in *Henry VI, Part II* is a detestable upstart, a lord of misrule; Indians who made war on Europeans were customarily regarded as treacherous savages; and slave revolts had potentially horrible associations. Now they coexisted in the costumes of history as emblems of universal human resistance to tyranny. The practical effect of this change should not be exaggerated: Forrest, like most of his party, disliked nonwhites and supported the continuation of slavery and the removal of Indians. The intellectual consequence may well have been a distancing of contemporary democratic thought from venerated traditions—truly, a revolt against culture—with the corollary assumption that there was a hidden history of subject peoples wherever one cared to browse in the past.

The past that most engaged American attention, however, was indeed American, a generation removed, and thought to be vanishing. The theatre, always sensitive to people's moods, furnishes countless examples. Some of the most successful comedians made their livings by imitating the dialects of Yankee artisans ("Deuteronomy Dutiful") or Western pioneers ("Nimrod Wildfire"). In melodramas the mother wit and innate integrity of rural characters, like "Old Catteraugus" Adam Trueman in Anna Cora Mowatt's *Fashion*, repeatedly foiled the schemes of those who plotted to get ahead in the shady world of sales and finance. Blackfaced tenors in the minstrel shows crooned nostalgically for the peaceful traditions of the old plantation. What was new on the stage was often validated by the well-publicized researches of actors in out-of-the way places among folks whose lives and speech were, as yet, uncorrupted by change.[5]

Poems and songs, often meant for recitation or performance on stage, exploited similar feelings about a disappearing past. Some are still familiar: "How dear to my heart are the scenes of my childhood. . . . And e'en the rude bucket that hung in the well"; "Woodman, spare that tree. . . . In youth it sheltered me, / And I'll protect it now"; "O give me my lowly thatched cottage again . . . / There's no place like Home!" Others were printed in a local newspaper or copied in a personal notebook—and forgotten. To men-

tion only one example, in 1846, Abraham Lincoln wrote a long poem entitled "My Childhood's Home I See Again."

> Where many were, but few remain
>   Of old familiar things;
> But seeing them, to mind again
>   The lost and absent brings.[6]

Political speeches conveyed the same message in different format and
setting. Presidential aspirants from Jackson to Lincoln boasted, not that they
lived in log cabins (that might have raised questions about their drive and
ability), but that they had been brought up in them and still cherished the
memories. Daniel Webster's variation on the theme strikes the twentieth-
century reader as preposterous:

> it did not happen to me to be born in a log cabin; but my elder brothers and
> sisters were born in a log cabin . . . at a period so early, as that when the
> smoke first rose from its rude chimney, and curled over the frozen hills, there
> was no similar evidence of a white man's habitation between it and the
> settlements on the rivers of Canada. Its remains still exist. I make to it an
> annual visit. I carry my children to it, to inspire like sentiments in them,
> and to teach them the hardships endured by the generations which have gone
> before them. I love to dwell on the tender recollections, the kindred ties, the
> early affections, and the touching narratives and incidents, which mingle
> with all I know of the humble primitive family abode. I weep to think that
> none of those who inhabited it are now among the living; and if ever I am
> ashamed of it, or if ever I fail in affectionate veneration for HIM who reared
> it and defended it against savage violence and destruction, cherished all the
> domestic virtues beneath its roof, and through the fire and blood of a seven-
> years Revolutionary War, shrunk from no danger, no toil, no sacrifice, to
> serve his country, and to raise his children to a condition better than his
> own, may my name, and the name of my posterity, be blotted for ever from
> the memory of mankind![7]

But Webster merely illustrates the rhetorical obligations of political leaders
in an age of widespread and ritualized nostalgia.

Some writers tried hard to recover traces of folklife as part of a program
inspired by like-minded writers in England and on the Continent. Themes of
protest and renewal coursed throughout many writings of the Romantic
movement in history and literature: protest against the abstractions of reason, the artificiality of cosmopolitan culture, the destructiveness of commerce and empire; renewal of faith, of language, of national feeling. Educated Americans knew that Johann Gottfried von Herder's repudiation of the

Enlightenment's emphasis on universal categories to define human nature and progress had led him to call for a more particular and historical interest in the life of the *volk;* that the brothers Jakob and Wilhelm Grimm transcribed stories told by peasants and retold them in literary form; that William Wordsworth and Samuel Taylor Coleridge sought to restore vitality to English poetry by bringing it closer to the language and feelings of the "common life"; that Walter Scott began his career as a collector of border minstrelsy and author of folklike lays and won great fame through historical novels exploring all levels of Scottish and English society of bygone centuries. In responding to such international influences, Americans found themselves seeking the authentic and particular out of motives that were at least partly imitative and trying to recover passing forms of life by the instrumentalities of forms of literature and the scholarship of a new era.

The border between the literary and the scholarly was indistinct. We may dismiss dozens of volumes of pseudo-antique verse, mostly imitating Scott. Let us note, however, that Washington Irving's "Rip Van Winkle" and "The Legend of Sleepy Hollow," supposedly found among the effects of an old-fashioned historian named Diedrich Knickerbocker, were not only literary successes but won their author acclaim as the American Grimm.[8] William Gilmore Simms, "the American Scott," ascribed the accuracy of his delineation of Indians to his travels among and conversations with them.[9] In collecting the chimney-corner tales of New England, Whittier was influenced by the work of both Scotland's Robert Burns and the Connecticut poet John G. C. Brainard, but also by town histories and scholarly studies of witchcraft and Indian lore.[10] Though many of his poems depended on the dialects, legends, and customs of a passing way of rural life, Whittier made no distinction between fact and fiction. In addition to the poems, he wrote prose collections, *Legends of New England* (1831) and *The Supernaturalism of New England* (1847), and magazine articles on similar subjects.

This was the age of the discovery of "the folk," not only in the United States but in Europe, too.[11] Concerted scholarly study of folklore in the United States began in earnest only later in the century, when it received support from universities and museums and sought to define itself in relation to literary history and anthropology. But the origins of the endeavor to preserve and appreciate folklore may be traced to the transformations of American life from the 1820s to the 1850s. In addition to the literary works of Irving, Simms, and Whittier—to whom could be added Cooper, Stowe, Hawthorne, and many others—evidence of the endeavor may be found in such works as *Lectures on Witchcraft* (1831) by the Salem, Massachusetts, legislator Charles Wentworth Upham; *The History and Antiquities of Boston* by the antiquarian bookseller Samuel Gardner Drake; the first edition of *English and Scottish Ballads* (1857–1858) by Harvard professor Francis

James Child; *Algic Researches* (1842) by U.S. Indian agent Henry Rowe
Schoolcroft; and *Annals of Philadelphia and Pennsylvania in the Olden Time*
(1830) by banker and railroad official John Fanning Watson. The last made it
his purpose "to rescue from the ebbing tide of oblivion, all those fugitive
memorials of unpublished facts and observations, or reminiscences and
traditions, which could best illustrate the domestic history of our former
days." The project won praise from Washington Irving: "he is doing an
important service to his country, by multiplying the local association of
ideas, and the strong but invisible ties of the mind and of the heart which
bind the native to the paternal soil."[12] In a nation of immigrants and emigrants, however, book-learning about lost native grounds may have been of
questionable patriotic consequence.

Most modern folklorists deny that the field is dedicated to tracing and
preserving incongruous survivals from simpler and inferior stages of social
evolution. They speak of varied processes of creativity in all versions of
social organization. Yet a conception of "a usable hidden past" often accom-
panies interest in folklore.[13] In its origins the American pursuit of folklore
referred to beliefs and customs unaffected, so far, by currents of change. It
was part of an endeavor to prolong acquaintance with all that the tide of
oblivion threatened to cloak in darkness. If folklore smacked of credulity,
that explained why it seemed doomed in the face of the subjection of social
institutions to the calculations of reason. By the same token, its persistence
indicated depths of the spirit that resisted change. Thus Whittier, while
deploring bigotry and error, claimed that persistent superstitions disclosed
"an under-current of intense, earnest thought—an infinity of Belief"—in a
New England too often caricatured as a region of railroads, factories, and
peddlers.[14]

Even when not concerned with folklore, much of the historical imagination of the era focused on the nearby, but receding, past, the days of
harmonious village and happy farmstead, "the ante-railroad times," as Harriet Beecher Stowe called them.[15] Sometimes this past was located in the
eighteenth century, two or three generations back. By the 1850s, however, it
had moved closer, and reminiscences were published of what life had been
like "thirty years ago."[16] Are we to believe from the flood of highly sentimental reminiscences that Americans really felt, however far they wandered,
close emotional connections with the past? There is no way to be certain.
Perhaps many felt with catholic-minded Walt Whitman: "Before I was born
out of my mother generations guided me."[17] It seems likely, however, that
many others, even as they polished memories of home and mother, felt no
connection between the preparations of preceding generations and their own
experience. Reiterated explanations of how different life was a few decades
ago often revealed strong feelings about parents and grandparents, but they

also suggested severed connections and new departures. In a sketch for newspaper carriers to give their patrons on January 1, 1838, Hawthorne dismissed conventional images of "Time" as an old man in ancient clothes, a frequenter of ruins and burial grounds, or a good fellow telling old legends, moving slowly in business and favoring old books. To the contrary, Time was a creature of fashion, mischievous, fickle, on the move, destructive.[18]

In *Past and Present* (1843), the Scottish essayist Thomas Carlyle uncovered in the year 1200 a once-living, organic world that put the economic world of the nineteenth century to shame. But Americans did not trace their past back so far, and such a contrast between feudal mutuality and the faithless frigidity of modern life was unavailable to them. Most backward glances extended only a short way, to the supposedly simpler communities of a generation before or, at most, to Puritan villages. Even workingmen, who shared something of Carlyle's anger at the ruinous effects of the "cash nexus" on a more secure system of economic relations, remembered their golden age as having existed in the late eighteenth century, when master, journeyman, and apprentice lived and worked in close proximity.[19] The hope of reversing sixty years of time, let along six hundred, was in any case forlorn.

There was some romantic glorification of the medieval past. But it was found not so much among labor reformers (except for a few communitarians) as among Southern defenders of slavery. Southerners sometimes went to absurd lengths, pretending their way of life was a throwback to the days of Walter Scott's *Ivanhoe*, with jousts, riding at the ring, and all the accoutrements of chivalry.[20] Some Southern writers claimed, in Carlylean terms, to uphold a feudal counter-current running against the damaging capitalistic tides. But it was hard, in a land of commercial agriculture, frontier expansion, democratic politics, and racial slavery, to find any convincing approximation of the idealized vertical hierarchy of medieval tradition. Even the cavalier past of the South was somehow thought to have prospered less than a century before. "Often in my evening reveries," begins the narrator of a historical romance set in the Virginia of the 1760s, "I endeavor, and not wholly without success, to summon from their sleep these stalwart cavaliers, and tender, graceful dames of the far past. They rise before me and glide onward—manly faces, with clear eyes and lofty brows, and firm lips covered with the knightly fringe: soft, tender faces, with bright eyes and gracious smiles and winning gestures; all the life and splendor of the past again becomes incarnate!"[21] The tone revealed those days to be beyond recovery except through fiction or in dreams. They belonged to the remote past of fantasy even though the Revolution that ended them occurred scarcely two generations before.

CHAPTER SEVEN

Holding On to History

If few Americans even in imagination could remove themselves to a graceful, harmonious medieval past, many confronted the question that Carlyle
explored in *Sartor Resartus* (1833–1834): how to fight against doubt and
affirm permanent spiritual truth in a world fractured by material transformation? *Sartor Resartus* appeared as a book in America, with an introduction
by Emerson, before it did in England. The resources Carlyle had seized on
during his crisis of faith were those Emerson and his American followers
learned to prize: nature, work, moments of insight, heroes of transcendent
force. In a nation that seemed constantly on the move and that took pride in
eliminating venerable forms of social, political, and religious hierarchy,
there was no hope of securing truth to the longstanding beliefs and practices
of historical communities. There was scarcely any way around recognition
that old forms of social organization were gone and the material conditions of
life were constantly changing; thus, one had to grapple with a conception of
truth outside tangible experience.

That truth endured in human consciousness was taught not only by
Emerson and other avant-garde thinkers but also in orthodox divinity
schools and in conventional textbooks on human psychology and ethics.[1] It
was also the lesson of thousands of ephemeral poems about fleeting thoughts
and drifting sands. Consciousness was timeless, a given, but it was also
repository to imperishable memories of absent loved ones and homes left
behind. It is an important fact about the formation of American culture that

63

both problems of belief and problems of affection were referred so frequently and vaguely to immaterial consciousness.

There was so much suspicion of "fashion" and such intense denunciation of the fickleness of public opinion, as we will notice more than once, that it was hard to put so much confidence in individual consciousness. The wish to find roots in the past was often irresistible. Yet how can anyone know a past so rapidly receding? Once the past is not of immediate acquaintance, there are only a few approaches that anyone can try. All have their limitations, and these were especially frustrating to Americans of the post-revolutionary era.[2]

One resort is to memory. This approach may be the most direct and personal, though one person's memories of the past usually depend on those of others for reinforcement and selectiveness. Except in societies that designate certain bards or elders to train their memories, the past approached through memory is usually of short duration. But it may be supremely important to the individual's feelings about who he or she is, the group that shelters this identity, the person's and society's future course. When Whittier recalled the old soldier's stories, when other Americans passed on stories about the conditions of life in their childhoods, when orators or journalists spun out descriptions of military valor or domestic simplicity, they were turning a fabric of memories into versions of history, a past that was codified and transmitted more than one actually remembered. The assumption behind much of this history making was that memories were fading, destroyed by change. As stoves and furnaces replaced open fires, and families no longer sat together before the flames, both Hawthorne and Lucy Larcom wondered, what would happen to the warmth from the past and stories shared across generations? And what would happen to collective loyalties? Would the motto "Fight for your hearths," asked Hawthorne, give way to "FIGHT FOR YOUR STOVES?"[3]

In written history, as Hawthorne also noted, knowledge of the heroes of past times atrophied. The knowledge furnished by historian or biographer was "analogous to that which we acquire for a country by the map," accurate enough, perhaps, and accessible to all who can read, but less vivid and affecting than that conveyed through "fire-side legends."[4] History that is read may give little feeling of the past, but in some ways it improves the past, giving it shape, detail, coherence, and explanatory power. The past we gain knowledge of is not exactly the present that anyone experienced.[5] And much that was keenly felt disappears without a trace or seems insignificant by later standards.

American readers sensed that they were losing the quality of the past in the midst of so much attention to recording history. That may help explain the popularity of historical fiction. It is not clear, however, that novels were required to be consistent with any past that actually had existed. To be sure, Scott was much praised for his credible, variegated portraits of historical situations. But in her 1827 bestseller *Hope Leslie*, set in John Winthrop's Boston, Catharine Maria Sedgwick explained that "the author's design" was "to illustrate not the history, but the character of the times."[6] In his preface to *Blithedale Romance*, set in the recent past at the utopian experiment at Brook Farm, Hawthorne warned against "too close a comparison with the actual events of real lives." He intended "merely to establish a theatre" for the imagined antics of his characters, an intention always hard to carry out in America, which lacked the remote, enchanted past of old countries.[7] Sedgwick and most historical romancers sought to claim more than this— she had committed herself to "patient investigation of all the materials that could be obtained"—but she still differentiated her work from "genuine history."[8]

Should historical writing be documented? Counsel was divided on this question. Authors and publishers who sought to reach a wide audience promised to keep history "exciting" and "entertaining." "We have no thought," said the *Virginia Historical Register*, "of going out of the warm and sensible world around us, to bury ourselves amidst the rubbish of antiquity—to dote upon dust."[9] Yet "doting upon dust" is not a bad description of the exercises of some historical societies, as we have seen, and much of the filiopietism of the era seemed to treasure the cold dullness of the past and to show little interest in narratives of derring-do. So many old papers were transcribed and collected that one study of the period speaks of "documania" as a "national obsession."[10] Americans praised this activity as indicative of proper respect for the past and proper regard for generations yet to come. Federal, state, and local governments contributed substantially to the effort. "To rescue from oblivion" was the stated purpose of most documentary collections, and many of them sold extremely well.[11] What was rescued from oblivion was, of course, disconnected from the present. This was not living history; though in one instance, the publication in 1840 of James Madison's notes on the Constitutional Convention, the bringing to light of what was formerly unknown had an unanticipated, disruptive effect in the present. Revelation of the compromises over slavery disclosed, in the minds of abolitionists, a dark, sinful history that needed to be purged.[12] For the most part, however, publication of old documents had no discernible effect on present moods beyond a complacent feeling that the past was in good order.

By the 1850s and 1860s, a new school of historical scholars, critical of the inaccuracy of romantic history and fiction, stressed their labors in old archives. In preparing his great work on the Dutch Republic, John Lothrop Motley explained, he relied on "the only foundation fit for history—original contemporary documents. These are all unpublished. . . . the most valuable of my sources are manuscript ones." With great diligence over many months, in London and The Hague, he had "read what no one else has ever been permitted to see."[13] Thus he could give his contemporaries a history that was unavailable before and one that made very different claims to truth than had most previous histories and novels. But this was a moment of change and contradiction. In a few years, Motley himself would seem old-fashioned to historians who sought to make a more scientific use of documents.[14]

Documents are only one kind of relic left over from the past. Awareness of rapid changes in the manmade landscape—the results of population movements, transportation improvements, commercial expansion, and the growth of cities—meant that the once-familiar was vanishing. That recognition was associated with all the poems, stories, and orations about log cabins and oaken buckets. Nevertheless, only historic sites linked to the memories of famous men inspired campaigns for preservation. Steps were taken to save Independence Hall in the 1810s, Fort Ticonderoga in the 1820s, Monticello and Old Ironsides in the 1830s, and Mount Vernon and the Hermitage in the 1850s.[15] Some of these efforts depended on state financing, though not on the same level as the documentary-publication programs; others, on philanthropic efforts, particularly by women. In spirit, they resembled campaigns to erect monuments, such as at Bunker Hill (started in 1820s), at Lexington (1836–1837), and grandest of all—and most frustrating in the slowness of its completion—the Washington monument in Washington (not completed till the 1880s). On a smaller scale, cemeteries began to feature monuments to departed worthies who might otherwise be forgotten.

The preserved past is an altered past. To see this, we need not join nineteenth-century English romantics like John Ruskin and William Morris in admiring the damage of time. When we side with those who seal and repair to keep the old looking new, we must alter what we wish to keep. Either way, things change. New uses have a similar result. Once Mount Vernon existed as a tourists' mecca and patriotic shrine rather than as a planter's home, it was irretrievably changed. This dilemma seems more painful to the very different historical mentality of the late twentieth century than it did to mid–nineteenth-century Americans, who seldom shrank from altering relics as they saved them from oblivion.

Some of the historic trees, buildings, and battle sites consecrated in this era actually had the significance assigned to them. Others were virtually fabrications. Consider the era's most extravagant historical creation: Plymouth Rock. Although the Pilgrims presumably stepped ashore at some location, there is no evidence that it was on a rock, let alone that rock now given hallowed status. But visitors streamed to see it, an edifice went up around it, painters interpreted the scene, and orators pointed to the rock as the foundation of American liberty and order. Alexis de Tocqueville marveled at the "veneration" of the rock. "I have seen fragments carefully preserved in several American cities. Does not that clearly prove that man's power and greatness resides entirely in his soul? A few poor souls trod for an instant on this rock, and it has become famous; it is prized by a great nation; fragments are venerated, and tiny pieces distributed far and wide. What has become of the doorsteps of a thousand palaces? Who cares about them?"[16] Tocqueville's emphasis on the soul may give a clue to Americans' acceptance of what to later eyes might appear hokey and contrived. With the past disintegrating everywhere, perhaps the best one could do was to collect some small pieces, however dubious their origin, revere them, and attribute to them spiritual meanings.

Since we inevitably change the past, regardless of our intentions, why not retailor it to suit present purposes? In the twentieth century the question makes us nervous because we think of the extreme measures of totalitarian governments and thought control, as satirized in George Orwell's *Nineteen Eighty-four*. In the mid–nineteenth century no one thought of employing government agencies to manipulate the truth on an Orwellian scale, but it was abundantly clear that the past could be turned to widely differing purposes. The past could be, as we have seen, a remote and glorious legacy that justified good order in the present, or it could be a record of conspiracy that required strenuous efforts at reform. It could explain characteristics of the American people that had emerged over time and thus were unlikely to change despite other kinds of transformation. Or it could reveal a protean quality inherent in all experience. Without assuming that they were insincere, we can see that some Americans were learning they could make the past whatever they liked.

The example of the early settlers of New England illustrates this possibility. In the first place, some of the most influential proponents of an American culture succeeded in popularizing the idea that the origins of the most civilized and progressive impulses in the entire nation were to be found in Plymouth and Boston. We will need to return to the ideological uses of this claim, but here let us note some of the varied elements of the American experience that the history of early New England was said to illuminate. To Lyman Beecher, the resolute evangelist who had come to Boston from western Massachusetts, the New England Fathers were in some ways "uncouth and uncourtly," but as such they remained a reproach to their descendants who were more "expert in the graces of dress, and the etiquette of the drawing-room." Their critical descendants could never "have felled the trees, nor guided the plough, nor spread the sail, which they did; nor braved the dangers of Indian warfare; nor displayed the wisdom in counsel which our fathers displayed; and had none stepped upon Plymouth Rock but such effeminate critics as these, the poor natives never would have mourned their wilderness lost . . . [and] the Pequods would have slept in safety that night which was their last."[17] To the conservative New Haven theologian Leonard Bacon, the Puritans were writers and scholars, predominantly from the middle classes, "which the progress of commerce and civilization, and free thought, had created between the degraded peasantry and the corrupt aristocracy." "And richly have their posterity . . . enjoyed, in well-ordered liberty, in the diffusion of knowledge, and in the saving influences of pure Christianity, the purchase of their sufferings, the reward of their virtues and their valor."[18] To Seargent Smith Prentiss, Bowdoin-educated Mississippi legislator, "the spirit of the Pilgrims" survived in the "indefatigable enterprise" with which Americans cultivated the land, built factories, and carried out a worldwide commerce.[19]

In *Hope Leslie*, Sedgwick imagined how New England's history would look if seen from the viewpoint of the Indians. This viewpoint also allowed her to explore how the conventions of Puritan society—like those of her own time—inhibited women's natural instincts and intelligence. In the course of turning traditional values upside down, she portrayed John Winthrop and his associates as gullible and unwise. Sedgwick was not hostile to the Puritans; she simply assumed the liberty to view them from a new angle, one that none of her sources could prove or disprove, and thereby to catch unnoticed qualities. To others Puritans were notable chiefly for their intolerance of dissent, their persecution of witches, and their merciless extermination of Indians—emblems of a joyless, bigoted, repressive spirit Americans must overcome.[20] Whether Americans glorified or debunked New England's ancestral past, no one entertained the possibility most attractive in the scholarship of recent years: New Englanders reflected the political and economic diversity of the agricultural regions, the religious fragmentation of the Protestantism, and the divergent beliefs of social classes of the English nation they came from.[21] Americans took Puritan leaders on their own terms as spokesmen for an entire society, as an orthodoxy of continuing relevance to the problem of cultural leadership in America, and proceeded to portray them however they in the nineteenth century wished.[22]

It is hard to know in any particular case whether someone changed the past to relieve the burdens of the actual past or whether the remoteness of the past made it seem weak and malleable. But one strong note heard from many quarters in this era was a wish to escape from the past. Such a wish may spring from various motives, including feelings that the accomplishments of past generations—the ancients, the revolutionaries—were so superior that moderns are enervated by thinking back on them. The past may draw attention away from what is admirable in the present. The glorification of past error may deter efforts to reform what does not deserve to survive in the present and the future. All of these feelings were expressed by American writers. After inspecting the Greek and Egyptian relics in the British Museum in 1856, Hawthorne worried: "The present is burthened too much with the past. We have not time . . . to appreciate what is warm with life, and immediately around us; yet we heap up all these old shells, out of which human life has long emerged, casting them off forever. I do not see how future ages are to stagger under all this dead weight, with the additions that will continually be made to it."[23] Contrast this reflection with his more familiar fear, as dramatized in "Earth's Holocaust," that moderns were so antagonistic to the past that they hastened to throw all the artifacts of the ages into the bonfire. In a nation where everything was changing, it was hardly possible to find middle ground between burdensome awe and reckless indifference to the past.

CHAPTER EIGHT

Anti-History

One striking feature of public controversy in the era was the elimination of the past. While poets wrote mournfully of the dead and orators acclaimed the deeds of the fathers, a very different agenda prevailed when it came to arguing cases and deciding issues in public.

Legal scholars have called attention to a "transformation" of the law in which customary privileges gave way to calculations of current use and social progress. Let us suppose the case of a property holder whose family had for generations enjoyed a river flowing through the estate. Now someone builds a mill upstream and impedes the flow of water. When the case comes to court, historic but unprofitable use is pitted against profit-seeking innovation. Traditionally, local courts decided in favor of historic custom, but by the second quarter of the nineteenth century the ground was shifting. The argument that the community benefits from uses of resources that were unfettered by the past was more likely to win the day.[1] In the U.S. Supreme Court, one of the notable achievements of Chief Justice Taney's Jacksonian majority lay in overturning the Marshall Court's previous respect for "vested rights." For years Jeffersonian republicans had asserted angrily that this term does not appear in the Constitution; thus, for the Court to honor the vested interests of those who gained by the perpetuation of the status quo amounted to a reactionary alteration of the basic law of the land. The best-known cases by which the claims of history were tested involved transportation monopolies—a bridge and ferry service threatened by competition—

and by the 1830s the vested rights of the old order had been undercut. The rights of new entrepreneurs and their projects were ascendant.[2]

Religious controversy focused, more often than not, on timeless testaments. Some Americans, notably Unitarian followers of William Ellery Channing, dared to interpret the Bible broadly to suit the exigencies of the present;[3] many more accepted a "populist hermeneutics" that gave individuals the right to interpret the plain language as it made sense to them.[4] Frequently there was an assumption—misguided, it may seem, in view of the proliferation of sects and interminable wrangling—that biblical truth was so obvious that all Christians would naturally agree on the essentials of scripture. With the exceptions of a few old denominations and their seminaries, almost no one took seriously the claim that the time-hallowed practices of religious communities deserved veneration in their own right, let alone that determining the meaning of scripture took linguistic sophistication and historical subtlety. Americans of many persuasions quoted the Bible, memorized it, flung it out in argument, and parted company over it, for the most part in a pastless void.

Much religious controversy concerned the so-called new measures of revivalism, which included such innovations as the "anxious bench" for potential converts, use of the second person to preach directly at sinners, and protracted meetings of a week or longer. From a traditional point of view, the novelty of these measures, as executed by professional revivalists and the squadrons of zealots who accompanied them, sufficed to condemn them. To the prevailing opinion, however, absence of historical precedent was inconsequential. God had not established "any particular form, or manner of worship," for all time, said the greatest revivalist, Charles Grandison Finney. Otherwise ministers would still be wearing the wigs and gowns of a previous generation. Without innovations the church would be impotent in an age in which "there are so many exciting subjects constantly brought before the public mind, such a running to and fro, so many that cry 'Lo here,' and 'Lo there.'" And why should God's work be done by stodgier methods than those of the courtroom, legislature, or newspaper office? Though the new measures were shunned by Unitarians, Episcopalians, "Sober-Side" Lutherans, and "Old School" Presbyterians, throughout most of American Protestantism accommodation of the new was the order of the day.[5]

Reform movements did their part to "dehistoricize" public argument. It was theoretically possible to argue that institutions and practices surviving from previous centuries deserved respect even if they needed modification. But that was not how most reformers argued. In opposition to the flogging of sailors, Herman Melville proclaimed that "the Past is dead, and has no resurrection. . . . The Past is, in many things, the foe of mankind; the

Future is, in all things, our friend."[6] Agents of the American Anti-Slavery Society were instructed to hold to the position that slavery was a sin regardless of circumstance. Emphasize "the inflictions of slavery on mind," Theodore Dwight Weld advised antislavery speakers; emphasize its interference with divine law, and avoid nitpicking arguments about time and place.[7] This was a good tactic since it nullified the arguments of cautious people who stressed that slavery had existed throughout human history, that it had been introduced to America over a long period of time, through no one's fault, and that it would take a long time to eradicate.

Feminist movements insisted that centuries of subjugation of women did not justify reluctance to elevate their status now. Sometimes feminists adopted and modified the arguments of the antislavery movement: timeless, divinely ordained rights were being violated. More often they took up the secular rhetoric of the Revolution and Enlightenment. Their most famous document, the "Declaration of Sentiments" of the Seneca Falls convention of 1848, was modeled on the Declaration of Independence, beginning with these words: "The history of mankind is a history of repeated injuries and usurpations on the part of man toward woman, having in direct object the establishment of an absolute tyranny over her." A bill of particulars followed: man has denied her the franchise; monopolized the best jobs; discriminated against her in education; weakened her self-respect; exploited her through inequitable laws; and so on. The "facts" of history, in other words, were stark conclusions about the deprivation of universal rights; no further distinctions were needed to make the case for the immediate granting of unjustly withheld equality.

Not all reforms rejected the past. Workingmen's movements referred back to a golden yesterday and, to some extent, "represented struggles to return to a past that had gone." But they were more likely to castigate inequality as a vestige of the past and to praise equal rights as a goal to be won in the future through concerted action.[8] Reformers who took up the cause of Indians tried sometimes to insist on legal respect for past agreements and customary rights. But reminders that the United States' gains had historically been the Indians' losses were unwelcome, and the cause was nearly futile. Many reformers accepted the proposition that involuntary removal from ancient lands was the Indians' only hope of progress and survival.[9] For the most part, arguments like those of the antislavery and women's movements were repeated wherever reform movements sought fundamental changes in accepted procedures and customary practices. That both religious and secular arguments could be turned to the same antihistorical end suggests that we are not dealing with a matter of specific intellectual influence; the point, rather, is that the past no longer seemed to restrict the social arrangements that men or women needed to accept.

The counterarguments of those who opposed reforms also became less grounded in history. To point to the long endurance of an institution or practice no longer seemed a forceful justification. After 1830, therefore, slavery was defended less often as an inherited, obsolescent evil and more often as a positive good. New-model versions of slavery should be extended as an alternative to the corruptions of democracy and callousness of capitalism. Similarly, modern marriage, though denying women most rights of citizenship, was championed as an ideal arrangement benefiting not only husbands and children but also the women themselves. The strongest recourse, perhaps, for those who sought absolute standards by which to defend the treatment of blacks or women, in a world where history no longer furnished reliable authority, lay in biology. In this same period elaborate versions of scientific racism were offered: the condition of slavery was natural and appropriate. Women were discovered to have a nature that barred them from the competitive exertions of public life and suited them to be queens of the home.[10] History might corroborate these points, but it no longer furnished the main support.

In spite of so many indications of the dehistoricizing of thought and argument, two of the most incisive commentators on American life saw too much heed being given to the past. "The whole of history is in one man," wrote Emerson. "There is no age or state of society or mode of action in history to which there is not something corresponding in his life." Whatever such pronouncements meant to his audience, to Emerson this was not a view that put much of a premium on specific knowledge of any particular history. Human nature and ethical law were what interested him. History was one access to the "one mind common to all individual men," and as such, it was always "subjective." Wisdom formulated in the past must today be verified anew.[11] "How dare I read Washington's Campaigns or Xenophon's before I have answered the questions of business or thought proposed to me?" he asked in 1839. "One of our illusions is that the present hour is not the critical, decisive hour," he asserted in 1857.[12] The intellectual leader of this era whose work was most influential for the rest of the century was also the most antihistorical.

Henry David Thoreau, his pugnacious ally, thought about time more deeply but was, in the end, equally antihistorical. He had a keen sense of the irreversible passage of time. He was an inquisitive digger in the dirt, learning from the arrowheads in his beanfield of "an extinct nation" that preceded him; he was conscious of blacks, free and slave, and Irishmen who inhabited the woods before him.[13] He spent many hours chatting with oldtimers about changes in farm life and accepted much of their misty talk about a day, not so long ago, of greater leisure and autonomy. His satirical portraits of his greedy, bustling neighbors and his appeals to Americans to simplify their lives were versions of that nostalgia for a way of life just at the reaches of memory that we have already observed.[14] Yet he also scorned the admonitions of old men and recognized the impulses that brought on change: "One generation abandons the enterprises of another like stranded vessels."[15]

Thoreau was not much impressed by America's history. He ridiculed the filiopietism directed at Puritans and revolutionaries. Throughout his works, however, runs a tension of attraction and conflict between the ancient world and the present. He nourished an old quarrel between ancients and moderns, a drive to be original, a fear that the lost golden age could never be imitated. "Some are dinning in our ears that we Americans, and moderns generally, are intellectual dwarfs compared with the ancients, or even the Elizabethan men," he reports. "But what is that to the purpose? A living dog is better than a dead lion."[16] Occasionally he sounded even more anti-historical than Emerson: "Why read history, then, if the ages and generations are now?"[17]

At the same time he was compelled to draw parallels, which he insisted went beyond parallels, between contemporary experience and the legends of Greece, Rome, and India. In the Maine woods he thought of "the creations of the old epic and dramatic poets, of Atlas, Vulcan, the Cyclops, and Prometheus."[18] An island in the Merrimack set him dreaming on Pindar's tales of Argonauts and Helius.[19] But these were not tales from history, and he made it clear that a pedantic regard for "historical truth" was too limiting. What counted was "a higher poetical truth," history turned into mythology, history that contained, not recorded fact, but "immemorial custom" like that of the Hindus. What was absent from the American fetishes about the past was that sense of long lasting connectedness found in cultures where myths move slowly through time and space. In those cultures, "fond reiteration of the oldest expression of truth by the latest posterity, content with slightly and religiously retouching the old material," gave "the most impressive proof of a common humanity."[20] By contrast, Americans were on their own, clutching at fragments of memory, drifting away from universal truth.

In some ways, it remains accurate to speak of the vital interest of Americans in history. They longed to have some equivalent to the ruins of Europe and took heart from studies of the Mound Builders and pre-Columbian relics that they could use to refute "the reproach [of] the excessive modernness and newness of our country."[21] They published quasi-folkloric fragments of a lost way of rural life, just at the edge of memory and stretching back into an indefinite time. They cherished pious memories of the "Fathers" of the seventeenth century and the Revolution. They collected records and relics and preserved them in tomes and cabinets. Schools and lyceums made historical knowledge accessible to increasing numbers of men, women, and

children. Multivolume scholarly projects gave a documentary basis to defini-
tive treatments of past eras. Novels captivated readers with a living past.

Despite such evidence of American preoccupation with multiple pasts,
collective memory no longer exerted a decisive influence on belief and
practice. Amid protestations of nostalgia and regret, the past was slipping
away. It was difficult to seize and keep hold of any part of it. The history
collected by historical societies was inanimate. Scholars began to create a
new past known only from documents. In the lyceums, history was eclectic
and miscellaneous, in some ways indistinguishable from any self-improving
activity. It did not supply a past directly relevant to the listener's identity.
Novelists filled this lack by creating emotionally affecting portraits of past
eras, but they made the past more remote and exotic rather than connecting
readers to a meaningful, inescapable previous history, especially a recent
one. They were free to change the past, and they reinforced feelings that the
recent past was of less interest than older ones. Pre-Columbian relics might
be claimed to show that the United States enjoyed "what no other nation on
the known globe can claim: a perfect union of the past and present; the vigor
of a nation just born walking over the hallowed ashes of a race whose history
is too early for record."[22] But this was to avoid the uncomfortable history of
Indian peoples who still survived, and no one convincingly asserted strong
links between the white American's present and the lost empires that left
such intriguing traces. These were not our Parthenon, Bury St. Edmunds, or
Alhambra.

No one could deny the warmth of memories of log cabins, beehives, and
gravesites on old farms, but the songs and poems that spoke of yearning
memories also accepted the reality of the business that took the songster
ever farther from those sites. Popular theologies neglected to harness the
generations together in providential union. Piety about the "Fathers" had its
genuine aspects; the assumption that current policy ought to be faithful to
the goals of those who sacrificed for us long, long ago became, as it continues to be, a touchstone of our politics and morality. But it was already true
that Americans "cut ourselves off from the benefit of a historical tradition,
properly speaking, by the veneration we show for the achievement of men
who are increasingly removed from the age in which we live."[23] That is,
selective focus on distant ancestors (of *some*) weakens respect and analysis
of all the successive actions and experiences of those who preceded us.[24]

What should we make of the repeated view that the present was "the
forcing-house of mediocrity" in comparison with earlier, more exciting, more
heroic days? Or that moderns were poor followers of nobler ancestors?[25]
Surely there is little evidence of Americans' actually preferring the past. In
some ways, in telling their countrymen that the present was the decisive
hour, Emerson and Thoreau were preaching to the converted. More accu-

rately, they identified beliefs people already acted on but were not yet comfortable with. It was scarcely possible to go forward in life without some conception of the past, and the pasts men and women cherished were generally those being left behind more than pasts being carried forward. Emerson and Thoreau essentially dismissed the feelings of conservatism, inferiority, or narrow-minded antiquarianism that droned in accompaniment to more antihistorical strains of the era.

Thoreau did experiment with forms of thinking about time and generations that seemed irretrievably lost amid all the chatter about history. His experiments were literary and had little influence, and the volume in which he presented them most beautifully was his most neglected work, *A Week on the Concord and Merrimack*. Americans have never, as a people, adopted a cosmological sense of time that connected them with other men and women throughout the ages. No reform movement could have altered their vision to that extent, and certainly no work of literature could. Nor could they recover, except in small groups, the sense of intergenerationally transmitted stories that is one way of establishing moral truths.[26] They were far more likely to think of truth as permanent and extrahistorical. Or they might come to doubt the security of truth outside the passing historical situation. Americans who survived these years of transformation were uninstructed by history and unprepared for much that they would experience.

In 1845, Whittier recorded his feelings while gazing at Chapel Grove, a stand of ancient oaks amid the factories of Lowell. His reflections may stand for the typical ambivalence of Americans preserving mementoes of the past while succumbing to, and even celebrating, the rapid pace of change. The trees looked "lonely and isolated, as if wondering what has become of their forest companions, and vainly endeavoring to recognize in the thronged and dusty streets before them, those old colonnades of maple, and thick-shaded oaken vistas, stretching from river to river, carpeted with the flowers and grasses of spring, or ankle deep with leaves of autumn, through whose leafy canopy the sunlight once melted in upon wild birds, shy deer, and red Indians!" So much that these senescent trees could remember was fading from human recollection. Whittier associated them with controversies in the Church of England in which Edward Pusey and the Oxford movement argued against modern developments and urged restoration of the liturgy, doctrines, and devotion of traditional Catholicism. By choosing an English reference, even one as topical in the 1840s as the Oxford movement, Whittier distanced his reflections from events in the United States. Yet we know he was always uneasy with the incongruity between his career in the literary marketplace and his simple Quaker heritage. Surely these reflections cast doubt on prospects of retaining any hold on traditional convictions. "Long may these oaks remain," he wrote, "to remind us that if there be utility in the new, there was beauty in the old, leafy Puseyites of Nature, calling us back to the Past; but, like the Oxford brethren, calling in vain; for neither in polemics nor in art can we go backward, in an age whose motto is ever 'ON-WARD.' "[27] In a similar mood he might as easily have disposed of Plymouth Rock or Mount Vernon as worthwhile, but ineffectual, attempts to keep an eye on the receding shore as the currents of change surged forward.

PART THREE

Travelers

All this so that Marco Polo could explain or imagine explaining or be imagined explaining or succeed finally in explaining to himself that what he sought was always something lying ahead, and even if it was a matter of the past it was a past that changed gradually as he advanced on his journey, because the traveler's past changes according to the route he has followed: not the immediate past, that is, to which each day that goes by adds a day, but the more remote past. Arriving at each new city, the traveler finds again a past of his that he did not know he had: the foreignness of what you no longer are or no longer possess lies in wait for you in foreign, unpossessed places.

—ITALO CALVINO, Invisible Cities

CHAPTER NINE

Ruins and Stumps

In a beautiful passage in *Democracy in America*, Alexis de Tocqueville wrote emotionally of a memory of his travels in upstate New York. "I remember . . . coming to the shore of a lake surrounded by forest, as at the beginning of the world," he wrote. "A little island rose from the water, its banks completely hidden by the foliage of the trees that covered it." He saw nothing on the lake to suggest a human presence, except an Indian canoe, which he used to reach the island.

> The whole island was one of those delightful New World solitudes that almost make civilized man regret the savage life. The marvels of a vigorous vegetation told of the incomparable wealth of the soil. The deep silence of the North American wilderness was only broken by the monotonous cooing of wood pigeons or the tapping of green woodpeckers on the trees' bark. . . .
> But when I got to the middle of the island I suddenly thought I noticed traces of man. . . . I was soon convinced that a European had come to seek refuge in this place. But how greatly his work had changed appearance! The logs he had hastily cut to build a shelter had sprouted afresh; his fences had become live hedges, and his cabin had been turned into a grove. Among the bushes were a few stones blackened by fire around a little heap of ashes; no doubt that was his hearth, covered with the ruins of a fallen chimney. For some time I silently contemplated the resources of nature and the feebleness of man; and when I did leave the enchanted spot, I kept saying sadly: "What! Ruins so soon!"[1]

81

The example was not well suited to the point Tocqueville was making: that a restless desire for wealth and independence was less dangerous to social order in America than in Europe. To accept that point one would need to know more about where the European settler had moved. There is internal evidence that makes the passage seem contrived and contradictory: the *green* woodpeckers; the canoe where there is no sign of man; the refoliation of fence and cabin; the enchantment and the sadness. But in a book that often seems interminably theoretical the reader is delighted to come across this little fairy tale out of European romanticism.

Fascination deepens when the passage is compared with Tocqueville's more immediate, and very different, account of this visit to Frenchman's Island in Lake Oneida. In his pocket notebook he jotted down notes about the "monotonous, lonely look" of the hill country outside Syracuse and a stop at a "detestable inn" in Fort Brewerton. Then he plunged into an immense forest where "delicious freshness" reigned. With Gustave de Beaumont and other companions he conversed about Frenchman's Island and the residents who settled there more than thirty years before. His emotion was intense even before disembarking from "a little boat" and pushing his way through "immense" trees and "rotting trunks." There were "traces of man," primarily an "old apple tree" and "a vine, gone wild again"; but "no trace" of the house. The travelers wrote their names on a tree and departed through silence broken only by the sounds of birds. The sketchy notes conclude: "This expedition is what has most vividly interested and moved me, not only since I have been in America, but since I have been travelling."[2]

It was too important an experience to set aside. A longer and more rhapsodic account (the date of composition is unknown) improves many details.[3] In the middle of a cruelly hot July day, the party followed a path into "one of those deep forests of the New World whose sombre savage majesty strikes the imagination and fills the soul with a sort of religious terror."[4] The scene was indescribable: a thousand streams untamed by man, an "incredible profusion" of every kind of plant, a floral dome overhead, trees of every age, reminders of life and death, "a sort of chaos." In the mythlike setting "a solemn silence reigned," and yet nature displayed "a creative force unknown elsewhere"—only man was absent. "It was as if one heard an inner sound that betrayed the work of creation and could see the sap and life circulating through ever open channels." After passing for several hours through "these imposing solitudes," the travelers heard the sound of an axe and came to a pioneer's cabin, "the rough dwelling of the precursor of European civilization," where they lingered a few moments in conversation. Then they made their way to a fisherman's hut on the banks of Lake Oneida. There was as yet no road or factory; the Indians were already driven away. And though this was no tourist site of "picturesque beauty," it was not by "chance" that they had come here. "For it was the end and object of our journey."

At an "impressionable age" Tocqueville had read a book about a young Frenchman and his wife, "driven from their country by the storms of our first revolution," who took refuge on an island in Lake Oneida. "There, cut off from the whole world, far from the storms of Europe and rejected by the society that saw them born, these two unfortunates lived for one another, each consoling the other for their unlucky fate." The story lingered in his memory, which associated it with enviable scenes of marital happiness; "even love itself came to be merged in my mind with the picture of the solitary island where my imagination had created a new Eden." Beaumont came to love the story as Tocqueville retold it for him, and they agreed, "the only happiness in the world is on the shores of Lake Oneida." Thus when unexpected reversals in French politics drove them to America, they both wished to look up these exiles, if still alive, or at least to visit the site. There was "nothing new" on Frenchman's Island: "we seemed to be revisiting a place where we had passed part of our youth."

The fisherman's wife informed them that the residents had already left when she came to settle in 1810. The Frenchwoman reportedly had died, and no one knew what had happened to the man. At that time their orchard and gardens could still be found, but twenty years later, to the eyes of the travelers who borrowed the fisherman's boat and explored the island, only faint vestiges of cultivation were visible. The scene was a reversal of what they saw elsewhere on their journey. Instead of man struggling to master nature, here the forest was "regaining its sway, setting out again to conquer the wild, defying man, and quickly making the traces of his passing victory disappear." Tocqueville testifies to the profound, almost "religious feeling" evoked in him, and he indulges in novelistic fantasy about the wretched man, rejected by society, forgetting "revolutions, parties, cities, his family, his rank and his fortune" in his wife's love, and then losing her to death. He must have been a kind of border figure, "neither a savage nor a civilized man . . . nothing but a piece of debris, like those trees in the American forests which the wind has had the power to uproot, but not to blow down. He stands erect, but he lives no more."[5]

Placed beside these other tellings, the vignette in *Democracy in America* seems more and more distorted. This is not an episode in the spread of democracy in the New World, but, instead, a sketch of the sorrows of marginal and exiled men of the Old. It warns us just how literary *Democracy in America* can be, how freely Tocqueville edited the substance and altered the meaning of what he saw. It puts us on notice that the French Revolution is centrally important in this classic account of American democracy. And for all its musings on chaos and Eden, on exile and solitude, the passage dramatizes the central issue emanating from the French experience and raised in reversed form in America—the fate of civilization. In the Old World, the issue was whether past achievements would be shattered by revolution; in the New World, whether civilization could be created anew.[6]

This story introduces themes we must explore at length. American culture was not easily understood, even by those who earnestly sought to define their places in a new world of intellectual endeavor. To comprehend it involved more than a rendering of history; it involved travel and exploration, often along a line where the familiar and the wild seemed to meet. In such explorations it was easy to imagine scenes of personal exile set against the breakdown of an old order. Whether democracy itself was a form of wilderness indifferent or hostile to the aspirations of the gifted was a recurrent question; yet it was also conceivable that America represented a new theatre for the advance of civilization, a relief from the tragedies of the Old World and a promise of dawning human creativity. In the minds of some travelers, in fact, we may see a shift of historical paradigms as they wander across new space, a shift from thinking of the end of Europe to thinking of the future of the world. This was a shift that required abrupt changes in values, journeys away from what was fixed in the glories of the past and must be held on to steadfastly, journeys toward acceptance of the varying, adaptive qualities of human nature and society. Dread of being cast adrift mingled with hope that, in the conquest of terra incognita, new adventures of the spirit might commence.

Democracy in America was only one of many explorations of America. Like twentieth-century revolutions, the American Revolution lured foreign travelers and occasioned a long series of reports on what life was like in a new nation. Inevitably, these reports were contrived and biased.[7] Direct observation of American life seldom caused a European writer to discard preconceptions. Those who wished to report on the rudeness of life among the democratic multitudes found plenty to complain of in the food, talk, and habits of town and agricultural laborers. Those who wished to mock the pretentiousness of upper-class manners in a land without aristocracy found no shortage of amusing details to recount in their narratives.

Many Americans resented these disparaging reports. Nevertheless, they came to be accepted as sources of descriptive data about America and to set the terms even for American thinking about the American condition and prospects for improvement. In spite of Ralph Waldo Emerson's celebrated "declaration of cultural independence" in the "American Scholar" address (1837)—"our day of dependence, our close apprenticeship to the learning of other lands, draws to a close"[8]—Henry Adams, a half-century later, still relied on the travelers' reports for his critical assessment of society and thought in America in 1800. He found it comfortable to use the lenses of

European class prejudices to focus on the provincial backwardness and pretension that stifled the American imagination and hobbled the march of civilization.[9]

It is tempting to dismiss all these reports as artifacts of European history, too hopelessly prejudiced to be taken as reliable evidence of American life. To do so would be to follow respected precedents. Social historians have insisted on professional suspicion of any "elite" outsider's account of "ordinary" life. More generally, we have learned that "ideology" causes misunderstanding: an observer with a worldview reflecting one set of values, experiences, and expectations cannot easily comprehend what someone of a different social position in different circumstances means by speech or behavior. Scholars examine travelers' accounts critically as "texts," and we are reluctant to accept literally what a passer-by records as significant. What Europeans said about America figures in recent historical writing principally as false observations to be cast aside upon close examination of more legitimate sources.

No doubt, the foreign travelers must be consulted with much caution. For that matter, *any* observation must be regarded critically in constructing a description of "actual" people, events, institutions: they are always at best secondhand, and travelers usually have to tell us what someone else told them. If our interest lies in intellectual and cultural life, however, the travelers' books may have important uses. Some of them are penetrating treatments of American customs and institutions from the vantage point of Europeans with clearly identified concerns and programs of their own. When Michael Chevalier visited in 1833, he was a young bureaucrat with a keen interest, nurtured by contemporary socialist movements, in industrial organization and human welfare; later he became an influential advocate of free trade. His *Society, Manners, and Politics in the United States* (1836) surpasses almost every contemporary American source on what we now think of as "the transportation revolution" and its consequences. It is easy enough to identify inaccuracies and dated preconceptions, but its analysis of systems of communication, patterns of governmental and economic interaction, and the bearings of social organization on the welfare of social classes are too insightful to discard. And they clearly owe much to the foreignness of the perspective of the observer.[10]

Even when they were not so penetrating, the travelers' reports often reflected the opinions of persons whose respect many Americans craved. That was especially true of liberal and literary circles in Britain. The outcry that followed Harriet Martineau's *Society in America* (1837) and, even more, Frances Trollope's *Domestic Manners of the Americans* (1832) testified to an extremely self-conscious concern about the international reputation of America in general and its urban, educated classes in particular. Martineau's chief offenses included her denunciation of slavery, her dismissal of Ameri-

can literature, and her scolding tone toward prominent leaders. Margaret
Fuller complained of Martineau's "presumptuousness"; Thurlow Weed called
her a "sour old crabapple"; and Charles Dickens said that he heard from all
sides, proslavery and antislavery, Whig and Democrat, such abuse of her
that he couldn't figure out what she had done wrong. "Mr. Dickens, don't
write about America," he was warned by one of his American hosts; "we are
so very suspicious."[11] Trollope appreciated the entire business as a game.
While she was in Cincinnati, Basil Hall's *Travels in North America* (1830)
was published, and in listening to incessant denunciations of his Tory prejudices she discovered that desire for approval and sensitivity to criticism had
been carried in America to faults. In Hall's generous reaction to American
critics, whom he declined to read lest he lose his pleasant memories of
America, she detected a magnanimous spirit that Americans would do well to
imitate, if they could learn to do so. For her part, she courted hostility by the
contempt with which she discussed one disagreeable aspect of America after
another: from stinking slaughterhouses to boring conventions, from "detestable" rot in the forests to the hysterical howling of women at a camp meeting,
from the "inferiority" of "national literature" to an arrogant "gentleman" who
took out a map to prove Britain smaller than one of the "least important
states" and then "placed his feet upon the chimney-piece, considerably
higher than his head, and whistled *Yankee Doodle*."[12]

If asked "the greatest difference between England and America," Trollope said she would answer: "The want of refinement."[13] Charles Dickens
was more sparing of judgment; it is easy to credit his protestations that he
liked America and wished to give no offense. But to sensitive American
readers he seemed not to like America enough, to give only the faintest
praise to its accomplishments, and to harp on its shortcomings. In *American
Notes* (1842), he paid compliments to Harvard professors, the "resident
gentry" of Boston, Lowell mill girls, high society in New York, and many
(though not all) charitable institutions. But he criticized some prisons and
asylums, and he detested slavery. While singling out "Universal Distrust" as
a great "blemish" on American society, he had more to say about a host of
minor nuisances: uncomfortable conveyances, tobacco spit, impertinent
questioning of strangers, offensive ribaldry. Although he expressed awe at
Niagara, he wrote with greater feeling of the dreariness of America as
observed amid the discomforts of a railroad car: "Mile after mile of stunted
trees: some hewn down by the axe, some blown down by the wind, some half
fallen and resting on their neighbors, many mere logs half hidden in the
swamp, others moldered away to spongy chips."[14] Thus the objective of
many subsequent writings was to disprove Dicken's libel of America. To see
only the stumps and not the cleared fields and framed houses was like
missing the forest for the trees.

The reception of the travelers' reports revealed more than the sensitivity of Americans. The exchanges between European writers and Americans, who were at the same time the subjects, critics, and (at least in part) the audience of the Europeans' reports, remind us that cultural life was not exclusively a national business. In these exchanges, terms were articulated for establishing the meaning and evaluating the achievements of America as problems of international significance. Trollope saw little hope of useful dialogue: "there is hardly a single point of sympathy between the Americans and us."[15] In her opinion, the English had nothing to gain and much to lose from pursuing the example of America. Other travelers disagreed that America was a model only of what should be avoided. They listened carefully to their informants, restated and clarified American concerns, told Europeans what they needed to learn and Americans what they were pleased to hear. In their view, America was important because it was the stage where Europeans continued to push westward, where the fate of the democratic revolution was being decided and the progress of civilization tested. Perhaps Europe should not imitate America, but there was no doubt where the future condition of races, classes, and sexes was undergoing its most interesting trial. This was the view of two European travelers whose reports will receive extended analysis in the pages that follow—the most influential, Tocqueville; and in some ways the most insightful, Fredrika Bremer.

CHAPTER TEN

Tocqueville: Wilderness and Civilization

In explaining why some works endure as classics, Frank Kermode has said that they are "patient of interpretation." The point is not just that they can be read on many levels but that over time they permit many readings.[1] Perhaps such an explanation helps to account for the remarkable, continuing influence of Tocqueville's *Democracy in America*, one of the most difficult and elusive works ever written about America. Lurking throughout this work are images of exile, drawn from family memories and children's stories and evident in his retellings of the trip to Frenchman's Island. Yet these images almost disappear within a sometimes ponderous analysis of the options facing European civilization as it came to terms with prolonged revolution. Tocqueville tailored his observations to conduct an argument with European audiences that were either too favorable to democracy or too hostile. He failed to define key terms and let them shift in meaning; he was forced to discard the hypotheses he began with.[2] His account was further complicated by the scantiness of his American experience, his preference for romantic sidetrips, and his reliance on American informants who were themselves ambivalent about the events of their lifetimes. And he never quite decided whether to describe America as wilderness or civilization, and Americans as half-savage degenerates or bearers of a new European social order. His Americans were forgetful of the past as they raced out into uncharted forests, but in traveling among them one was constantly returning to civilization.

We cannot know all that is meant by Tocqueville's remark that at French- **89** man's Island he and Beaumont seemed to be revisiting scenes of youth. We would have to know much more about his childhood and relations with his father. In general terms we may speak of his ambivalence. He possessed the feelings of a scion of a noble family and class hurt by the French Revolution. His parents, as newlyweds, had been imprisoned for several months during the Terror; close relatives were beheaded. His father was never an émigré but lived in inconspicuous quiet through all the days of Revolution and Bonaparte. The father entered public life only with the restoration of the Bourbons, from whom he received a series of increasingly important posts and honors; he refused to accept the overthrow of the Bourbons in the Revolution of 1830 and returned to obscurity. Alexis, however, took the oath to the new monarch Louis Philippe in 1830, and it is not entirely clear which was the stronger drive behind his trip to America—Orléanist suspicion of him because of his association with his family, or family displeasure at his turncoat acceptance of the new regime. Though Tocqueville went to the United States to take a critical view of democracy in the one nation where it flourished, he showed little doubt that the direction of change was irreversibly toward democracy.[3]

After returning from his nine-month journey in the United States, he had to collaborate with Beaumont on a report on prisons that had furnished the pretext for their voyage. He had other commitments, including the legal defense of a friend and a trip to England, which delayed work on the book on democracy until October 1833, when he started outlining in a garret in Paris. He had a draft manuscript to show friends by July, and the book was in print, in two volumes, by January 1835. This was Part One of the eventual work, and it was completed in a burst of intense labor. It was so highly acclaimed that it raised the stakes for the promised second part, which was to be a grander philosophical treatment of equality in the modern world. Although many obligations cut into his time—he was married, inherited an estate, was elected to office—he clearly encountered something like a writer's block as he tried to write the second installment. He spent much time in reading Western classics—Plato, Aristotle, Plutarch, Aquinas, Machiavelli, Montaigne, Montesquieu—and it was hard to find the right room to write in. Much of the work was done in 1838, but he did not let go of it until early in 1840. Part Two, also in two volumes, remained heavily concentrated on the United States, though it made use less of his observations (the vignette on Frenchman's Island appears near the end of Part One) and more of his predictions and speculations about the consequences of democracy.

In short order, the volumes established the author's fame. He was elected to the Académie Française in 1841 when he was still only thirty-six. His subsequent writings, which seldom referred to the United States and were not much read there, established him as one of the foremost commentators on a half-century of revolution. He also played a prominent role in public affairs, even serving as foreign minister of the revolutionary government of 1848 before the 1851 counterrevolution of Louis Napoleon drove him into retirement.[4]

Tocqueville wrote for the leaders of informed European political opinion in an age of revolution and resistance. Most of all, in every work, he addressed those who cared about France. To those of his own class who harbored memories of the ancien régime he depicted the advantages of a democracy that was to some degree inevitable: contentment, obedience, harmony, and peace. To the republican ideologues who embraced democracy uncritically, he stressed what was lost from the old order: intelligent leadership, individual distinction, spirituality, refinement, cordial bonds between society's ranks.[5] These tensions in his work can make his writing frustratingly unclear: even when discussing the United States, his mind was on France; and in the French context he had somewhat conflicting messages to give to opposed sets of readers. He addressed both sets because he cared about both. The best imaginable future was one in which responsible aristocrats and republicans would cooperate to accept the advances of the people in the least destructive way. If the great issue for French society was whether the rising middle classes would be allied with the old privileged classes or with the people, Tocqueville clearly favored the former—but he had no illusion that the people could be ignored.[6]

It is enlightening to compare his views with Karl Marx's. The bourgeoisie, according to the *Communist Manifesto* (1848), "has pitilessly torn asunder the motley feudal ties that bound man to his 'natural superiors,' and has left remaining no other nexus between man and man than naked self-interest, than callous 'cash-payment.' "[7] Tocqueville took no notice of Marx, but in many ways they started from the same realizations. Both were obsessed with the continuing revolution; both linked it to capitalism's long and ultimately triumphant assault on the feudal order. Only their ends were very different. For Marx, class cooperation and harmony were a cruel hoax; for Tocqueville, they were a cherished hope. "All that is solid melts into air, all that is holy is profaned," says the *Communist Manifesto*, "and man is at last compelled to face with sober senses his real conditions of life and his relations with his kind." From personal struggles with depression, Tocqueville knew much about the dissolution of conviction, and the shattering of illusions. In this new age, he wrote, "nothing any longer seems either forbidden or permitted, honest or dishonorable, true or false."[8] In a world at sea the deterioration of religious beliefs was especially frightening. Doubt invaded the mind, opinions were ever-changing, the soul was enervated, and in a desire for stability people tired of seeing "everything on the move" and were prepared to "hand themselves over to a new master."[9]

Nowhere is his historical perspective clearer than in the introduction to *Democracy in America.* After preliminary remarks about the "novelties" he encountered in America and his subsequent perception that "that same democracy" was racing forward in Europe, at which moment he "conceived the idea" of the book, he turns to a sketch of the previous seven centuries. A feudal order based on landed property had steadily deteriorated. Men who would otherwise have vegetated as serfs became clergymen or lawyers; then came commerce and intellectual enlightenment so that men of wealth and education entered the affairs of state. Nobility and Crown in competition with each other gave the lower classes a share in government. New forms of property-holding and new inventions hastened the process of "levelling." The invention of firearms, the insurgency of Protestantism, the discovery of America—virtually every movement and event for centuries had diminished social inequality. As noblemen fell and commoners ascended, the distance between them began to disappear, "and soon they will touch." Tocqueville sounds nearly as deterministic as Marx. The progress of equality was, he wrote, "something fated" or "imposed by Providence." It was irresistible, advanced both by those who favored and those who opposed it. It was as clearly part of God's design as the orbiting of the stars. The entire book was written in a state of "religious dread" occasioned by viewing this centuries-long progress and the "ruins" it had created.

A new political science, he believed, was needed to adapt government to new circumstances, but there was very little evidence of responsible governmental action or political thought. Tocqueville offers a devastating survey of "the world of the mind," a world of "strange confusion" in which religious people who ought to cherish equality instead oppose it, while democrats who ought to support religion instead attack it; lovers of the people embrace slavery while enemies of the people praise freedom; friends of labor oppose the advance of civilization, while those who take a narrowly materialistic view of human wants are hailed as champions of civilization. In this world of illusion and disconnected thoughts, devoid of clarity and guidance, the "good things of the old order" are perishing without giving way to the best rewards of democracy and equality.

In addition to a sweeping view of history and a scathing look at intellectual controversy, the introduction features three passages that together provide a scaffold from which to examine the past, the present, and an optimal future. The first[10] concedes that feudalism, despite its inequality, ostentation, and misery, permitted "several types of happiness which are difficult to appreciate or conceive today." While the nobles checked the king's power, no one questioned the essential legitimacy of authority. As a result, says Tocqueville, there was greater incentive to use power justly and benevolently. Since abuses were considered "inevitable ills sent by God," there was less rancor and more of "a sort of goodwill" between classes. Mostly the "happiness" of this state resulted from its "stability" in contrast to the disintegration that followed, though Tocqueville alludes vaguely to its "glory" (which probably refers to patronage of the arts and religious devotion). The second passage[11] describes a utopia based on "reciprocal courtesy." The principal features of this utopia would be universal respect for law, which everyone would see as necessary (though no longer as sacred), and free association, which implies a model of citizenship in which "in order to enjoy the benefits of society one must shoulder its obligations." In this society of the future, some blessings of the old order are exchanged for new benefits: generally there would be less glory, pleasure, passion, and intellectual distinction for the few and more widely diffused contentment, education, politeness, and orderliness among the many. Citizens would see that their "private interest was mixed up with public interest"; that is, a kind of enlightened selfishness would replace the mystifications of the past. "The nation as a body would be less brilliant, less glorious, and perhaps less strong, but the majority of the citizens would be pacific not from despair of anything better but from knowing itself to be well-off." Here was a utopia of "calm and rational feeling" to contrast with the current state of confusion and terror.

Was this utopia merely a dream, or could it be realized? That is where the third passage[12] comes into focus. It is a sketch of the United States, where the "social revolution" had taken place to an advanced degree, reaching "almost complete equality of condition," but without the violent conflict of Europe. Initially, at least, the peacefulness of America appears to be its extraordinary virtue. In fact, one could say that America enjoyed the results of social revolution "without experiencing the revolution itself." This famous statement has sometimes been twisted by later commentators into a claim that America is so exceptional as to have little in common with Europe. Tocqueville actually believed that the American experience had the utmost relevance to Europe. While American forms of government and social institutions should not be simply adopted, there was much to be learned from a nation where what lay ahead for Europe already existed in daily experience. "I saw in America more than America," wrote Tocqueville, who saw "the shape of democracy itself." In other words, America represented a kind of midpoint between feudal stability and glory on one hand, and the calm and rational utopia on the other. *Democracy in America,* the book in which Tocqueville proceeds to tell the results of his study of the United States, is in this sense a lengthy answer to the question that might well be asked of anyone who projects a future state of social improvement: what grounds in observed human experience do you have for believing, and asking others to believe, it possible?[13]

The imaginary utopia involved trade-offs. America, the middle ground, also exemplified many of the losses entailed in the rise of democracy. "Anyone who supposes that I intend to write a panegyric is strangely mistaken," Tocqueville wrote;[14] and indeed he was so insistent on correcting the opinions of readers who were too enthusiastic about democracy that he may well have exaggerated the disturbing tendencies that he attributed to America. It was a land of mediocrity, materialism, selfishness, envy, and conformity; it exhibited the dangers of obnoxious conceptions of equality that might someday induce people to relinquish liberty and introduce modern forms of despotism. In a letter to his English translator Tocqueville acknowledged that "I felt it my duty to stress particularly the bad tendencies which equality may bring about in order to prevent my contemporaries [in France] surrendering to them." He complained that the translation of Part One distorted even this emphasis: "You have, without wanting it, following the instinct of your [British] opinions, very lively colored what was contrary to democracy and rather appeased what could do wrong to aristocracy."[15]

One interesting question, therefore, is why this first part, in particular, was acclaimed in America. For this book, directed at French readers, was a great success in the land it studied. It was swiftly converted into school editions and presented as an authoritative account of American institutions.[16] One explanation for the book's success is that it reflected faithfully the views of the Americans Tocqueville conversed with and placed them in a serious international context. Though it contained very little first-hand observation of people or events—far less than other travelers' reports—Part One rested quite securely on what Tocqueville had heard while in America.

These conversations were not quoted directly, out of respect for his *rapporteurs,* who might have spoken more freely with a transient guest than they would with their fellow Americans. "I have noted down all such confidences as soon as I heard them, but they will never leave my notebooks," he promised.[17] But in recent years they have been published and translated, and we can see the sources of the complaints about democracy that are transmitted in *Democracy in America.* These complaints were widely felt by the kinds of men he met, mostly Whigs in politics, prominent educators and church leaders, lawyers and physicians, generally respectable and well-to-do. He heard so often that the people choose leaders who resemble themselves rather than truly qualified men that it would be hard to assign provenance for this view. He was especially struck by the explanation given by a Maryland gentleman, Ebenezer Finley, of the role played by "the upper classes" in extending the franchise and "pressing democracy to the utmost limits." They had found it necessary "to flatter the people" and bid for their votes by "granting new privileges" in order to compete for office. Thus the logic of democratic politics forced them to hasten a state of "all-embracing change" that contradicted their true views and interests.[18] He heard again and again of Jackson's incompetence and corruption as signs of the flaws of democracy. It was the historian Jared Sparks, later president of Harvard, who first told him that the majority tyrannizes over minorities.[19] While he learned that the rights of the individual were the essential counterweight to the power of the majority in the American system, he was also informed that the regnant masses were less respectful of those rights than were the discontented elites.

By converting such complaints into a grand account of the workings of democracy in the modern world, Tocqueville was bound to please the leaders of the educated classes in America. In fact, he stayed remarkably close to the terms used by Madison and Hamilton in the *Federalist,* a volume that he admired and studied carefully. His reading program while writing *Democracy in America* even resembled Madison's preparation for the constitutional debates. In the *Federalist* he found a concern like his own to weigh American political institutions against standards worked out over centuries of European thought. There he found an effort to select from a spectrum of forms of popular government one that did not press democracy to its utmost limits. There he found a congenial insistence that leaders should not be chosen for their sameness with the people but for their breadth of vision and enlightened respect for the public interest. There he also found a warning that majorities can be oppressive if not tempered and deflected. But, of course, Tocqueville had also learned that democracy was irrepressible; there was no going back to the world of the *Federalist.* Thus the question he raised was what could be done *now* to temper the excesses of democracy. His book's success in America owes something to the feeling among those who shaped educated opinion that he revised familiar concerns to make them relevant to a new age.

Part Two received much less notice in the United States. In general, it strayed farther from Tocqueville's conversations with Americans and more conspicuously imposed on the American experience abstract considerations based on his endeavor to map out the logic of historical change in Europe. Part Two includes, alongside analyses of the disintegration of feudal bonds and the emergence of new forms of individualism, speculations about the future of American culture. Some of these speculations, based on his assumptions that equality wars against depth and distinctiveness of thought and feeling, are notoriously wrong. His comments on philosophy do not stand up well against the example of Emerson; his comments on poetry do not compare well with the examples of Whitman or Dickinson; his comments on religion underestimate the depth of feeling and commitment in numerous sects. The United States was by no means as uncongenial to the idealistic, the self-exploring, the beautiful, and the devotional as his logic maintained

it had to be. He overlooked the way in which practical, materialistic aspects
of American society inspired sensitive souls to seek to reform or redeem it.
Nevertheless, the complaints he made might well have been heard among
some of the Whigs he talked with. The view of America as a society at war
with artistic refinement and spiritual depth was already current among disgruntled members of the social and intellectual elites, just as it has continued to be a standard complaint in some intellectual circles ever since.[20]

While Tocqueville held out little hope of "glory," he was struck by the
tenacity of civilization in its confrontation with the wilderness. He assumed,
apparently, that Americans who had achieved some degree of civilization
would stay where they were—in the East—and thus the Western frontier
would be peopled by European newcomers. In *Democracy in America* he
described this as the general supposition, but incorrect. He discovered, to
his surprise, that poor immigrants, without capital, unaccustomed to the
climate, generally remained in "the great industrial zone" along the seaboard, while Americans left their homes and headed west. Jared Sparks
informed him, for example, that landed estates were no longer divided in
Massachusetts; the eldest son inherited the whole, and the young all left for
newly opened land. Tocqueville made note: "the bearings of the fact immense." Another informant told him that most of the residents of Illinois
came, not from the East, but from the relatively new state of Ohio. Here was
another significant fact: already the "new generation" in Ohio "does not find
enough opportunities of getting rich there, and is setting out on the march to
lands newer still."[21]

This fact was not strictly relevant to the questions of European policy
that concerned him, and there is reason to think that he was uncertain what
new interpretation to offer. We have seen that in *Democracy in America* he
distorted his experience at Frenchman's Island in order to use it as an
example of the restlessness of Americans leaving ruins behind them.
Throughout his notebooks he made it clear that he viewed this restlessness
with some distaste. A single American man might try ten different trades
and occupy twenty different homes. He had no settled habits, no stabilizing
memories, no sustaining bonds.[22] While it might be thrilling to imagine this
condition for a cultivated, political European, Tocqueville was more uncertain about a white man living like an Indian just outside the line of civilization in Michigan and had little but disgust for the uncouth, "half savage"
men of Kentucky and Tennessee.[23]

For the most part, however, he spoke positively of westward migration.
His West was, in part, the Eden of fantasy glimpsed at Lake Oneida. In
Democracy in America he reports: "there are still, as on the first days of
creation, rivers whose founts never run dry, green and watery solitudes, and
limitless fields never yet turned by the ploughshare."[24] The availability of

this land spared the United States some of the problems of Europe. It dispersed the population and prevented concentrations of people with unsatisfied needs. It created opportunities: in 1830, he reported, there were thirty-six Connecticut-born congressmen, thirty-one of them representing Western states. "If those thirty-one had stayed in Connecticut," he thought, "in all probability they would have remained humble laborers, not rich landowners, and would have passed their lives in obscurity, not able to venture on a political career, and instead of becoming useful legislators, they would have been dangerous citizens."[25] Moreover, the land and the reslessness it stimulated occasioned (Tocqueville assumes the causal connection) an abundant material prosperity that eliminated radical opinions from the political field.

Tocqueville tells a story, inverting the tale of the exile at Lake Oneida, to illustrate "the power of material prosperity over political behavior." In a forested part of Pennsylvania he sought hospitality at the home of a rich man, who turned out to be a French émigré once notorious as "a great leveler and an ardent demagogue." Now this man spoke like a conservative economist, praising property, hierarchy, law, and public order. He even referred casually to the authority of Jesus Christ—striking evidence of the way personal beliefs changed to suit one's fortune. The fickleness of human reason, so alarming elsewhere, in a prosperous nation was a support to social peace.[26] But the bountiful land offered herself, not to the savage or barbarian, but only "to man who has already mastered the most important secrets of nature, united to his fellows, and taught by the experience of fifty centuries." There might be a high degree of relativism in beliefs of individuals, but the civilization whose westward march awed Tocqueville was essentially European.

Before analyzing the view of history that Tocqueville derived from his conversations and observations, it is important to mention what he saw as a major exception. The South simply did not fit the patterns he chose to emphasize. Wherever he went, he was told that Southerners lacked the commercial and industrial energy so noticeable in the North. Educational and other public institutions were deficient in the South, and political life was more "disordered, revolutionary, and passionate." As he passed down the Ohio River he imagined he could see these differences between bustling Ohio and torpid Kentucky.[27] To be sure, the South maintained some traits that ought to have been appealing to Tocqueville because of his nostalgia for the old order. He was told that it exhibited less enterprise and more "chivalry," and this ought not to have been a comparison all in the North's favor. To explain this apparent lapse, we may notice that all his informants, including the Southerners, found the South wanting. We may also acknowledge his profound antislavery feeling. But we also need to observe that he very carefully balanced his memories with a kind of relativism about the future. There were no absolutes derived from the past, no more for him than for the French leveler, and in the present there was much to be said for an energetic and orderly society, one that educated its citizens, developed transportation facilities, and spread civilization westward.[28]

The historians Charles and Mary Beard, in a perceptive interpretation, called *Democracy in America* a "great work" in which the fundamental conception was "no less comprehensive than the idea of civilization."[29] In fact, this theme was even stronger in his notebooks where there was less need for tactical criticism of American democracy. There he acknowledged that Americans exhibited the energy by which "great nations" are made and that Americans "in mass" were the most enlightened people in the world; indeed he spoke of "their high civilization."[30] He was, at the same time, disturbed by the "ever moving" torrent of social change and the corrosive effects of materialism and individualism. There was no comfort in the thought that "the woof of time is ever being broken" in a democracy; the chain linking society together was sundered.[31] This tension runs throughout his view of history. The decline of old, familiar ways of life prompted "religious dread," but the same emotion was inspired by the transmission of civilization across an edenic land. If America presented an alarming specter of ills to be feared from democracy, it also displayed sublime scenes of triumph for a civilization that he thought of as stemming, in the first instance, from New England and, more deeply, from Europe.

In the present-day pluralist milieu, Tocqueville's uncritical acceptance of a New England version of America's history may seem unfortunate. The modern reader will label as inaccurate, even mythical, much that Tocqueville offers as straightforward explanation. To start with, he speaks glibly of the American colonists as all of "the British race," united in national character, and sharing a single language, while today we are much more conscious of ethnic and cultural differences in colonial America, even among those who came from Britain. He offers generalizations, which today seem doubtful, about the initial equality and the "germ" of democracy among emigrants to New England. He asserts the supremacy and independence of townships in a ways that is probably exaggerated for New England and overlooks the weak, ambiguous status of municipalities elsewhere. He accepts New England's Federalist biases on subsequent historical issues, such as the troubles of the confederation period and the election of Andrew Jackson, thus distorting many constitutional issues of direct relevance to his inquiries. At every turn he contrasts the motives, attitudes, and accomplishments of a highly abstract North with those of an equally abstract South, thus missing much of the complexity of colonial and early national development.

While there were undeniable differences between New England and

Virginia, the repeated praise of the former and disparagement of the latter is to the modern eye oversimplified and irritating. Virginia was devoid of "noble thought or conception above gain," for example, while New England was a shining light to all humanity everywhere. And the view of American history that these contrasts uphold would today be dismissed by many as ideologically distorted. It was in New England, he wrote, that the "main principles now forming the basic social theory of the United States" took shape.

> New England principles spread first to the neighboring states and then in due course to those more distant, finally penetrating everywhere throughout the confederation. Their influence now extends beyond its limits over the whole American world. New England civilization has been like beacons on mountain peaks whose warmth is first felt close by but whose light shines to the farthest limits of the horizon.[32]

This regional bias is easily explained if we remember Tocqueville's sources of information. Not only had he conversed primarily with New Englanders and others (including Southerners) with New England sympathies, but he had read deeply in William Bradford, Cotton Mather, and other historians with a strong providential view of Massachusett's mission in the world.[33] He was also greatly influenced by two New York sources—*The Federalist* and Chancellor Kent's *Commentaries*—both of which must have reinforced his sense of historical conflict between national civilizing forces and "unorganized" anarchic elements.[34] That sense of conflict, rather than any prejudices in favor of New England, informed his sense of American history.

The vision of New England as a beacon of higher civilization, with purposes that went beyond the pursuit of gain (without excluding it), was powerful and attractive. It had gained strength over two centuries and was carried out of New England by travelers who left home for many different reasons but saw themselves as agents of social and spiritual improvement wherever they went.[35] For those Americans, and their European visitors, who wished more for America than simply the survival of democracy—that is, for those who wished to see a progress of culture and enlightenment—there was hardly any alternative vision besides that furnished by New England historians. Thus there were many Whiggish Americans who, like Tocqueville, found comfort and inspiration in a version of history that began with the New England town and proceeded toward the conquest of the continent.

Democracy in America begins with this scheme of Puritan influence, and Tocqueville plainly admired memories of the colonial past that strengthened feelings of civic obligation. But he insisted on the relevance of the longer

European past as well. No people could "found a society with no other point of departure besides themselves";[36] whether they wished it so or not, the Puritans and then the Americans must be seen as an extension of European civilization. This theme runs throughout the notebooks. Not only was he impressed by accounts of young Easterners going west to build schools and churches, but he was also motivated to gain personal experience of life at the margin between familiar society and raw wilderness. When he sometimes spoke contemptuously of those he found "half savage," he was of course adhering to European measures of civilization. But he was always aware that the Indian-fighting pioneers were "marching before the immense European family" who would follow with the sound of axes, the building of roads and towns, and eventually the erection of cities.[37]

Tocqueville and Beaumont were eager to find and cross the line separating civilization and wilderness, the line that marked "the utmost limits of European civilization." The quest took them in the summer of 1831 across upstate New York to Buffalo, then by steamboat to Detroit, where they interviewed a United States land officer who pointed proudly to his map and showed all the places where settlement was under way. When he told them not to go past Pontiac, where the road stopped and "impenetrable forest" began, they were filled with "joy at having at last discovered a place to which the torrent of European civilization had not yet come."[38] They headed to Pontiac and beyond to a trading post where they secured an Indian guide who led them by foot, horseback, and canoe on a circuitous path back to Detroit, whence they took another steamboat to Green Bay and Mackinac and thence back to Detroit again with passages in the forest along the way. Although this trip was probably the high point of Tocqueville's trip to America, few details of it can be found in *Democracy in America*. Evidence of his emotional pursuit of the adventure and his intense response to what he experienced must be found in a long and artistically composed essay, "A Fortnight in the Wilds," that deserves a much wider reading than it has received up to now.[39]

As we have noticed, exile and abandonment were preoccupations of Tocqueville's thought, forming a kind of counterweight to his appreciation of the monuments of ancient civilization in Europe. "A Fortnight," like the account of Frenchman's Isle, experimented with a wide range of feelings about the rivers and forests as both Edenic and menacing. Moments of stillness and awe are compared with oceanic feelings in the middle of the Atlantic. There are remarkable descriptions of Indians differentiated not only by tribal ties and their relation to the wilderness, but also by their accommodation to the many nationalities and religions they had been exposed to. They did not live up to expectations shaped by his reading of Cooper and Chateaubriand. Some were drunk; others, wasted by disease.

The hypocrisy and inhumanity of white Christians prompt Tocqueville's scorn, while "civilized" savages and gentle "half-castes" earn his sad respect, for no good awaits them on this earth. What makes the wilds so remarkable, or so it seems at times, is that they are not wild at all. They are a laboratory of miscegenation and human adaptation, challenging to Tocqueville's belief in separate and enduring traits of national character.[40]

Yet the focus of the essay is neither on the feelings of oceanic solitude nor on the relations of Europeans with Indians, but on the triumph of civilization over the forest. A gunshot through the silence reminds the traveler of the "fearsome war cry of civilization on the march." There is no doubt of the outcome: "The noise of civilization and industry will break the silence of the Saginaw," and the irresistible push of "the great European settlements" will eliminate these scenes of "primitive splendour." He continues:

> It is the consciousness of destruction, this *arrière pensée* of quick and inevitable change that gives . . . such a touching beauty to the solitudes of America. . . . Thoughts of the savage, natural grandeur that is going to come to an end become mingled with splendid anticipation of the triumphant march of civilization. . . . One's soul is shaken by contradictory thoughts and feelings, but all the impressions it receives are great and leave a deep mark.[41]

Tocqueville had expected to find history recreated in geography, with a vast chain of social conditions "descending step by step" from civilized opulence to primitive savagery. Instead, he found among those of European descent "one society only," with variations of wealth to be sure, but in other respects "levelled out": "The man you left behind in the streets of New York, you will find again in the midst of almost impenetrable solitude." In his notebook he put it thus: "The Americans in their log-houses have the air of rich folk who have temporarily gone to spend a season in a hunting-lodge." Consequently, the effect of travel was one of abrupt changes, like crossing a line between civilization and its opposite. It was a "striking emblem of American society" that the travelers could emerge in New York from the stillness of the forest to see, suddenly, "the elegant spire of a clock tower, houses striking in their whiteness and cleanness, and shops."[42] Chaos or paradise, the wilds of Michigan and beyond were destined to make room swiftly for order and commerce.

Tocqueville was occasionally overcome by memories of France. "A year ago today we made a king," he jotted in his journal at Sault-Sainte-Marie. The revolutions of Europe, indeed all events of "the well-policed part of the world," seemed remote to the traveler in the wilds. But for a while "memories of July 21" broke the quiet.

The cries and smoke of battle, the roar of guns, the rattle of rifles, the even more horrible ringing of the tocsin—that whole day with its delirious atmosphere, seemed suddenly to rise out of the past and to stand before me like a living picture. This was only a sudden hallucination, a passing dream. When I raised my head and looked around me, the apparition had already vanished; but never had the silence of the forest seemed so icy, the shadows so sombre, the solitude so absolute.[43]

At times he may have felt as though he had really broken away, like the exile on Lake Oneida. In Europe one could get lost in the woods, but always "some sound of life"—a bell, a barking dog, a footstep—could be heard to give reassurance of surrounding society. In Michigan at times no comforting sounds could be heard.[44]

But Europe was never really far away. "Those who dwell in isolated places" in America, he noted in his account of the fortnight in the wilds, "arrived there yesterday. They came bringing with them the morals, the ideas and the needs of civilization." They bring tastes for "French fashions," designs of French boulevards, and needs for goods from "the factories of Lyons." They receive weekly mail and read newspapers. In a log house may be found the Bible, a prayer book, even works of Milton and Shakespeare.[45] When he turns to this observation in Part Two of *Democracy in America*, his account is revised and inconsistent. By that time the logic of his book obliged him to emphasize the decline of glory in a democracy. Therefore he stressed the "dim," transitory, uninformed, and derivative qualities of American literary taste and literary production. It counted against America that the authors favored there were mainly British. American writers "paint with borrowed colors," and readers awaited English judgments before offering their own. Yet he was also obliged to mention the existence of "a large number of people who take an interest in things of the mind," in however derivative a fashion. "The literary inspiration of Great Britain darts its beams into the depths of the forest of the New World. There is hardly a pioneer's hut which does not contain a few odd volumes of Shakespeare. I remember reading the feudal drama of *Henry V* for the first time in a log cabin."[46] Surely this attachment to the literary standards of an aristocratic nation is not something altogether to be scoffed at, especially if we recall the scheme of history that *Democracy in America* commences with. The retention of tastes and habits from the past in the democratic conquest of the wilderness might well be interpreted as a hopeful sign of the persistence of Europe.

There is no point in trying to reconcile Tocqueville's ambivalences and contradictions. The importance of "A Fortnight in the Wilds" is that it captures facets of his American experience that are nearly lost in the convolutions of *Democracy in America*. The former belongs much more to the genre of travel writing, which follows its own conventions. The traveler is able to report more favorably on the shifting moment in history when civilization confronts nature, while the new kind of political scientist who wrote *Democracy in America* is compelled to see bitter losses as an old glorious order is razed by democracy. "A Fortnight in the Wilds" anticipates the work of other writers, American as well as European, who sought to understand the abrupt changes taking place by traveling and reporting on life at the margins of American society.

Although Tocqueville wrote for Europeans, in his works we have encountered two themes of recurrent and interlocking significance to other travelers and reporters: the legacy of New England and the settlement of the wilds. In fact, many of Tocqueville's best-known comments on the American character may be subsumed under these headings. While the conformity, the practicality, and the restlessness of Americans had a negative appearance when viewed through the lens of European political turmoil, they appeared more benign when seen as part of a story of the extension of civilization. The "habits of the heart" that softened individualism through family ties, voluntary organizations, and religious affections played a part in this same inspiring story. If Tocqueville stressed at times the crude, the egotistical, and the inadequate in the American civilization and character, so did other travelers. That might even be called the fundamental intellectual inquiry of Americans: to assess just how much was being lost in the movement out of a recent colonial past, just how much was being oversold in Americans' boastfulness about their dreams and attainments.

Few Americans could accept the view that the pinnacle of intellectual glory was reached under feudal aristocracy. Many Americans expected notable achievements, for which Tocqueville held out little hope. To the blessings of middle-class democracy, mixed as they might be with perils, they aspired to add the benefits of culture. What might be the goals and characteristics of this culture is one of the issues we must attend to. But Tocqueville's comments on the westward transit of civilization captured one source of American inspiration. In this regard we may note the single sentence from *Democracy in America* that Ralph Waldo Emerson quoted in his notebooks. America's most influential nineteenth-century public moralist made this note on America's most famous European traveler in April 1841: "America & not Europe is the rich man. According to De Tocqueville, the column of our population on the western frontier . . . advances every year a mean distance of seventeen miles. He adds 'This gradual & continuous progress of the European race towards the Rocky Mountains has the solemnity of a providential event; it is like a deluge of men rising unabatedly & daily driven onward by the hand of God.' "[47]

CHAPTER ELEVEN

Bremer:
Home and Citizenship

Fredrika Bremer carried from Europe no exciting memories of revolution or stories of exile. She was never lost in the solitude of the American forest. She spent little time with Indians. She did not fire a gun or kill any game. Although her *Homes of the New World* is longer and more detailed than *Democracy in America* and was nearly as popular in its own day, scarcely anyone reads it any more. Tocqueville discoursed more authoritatively on political institutions, a field women were excluded from in the nineteenth century. While Tocqueville's name is inescapable in discussions of American culture, Bremer's is close to forgotten.

Recent feminist scholars help us see and understand such differences. Stories of male journeys in the forest (or on the ocean or river) among men of other races have been accepted, too exclusively, as the mainstream of American literature. These are the stories that explore the meaning of America through the adventures of young men who break from home and test themselves against the wilds. Given privileged status in classroom and interpretative texts, they have an influence from generation to generation as the "best" American authors retell the same old tales. Meanwhile, the themes of successful female authors seem too local and domestic, or too global and idealistic, to find a place in courses and books on the quest for an American identity. So they gain no lasting respect or influence, and the woman who seeks a literary career is deprived of a tradition of female precursors.[1]

Plainly this analysis fits well when we compare Bremer's experience and

influence with Tocqueville's. But the fit is only partial. It applies to the
personal adventures and political expertise of the two travelers, but it applies
less well when we turn to the great themes of New England culture and
civilizing the West. Those themes belonged to women as much as to men,
perhaps even more, inasmuch as women could not break loose from the town
and trek in the wilds. Bremer focused on precisely those themes, which were
also central to Tocqueville's work, and discussed them in subtle and reward-
ing detail. *Homes of the New World* deserves attention as a major and neglected
work on the progress of culture.[2] But we will find it a gendered report, one that
makes it clear that *Democracy in America* speaks from a gendered perspective, too. Not only does Bremer's work acquaint us with women's roles in
developing American culture, but it takes less interest in restless emulation
than does Tocqueville's, and it voices a deep preference for social harmony
that was considered a female attribute. As we will see, it also raises important
issues concerning women's domestic and public responsibilities.

Bremer was the daughter of a prosperous ironmonger and enjoyed the
advantages of a good education, musical and artistic training, and foreign
travel as she grew up. But her parents were strict and fussy, and her
childhood was not happy. When she was three, her family moved for political reasons from Finland, where they had lived for several generations, to
Sweden—thus she did have some memory of dislocation. She took solace in
writing verse and in charity work among the poor and sick, two forms of
expression that were open to young women. Though she did not act on a wish
to devote her life to hospital work as a "Sister of Charity," the proceeds of
her first book went for assistance to the rural poor, and all her writings
conveyed a warm interest in benevolent causes. In novels of the 1830s, like
The Neighbors and *The Home*, she concentrated, as the Swedish Academy
put it in awarding her a gold medal, on "the interior of social life, often
hidden from the eyes of the public."[3] By the time of her visit to the United
States in 1849, she was more concerned with the legal and social restrictions
that prevented women from benefiting society outside the home as "lecturers, professors, judges, physicians, and functionaries in the service of the
state."[4] Her strongest feminist work, *Hertha* (1856), was criticized as a
deviation from her earlier, gentler sentiments. The American edition carried
a dedication pointing out that even in the New World, "where the women are
indulged and left fancy-free more than in any other country on earth,"
women's minds were not allowed adequate development for the great missions they might undertake.[5]

Her novels had already been translated into English and were well
known in the United States.[6] Her visit was an important cultural event, and
nearly everywhere she went the homes she stayed in were those of prominent
writers and patrons of the arts. During her initial stay at the Astor House,

"one of the largest and best hotels of New York," she spent a few moments gazing at Barnum's museum and the "republican intermixture" on Broadway, but she was swiftly taken to a literary soirée, kept up late, and worn out by her friends' demands on her time. In her second day in the United States she was whisked up the Hudson River to the villa of Andrew Jackson Downing, where everything was tasteful and serene. "In food, in fruits, as well as in many small things, prevails a certain amount of luxury, but which does not make any outward show."[7] But visitors followed her there, including editors and publishers who wished her to write for them, and invitations to visit other homes poured in. Back in New York, she stayed in Marcus Spring's pretty "Rose Cottage" in Brooklyn and wrote rhapsodically of the wooded grounds and garden and of the happy lifestyle that allowed Spring to go back and forth between business in New York and his sheltered family circle. In Concord she stayed with Ralph Waldo Emerson; in Cambridge, with James Russell Lowell; and elsewhere in New England, with equally illustrious hosts.

She has much to say, not only about the varied but always confortable residences, the kindness of her friends, and the "incessant shower"[8] of social events, but also about long conversations with writers and intellectuals (Washington Irving, George Bancroft, Louis Agassiz, Nathaniel Hawthorne, Bayard Taylor, Henry Wadsworth Longfellow) and reformers (Bronson Alcott, Adin Ballou, Elihu Burritt). The Springs took her to a socialist community at Raritan Bay, New Jersey (where she went to work in the bakery). Charles Sumner took her to visit a prison and an asylum. She heard the preaching of Theodore Parker and Father Taylor. She visited Lowell's factories. William Lloyd Garrison arranged an interview with the escaped slaves William and Ellen Craft, and Samuel Gridley Howe invited her for dinner with his deaf and blind pupil, Laura Bridgman. In her first few months in the North, in short, Bremer had remarkable opportunities to acquaint herself both widely and in depth with American thought and culture. She was much less critical than other vistors. Arriving two decades later than Tocqueville and meeting more forward-looking reformers than backward-looking gentry, she presented a more favorable portrait of the culture that Americans were creating. She did not agree with those who found the nation utterly materialistic and prosaic. Others called America a "realist country," she noted, but "there is here much more poetry, much more of the romance of life, than we have imagined."[9]

These travels were distinguished by frequent and extended conversations with intellectual women. Included, of course, were the wives of Downing and Spring, though the "cultivated mind" of the former and the intense Quaker "inward life" of the latter expressed themselves mainly in private.[10] Bremer also met the Hartford poet Lydia H. Sigourney ("a very kind little sentimentalist, but a very agreeable lady") and became very friendly with another poet, Anne Lynch, who was at the center of New York's artistic circles. She spent many days with two writers of fiction, Catharine Sedgwick and Caroline Kirkland, both of whom proved to be lively, stimulating friends. With Sedgwick she had earnest conversations on writing "for what I will call people of lower degree in society . . . because here . . . one can not properly speak of a working class" and on the way an author's works "constitute a history of that author's development," even a form of autobiography.[11] Kirkland, beneath the humor of her work, concealed great depth of character: "She is one of those natures in which the feminine and manly attributes are harmoniously blended."[12] Bremer learned to admire Lydia Maria Child, not only for her fiction, but also for her works of charity with poor children.[13] Bremer also spent enjoyable time with the actresses Charlotte Cushman and Fanny Kemble, both intelligent and spirited conversationalists as well as powerful performers. Indeed, the "most agreeable" hours in Boston were spent at public readings of *Henry V* and *Julius Caesar*, in which Kemble excelled in the heroic, masculine roles.[14]

The circle of women friends expanded throughout Bremer's travels in America. Kirkland introduced her to a woman named Haynes who had been a missionary in China and now ran a girls' boarding school in New York.[15] The physician Harriot Hunt in Boston introduced several " 'emancipated ladies,' as they are called," including the lecturer on physiology, Paulina Davis.[16] Bremer heard Lucy Stone speak against slavery—not very well, Bremer thought, because she repeated what men said rather than speaking as a woman.[17] She did not meet Elizabeth Blackwell, but women in Philadelphia told her about the medical college that Blackwell was opening, and she eventually visited it.[18] Nor did she meet Margaret Fuller, who had been in Italy and died at sea, but she had important conversations about her.[19] She spent much time with Dorothea Dix in Washington and learned how Dix had sought a noble field of action and found it in work on behalf of the mentally ill.[20] She not only met Lucretia Mott but saw her in action at a public lecture by Richard H. Dana, "a distinguished *littérateur*" who spoke on Shakespeare and "instanced Desdemona as the ideal of women of all ages." At the end of the lecture Mott arose and said, "Friend Dana, I consider that thou art wrong in thy representation of what woman ought to be, and I will endeavor to prove it." She asked the assembly to meet her at a later day in the same room and, at that time, "delivered an excellent lecture, permeated by that love of truth and integrity which is the very foundation of Quakerism."[21]

For the most part, Bremer is not self-conscious about being in a separate sphere in describing meetings with women. The company in which she traveled and conversed was usually mixed. Nevertheless, in describing and evaluating women, she especially liked "sensible," "feminine" qualities.

She tells more about the appearance and character of women she talked with, and about her feelings in their presence, than about the substance of their discourse. She believed that "the highest object of [Margaret Fuller's] soul was gained in her happiness as a mother."[22] A "young and really gifted poetess, Miss C.," whom she met in Washington, she had little use for; she "is too much of an Amazon for my taste." Another "gifted authoress" in Washington, one "who has begun to excite attention by her novels," was "too much wrapped up in herself."[23] But when she spent time with women who were both intelligent and gentle, accomplished and altruistic, she felt a kind of loving fulfillment that was too often denied European women. Most moving was her experience in a large circle of women in Mobile, especially Octavia Le Vert, with whom she discussed transcendentalism and Mormonism amid "delicious" semitropical scenes and whom she loved as dearly "as a young sister."[24] In Philadelphia she fell "desperately in love"—so deeply that it seemed a desecration even to record the name—with a young singer who had been "Fanny Kemble's 'pet' " and who personified "the girl of the New World," with "a glorious young-womanly character richly endowed . . . with that spark of inspired life which is so enchanting and so infinitely revivifying."[25]

It was not simply the women, but the pleasant homes she stayed in and the affectionate couples who entertained her, that prompted deep reflection on losses in her own past. These losses are never clearly explained but are referred to as memories buried in the recesses of her imagination "for more than fifteen years" or "dim shadows" that "have for twenty years existed in the background of my soul."[26] This beloved novelist of domestic life was in some ways a lonely pilgrim trying to understand the sources of unfulfillment in her life and in the lives of other women.

Her project in coming to America, as she conceived it, was to get above the private subject matter of fiction and to "occupy myself with public affairs." Though we will need to return to her observations on women and homes in the New World, we must note at once that these topics were intended to lead into broader subjects: "the popular life, institutions, and circumstances of a new country"; and the prospects for humankind as revealed in the New World. Bremer's preconceptions led her to ask, not where American democracy fit in a scheme of historical devolution and conflict, but whether American society was more just and encouraging to the potentialities of human nature than was Europe's.[27]

Her travels were extensive. After New York and New England in the autumn and winter of 1849, she sailed south to Charleston and Savannah (March through June 1850), then came back north as far as Philadelphia, spent a month in Washington, vacationed for a fortnight at Cape May in New Jersey, and crossed New York to Niagara Falls by early September. In mid-

September of 1850, she was in Chicago; most of October was spent in Minnesota; and in November she crossed Iowa in a covered wagon, then went down the Mississippi to Saint Louis and moved on to spend several weeks in Cincinnati. The winter was spent on the Gulf: New Orleans, Mobile, and three glorious months in Cuba (where she had a reunion with another famous Swede, Jenny Lind). In May 1851, she was once again in Charleston and Savannah, with an excursion into Florida. She never got to Tennessee, though twice she tried. In 1850, she was told that the roads were too bad; in 1851 the Tennessee River was "dried up" and unnavigable.[28] After crossing North Carolina by railroad, she did fulfill her goal of seeing Virginia in June, dividing her time between Richmond and Charlottesville. She then sailed down the St. James River to Baltimore and reached Philadelphia by train for a three-day stay before heading north. The remainder of her trip began at Rose Cottage in Brooklyn, whence she proceeded to Boston, Concord, Nahant on the Massachusetts coast (August 1), the White Mountains (August 10), the Berkshires, Saratoga, and back to New York for her final weeks in America in September 1851.

What did these travels teach her? She offers relatively little commentary on politics in what she grandly described as "the world's greatest governmental culture."[29] Like Tocqueville, she heard Whig complaints about "the election of low and truthless agitators" and "the difficulty for the best men to get into government," but she tended to dismiss these problems as limited to a "transition-point" in the progress of "popular education."[30] She disliked the behavior of political parties but thought them equivalent to European parties in the stubborn distrust with which they opposed one another's position.[31] Her fundamental impression of American politics was favorable. She sat and listened for days to debates in the Senate over the measures that came to be known as the Compromise of 1850. While she thought some speakers "scream too much" and proslavery speeches made her uncomfortable, she felt great admiration for Daniel Webster and Henry Clay and recorded vivid impressions of other speakers. "No country on earth," she wrote, "can at this time present an assembly of greater talent or of more remarkable men than may be met with in the Senate of the United States." What was remarkable was to see "picturesque" regional types joined in a national forum to discuss "public questions, which are interesting to the whole human race."[32] While representatives of the states could squabble like children, the system avoided the sense of limitation that made European politics sad and hopeless.[33]

If her remarks on American politics are generalized and superficial, however, her observations on slavery are extensive and complex. They are informed by tension between her clear antislavery opinions, reinforced by her affection for Northern reformers, and her sympathy for the enlightened

Southerners whose homes she visited. In the end, her own position seems ambiguous and inconclusive. She criticized abolitionists for setting back antislavery by their "unreasonable" demands. She criticized Southerners, especially the educated ones, for evasiveness and temporizing on the subject of slavery: "I scarcely ever meet with a man, or woman either, who can openly and honestly look the thing in the face." Yet she was credulous about colonizationist talk of turning slavery into a civilizing influence by deporting freed blacks: "Slavery is an evil; but under the wise direction of God it will become a blessing to the negroes." In an appendix she expressed her differences with Harriet Beecher Stowe, whose *Uncle Tom's Cabin* overlooked the optimistic development of "Christian communities" among the slaves. "My own hope rests . . . in the nobler South; my earnest wish is, that it may take the emancipation question into its own hand."[34]

She plainly loved the climate and landscape of the South and the hospitality of its homes. She saw and believed the best of those whose pleasant conversation she enjoyed. She was impressed by the loving kindness of house slaves who appeared to serve out of instinctive devotion and subservience. (She was reminded of the same "beautiful expression in the eye of the dog.") Between Octavia Le Vert and her "clever, handsome mulatto" Betsy, for example, existed "the ideal of the relationship between a lady and her female slave." Betsy lived only to see her mistress happy and admired, dressed her hair "*à la* Mary Stuart" every day, and rattled on about the fine impression made by her lady when she traveled. Yet Le Vert's heart still did not "confuse good and evil. . . . she simply and earnestly expresses her conviction that slavery is a curse, and on this subject we are perfectly harmonious."[35]

Slavery looked more obnoxious at a distance from her Southern friends. It was horrifying to see a slave pen in Washington, to witness the sale of a young girl and the separation of a mother and child in New Orleans. In a Richmond jail she saw a series of horrid sights, including a man separated from his wife and children by a master who planned to sell him further south. This "bad rascal," as the keeper called him, had borrowed an ax and cut off the fingers of his right hand in order to lower his value and spite his master. Bremer spoke with this man, his hand in bandages, about Christ: "if he had known him, he would not have done this act; . . . even now he ought not to feel himself abandoned, because He who has said 'Come unto me, all ye that are weary and heavy laden,' . . . would console and recreate even him." At first the man's countenance was dark, but slowly it "brightened up, and at the close looked quite melted." Why had no one come to preach to this soul, "still open and accessible to good," the gospel of mercy?[36]

This conversation will not win Bremer much respect from modern readers. Nevertheless, the qualities of her personality that suppressed judgment of her slaveholding friends enabled her to talk sympathetically and at length with slaves. She admits the limitations on these conversations. One day, for example, some slaves told her how hard it was to get enough to eat. Her white host called this a lie, but the thought nagged her that it might all be true, at least in some cases, in an institution that gave some so much "irresponsible power" over others. The next day she took a solitary walk and encountered slaves with cornbread and pots of beans, which she tasted and found "savory," though highly seasoned. As the men ate contentedly, she told them that "the poor working people in the country from which I came" seldom had food as good as theirs.

> I was not come there to preach rebellion among the slaves, and the malady which I could not cure I would alleviate if it was in my power. Besides which, what I said was quite true. But I did not tell them that which was also true, that I would rather live on bread and water than live as a slave.[37]

She was less encumbered when she observed black religion. On this subject she is a first-rate reporter on antebellum black life. She gives detailed descriptions of a Methodist camp meeting of blacks and whites in a grove outside Charleston, a black Baptist church service in Savannah and the preaching of an old black preacher in the same city, the slaves' evening worship in Charleston, Methodist services for Washington's free blacks, African Methodist and Baptist services in Cincinnati, a "real African tornado" in a black church in New Orleans, a ringdance in Havana.[38] No other foreigners, and few Americans, could supply such convincing detail on both preachers and congregations, on preaching, on singing and testifying.

The tension of her own response, though it does not mar her reliability as a witness, is important. On one hand, she interpreted "the inbreaking light of Christianity among the children of Africa" as due to the efforts of white instructors.[39] The spread of the gospel was relieving the gloom of slavery and laying the basis for future harmony among the races. On the other hand, she could not help but recognize that the Christianity of the slaves was a different religion from that of whites. In Cincinnati a black preacher proposed to speak "of our nation, my brethren; . . . I regard our nationality." He proceeded to draw "a very ingenious parallel between the captivity of the Israelites in Egypt and the negroes in America, and those trials by which Providence evinced His especial solicitude about the chosen people." As he enumerated the signs that God favored his enslaved people—increasing numbers of free blacks who bought houses, built churches, and improved in knowledge, and increasing alarm among their oppressors, who wished to deport them to Africa—the congregation shouted, clapped, and stamped their feet.[40]

Bremer heard enough undertones of nationalism among blacks to be disturbed by the shortsightedness of the nation's lawmakers.[41] She suggested that blacks be allowed to form "small, free, Christian communities for themselves, like the Shakers, Dunkers, &c., who live an independent life in the great community, without taking part in its affairs, and without disturbing them." This possibility answered the objection that even the Northern public would never give them political rights. "It is not difficult to see from the negro character that they would trouble themselves very little about the government of the United States, if they could merely have their churches, their festivals, their songs and dances, their own independent ministers and churches."[42]

When Bremer's opposition to slavery faltered, the reason was her recognition of irreconcilable differences in a nation where she preferred to see harmony and unity. In any case, while she records many observations of slavery, she envisioned a future for blacks far outside the developing American civilization that was of greatest concern to her. It may be complained, accurately, that her perspective on white society was also distorted by dependence on a certain kind of well-to-do family to be her hosts and guides. *Homes of the New World* includes some interesting descriptions of poor "clay-eaters" in the Georgia woods or of poverty seen on the almost obligatory tour of the Five Points in lower Manhattan, the Old Brewery, and the Tombs.[43] But there are few of these passages, not at all comparable to the observations of slavery, and they describe sights (one is tempted to say tourist attractions) that her cultivated friends brought her to see. On her travels she was happy to contrast the comfort of her stateroom or the ladies' saloon with the external world of unruly immigrant children, men hunting, and women who "smoked their pipes and blew their noses in their fingers, and then asked how one liked America. Ugh! There are no greater contrasts than exist between the cultivated and the uncultivated ladies of this country." It was inevitable, she insisted, for a traveler, no matter how democratic, to "become aristocratic to a certain extent."[44]

For the most part, she concentrates on her "cultivated" hosts, and her commentary on America is overwhelmingly favorable. Not only was she "compelled to feel that any thing more agreeable than a lovely, refined American woman is scarcely to be found on the face of the earth," but a "blending of brotherly cordiality and chivalric politeness" made "the man of the New World the most agreeable companion that a lady can desire."[45] A glow of appreciation suffuses most of her remarks on American civilization.

Even in the relatively new city of Cincinnati, where the arts were at a beginning stage, there were lectures and musical series, an observatory, an art union, many other cultural institutions, and vineyards and villas where good conversation took place on history, geography, mythology, drama, piety, and benevolence. She did not adopt the critical stance of other Europeans in assessing American culture; she did not share Tocqueville's view of the inevitability of mediocrity in a democracy. In Cincinnati, as in America generally, she honestly noted shortcomings in the fine arts—both in the artists' execution and in the public's support—without gloomy theorizing. She proceeded swiftly to a work that she could praise, the first marble bust by Hiram Powers. This work, Bremer thought, ought to be named *Galatea*, "because Pygmalion Powers has infused into her a vitality which requires only a divine indication to breathe; or, rather, it ought to be called the *American*, because the peculiar beauty of the features, the form and action of the head and neck, are those of the American woman. There is none of the Greek stiffness in it; it is a regularity of beauty full of life and grace . . . yes, thus ought she to look, the woman of the New World, she who, sustained by a public spirit full of benevolence, may without struggle and without protest develop the fullness and earnestness of her being." After gushing on about how this creature should carry herself with a mixture of firmness and gentleness, and how she must "work," Bremer concluded that she already had seen a few actual instances of American women who matched this artistic ideal.[46]

Bremer agreed with Tocqueville that "egotism" was "the most dangerous monster of the New World."[47] Her hope was for men and women to develop their powers to the fullest while becoming more benevolent, even self-abnegating. Thus it was not a society of enlightened self-interest that she looked for, as Tocqueville did in his search for a principle to replace the glory that was past. But her thinking was also influenced by the political turmoil of Europe, where disappointed expectations had induced people "to sink back again under a despotism which knew better what it aimed at." She had turned to America "to establish a new hope." She sought glimpses of "the new human being and his world; the new humanity and the sight of its future on the soil of the New World."[48] Her hope centered first on the culture of New England, which she did not see as merely an extension of Europe, and second on the emerging civilization of the West, which she sometimes saw as a near-realization of the millennium.[49]

Downing told her, almost at the start of her journey, that "the reformers and lecturers who develop the spiritual and intellectual life in America, and call forth its ideal, come from the Northern States, from New England, and in particular from Massachusetts, the oldest home of the pilgrims and the Puritans."[50] Though the South was more "romantic" and paradisal and in some ways she liked it more, she never found reason to question what she had been told. The South was not as admirable a culture in its own right, and it was not a source for the westward extension of civilization.[51] The writers of the North gave her new terms in which to imagine the mission of America.

On one of her early evenings in America, Downing read aloud parts of James Russell Lowell's "Prometheus," in which the poet of the New World distinguished himself from Aeschylus and Shelley by emphasizing, not revenge or selfish defiance, but resistance to tyranny and the promise of "freedom and happiness for the human race."[52] Emerson virtually gave her the language in which she spoke of the "new man," self-reliant, a believer in beauty and ideals, setting off in new directions, whose works she had come to discover. She discussed Emerson in the Downing circle, copied pages of his pronouncements into her letters to Sweden, spent several days with him in Boston and in "the pretty little Idyllian city of Concord," and struggled with nagging feelings that his religion was too un-Christian and his teachings too vaporous. She never doubted that he gave voice to America's search for its highest calling.[53]

Emerson was only one voice, however; an individualistic one. Bremer thought there were "two principal tendencies of the age," one of which "would perfect society by means of each separate human being perfecting himself." Bremer was more in sympathy with the other, which sought to "perfect man and human nature by means of social institutions."[54] Throughout her book it was confidence in the progress of popular education, more than anything else, that enabled her to overlook American shortcomings and anticipate a brighter future. The great champion of social improvement, as Downing told her in an early conversation, was Horace Mann, tireless advocate of public schools in Massachusetts and the nation. She talked with him in Washington, where he served in Congress, and was thrilled by his "heroic nature" and "faith which might remove mountains." She was almost equally impressed with the political economist Henry Carey, whom she also met in Washington, where he spoke appealingly of strengthening "the basis" on which republican government rested by means of public education. She did not really understand his vision of economic growth ("an island which will very well support ten persons," she countered, "never can support equally well ten hundred"), but she was inspired to converse with men who thought earnestly about the relationship between government and human welfare.[55]

Most inspiring of all was Downing himself, who was several times her host, traveled with her on several of her circuits, and introduced her to friends who entertained her in the South and West. By his own modest account, he was "a self-made man" who was fortunate in life: "I came at a time when people began universally to feel the necessity of information about building houses and laying out gardens." Bremer admired his success ("nobody, whether he be rich or poor, builds a house or lays out a garden without consulting Downing's works"), though she occasionally teased him for "being more exclusive and aristocratic in his beautifying activity than became an honest, downright republican." While Downing's love of beauty signified "inward" cultivation of the kind hailed by Emerson, his acceptance as an expert on architecture and horticulture showed how well he understood the feelings of middle-class men and women, especially the young. "Every young couple who sets up housekeeping" bought his books.[56] Thus he was associated with qualities Bremer admired most in American civilization: the beauty of the homes of families who were not born to wealth, and, as she imagined, the effects of beautiful, contrived surroundings on their souls.

At the end of her two years in America, she took pleasure in Downing's increasing influence. His business was greater than ever (and he conducted it with ease, "*con amore*, as Jenny Lind seems to sing"). He was consulted about the White House grounds and other projects in Washington as well as on the initial planning of Central Park in New York. She was pleased, also, that in his writings he had begun to take "a far higher stand" than formerly on the effects of public institutions on the republican population. She extracted a long section of an article he published in answer to "ultra-democratic" elements and "social doubters" who believed a public, central park would benefit only the "upper ten" who wished to ride in their fine carriages, or that it would be "usurped by rowdies and low people." This opposition rested on ignorance of beautiful parks in France and Germany where entire urban populations, hundreds of thousands of people, passed afternoons and evenings together in enjoyment of refreshing scenery, sharing delight in the same art and music, participating in "the social freedom of a community of genial influences."

Why should Europe, Downing asked, exhibit a better understanding than republican America of "the elevating influences of a wide popular enjoyment of galleries of art, public libraries, parks and gardens, which have raised the people in *social* civilization and social culture?" "Popular refinement" was truly a republican idea, which ought to find greater favor in America than overseas. It reached beyond the common school and the ballot box by offering to the working classes the same opportunities as were available to the rich.

> The higher social and artistic elements of every man's nature lie dormant within him, and every laborer is a possible gentleman, not by the possession of money and fine clothes, but through the refining influence of intellectual and moral culture. Open wide, therefore, the doors of your libraries and picture galleries, all ye true republicans! Build halls, where knowledge shall be freely diffused among men, and not shut up within the narrow walls of narrow institutions. Place spacious parks in your cities, and unloose their gates as wide as the gates of the morning to the whole people. As there are no dark places at noonday, so education and culture, the true sunshine of the soul, will banish the plague-spots of democracy.[57]

Acquaintance with Downing and his friends led Bremer to broaden her own interest in the home and to extol the larger New England project of extending civic culture. She detected the emerging significance of "culture" in America, not simply as a sign of distinction for those who had made it, but more grandly as an emancipation of the "gentle" qualities repressed within the souls of all humankind. Later in the century it would seem clear that "culture" could serve purposes of social control or reinforce invidious distinctions between rich and poor. What the Swedish traveler reveals to us, however, is the innocent enthusiasm for the spreading light of culture over dark places of society that motivated some progressive, humanitarian leaders of America's educated classes.

Parks, museums, and libraries were restful and stable centers in a nation that seemed, to the European traveler, to be always in motion. Bremer was struck by American uses of the telegraph for every kind of communication ("even affairs of marriage, I have heard"), and in the United States Patent Office she observed how many of the machines on display were "for the acceleration of speed." The great feature of life in this country was "the circulation of life and population," for short visits as well as long treks to new homes. She was impressed by her host in Missouri, Senator David Rice Atchison, a "well-informed young man" who had given five hundred "stump speeches" to develop interest in laying down a railway to the Pacific. All the travelers were "like shuttles in the weaver's loom," darting to and fro, north and south, east and west.[58] What she saw was, not menacing restlessness, but the weaving of a new civilization. That is why the West was such an important part of her journeys. That is why she was so impressed by the cultured life of Cincinnati.

The point for her was not that the wilderness was half-savage; it was that the American was transporting civilization where it did not previously exist. "Wherever Americans establish themselves, the first buildings that they erect, after their dwelling-houses and places of business, are schools and churches." Log houses gave way to cottages and villas; then followed capitol buildings, academies, asylums, "institutions of all kinds." The early evidence of civilization was "*material . . .* , but the spiritual growth follows in its footsteps."[59] Nowhere in the world was so much done "for the public" by private individuals as in the United States, "in particular in the free states." Nowhere else was "intelligence" so closely joined with "active human-love."[60]

Amid all the other activity in the civilizing of the West—the building of institutions, the flurry of newspapers and politics, the destruction of forests, the creation of canals and railroads—"husbands build beautiful homes for their wives, plant trees and flowers around them, and woman rules as a monarch in the sacred world of home."[61] Although this image is likely to undermine Bremer's credibility as an advocate of women's rights to some modern readers, it was central to her thoughts about the West. It emerges from a progression of specific descriptions of scenes in the West. On the banks of the Mississippi, in Iowa, she visited a new log house where a "young, strong, earnest mother" held her plump baby boy. The husband was "out in the forest." Two cows grazed in the meadow. There was "a degree of comfort" in the house; in particular, she noticed a Bible, prayer books, and anthologies of literature. Here were the calm, reverent people who were establishing society in the wilderness.[62] In Saint Paul, which was less than two years old, she stayed in the house of Governor Alexander Ramsey "and his pretty young wife." The house was rough and used for business, but Ramsey was building "a handsome, spacious house, upon a hill, a little out of the city."[63] Then came Saint Louis and Cincinnati, where civilization was farther along; and she could write in her most millennial terms of the type of home that characterized this nation from Massachusetts to Minnesota: "Order, comfort, embellishment, and an actual luxury of trees and flowers, distinguish the home of the New World. And this house is the earliest world of the child, of the new man."[64]

In light of her glowing praise of home and motherhood, it is almost surprising to find that Bremer repeatedly tried to describe the shortcomings of America's women. Perhaps she had Tocqueville in mind (though she never mentions him) when she wrote that "the women of America do not, *in general,* equal that good report which some European travelers have given of them."[65] Certainly she was echoing, in part, dissatisfaction she heard from Americans about the inadequacy of female education. Criticisms of American women appear often in *Homes,* and they usually are linked to specific conversations and observations. They offer an opportunity to extend comparisons between her work and Tocqueville's more famous *Democracy in America.* They also allow us to focus more precisely on her conception of the relationship between culture and citizenship.

Tocqueville devoted a series of chapters to the influences of democracy on the family. Many of his comments are self-revealing. He speculated that relations between father and son were more trusting and affectionate once the father was shorn of aristocratic prerogatives; brothers became more harmonious and intimate once the privileges of the first-born were removed and there was "no cause for friction." In his comments on women he focused more specifically on America. He commented, accurately enough for the social classes he met, on the relative freedom with which girls thought and acted on their own as they grew up and the abrupt cessation of independence that greeted them in marriage. Much of his commentary had to do with the prevention of premarital and extramarital sex in America and the loss of warmth and charm, as he saw it, that accompanied the better morals and judgment of educated women in democratic countries.

His most often quoted chapter reproved European advocates of women's rights who forgot "the divergent attributes" of the sexes. In the United States, he maintained, democratic equality was not understood to imply that women should have the same functions, rights, and duties as men. Instead, Americans kept men and women in "clearly distinct spheres of action"; women "never" managed businesses or interfered in politics, but they were also shielded from rough physical work. There was no endeavor to "destroy all power": men were understood to have "the right to direct" their spouses, and women liked it that way. He had "never" found that American women felt their husbands had usurped their rights. To the contrary, "they seem to take pride in the free relinquishment of their will. . . . That, at least, is the feeling expressed by the best of them." What women gained was release from the "contempt" that European men expressed even while flattering them. They gained greater freedom from seduction and rape, both of which Europeans regarded more leniently. In a famous peroration, Tocqueville claimed that Americans, while continuing "the social inferiority" of woman, "have done everything to raise her morally and intellectually to the level of man." While never leaving her domestic sphere, she enjoyed a higher station than elsewhere. And for reasons that are unclear, since he does not discuss politics or economics in these chapters, he adds, "if anyone asks me what I think the chief cause of the extraordinary prosperity and growing power of this nation, I should answer that it is due to the superiority of their women."[66]

Tocqueville's diaries and notebooks contain no evidence that he spoke much with American women. When he spoke about them, the topic was usually chastity.[67] His analysis of how they were treated and how they felt is highly suspect. His great advantage over Bremer is that he is at least clear about what he claimed to see, which was what for personal and theoretical reasons he wanted to see. As so often happened with his new political science, the social description was actually dictated by *a priori* consider-ations. Nevertheless, his view of woman's higher station in a separate sphere was in accord with widespread rationalizations of why the universalistic Enlightenment doctrines about human rights and political participation, at a time of economic mobility and extension of the franchise, were limited in their application to women.[68] Tocqueville's peroration was quoted by promi-nent American women who thought it could be used to good account in the improvement of woman's lot in certain areas, such as employment in "moral" fields like schoolteaching.[69] Historians of the period have some-times thought that the notion of "separate spheres" actually fit the realities of women's lives in the period, giving them higher status in some respects while narrowing their economic and political options. But no one today would maintain that the spheres were as rigidly maintained as Tocqueville implied by his repeated use of the word *never*, nor was women's education as perfect as he claimed.[70]

It should be noted that Tocqueville visited the United States almost two decades before Bremer. He knew nothing of the women's rights advocates who assembled in Seneca Falls (1848), nothing of the women in the American Anti-Slavery Society and other movements that "interfered" in politics, nothing of the "emancipated ladies" who insisted on public professional roles for women. Even in the early 1830s he might have learned more about women writers than he did (one of his more preposterous claims is that "few novels are published in the United States" because voluntary marriage made sexual temptation and transgression intolerable in society and unattractive in fiction).[71] What is remarkable, perhaps, is that Bremer, who was aware of emancipated women, active reformers, and celebrated writers and who spent so much time with accomplished women, found American women to fall short of expectations.

In the gallery of the Senate she studied typical American women whose "elegant toilets" and "very lovely faces" were admirable. But they wished to "show themselves there—only to be seen. . . . I am obliged to say silently, regarding their expression, 'How unmeaning!' " The men of America surpassed the women in both "real development and good breeding."[72] After a bridal party in Cincinnati, she recorded a similar view, which became a touchstone in all her thinking about America. The women's "toilets" were beautiful; they dressed with good taste. But they behaved with as much artifice and vanity as ladies in Europe's capitals, "and far more than in our good Sweden." Sometimes they drove their husbands to despair and drunkenness with their extravagant desire for luxuries. And there was something missing even in their beauty. It was superficial. It lacked any suggestion of repose, grace, depth of being.[73]

To explain such deficiency, Bremer referred to the separate education that Tocqueville praised lavishly. There was, to be sure, much to commend. Blackwell's college for female physicians was exemplary, for surely there were branches of medicine consistent with women's "natural tendencies."[74] There were good drawing schools. The increased demand for female schoolteachers had given rise to excellent seminaries, and the crowds of women entering that profession were exempt from her criticisms. ("Even Waldo Emerson, who does not easily praise, spoke in commendation of them.") Because of women's value as teachers, educational institutions for women were generally superior to those in Europe. But this change did not benefit the majority of women. Young girls, she concluded from a visit to the female academy of Rutgers, had too much attention paid to their poetic effusions before they gained sufficient experience in life.[75] They were denied the chance to learn "industrial employments," especially bookkeeping, a subject offered women to great advantage in France. For most of those shallow women with beautiful, "unmeaning" faces, the problem was an education that was merely "scholastic," offering no "higher training for the world and social life."[76] Their education was "effeminate," conducive to physical weakness, preparation for days of inactivity that really amounted to "a sort of harem-life." America had not fully made a commitment to give all citizens the best possible chance to use their natural human talents.[77]

Women had all the power in the home that they could wish.[78] On this point Bremer agrees with Tocqueville. But the stultifying routine of their lives limited the good that they could do even as mothers. While speeches, songs, and stories glorified the influence that mothers exerted over the minds and souls of future citizens, the "thoughtlessness, insipidity, vanity, and pretension" of many American women was worrisome. They were too self-involved to be anything but indulgent and neglectful of their children. They lacked the sternness and strength that classical writers had thought necessary to bring up republican children. They lacked the depth of character and civic spirit that the same task required in modern times. It was not just that their schooling was inadequate. There was reason to wonder whether "that great freedom, which is early permitted to young women," was consistent with their highest development. Such freedom was not likely to have good results in a society in which men, contrary to Tocqueville, were gallant but not truly respectful. Men were polite and even compliant, but regarded women, all the same, "more as pretty children than as their reasonable equals, and do not give them their society when they seek strengthening food for soul and thought." Women married young in America; they knew that men prized "the merely agreeable and outwardly attractive in the sex"; and their characters were not strong when they found themselves mothers. No wonder they were so poorly prepared for the one task they were supposed to find most ennobling.[79]

What was missing, in the final analysis, was an adequate conception of citizenship. To explain what she meant, Bremer fell back on flights of vague rhetoric that appear almost evasive, particularly when she refers to the women's rights conventions of the era. She applauds these conventions, rejoices at the support many "distinguished men" give them, and regrets only some (undisclosed) "lesser" planks and the occasional "tone of accusation and bravado." But she does not take a stand on suffrage, let alone divorce or women's property rights. She hails the movement only as evidence of transition toward changes that are bound to come.[80]

She reports that even women's rights advocates agreed with her on "that deficiency of many-sided development" too often characteristic of American women. She thought woman required, "not a less, but, on the contrary, a higher esteem for home and her vocation"; yet as long as home was considered narrowly as a retreat for an inferior sex, women would not do well even in the restricted responsibilities entrusted to them. In the New World, and in the Old as well, "woman still stands almost isolated in the home and in social life, with no place of fellow-citizenship, without any higher consciousness of the connection which exists between this and the life of the home, or of the connection between moral and religious (or the higher political) questions, and social questions and political life." She repeats such words several times: "the citizenness is not as yet fully awakened within the community"; as long as the influence of "the female consciousness" was not valued in "the councils of the community" it would remain weak in the home, which would continue not to educate "citizens and citizennesses."[81] The last quotations appear in Bremer's account of a return visit to the Raritan Bay phalanstery, where she was impressed by the "thoughtfulness and gentleness" of women joining in work essential to the community. This was very much in contrast with the lives devoid of public consciousness that she saw among women elsewhere.

There is little point in trying to infer what Bremer specifically meant by citizenship when she fails to say so herself. She was only a casual visitor to Raritan Bay, not an advocate of community living. She was writing to Swedes who were much more adamantly opposed to women's rights than Americans were,[82] and some vagueness may have been tactically wise. She was at a stage of transition in her own intellectual growth toward an advocacy of women's rights that would jeopardize her popularity as a fireside novelist. Her fundamental point was that republican society ought to call on everyone to be concerned about the welfare of the community as a whole. Women, given no role in public affairs, would fail to "develop" (a favorite word, as we have seen) fully and would fall short even in their narrowly defined duties. In discussing the family, Tocqueville praised Americans for applying the political economists' idea of the division of labor; the person who performed one small task in the making of pins did not need to know anything about their manufacture or marketing.[83] Bremer spoke, not of political economy, but of "the great Christian Commonwealth."[84] To her, a conception of citizenship demanding that all should understand and help in the pursuit of common goals was essential if the great work of public education and social improvement were to proceed.

Bremer's view of citizenship was not completely new. Aristotle and other classical writers asserted that citizenship led to the ethical improvement of the citizen. But before her time this assertion was seldom stretched to call for an enlargement of the citizenry to include unfranchised groups like women. Her view owed much to her conversations with American women. It was related in obvious ways to the program of popular education and cultural advance associated with men like Mann and Downing. It hinted at important new departures in the idea of the citizen in America. It differed greatly from the views of the Fathers of the late eighteenth century: not only was it more inclusive but it also emphasized the role of citizenship in developing the potential of those who needed to fulfill its duties, an emphasis unimportant to the Fathers. This view of development could be extended to other groups besides women. Her view prefigures the analysis offered several decades later by Jane Addams of the discontents of educated women who had too little asked of them, of the part to be played by these women in improving the lives of less fortunate members of the community, and of the enhanced sense of social cohesion that would follow from a reinvigorated and enlarged conception of citizenship.

Bremer shared with Tocqueville an appreciation of the legacy of New England and the civilizing of the West. But she did not travel or write in religious terror, and she expressed a more confident expectation about the example of democratic culture to be shown the world by America. While she offered important criticisms of barriers to women's development, what is most memorable about *Homes of the New World* is its enthusiastic description of the building of a new civil society that was both domestic and progressive as homes and schools, churches and libraries were erected in America.

CHAPTER TWELVE

The Opening of the American Mind

The travelers who wrote books about America reflected a belief that travel was enlightening. Both Tocqueville and Bremer traveled to other lands besides the United States and wrote about their experiences, and the Europeans who read their books also read other works by other travelers. The readers traveled, too. In early modern Europe, travel had been a sign of privilege and wealth; the man who had been abroad had experiences to relate and, often, collections of refined or curious objects that distinguished him from those who were stuck forever in one locale. By the nineteenth century the Grand Tour had become a well-established ritual for wealthy young people who visited the cultural capitals of Europe, and sometimes went farther afield, as preparation for a lifetime of social leadership.

Naturally enough, Americans traveled in Europe.[1] Some of the well-to-do pursued the Grand Tour to show their social standing and to gain the cultural polish that was so hard to acquire in a new and distant nation. Some went to acquire training in fields like painting and sculpture that were undeveloped in America. Some American writers—among them, Hawthorne and Irving—went overseas on diplomatic assignments, while others—including Cooper and Longfellow—spent years in pursuing their literary business, enjoying the leisure of travel, exposing their children to the culture of Europe, and collecting material for future works. Others went for shorter periods, much as Tocqueville and Bremer came to America, and with specific assignments (to lecture, perhaps, or to inspect parks and architecture), but with the intention of composing books about their travels. Nearly always, these books followed familiar conventions: passages on the sea journeys at the beginning and end, with a chronological account of the sites and monuments, parks and city-scapes, meetings with distinguished writers and records of other conversations in between.

The results of American travels in Europe include reams of popular poetry, inspired by the legends and monuments of the Old World, and successful novels, such as Washington Irving's *The Alhambra* (1833). They also include works of travel, such as Cooper's *Sketches of Switzerland* (1836), Frederick Law Olmsted's *Walks and Talks of an American Farmer in England* (1852), Hawthorne's *Our Old Home* (1863), and Emerson's *English Traits* (1856). Reports on Europe were also features of the lecture circuit. Bayard Taylor, one of the most popular lecturers, added reports on Africa and Asia as well. No lecture was more popular than Wendell Phillips's "The Lost Arts," which continually reminded listeners that anyone could profit-ably visit ancient scenes and reflect on the skills that moderns had not yet mastered.

Americans who spent much time in Europe were apt to discover that their hosts regarded them as uncouth and ultrademocratic folks to whom the splendors of proper civilization were really inaccessible. If it was so hard for Europeans to speak about America without condescension and for Ameri-cans to perceive Europe without naïveté, someone might have advised call-ing off the effort or at least questioning whether there were international standards of inquiry and analysis that could make communication and com-parison worthwhile.[2] But few were inclined to do that. Tocqueville and Bremer, who were among the kindest observers of America, assumed that America's relation to European history as a haven for immigrants and an experiment in republican government made travel there, not just another series of tourist stops, but an exercise in learning about the future. Similarly, America's talented and thoughtful writers who visited Europe often saw opportunities for comparisons and contrasts, not all in favor of either conti-nent, that might have instructive benefits surpassing the usual broadening consequences of travel.

There were exceptions. Taylor's journeys "afoot" did not reach much beyond the traditional exercises in graphic daily reportage, and no travel writer was more popular in the United States. One critic noticed, however, the self-consciousness with which most nineteenth-century Americans wrote about Europe: "What shall I, as an American, do about Europe?" they seem to ask.[3] In some cases travel in Europe accentuated resentful feelings that artistic and intellectual distinction was difficult to attain in a "prosaic," materialistic new nation. In his admiration of the grace, charm, and intellec-tual openness of Europe's capitals, Cooper wrote bitterly of his countrymen's "secret, profound, and general deference" for money. "Men will, and do, daily, *corrupt themselves* in the rapacious pursuit of gain," and the "*millionaire*" had become the most esteemed member of a society in which fine art and literature barely survived.[4] Though Cooper protested against European underestimation of the solid virtues of Americans, he admired American energy less than Tocqueville did, and he had harsher things to say in indictment of American inhospitality to intellectual distinction.

But travel in the Old World could equally well heighten appreciation of America's leading role in the advances of republicanism and reform. In the mid-1840s, Henry Clarke Wright sent weekly dispatches to the antislavery newspaper *The Liberator* on his travels in Great Britain and on the Continent. Wright, one of the most radical of American abolitionists, was a critic of the military state, ecclesiastical institutions, and the oppression of women, as well as of the evils of slavery. The Europe he saw teemed with policemen and beggars; the familiar tourist sights were reminders of the lingering tyranny of aristocracy and bigotry. Though he followed the same conventions as other travel writers, he had no love of cathedrals and courts, crown jewels and midnight masses—all were emblems of the haughtiness of the rich and subservience of the poor in lands where women labored in the fields, men drank too much, and barracks were everywhere. He admired some things, particularly the playing of Johann Strauss's orchestra in the People's Garden in Vienna. But he gathered reports that Europe was on the eve of violent revolutions worse than sober, egalitarian Americans could imagine. In some respects, travel in Europe intensified and universalized his radicalism, but it also pointed to the relative superiority of the American social order.[5]

Emerson seldom took much part in antislavery agitation, let alone the "non-resistance" movement of which Wright was a key leader and that critics denounced as "no-governmentism." Yet on a trip to Stonehenge, interrupted by a rainstorm, Emerson was twitted by Carlyle and other companions about the intellectual mediocrity of America. Could he name a single "American idea—any theory of the right future of that country?" After some thought he "opened the dogma of no-government and non-resistance, and anticipated the objections and the fun, and procured a kind of hearing for it." He gibed his companions about "the bankruptcy of the vulgar musket-worship" and concern for "the secure tenure of our mutton-chop and spinach." Carlyle pretended to be so afraid of his wickedness that he would not walk before him.[6]

Almost all travelers concluded that the United States, for all its deficiencies when compared with the glories of the capitals of Europe, also lacked the extremes of wretchedness and gaudy wealth, of brutal ignorance and stratified intellectual distinction. "The people [of England] all seem to be enjoying life more, or else to be much more miserable, than in America," wrote Olmsted. In comparison with other countries, he went on, "the people of America have less of pleasure and less of actual suffering than any other in the world." Americans were notable for the "hopefulness" visible in every face, but also for their discontents and the absence of "virtuous pleasure" in their lives.[7]

Yet if America seemed solidly and enviably middle-class in contrast with Europe, it also seemed in some ways incomplete—to lack the ruins and monuments of the past, the abundance of comfortable satisfactions, the signs of a fully developed culture. The problem of America, as defined by Tocqueville, Bremer, and other Europeans, could be conceived in terms of the prolonged resistance of the wilds to civilized endeavor, or it could be conceived in terms of the home. After conversing about no-government, Emerson found himself asked about "American landscapes, forests, houses—my house, for example," and the questions were "not easy" to answer.

> There, I thought, in America, lies nature sleeping, overgrowing, almost conscious, too much by half for man in the picture, and so giving a certain *tristesse* like the rank vegetation of swamps and forests seen at night, steeped in dews and rains, which it loves; and on it man seems not able to make much impression. There, in that great sloven continent, in high Allegheny pastures, in the sea-wide sky-skirted prairie, still sleeps and murmurs and hides the great mother, long since driven away from the trim hedgerows and over-cultivated garden of England. And, in England, I am quite too sensible of this.

Fortunately, it was dinnertime; the company had to dress and be on "good behavior," and he got off with "very inadequate details" in lieu of a proper answer.[8]

What he says, of course, reeks with ambivalence. There is something seductive in the gothic, sloven scenes that he imagines, as well as something unfulfilled, disorderly, and inadequate. As so often, Emerson's writing pulls in two directions at once. Americans were less unambivalently thrilled than their European visitors were by prospects of a continent completely reduced to order. Yet it is a passage that encapsulates many of the meanings literate Americans discovered in Europe: images of themselves as rooted in an old homeland, living now in a state of semi-fulfillment, searching for deeper understanding of self and locale, nature and civilization. When they turned to writing about America, they produced no classic equal to *Democracy in America* or even *Homes of the New World*; the greatest attempt was, as we shall see, never completed. They were less sure of their footing, perhaps, because they wished to compare what they saw, not simply with an existing society in the Old World, but with a civilization whose outlines would be clearer in the future.

To a striking extent, intellectual activity in antebellum America consisted of travel and writing or speaking about travel. This is true especially of the branch of intellectual activity that was most self-consciously American, that wanted to understand what it meant to be an American and the extent to which American civilization had progressed. Several decades ago, when the best way of penetrating American culture seemed to be through the myths and symbols that it nourished, scholars called attention to images of the American Adam and the earthly paradise he inhabited.[9] To those images might be added many others, even more closely connected with journeys to knowledge, faith, or culture: Jason, Odysseus, Aeneas, and the Chosen People of the Old Testament. We might add saints and pilgrims, voyagers and adventurers, Childe Harold and Don Quixote: all those who revealed that knowledge is peripatetic and cosmopolitan, that it requires exertion and raises the risk of deception. (Anyone who has tried to teach works by antebellum authors to today's students knows that even the simplest texts are difficult to those devoid of knowledge of the classical and biblical traditions.) Most directly, Americans knew the stories of early colonists of North America, especially of New England. They knew the tales of discovery, exploration, and settlement, of coming across new things and trying to reestablish old things, that have always figured strongly in the imagination of Americans.[10]

To travel, or to read about travel, was, after all, the appropriate way to learn about and to present knowledge about a nation on the move. That America was incessantly mobile was not an observation unique to Tocqueville; it was what Americans reported about themselves. That all the traveling Americans were shuttles weaving a new civilization was not Bremer's private fantasy; Americans believed it to be true. Both in the world of intellect and in the larger economy there were trades that required mobility and versatility. In one of his best travel books, *Eldorado* (1851), Bayard Taylor described meeting college graduates and men of "genuine refinement and taste" among the forty-niners in the gulches of California. They looked as dirty and sunburnt as trappers or mountaineers, but only a year before they had been "patientless physicians, briefless lawyers and half-starved editors." They represented an "infusion of intelligence which gave the gold hunting communities, notwithstanding their barbaric exterior and mode of life, an order and individual security which at first sight seemed little less than marvellous."[11] If this could be said of those who failed and vaulted west, how much more was it true of those who traveled successfully in fields like medicine, law, or literature. Those who were on the move, even as they pursued their own self-interest, were also the bearers of civilization.

The questions, then, to be explored in American travel were, what kind of people did you see, and how were they living? Answers to these questions often took the form of presenting one of two stereotypes of American character. Taylor encountered among the Mississippians, Arkansans, and Missourians who boarded ship with him at New Orleans on the way to California one of the "new varieties of the American." They were "long, loosely-jointed men, with large hands and foot and limbs which would still be awkward, whatever the fashion of their clothes." Their appearance was menacing:

> Their faces were lengthened, deeply sallow, overhung by straggling locks of straight black hair, and wore an expression of settled melancholy. The corners of their mouths curved downwards, the upper lip drawn slightly over the under one, giving to the lower part of the face that cast of destructiveness peculiar to the Indian. These men chewed tobacco at a ruinous rate, and spent their time either in dozing at full length on the deck or going into the fore-cabin for "drinks." Each one of them carried arms enough for a small company and breathed defiance to all foreigners.[12]

In this type we recognize men much like the Tennesseans in whom Tocqueville saw the devolution of European culture in the direction of savagery. Similar descriptions were given of "pukes" from Missouri or of Hoosiers or Suckers. Not everyone agreed on the devolution: both Margaret Fuller and Emerson saw lots of similarities between these folks and the peasants of the Old World.[13] In any case, these American types called into question any link between westward movement and social progress.

The other stereotype was the literate, progressive farmer. In a public letter to a British abolitionist, "Old England and New England Laborers on Land Contrasted," Henry Clarke Wright described such a man whose hospitality he was enjoying in Princeton, Massachusetts. This man owned his farm and employed a young man who in due time would start his own farm, marry, and raise a family. He had been a legislator. He owned books and subscribed to six periodicals. He was temperate and up-to-date on the reforms. His family's diet included a rich variety of foods, and their home was floored with handsome boards. They had a piano and good music.[14] Here was a good citizen and an emblem of the upward progress of civilization—the original of the model being copied in villages and towns and throughout the West.

Literary history has given inordinate stress to one theme in nineteenth-century American culture: signing off from civilization, like Melville in the Marquesas, lighting out for the as-yet-uncivilized territory, like Huck at the end of his adventures. This theme, most familiar in great works of fiction, shows up in lectures and travel writing, too. Henry David Thoreau's brilliant lecture, "Walking," for example, spoke in favor of "freedom and wildness, as contrasted with a freedom and culture merely civil," and recommended exercises to get outside the world of domesticity, trade, and politics.[15] Taylor's accounts of travel in Africa, India, and China conveyed the thrill of getting outside the ordinary and the familiar. Washington Irving's *A Tour of the Prairies* (1835) and Francis Parkman's *The Oregon Trail* (1849) related to curious Eastern readers what life was like beyond the line of settlement. Margaret Fuller's *A Summer on the Lakes* (1844) resembles Tocqueville's endeavor to see the wildness of the West. In works like these, wildness may at times appear inviting, and few authors could avoid the traditional satirical device of showing the occasional superiority of the Indians' mores to those in supposedly civilized society.

In Parkman's hands, however, the uncivilized West became a kind of wasteland of physical hardship, loneliness, monotony, and pointless slaughter. Alone in a canyon, Parkman found himself dreaming of scenes of refinement in Europe. Even Thoreau, who associated the westward impulse with Columbus, imagined in the building of homes along the Mississippi and the dredging of swamps in Massachusetts acts of heroism and redemption. The wilds were fascinating because of the certainty of their approaching settlement. What made possible Taylor's adventures in exotic lands was the existence of well-dressed audiences waiting to hear his reports and buy his books. The writers' rejection of civility was never anything more than temporary, even artificial.

This was an era, not only of westward expansion, but of urban growth, and there was perhaps as much curiosity about the latter as about the former. The conventions of travel writing could be adapted to this purpose. When the cities were described by travelers, it was usually in attempts to explore scenes of wretchedness and drunkenness. Solon Robinson's *Hot Corn: Life Scenes in New York Illustrated* (1854) depicts the miseries of New York's poor from the point of view of a benevolent Christian reformer, a man from the West who assumes that if such scenes were familiar they would become things of the past. Some of the best-selling novels of this era, particularly George Lippard's *The Quaker City* (1844) and *New York: Its Upper Ten and Lower Million* (1854), approached great cities as *terrae incognitae* in which polite and well-meaning people were unaware of villainous conspiracies responsible for great crimes. But experienced guides could conduct the reader through labyrinths of misery, evoking tears and shouts of outrage as unfamiliar scenes passed by, almost as in the cinema of the next century.

Quite a few novelists worked over stories of violence, inebriation, and lust in the cities, but few took on the literary world itself.[16] Travel writers had almost nothing to say about the people and institutions that constituted a reorganization of intellectual life: the clergymen and editors, lecturers and reviewers, museums and colleges, libraries and historical societies, salons and clubs of Boston, New York, or Philadelphia. For the aspiring poet Bayard Taylor, the meanings of a change from a small town to New York are well documented. He spent a year editing a weekly newspaper in Phoenix-ville, New York, where he accumulated debts and felt stultified. In late 1847, filled with what an early biographer called his "indomitable desire for growth," he responded to William Cullen Bryant's words: "The intellect is incited to greater exertion [in New York], is invigorated by collision with other intellects, and finds more abundant aliment." It all came true for Taylor, who swiftly found himself in great demand by the magazines, enjoy-ing *conversaziones* at the home of Anne Lynch, reading widely, and rapidly ascending to fame.[17] Success in New York gave him entrée to a far-flung network of intellectual contacts. Though a traveler to exotic realms, he had personal connections with everyone he needed to meet.[18]

Taylor did not like the title he was commonly known by: "the Great American Traveler." He was a poet, critic, and translator whose most impor-tant work was probably a translation of Goethe's *Faust* (1871), which he worked on for decades. He wrote a dozen books of travel, however, and edited a half-dozen others, and his lectures and poems often had a basis in travel. Although most of these works were about far-off places, he also wrote about trips to Mammoth Cave, upstate New York, and Colorado, as well as a second trip to California. They are by no means works of deep analysis, but they did raise in an accessible way some fundamental questions about human possibility. He recommended learning about other peoples as a method to "gather into our own the aggregate experience of Man." After seeing the size of pumpkins and beets in the San Joaquin Valley in 1859, he wondered: "if plants change, wherefore not men? And if so, how? Or is the change only in the hidden roots of our character, not in the boughs and blossoms which we show to the world?"[19] Here were his attempts to address questions of human variability that could eventually undermine the certain-ties of nineteenth-century faith. But Taylor, like most successful public men of his time, was optimistic: "He saw whatever illustrated life, hope, vigor, courage, prosperity," said the philosopher Josiah Royce years later of his *Eldorado*.[20]

The progress of civilization was usually illustrated, not by the growth of cities (though that was certainly an exciting aspect of California) but by the quality of farms, homes, towns, and especially roads. Travel literature, American-style, was much concerned with the ease or difficulty of getting from one place to another. American writers preferred to go to places where civilization was in the making, and they judged what they saw by the extent to which order had replaced chaos along the way. There were nay-sayers. Leaving a little town in Illinois, Margaret Fuller reflected that "there was neither wall nor road in Eden, that those who walked there lost and found their way just as we did, and that all the gain from the Fall was that we had a wagon to ride in." In her view, "what is limitless is alone divine." But this was surely an affectation. She herself admired another town, Geneva, because it reminded her of a New England village; it was even graced by Unitarian preaching. Such "points of light" were needed among the "swarms" of uncouth settlers. While she criticized women who brought pianos to the wilderness, she thought singing in parts, even "a fine Italian duet," was a perfect recreation in a log cabin. Her companion was closer to the prevailing view when he defended the Greek belief that "limits are sacred: that the Greeks were in the right to worship a god of limits."[21]

Caroline Kirkland is more representative than Fuller. A key figure in the literary circles that Bremer and Taylor enjoyed, she had lived for six years in Livingston County, Michigan, where her husband hoped to see a new city spring up around their lands. The venture collapsed in the depression of the late 1830s, but it laid the basis for her largely autobiographical *A New Home—Who'll Follow?* (1839) and other works that established her reputation as an "early exponent of frontier realism."[22] *A New Home,* her account of "journeyings and tarryings beyond the confines of civilization," was so close to fact, she said, that she thought of setting it forth as "an unimpeachable transcript of reality . . . a sort of 'Emigrant's Guide.' " Though some of the humorous dialogue that has won it praise may have been fictionalized, the main story it tells is one of impatience for signs of refinement and acquiescence in the slow pace with which civilization actually makes its way. The image it begins with is of "a Michigan mud-hole" that stops her carriage and casts her, flimsy shoes and all, into a vain search for a dry footpath to take her to what turns out to be a dismal log hotel. Even at the end of the book, three years later, the town lacks elegance and convenience. To live there is a practical course in "Equality" in which one learns to forgo "refined indulgences" and feelings of superiority and condescension. But there is the weekly mail, the center of anticipation and happiness for one who has "left behind hosts of friends, as well as many other very comfortable things."[23]

The roads, more than anything else, provided Frederick Law Olmsted a basis for the comparisons he made between North and South. He brings to mind the landscape historian John Stilgoe's comment: "Outsiders focused their anger on abused slaves and eroded, abandoned fields, but the very alienness of the southern landscape unnerved them more."[24] The proximate origin of Olmsted's ideological viewpoint lay in New England: he was an Easterner who disliked the rush of population westward because it threatened to leave no settled, tightly clustered landscape anywhere. He held fast to the vision of united villages with improved lands around them in contrast to the slovenly wilderness that still surrounded them at a distance. The origins of the vision go back much farther into European tradition, which had helped define the purpose and habits of Northern colonists.[25] Yet he was by no means a conservative traditionalist. A recent study considers him a utilitarian, and certainly he admired the concerted efforts of both entrepreneurs and engineers to transform the environment and subject it to human uses.[26]

Olmsted did not see the South as all of a piece. As we noticed in Chapter Four, he was obliged to acknowledge that some Southern aristocrats really were superior to the Northern upper classes, and that the "common farming and laboring people of the North" lacked adequate culture and good manners.[27] Furthermore, he accepted a distinction between progressive and backward people in all lands: "The calculating, indefatigable New-Englander, the go-ahead Western man, the exact and stern Englishman, the active Frenchman, the studious, observing, economical German would all and each lose patience with the frequent disobedience and constant indolence, forgetfulness and carelessness, and the blundering, awkward, brute-like manner of work of the plantation-slave."[28] He recognized that some parts of the South were further developed than others. The roads and railroads of Georgia, for example, were "exceedingly well managed,"[29] and he was impressed by some farms and factories in Virginia. He tended to think, however, that the landscape looked best where it was owned by emigrants from the North or England, and that the system of free labor was unquestionably more productive in all circumstances.[30] No part of the South impressed him so favorably as German communities near San Antonio, where he found none of the "indolent and inefficient habits" that stifled domestic and communal feeling and deterred beneficial settlement. There one might even hear "teamsters, with their cattle staked around them on the prairie, humming airs from 'Don Giovanni,' " or repeating passages from Dante and Schiller "as they lay on the ground looking up into the infinite night."[31]

His basic impression of the South, despite the many exceptions, was of temporary conditions. The physical condition of the roads and the appearance of the land alongside them testified to the region's moral impoverishment. These were not roads that led from one compact settlement to another. They were not bordered by neat fields. By the roadsides lay undrained swamps, scrubby soils, crude houses (even those of planters more often than not), and scattered crossroads stores. Olmsted lacked any appreciation of the uses that Southerners made of their roads. It was a land of "stagnation."[32] He expressed contempt for the rural folk who congregated on market days: "The 'wild Irish' hardly differ more from the English gentry than these rustics from the better class of planters and towns-people." He hated the "drawling whine" with which one man pestered him to sell his horse (though he acknowledged that "the worst of the New-Englanders" also spoke with a "nasal tone" that was "intense and painful."[33]

One conversation may stand for much that Olmsted abhorred. As he rode through the Mississippi Delta, a group of men in a tavern, apparently unaccustomed to seeing strangers, stared at him. A rough-looking man with a pistol sticking out of his trousers jumped on his horse and overtook Olmsted, who asked: "Can you tell me how far it is to Woodville, Sir?"

"I don't know."

"Have you no idea of the distance?"

"You won't get beyond there to-night."

"Can I be sure of getting there before dark?"

"No place for you to stop this side of there, I reckon."

"You can't tell me about how many miles it is there?"

"No."

The man spoke "sneeringly" about the "big bugs" who owned most of the land and large numbers of slaves and about the deterioration of the soil, once called "the gardying of the world" but now much less productive. Then he reined off at a fork in the road and said, "without turning his face at all toward me: 'If you are going on to Woodville, that's your road—this is mine,' and rode off, making no reply to my good-bye."[34] We recognize here a version of what became the "Arkansas Traveler" stories and many other jokes about the unresponsive answers given by rural people to a citified traveler's questions, jokes that were not restricted to the South but had their counterparts in the outreaches of New England. But for Olmsted the encounter was a disturbing example of Southern ignorance. After this conversation he asked twelve other persons, white and black, the same questions and got no better answers. It was a land of incivility, ignorance, carelessness, and waste.

Roads were in some respects strange objects to choose as signs of civilization. In European tradition, they represented the triumph of human intention over the chaos of the wild, but they were also the domain of gypsies, traveling folk, and the Devil. They led away from the settled, familiar order and toward the threatening and unknown.[35] Certainly Northerners who praised roads did not have in mind the forces behind a high rate of migration out of New England; it was not the facility of movement away from civilization that they meant to praise.[36] The roads that Olmsted valued were the kind that connected familiar places, the kind that citizens of towns donated time and labor to maintain; their absence in the South or West meant an absence of civic nexus. The same view was expressed by the prominent Hartford theologian Horace Bushnell in an 1846 lecture on the "moral connections" of travel, published in pamphlet form with the title "The Day of Roads." "The

Road is that physical sign, or symbol, by which you will best understand any age or people," said Bushnell. "If they have no roads, they are savages; for the road is a creation of man and a type of civilized society." Wherever law is weak, where trade is feeble, where education and religion are stagnant, roads will be poor and impeded by fortresses and drawbridges. Wherever "there is motion in society," where "there is activity, or enlargement, or a liberalizing spirit of any kind," then "you will see it by the roads they are building."[37] The point could be illustrated from biblical times and ancient history, but Bushnell was especially impressed by the numerous road-building projects throughout Europe and, of course, in the United States. The final death of militarism and aristocratic privilege was foretold in the increased communication and wealth and the freedom of thought that roads would bring. Governments existed for the benefit of all, popular education must now advance, and "social revolutions" were afoot that might well have the holy purpose of leading toward "the coming reign of Christ on earth."[38]

The proper policy of governments in the modern "day of roads," according to Bushnell, was "to assist and encourage industry" and "to make every man as valuable as possible to himself and to his country."[39] The breakdown of archaic hierarchy, the expansion of wealth, and popular education were all realities of modernity, of which roads were the signs. Obviously this was a faith or an ideology shared by certain groups of cultivated citizens in the post-revolutionary era. But we should note that in America some groups rejected it, especially the parts of it requiring governmental funds. Democratic politicians detected an infernal stratagem by which elites sought to hold onto privilege, use the government for their own corrupt ends, and set class-biased standards for advancement in the new era. In a famous speech in the House of Representatives in March 1830, James Knox Polk denounced internal improvements as a "sponge" for soaking up the corrupt proceeds of an unfair economic system.[40] Education was always controversial among its alleged beneficiaries. Even those who wished the creation of roads, canals, and railroads in advance of settlement to facilitate the movement of agricultural goods might well repudiate the New England village ideal and the ideology cherished by Olmsted, Bushnell, and other proponents of advancing culture. One element of conflict in the era's intellectual life was that a policy proposed by some as liberalizing, anti-hierarchical, and revolutionary was, in the eyes of others, an illiberal vestige of a passing day.

In this kind of ideological controversy, symbols were all-important. Both Bushnell and Polk made that clear. For Northern intellectuals—and some European travelers—the North and the South became the great objective manifestations of conflicting attitudes toward the progress of civilization. When the twelve-year-old Henry Adams went to Washington with his father in 1850 he saw

the sudden change that came over the world on entering a slave state. . . .
The mere raggedness of outline could not have seemed wholly new, for even
Boston had its ragged edges, and the town of Quincy was far from being a
vision of neatness or good-repair; in truth, he had never seen a finished
landscape; but Maryland was raggedness of a new kind. The railway . . .
rambled through unfenced fields and woods, or through village streets, among
a haphazard variety of pigs, cows, and negro babies, who might all have used
the cabins for pens and styes, had the Southern pig required styes, but who
never showed a sign of care.

Washington itself showed evidence of neglect in its dirt streets, ramshackle
houses, and the "unfinished square marble shaft" of the Washington monument. Truly, slavery was "a nightmare, a horror, a crime, the sum of all
wickedness!"[41] When the abolitionist poet Whittier traveled to Harrisburg in
1839, he was stirred by the spectacle of "a rich and beautiful country
exhibiting the *free-labor* system to excellent advantage." He watched "hardy
farmers . . . sweeping with their scythes the heavy grasses of their meadows"; yellow wheatfields "relieve[d] the dark green of the vallies." But he
could not keep his mind off scenes further south where the valley stretched
"far away into the land of slavery": "I could not but contrast in imagination
the unpaid and miserable laborers of one portion" of the valley "with the
happy groups of freemen, reaping the bountiful harvest around me;—in the
midst of greenness and beauty, and the abounding munificence of nature,
and within hearing of the cheerful voices of contented and well-rewarded
industry, my heart was pained within me—a shadow from the land of oppression fell over the sunny landscape."[42]

To what extent did Southerners accept this ideology contrasting the
finished and unfinished landscape? White farmers, rich or poor, who built
houses far from those of others, who left land uncultivated and animals free
to wander, and who resisted the expenses of schools, showed their attachment to scenes that to Whiggish eyes looked ragged.[43] The contrast between
Northern and Southern society was by no means imaginary. Yet both Tocqueville and Bremer reported that many of the "best" Southerners drew the
same contrast and deplored it, without seeing any way for the South to
escape. Southern intellectual life had long been permeated by New England
influences, from tutors who came in colonial days to teach the children of
the gentry, to professors and clergymen who moved south in the nineteenth
century. To a surprising extent, the intellectual defense of slavery was de-
vised by transplanted Northerners, often conservative Federalists who saw
slavery as one more emblem of traditional privilege undergoing assault by
commercial and democratic forces, or by Southerners educated in the
North.[44] The South had articulate champions of a region forever agrarian or

forever aristocratic—remember the lawyer Allison whom Olmsted met in Nashville. This viewpoint was not necessarily inimical to preferences for a more settled landscape; in fact, it might regard the unfinished South as a victim of democratic greed. Certainly, there were Southern intellectuals who sought to promote improvements in transportation and education while also defending slavery,[45] and in the same spirit, editors of the *Southern Literary Messenger, De Bow's Review,* and other publications tried to nourish a literary culture equal to, and separate from, New York's and Philadelphia's. In a growing number of towns in the South, a network of civic, educational, and religious organizations much like those to be found in New York or Ohio was emerging.[46] In these towns men and women entertained visions of civic progress fully consistent with those fostered in the North.

It is important to note that Northerners like Olmsted did not criticize the landscape and society of the South out of a conviction that the rest of the nation was faultless. They found the South wanting on the basis of an ideology that called for progressive improvement everywhere. Olmsted later realized, in fact, that the "most manifest general evil resulting to society from Slavery was that it aggravated and prolonged the hardships and disadvantages of a pioneer condition of society." This "truth" made a strong impression during his travels in the South and provided the basis for a "line of thought and observation" that continued throughout his subsequent work. We have seen that he left Nashville with a program for improving the level of culture in the North through projects such as magazines, schools, and parks. When Downing died in 1852, Olmsted succeeded him as the premier landscape designer in the nation. By the late 1850s he had come to believe that the culture of the United States required new understanding. During the succeeding decade he compiled notes and drafted passages for what might be called the nation's first great cultural history, though he was never able to finish it and it exists only in voluminous fragments.[47] This searching meditation on the civilization of the United States as discovered through travel, had it been completed, would have taken its place as the outstanding such inquiry by an American.

Much of the difficulty in understanding American culture Olmsted attributed to the misleading influence of European, and especially British, travelers. Most of them had passed through too quickly to study the "multitudinous counter-currents" of American life. Their observations were distorted by their biased purpose: to find evidence of "the failure of Democracy." They were content with the most superficial proof of what they already believed: that only a government with an aristocratic element favored "the civilization, happiness and virtue of the people." In addition, they generally relied for information on rich Americans who knew a lot about commerce but had not taken much time to think about any other matter except as it affected their business. One problem that became obvious in the United States during the Civil War was how little public leaders really knew about "the popular character."[48]

Though British commentary was nearly worthless, travel was still vital to understanding America. Olmsted pointed out that he had resided at length in four states and journeyed thousands of miles, often on horseback or by foot, in most of the other states. The manuscript was compiled in California. He had also traveled over forty thousand miles outside the United States, resided for a year in England, and walked throughout that country.[49] He could argue from observation that many of the foreigners' criticisms of the United States actually applied more pointedly to England. The United States had not replicated the civilization of the true English gentleman; that much could be conceded. But we also had fewer dandies who deceived themselves and others by imitating the dress and manners of gentlemen, fewer men who were polite and chivalrous in certain contexts and brutal and licentious in others, fewer hypocrites who fawned on their superiors while lording it over those below them, fewer of those "alternately insolent and obsequious" characters portrayed so memorably in Dickens's novels. Though he loved England, particularly for its landscape, Olmsted had learned to appreciate "the greater essential good nature of the American."[50]

He was certain, moreover, that the ordinary American had attained a much higher level of civilization than equivalent classes in Europe who had not migrated to the New World.[51] This was remarkable in view of the wretched or vicious condition of most of Europe's seventeenth-century emigrants and the continuous "decivilizing" tendencies in American society ever since. Though he was a traveler himself and a keen observer of the migratory habits of his countrymen, Olmsted simply assumed that many valuable "civilized" qualities depended on settled forms of social existence. He repeatedly asserted that there were two tendencies in American history (as in all human societies), the first of which was civilized and stationary, while the other was migratory and, variously, "barbaric" or "bohemian," which came to the same thing. This second set of tendencies destroyed civilization; the vices and shortcomings that travelers criticized in America, "so far as true, can all be traced to frontierism."[52]

His horror at "decivilizing" tendencies in America prompted Olmsted to compose passionate attacks on supposed achievements in popular religion, education, and science.[53] But there was also much to praise in comparison with England, and some worthwhile characteristics seemed to be essentially American. In their strong drive to improve themselves, Americans differed from the English. Americans were less passive and helpless, more adaptive, "or as our American phrase is, forehanded," in the face of change.[54] "More completely emancipated" from the "mental hamper of the feudal system,"

Americans were able to see their own interest in what benefited the community, while the English history of popular opposition to the improvement of roads reflected an abiding negative attitude toward civic affairs.[55] The frontier conditions of the United States, however disturbing in some respects, had the positive consequence of depleting peasant hostility to progress.

What made the United States both distinctive and admirable was its commitment to democracy. The American idea of government surpassed the English in justice; it also created deeper feelings of loyalty.[56] Family affection was stronger in America than among the peasantry who stayed in the Old World. Yet there also was a characteristic independence of spirit and even a pervasive "childlike" impulsiveness among Americans. Early marriage and a basic disposition to listen seriously to children served to break down the diffidence and stolidity of the European past. The results were paradoxical but "agreeable": an "indifference to strangers" accompanied by a willingness to help. If you asked a Californian for "advice about the roads," for example, he was more likely to answer "in a painstaking and truthful way, though with a perfectly independent and perhaps surly manner, than in any other part of the world."[57]

"This then is American," Olmsted wrote of the progressive tendencies he detected in our history; "the other things are remnants of European decivilization"—that is, the frontier's erosion of what little civilization had come over. As American history had proceeded, barbaric isolation gave way to stronger bonds fastening the individual to family, community, and nation; and now, he hoped, would come greater benevolence and religious tolerance. But the direction was clear: "As a general rule, . . . the longer the period in which men have been subject to that class of influences which are peculiarly active in America, and the less they have been subject to that class of influences which are more active in Europe, . . . the more nearly will they be fitted and inclined to live in communities in which every individual on the whole during his life is of service to and is served by every other therein." In these communities "all the intelligence and other forces of those who constitute them are employed with the least waste and to the highest ends."[58] Coming after so much thought from a man who had traveled so widely, found so much to criticize, and seen so many obstacles to civilization in America's past, this optimistic vision seems almost breathtaking. In this vision the attachment to the European past that Tocqueville and his American informants brought to all judgments of American society dissolved, and belief that an excellent civilization would emerge because of democracy, not despite it, gained unprecedented confidence.[59]

CHAPTER THIRTEEN

Ambiguous Argonaut

Olmsted's vision of progress exemplifies one of the two tendencies that Fredrika Bremer noted in American intellectual life—the quest for social improvement though collective effort. The second tendency we may associate most of all with Henry David Thoreau, one of America's great apostles of individualism. Thoreau dissented from most schemes of improvement that his countrymen put forward. He despised the shallow, greedy motives released by economic development and the alienation from nature that characterized most so-called progress. But his dissent, though often sardonically expressed, was limited. No one appreciated the manmade landscape with deeper feeling than he did, and no one's belief in the need for moral culture was more intense.

Thoreau, who won little fame in his own day, occupies an honored place in the American imagination primarily because of his essay "Civil Disobedience" (1849) and, even more, *Walden* (1854), works long recognized as inescapably important in the American canon. They establish the familiar images of Thoreau in jail for failure to pay his poll tax during the Mexican War and in his cabin living in solitude away from the harried lives of Concord's other residents. They prepare us to see him as a rebel, nay-sayer, lover of nature, advocate of simplicity, critic of what for others passed for civilization. While his neighbors drained swamps, introduced new crops, extended their working hours, and worked hard to bring produce to Boston, he preached a contrary message of leisure, unacquisitive habits, limited

141

goals, closeness to nature, and self-fulfillment.[1] Surely he was not someone
who cared about improved transportation. One of his poems celebrated an
abandoned road: "Nobodys repairs it, / For nobody wears it," but "You may
go round the world / By the Old Marlborough Road."[2] Another fragment
asks:

> What's the railroad to me?
> I ne'er go to see
> Where it ends.
> It fills a few hollows,
> And makes banks for the swallows,
> It sets the sand a-blowing
> And the blackberries a-growing.[3]

So persistent is the image of Thoreau's *Life in the Woods*, to use the
subtitle of *Walden*, of the daydreaming rebel or the poet unconcerned about
society, that teachers and critics enjoy pointing out problems in Thoreau's
pose. Some almost accuse Thoreau of disingenuousness or even deception.
They point to his endeavors to write successfully for the public, the proximity of his cabin to Concord, his dependence on the cultivated people in that
commercially important town—all as signs of his bad faith. Life in the
woods did not prevent him from strolling into Concord "every day or two" to
pick up news or gossip. He watched commercial ice cutters and saw the
smoke of a locomotive from his cabin. Though he wrote with fascination of
the West, he never went farther than New Jersey until the end of his life.[4]
What is at issue, however, is more the persistent misreading of Thoreau than
his own deceptiveness. He himself reports on the ice cutters, the locomotive, the strolls to town; these are not matters deceitfully left out of his
account. He is frank about leaving Walden Pond when he realized he had
fallen into routine: "I had several more lives to live, and could not spare any
more time for that one."[5] He never recommended a permanent way of living
for anyone. Nor did he urge any program of westward travel or emigration.
His emphasis was on inward moral improvement wherever one lived.
"Surely, O Lord, he has not greatly erred, / Who has so little from his
threshold stirred."[6] Like most complex works of art, *Walden* is elusive and
ambiguous, and it has been more convenient for admiring readers to stress
the arrangements its author lived by than the exhortation to self-improvement dramatized by his experiment.

In fact, *Walden* provides a radical critique of contemporary American
culture. Some of his complaints were by no means unusual. Thoreau sounds
like many of Tocqueville's informants when he writes of "this restless,
nervous, bustling, trivial Nineteenth Century."[7] In praising simplicity and
sincerity and disparaging fashion he works with contrasts common to the

moral thinking of many of his American contemporaries. But he did not join most of the intellectual elite in celebration of the progressive development of culture. In an age that stressed the socialization of the young and the internalization of conscience,[8] he questioned whether age had anything to teach to youth, urged everyone "to find out and pursue *his own* way, and not his father's or his mother's or his neighbor's instead," and gave antisocial advice: "Grow wild according to thy nature."[9] In an age that glorified improvement and civilization, he carried out his little satire of living by the pond: "if we stay at home and mind our business, who will want railroads? We do not ride on the railroad; it rides upon us."[10] In an age of patriotic fervor and revolutionary enthusiasm, he enjoyed watching a battle of black and red ants and found it superior to every fight in Concord's history.[11] In an age of reform he expressed contempt for those who made a profession of "Doing-good." It was their "private ail" that motivated them to lives of interference.[12] In an age that celebrated America's expanding mission in the world, he was more interested in "the now almost exterminated ground-nut" that he dug up, a "humble root" passed over "in these days of fatted cattle and waving grain-fields," but likely to revive and flourish when "wild Nature" reigns again.[13] The Thoreau of *Walden*, at least, was detached from the ideology of spreading civilization.[14]

In some respects it is misleading to consider Thoreau an author who wrote one masterpiece. *Walden* itself may be better understood if read in conjunction with *A Week on the Concord and Merrimack Rivers* (1849), *The Maine Woods* (1864), and *Cape Cod* (1865). The experiences out of which he made his books were interwoven; and while the last two appeared in book form after his death, he was never in the habit of finishing one project before turning to the next.[15] He always presents himself as an outsider, but in *Walden* he poses as an exile from civilization, while in the other three books he appears as a traveler in the world Americans were building and a reporter on how they were changing their environment. We learn to see him as an incisive, if dissenting, observer of the landscape as a key to the American intellect.

Even in *Walden* his celebration of the wilderness is ambiguous. On the one hand, nature is timeless and distinct from what man has wrought. On the other, it can only be known in terms of the made environment from which it recedes. In order to illustrate the point that "only as towns began to appear did the wilderness motif take form" in American thought, John Stilgoe offers a well-known quotation from Wallace Stevens's "Anecdote of the Jar":

I placed a jar in Tennessee
And round it was, upon a hill.
It made the slovenly wilderness
Surround that hill.[16]

This is a point that the poet at Walden understood. His overgrown beans were "the connecting link between wild and cultivated fields; as some states are civilized, and others half-civilized, and others savage or barbarous, so my field was, though not in a bad sense, a half-cultivated field." Again, describing his surveyor's habit of imagining houses on sites around Concord, he wrote: "Wherever I sat, there I might live, and the landscape radiated from me accordingly."[17] In *Walden* the ironic stress is on the isolation by which he redefines civilization and wilderness for his own purposes, but the other books reveal a keen sense of the defining acts of other Americans who altered the wilderness and remade the environment. "The civilized man," he observes in *Maine Woods*, "not only clears the land permanently to a great extent, and cultivates open fields, but he tames and cultivates to a certain extent the forest itself. By his mere presence, almost, he changes the nature of the trees as no other creature does."[18]

All Thoreau's books are reports of travel. "I have travelled a good deal in Concord," he boasts in *Walden*, though in that satirical work, which discounts much that other people hold important, he collapses two years into one and follows the movement of the seasons. The other three books follow more strictly the conventions of travel writing: chronological organization, notes on guidebooks and maps, allusions to the military past, comments on buildings and towns, descriptions of Indians, accounts of occasional adventures (such as losing touch with his companion overnight in desolate forest along the East Bank of the Penobscot), and elaborate descriptions of scenery, improved with references to classical literature. But it was not, of course, Niagara or Carcassonne that he described, though he regularly compared the scenes he chose to explore with those to which "the tide of fashionable travel" dragged other visitors.[19] "I never voyaged so far in all my life," he brags, comically, in *A Week*. "You shall see men you never heard of before," he adds, "greater men than Homer, or Chaucer, or Shakespeare, only they never got time to say so; they never took to the way of writing. Look at their fields, and imagine what they might write, if ever they should put pen to paper."[20] With greater truth, perhaps, he says of going even a short distance from the fire into the "*standing* night" of the Maine forest: "You come back with the air of a much travelled man, as from a long journey, with adventures to relate."[21]

The lands he journeyed through varied greatly. He walked through scenes of nearly barren waste on Cape Cod, grim scenes that he repeatedly described as "chaos." He begins by visiting the site of a shipwreck where singleminded men and women were picking up seaweed, to be used for fertilizer, from among the corpses. From there he proceeds to describe poor soils, blasting winds, stunted trees, poisonous clams, infestations of ticks, dead whales, shark-mangled carcasses; an entire universe "where man's works are wrecks."[22] This was not the settled landscape whose back roads he felt comfortable on, and human efforts to exalt existence in this environment—especially the camp meetings—invite his scorn. In Maine he hiked through soggy forest, canoed on rocky rivers and stormy lakes, and climbed Katahdin. Though he had much to report on houses and villages ("it is difficult to conceive of a region uninhabited by man"), there were moments when he was aware of his distance from civilization and of passing through "primeval, untamed, and forever untameable Nature. . . . Here was no man's garden, but the unhandselled globe."[23] That conflict between nature's wildness and man's work becomes the powerful theme of the book, which alternates between moods of disgust at the shabbiness of America— travel by foot, he says, and ask whether America is really civilized, "tell me if it looks like a discovered and settled country"[24]—and anger at scenes of devastation. "Maine, perhaps, will soon be where Massachusetts is. A good part of her territory is already as bare and commonplace as much of our neighborhood, and her villages generally are not so well shaded as ours." *A Week* follows the rivers through scenes of commercial development up into New Hampshire. Closer to *Walden* in its satiric detachment from the bustle of the nineteenth century, it turns a boat trip into a spiritual voyage outside the ordinary confinements of time. Though each chapter covers a day's action, there are excursuses on the futility of reform and improvement, the transience of popular religion, the wisdom of the ancients and Asian seers, and the universal truths symbolized, however dimily, in nature. At the same time, his purpose is to read the landscape and to clarify awareness of the constructed distinction between the civil and the wild. "The wilderness is near as well as dear to every man," he reports. "Even the oldest villages are indebted to the border of wild wood, which surrounds them, more than to the gardens of men. There is something indescribably inspiriting and beautiful in the aspect of the forest skirting and occasionally jutting into the midst of new towns, which, like the sand-heaps of fresh fox-burrows, have sprung up in their midst."[26]

Nevertheless, the destruction of nature discloses the cant in what is taken to be progress. Factories and dams blocked the rivers, kept shad and other fish from migrating, and put fishermen out of work. Railroads broke the sod and exposed sand to the wind, "till it has converted fertile farms into deserts" near the Merrimack.[27] Even deep in the Maine forest there were harmful dams, built by lumbermen to float huge pines for the housing trade in Massachusetts. The pines were already gone from much of the territory that Thoreau covered—but the dams lasted past their use. Much of the fury in *Maine Woods* derives from descriptions of the "war against the pines," the greed and deceit of men who searched for good trees across vast distances, the almost chaotic wastefulness of twisted pines that never made it down-

stream.[28] Accounts of his Indian guides' slaughtering moose intensify the
fury: most of the meat was unused, and the scene was "too much like going
out by night to some woodside pasture and shooting your neighbor's
horses."[29] All the incongruous signs of civilization amid the trees spark
indignation: fence wood bundled together in the water, a ring bolt clamped
into a rock, a brick lying in the brush, the marks of an ax, a stack of hay.
Worst of all was a handbill wrapped around a pine stump and advertising a
tavern-store so that "even the bears and wolves, moose, deer, otter, and
beaver, not to mention the Indians, may learn where they can fit themselves
according to the latest fashion, or, at least, recover some of their own lost
garments."[30]

The source of anger was not so much that nature was being ravaged—as
we have seen, Thoreau appreciated the creation of a line between town and
wilderness. It was the materialism, commercialism, and spiritual emptiness
of the "civilization" subjecting nature to its uses:

> The Anglo-American can indeed cut down, and grub up all this waving
> forest, and make a stump speech, and vote for Buchanan on its ruins, but he
> cannot converse with the spirit of the tree he fells, he cannot read the poetry
> and mythology which retire as he advances. He ignorantly erases
> mythological tablets in order to print his handbill and town-meeting warrants
> on them. Before he has learned his a b c in the beautiful but mystic lore of
> the wilderness which Spenser and Dante had just begun to read, he cuts it
> down, coins a *pine-tree* shilling (as if to signify the pine's value to him,) puts
> up a *dee*strict school-house, and introduces Webster's spelling book.[31]

Thoreau is an ironic commentator on the ideal of the New England
village hallowed by the past. He confirms what other observers reported
about the eruption of towns like mushrooms in the clearing. Heading toward
Moosehead Lake, he comes across "more than a dozen flourishing towns,
with almost every one its academy," none of which appeared on his 1824
atlas. Beyond Moosehead was a string of towns in the making, clearings with
a few log huts: "There are forest schools already established,—great centres
of light."[32] He even finds occasional confirmation of Bremer's and Tocqueville's observations on the books pioneers carried with them. In a settler's
cabin he finds a cheap edition of the *Wandering Jew* and a few junky novels;
in a lumberer's cabin, some pages from the Bible and two antislavery
orations—one by Emerson was said to have converted two men to the
Liberty Party.[33] Close to civilization, there was "a very neat dwelling, with
plenty of books, and a new wife, just imported from Boston."[34] More valuable, however, were "small cent picture-books" for children and newspapers
for adults—important items to carry as these were "the only currency that

would circulate."[35] For the most part, Thoreau's tone was mocking. The rude, nascent villages were populated by "wiseacres" and "tavern loafers,"[36] and the schools were subsidized by grants of forest land, thus depending more on the devastation than the comprehension or appreciation of nature.

What Thoreau witnessed was not so much the progress of civilization as the spread of money-grubbing motives that demeaned human nature. Traveling on the Merrimack, he heard gossip about buried wealth, some of it plowed up by lucky farmers. He concluded: "There is money buried everywhere, and you have only to go to work to find it."[37] In the early nineteenth century, especially in northern New England, rumors persisted of treasures left buried in the earth by pirates and adventurers. In 1842, for example, Francis Parkman discovered that "some fools" with a divining rod had dug up the banks of Lake George near the ruins of Fort William Henry. In *The Pioneers* Cooper described a "dissatisfied, shiftless, lazy, speculating fellow" killed in a forest fire while treasure-seeking near Cooperstown, New York. There were many such episodes in Maine, often led by seers and prophets, and the founders of Mormonism in New York sought treasure through use of magic stones. To the modern historian it is easy to see in these episodes an avid rural response to dreams of "unlimited good" unleashed by revolution and economic change.[38] It is interesting to note how frequently the poet Thoreau referred to the gold-seeking motives of his countrymen. He enjoyed walking on the old road "Where they once dug for money, / But never found any." The "dreams of mines of treasure," sought with a "divining wand," reveal "How little curious is man" about the important mysteries of life. Thoreau will leave his wealth "Buried in seas in mines and ocean caves" and live proudly in poverty.[39] And in an epigraph to *A Week* he writes:

> I am bound, I am bound, for a distant shore,
> By a lonely isle, by a far Azore,
> There it is, there it is, the treasure I seek,
> On the barren sands of a desolate creek.

Thoreau does not always repudiate the village ideal. Often he steps forth as a respecter of the ideal, which the spirit of trade, the digging for wealth, has left in ruins. Sanctimoniousness about the New England past cannot conceal the damage. Americans must recover an expanded sense of time and an enlarged view of culture. Recent research has suggested that Thoreau initially took seriously the writer's role as a kind of critic-educator with a good influence on civic improvement. The poor reception of his early works depleted his belief in his abilities and the public's readiness for these civic efforts. The estrangement he felt led to a rewriting of *Walden* that made it more private and difficult of access, a work for the cognoscenti rather than the public.[40] Therefore, the expanded viewpoint that he calls for he nevertheless doubts is likely to be achieved. It would be good if human beings labored with respect for "immemorial" truth, if they developed their poetic faculties, if they sought meaning in nature instead of merely utilitarian ends, but these are considerations that lead more often to bitter irony than to action. After making fun of woodmen bragging about a deal in which "somebody cleared twenty-five dollars," he changes course and wishes he was one of them: they live "a solitary and adventurous life," like Western trappers, "let their beards grow, and live without neighbors."[41] At the conclusion of *Cape Cod*, wrongly predicting that "the fashionable world" will never go to land's end, he praises a lighthouse or fisherman's hut as an excellent "hotel" to visit: "A man may stand there and put all America behind him."[42]

When Thoreau, especially in his later writings, praised wildness and disparaged the "merely civil," he sometimes seemed to renounce the centuries of Western civilization in which the distinction between savage and well-ordered modes of living attained so much importance. Thus he seems to have little in common with other travelers who found in the advance of civilization the meaning of America. To some extent that is true, but his words are usually double-edged. There remains a sense in which he takes order and civility seriously; only the formulas used by Americans to describe them does he concider facile and deceptive and needing to be punctured. He disparages the "cheap civility" of a trading nation, but a true "magnanimity" he praises.[43] "There is reason in the distinction of civil and uncivil," he mused at the mouth of the Merrimack. He had just met a brawny New Hampshire mountain man, unkempt and weatherbeaten, and parted by shouting in answer to a question about hunting, that "we had shot a *buoy*." The reference was to a misadventure in navigating, but it left the man "for a long time scratching his head in vain to know if he had heard aright." In this case it was the educated travelers who spoke elliptically and puzzled the less cosmopolitan folk they met. Still, Thoreau takes pains to insist on the sincerity of their conversation, up to that point; "his rudeness [was] only a manner." He admits that "we sometimes meet uncivil men," living inhospitably near mountain paths, "whose salutation is as rude as the grasp of their brawny hands, and who deal with men as unceremoniously as they are wont to deal with the elements." To become more "like the inhabitants of cities," all they need to do is "to extend their clearings," improve their view of "the civil plain or ocean" below, and change their diet from wild meat and acorns to cereals. Yet Thoreau insists that "true politeness does not result from any hasty or artificial polishing" but depends on natural character and proper experience ("a long fronting of men and events, and rubbing on good and bad fortune").[44] He is not quite as hard on the yokels as other travelers, but he clearly does not dismiss the importance of civility.

His opinion of civility, however, is so equivocal that it is not easy to decipher "a tale to the purpose" that he relates "while the lock is filling." It is a tale of walking one evening up the Connecticut River into the mountains and looking for shelter. He had been warned that he would encounter "a rather rude and uncivil man," but his experience was mixed. On one hand, the man he met was "not so rude as I had anticipated," for he kept cattle, made maple sugar, and had a home with children, hired hands, and dogs. On the other, he was frustratingly uncommunicative, leaving his guest to fend for himself, and had an exaggerated, almost superstitious, sense of the advantages of his dwelling. Yet his pride that he had "tamed and civilized that region" was commendable enough. Dealing with him "as if to me all manners were indifferent," Thoreau was able to ignore his coarseness and incivility and discover that he had "a sweet, wild way with him," even "a gleam of true hospitality and ancient civility." He was much better than an old man Thoreau met the next morning, picking berries, praying aloud, and absolutely unresponsive to a stranger's questions.[45] If there is no simple reading of this tale, it surely indicates Thoreau's preference for a behavioral middle ground instead of the get-ahead frenzy of villagers he met and the idleness of loungers along his way.

In fact, Thoreau tells us that his observations confirmed traditional views of the stages civilization passes through. He makes it clear, of course, that "there is in my nature . . . a singular leaning toward all wildness."[46] He has high praise for the pioneer as a man with "information more general and far reaching than the villagers'."[47] And in Maine he has a vision of oxen standing on top of stumps as a mocking image of "the fact that the pastoral comes next in order to the sylvan or hunter life."[48] Yet he knows there is something to appreciate in the progression toward the pastoral. For what comes after, the commercial and urban, he has distaste, but he is content to celebrate the farmer's incursion into nature: "The white man comes, pale as the dawn, with a load of thought, with a slumbering intelligence as a fire raked up, knowing well what he knows, not guessing but calculating, strong in community, yielding obedience to authority." The farmer brings his knowledge and seriousness of purpose to the task of "building a house that endures, a framed house." In concert with others he creates towns like this one on the Concord:

> the fields on either hand had a soft and cultivated English aspect, the village spire being seen over the copses which skirt the river, and sometimes an orchard straggled down to the waterside. . . . It seemed that men led a quiet and very civil life there. The inhabitants were plainly cultivators of the earth,

and lived under an organized political government. The school-house stood
with a meek aspect, entreating a long truce to war and savage life. . . . the
era in which men cultivate the apple, and the amenities of the garden, is
essentially different from that of the hunter and forest life, and neither can
displace the other without loss.[49]

This sense of inevitable trade-off ought to be kept in mind as the necessary counterpoint to Thoreau's expressions of his personal preference for the
wild. One of the most striking features of A Week is its glowing descriptions
of the landscape: The "pageantry" of a village in the "mild and quiet"
Sunday morning light; the "antique look" of a canal; the banks of the
Merrimack "divided into patches of pasture, mowing, tillage, and wood-
land"; the "half-civilized and twilight aspect" of an old mill and cabins
among the trees; "the actual luxury and serenity," almost Arcadian, of small
houses scattered on the shore; groves that "appeared naturally disposed,"
even though the farmer who left them standing "consulted only his convenience."[50] In Maine Thoreau saw opportunity for a skilled Massachusetts
boy to go to work, "with a trunk full of choice scions, and his grafting
apparatus," on scraggly apple trees.[51] He recommends Maine to the immigrant as an escape from urban poverty and charity; it is a land where "the
possession and exercise of practical talent merely are a sure and rapid
means of intellectual culture and independence."[52] And he expresses relief
at returning from the forest into

> our smooth, but still varied landscape. For a permanent residence, it seemed
> to me that there could be no comparison between this and the wilderness,
> necessary as the latter is for a resource and a background, the raw material
> of all our civilization. The wilderness is simple, almost to barrenness. The
> partially cultivated country it is which chiefly has inspired, and will continue
> to inspire, the strains of poets, such as compose the mass of any
> literature. . . . Perhaps our own woods and fields . . . with the primitive
> swamps scattered here and there in their midst, but not prevailing over them,
> are the perfection of parks and groves, gardens, arbors, paths, vistas and
> landscapes. They are the natural consequence of what art and refinement we
> as a people have,—the common which each village possesses, its true
> paradise, in comparison with which all elaborately and willfully wealth-
> constructed parks and gardens are paltry imitations. Or, at least I would
> rather say, such *were* our groves twenty years ago.[53]

What made Thoreau skeptical was the mania for "improvements" in agriculture and for commercial development in general, a mania that threatened the
pastoral pace of life, the poetic temperament, the continued existence of
unused land near groves and fields, the scenes of darkness intermixed with

light. He had reservations other travelers failed to express about the destruction of the village ideal by the movements of families thought to be extending its reach. But his view of civilization, like that of so many of his contemporaries, remained agricultural and communal.

There is no mistaking Thoreau for a representative of the prevailing vision of intellectual progress. If nothing else, his silence about women and homes casts him outside the mainstream. A caustic note runs throughout his work and limited his audience in his lifetime. He saw shoddiness where others saw accomplishment, cultural deficiency instead of the improvement of intellect, narrowness of spirit instead of democratic vision, desperation instead of confidence. He was likely to see stumps and devastation where others saw the building of civilization.[54] But when he stressed the shoddiness and narrowness of antebellum realities, he often did so in comparison with ideals of true progress not too remote from those cherished by politer intellectual contemporaries. When he has fun with the horrors of a logging road, for example—"If you want an exact recipe for making such a road, take one part Mud Pond, and dilute it with equal parts of Umbazookskus and Apmoojenegamook; then send a family of musquash through to locate it, look after the grades and culverts, and finish it to their minds, and let a hurricane follow to do the fencing"[55]—he raises a standard similar to that of Kirkland, Olmsted, and Bushnell. He also gives us glimpses of the reality, to him a fading reality, of the serene village with its church spire, and husbandmen passing down roads and across bridges, toward home. His was, in short, a dissent that reaffirmed the importance of what others celebrated. He is one more instance of the intellectual as traveler, one more believer in the urgency of cultural improvement, even though his moral judgments of his compatriots took him to swamp, to sand dune, to land's end.

PART FOUR

Life as a Masquerade

To allegorize life with a masquerade, and represent mankind generally as masquers. Here and there, a natural face may appear.

—NATHANIEL HAWTHORNE, *American Notes*

CHAPTER FOURTEEN

City of Unwork

The story of the spread of good roads, pleasant homes, and polite citizens was only part of what travelers observed and pondered in America. Instead of rising popular intelligence, refinement, and culture, it was possible to see only artifice and superficiality. Sometimes travelers reported on America as a land of unrestricted theatricality and all too frequent fraud. Frederick Law Olmsted, for example, blamed the frontier for creating "a warrior state" in which "masks and ambuscades, stratagems and other forms of deceit" replaced "all ordinary morality."[1] But what of life east of the frontier? In the developing towns and changing countryside, was it possible to live earnest moral lives without pretense or deception? Among those whose lives were changing dramatically in democratic America, was there anything fixed and trustworthy, or was all behavior tinctured with artifice?

One of John Greenleaf Whittier's sketches in *The Stranger in Lowell* (1845) introduces such questions. As the book's title suggests, Whittier presents himself as a sojourner in a city of the new industrial order, a would-be writer striving for a position in society, a young man from the country in quest of a career. The early essays depict a model mill town. To the world's inquiry whether America could erect mills, assemble a work force, and dispatch textiles into the world's markets without duplicating the squalor and misery of Manchester, the young Quaker poet-editor's answer was a cautious yes. In this Lowell the wheels spun busily, and the lights glowed merrily. "With a little effort of fancy, one could readily transform the huge

155

mills, thus illuminated, into palaces lighted up for festival occasions, and the figures of the workers, passing to and fro before the windows, into forms of beauty and fashion, moving in graceful dances." The stranger kept a reformer's agenda. He called for a shortening of the workday, but he praised Lowell for placing women's work on a level of equality with men's.[2]

Like many books of the era, this one pasted together essays written and printed separately. Of the eighteen essays, about a third comment directly on Lowell and industrialization, with many of the rest on Whittier's favorite theme of the folklore of New England farms and villages in the recent past, and others on Mormonism, Second Adventism, Swedenborgianism, and new departures in religion. Intentionally or not, some of these essays convey a nostalgic communalism at odds with the praise of the textile works. By far the most interesting is "A Yankee Zincali" (the title shifts in Whittier's collected works to "Yankee Gypsies"), which provides glimpses of a vanishing America that one wishes were more fully documented.[3] As it stands, the essay exists as a clever literary exercise brushing against issues of moral obligation in a world of deception.

The sketch begins with the writer-narrator's irritation with some cold, rainy fall weather. The scene is contrived and ornamented; the irritation calls up allusions to Shakespeare and Dante. A rap at the door brings in a poor dumb wretch with papers identifying him as an Italian shipwreck victim in need of charity. The writer suspects, however, that these papers were "purchased from one of those ready-writers in New York who manufacture beggar-credentials at the low price of one dollar per copy, with earthquakes, fires, or shipwrecks, to suit customers." Then he realizes this mute is no stranger: "Pietro Frugoni, I have seen thee before." He has met him as a sanctimonious traveling preacher, as a Penobscot Indian bereft of both his hands, as the father of six children "pisened" by "marcury doctors," and as a feverish unfortunate back home after a disastrous emigration to the Genesee country. His real identity "under all disguises" is Stephen Leathers; greeted by that name, he quickly explains that he was merely trying to help "a poor furriner" unable to "make himself understood" in America. "Well and shiftily answered, thou ragged Proteus. One cannot be angry with such a fellow," who in any case rapidly disappears on "his benevolent errand."

The writer thanks this visitor for breaking the gloominess of the day and transposing him to "pleasant and grateful recollections" of "the dear old landscape of my boyhood." The farm in the valley, meadows and stream, sentinel poplars and oak forest beyond them, carriage path with rustic bridge—all flow back in memories that the writer compares to a picture that a traveler might carry with him upon leaving home. For it was as a boy that he had first seen not only this Leathers but a host of "old stragglers" who used to disturb "the generally monotonous quietude of our farm-life."

The writer proceeds to sketch thirteen more of these beggars of childhood memory. They come in waves of reverie. First appear three who resemble the revelers at Poosie Nansie's in Burns's "The Jolly Beggars": a haunted, mute, "wild-haired" woman who came for warmth and food; a phony herb doctor who "used to counterfeit lameness"; and a tottering old man with a huge, mysterious pack. Then come five instances of a "class of peripatetic philosophers— half pedlar, half mendicant"—bearing newspapers and pamphlets, needles and soap, sermons and songs. The first of these claimed to have been crippled when he worked on a farm owned by the governor of a nearby state. After winning the heart of the governor's daughter, he was thrown out a window for not knowing his place. The second was a once-successful parson destroyed by drink. The third was both "a Yankee troubadour,—first and last minstrel of the valley of the Merrimac,"—and skilled at quoting scripture. The others also sang, the fourth giving the writer his first acquaintance with Burns's ballads, the fifth humming the comic dialogue (still familiar in the 1990s), "Our gude man cam hame at e'en," in which an unfaithful wife attempts to persuade her husband that all the signs of her lover's presence are nothing but domestic commonplaces ("Ye auld fool, ye blind fool . . . 'Tis naething but a milking cow / My mamma sent to me"). The singer then worked his own ruse, running off with a horse that caught his fancy. Next appeared three "gaberlunzie men" carrying their belongings on their backs and looking for barn or haystack to pass the night in: a "harmless old pilgrim"; a drunken, gruff giant; and a black-bearded, sullen Italian—all frightening to a boy's eye. Finally appeared two examples of an entire "tribe of lazy strollers" who kept a city of their own, a kind of anti-utopia, in Barrington, New Hampshire. Of these the writer describes only "an old withered Hag," known as Hopping Pat, and her grandson, a pretentious preacher accompanied by a tame crow. These were, like Leathers, the ones who "came to us in all shapes and with all appearances" in order to conceal, "under well-contrived disguises, their true character."

These memories evoke two themes of direct relevance to Lowell and the changing economic scene: the passing of a traditional order and the moral obligation toward the unfortunate. Though these visitors come in with a rap at the writer's door, they are swiftly trapped in the past tense and associated with picturesque scenes on the boyhood farm. When the storm subsides, the sketches end, and "in the beautiful present the past is no longer needed." Before leaving, these figures raised an important issue: when is charity justified? Presumably neither with a Leathers who dissembles his own errand of mercy nor with those whose "low vices" disqualify them from even his mother's tenderhearted benevolence. But the writer does recall affectionately that, "whatever the temperance society might in such cases have done," his family had enjoyed giving some of these poor creatures a pitcher of cider. The best of them were "wandering tests of our benevolence."

Even the tricky Leathers exercised the faculties of conscience. His visit launched a struggle:

> Every man, the Mohammedans tell us, has two attendant angels,—the good one on his right shoulder, the bad on his left. "Give," says Benevolence, as with some difficulty I fish up a small coin from the depths of my pocket. "Not a cent," says selfish Prudence; and I drop it from my fingers.

Think of the traveler's woes, says the first; he's an impostor, is the reply. And if Prudence properly dismisses Leathers, we are given a sweet anecdote of Whittier's mother befriending a forlorn, rejected straggler, who appreciated her trust and left the family with "the blessing of the poor." These are familiar matters in intellectual history. A conventional account of them would refer to the moral sense, faculty psychology, and the influence of Scottish philosophical traditions in America. Whittier accurately refers to Islam for the same tribunal theory of conscience, and we may note that there are other belief systems in which alms-giving is a test of devotion. These are issues of basic human concern, and not even in the new economic era in America were they confined to the domain of philosophical abstraction.[4]

Surely, an increasingly complex economy tested feelings of sympathy in puzzling ways. The key problem for public charity in previous eras was the vagrant poor. Everyone recognized the necessity of occasional assistance to the unfortunate who belonged in a community, but no town wanted to tolerate incorrigible idleness or to get stuck with the costs of relieving those who came from elsewhere.[5] In the mobile society of the 1840s there was all the more reason to be wary of shiftless, deceitful folk who might take advantage of suckers. This may explain the negative attitude Whittier repeatedly expresses toward dissemblers among the beggars. There is even a menacing sexual dimension to their visits, as when one inebriate sat down next to the "aged" grandmother and started "paying his addresses to her."

Why, then, is the writer's tone sometimes more positive? This is so, not only in reveries about his boyhood, but also in a brief account of a visit to Barrington. The scene was as barren as Lowell was teeming: "a lonely, half-ruinous mill . . . scraggy hills . . . dwarf pitch-pines." The city of beggars made do without fences or walls to separate the "ragged cabins"; there was nothing to protect property or limit freedom. Barrington had no need of property divisions because its residents could count on benefiting from the work of others. "That comfortable philosophy which modern transcendentalism has but dimly shadowed forth—that poetic agrarianism, which gives all to each and each to all—is the real life of this city of unwork." It is not entirely clear how we are supposed to react—with contempt or envy? But the last word is to compare them with Indians, vagabonds, the dispossessed:

Other hands may grasp the field or forest,
Proud proprietors in pomp may shine;
Thou art wealthier,—all the world is thine.

No one would mistake antebellum portraits of heroic Indians for strong social criticism. They rendered the Indian "safely dead and historically past" while the world stayed securely in the grasp of others.[6] Similarly, the Barrington utopians supply a humorous bit of nostalgia to be indulged while the world goes about its business.

These are wonderful materials, though Whittier's tone may be unsure. It is tempting to wonder what Hawthorne or Thoreau might have made of these "dingy" stragglers. What Whittier does, in the end, is to distance his readers from them by constant, even tedious, reminders of the cultural knowledge that he and his literary audience, unlike the wanderers, possess. A cripple is "like Vulcan on the rocks of Lemnos"; pale supplicants are "like Sterne's Monk." Singers are compared to stars of the concert stage; the Barrington residents, to English paintings of gypsy life. These allusions betray the importance to genteel readers of seeing signs of their own distance from a rural past that the sketches pretend to ennoble. Sentimentalized writing about gypsies, tinkers, and beggars is not so much intended to encourage sympathy for those who have been dislocated or dispossessed as to signify the kindly—but largely literary—dispositions of its readers.

For present purposes there is one other point to stress: the suggestion that the past and the marginal folk are protean and thus by implication that the present and those who are actively making it are straightforward. Whittier's essay concerns many things, but surely it is the disguises of Leathers and his ilk that render them such fascinating contrasts to those who own property and put up fences. Might there not be elements of fantasy and denial in this view? By 1845, many others besides old-time gaberlunzies were on the road. It was always hard to be sure of the character of anyone who came from somewhere else, even if he carried a carpetbag instead of a basket or sack. Even the straightest appearance might turn crooked if inspected with enough suspicion. These issues, concealed here in fun and reverie, are common to many accounts of excursions in America.

CHAPTER FIFTEEN

Excursion

A good approach to the public masquerade in post-revolutionary America, the anti-culture of sham and illusion, is via Nathaniel Hawthorne's notes of a tour of western Massachusetts in 1838. These notes were not written for publication. Partly, they recorded what might prove useful in later fiction; partly, they satisfied a friend's request that he keep a record of the trip. Some of the characters whom he met found their way into "Ethan Brand" (1850), and a few details entered *The House of the Seven Gables* (1851). After his death his widow edited some portions of this and other notebooks and published them in the *Atlantic* and in book form.[1] Nevertheless, the notes are not fiction, and they afford an informative view of life along the road as seen through a writer's imagination.[2]

Hawthorne left Salem by stage on July 23, and in Boston took the railroad to Worcester, where he stayed at the Temperance House. He noticed a little boy who had been selling custards at the depot and was starting back the several miles to home. Along the way Hawthorne was interrogated, as were other travelers, by an old Unitarian merchant. Apparently this man thought his age and good intentions entitled him to ask impertinent questions. Hawthorne regarded him with the suspicion that he usually had for reformers. "I want to do you good," quoth the merchant. "Well, sir, . . . I wish you could, for both our sakes; for I have no doubt it would be a great satisfaction to you." (80) The landlord was a decent and serious man who gave him some business cards to distribute during the rest of his journey.

161

On his way to Northampton by stage, after an early morning departure, Hawthorne conversed with an irritable stage driver, under pressure to make good time without injuring the horses, and with a grocer and his son, who were figuring out how to visit Niagara while missing as few days as possible from their shop. He recorded little about two "rather good looking" ladies, but much about a peddler who carried an open basket full of bottled "essences"—aniseed, cloves, red cedar, wormwood, hair oil, cologne—and a large tin box filled with combs, jewelry, and other dry goods. Some bottles were mislabeled to appear foreign; others claimed effectiveness against all sorts of human ailments. The peddler was fairly new at the trade and did not yet go on a wide circuit. His business was limited by how much he could carry. But he contemplated a trip west that would require planning ahead and shipping some of his wares to various locations. He enjoyed seeing the world and meeting people; peddling was better than farming. And he spoke freely with Hawthorne about the risks and requirements of his line of work. At a bumpy spot in the road he had lost a load of bottles: "What a waste of sweet smells on the desert air." It was necessary to have an even temper: though customers might provoke him, he had to remember that he needed to retrace the same road for future sales. "The pedlars find satisfaction for all contumelies, in making good bargains out of their customer." (81)

Hawthorne also met an elderly, "country squire looking" judge. But most encounters in these first days of the trip gave evidence of widened markets and increased commerce. The little boy could convert eggs and cream into custards to vend at the depot; the peddler could give up farming. The landlord's cards, the grocer's calculations, the driver's irritation—all were signs of a new economic era, as was the peddler's recognition of the importance of controlling his temper under fire. Alongside the road the villages looked drowsy, especially when the coachman delivered mail to a yawning postmaster; and the forest looked "desolate" and threatening, "as if, should you venture one step into its wild, tangled, many-stemmed, and dark-shadowed verge, you would inevitably be lost forever." (82) A tame crow pursued them and tried to get at some fish they were carrying to a tavern along the route. (90)

Between Northampton and Pittsfield, Hawthorne was stuck with a scornful-looking young man who had been a schoolteacher in Pennsylvania and now had taken an agency for a "destitute church" in need of rebuilding. He "attacked" Hawthorne for a donation. This unpleasant passenger was going to visit his married sister, and when he got off and saw her, "there was a broad smile, even laugh, of pleasure, which did him more credit with me than anything else." As the young man received a kiss from his "comely" sister, one of the remaining passengers made a suggestive remark ("I should like to share it"). (83) On the next leg of his journey Hawthorne was preoccupied with newlyweds, a New York shopkeeper and his genteel-looking "lady," happily complimenting one another's "comeliness" and exchanging playful pats and taps. "The driver peeped into the coach once, and said he had his arm round her waist. . . . It would be pleasant to meet them again next summer, and note the change." (86) The driver had once emigrated to Ohio but returned to see whether the Berkshire air might benefit his wife's health. She was dying of consumption, and he vowed never to remarry.

Pittsfield, Massachusetts, was a thriving courthouse town with an academy and attractive marble buildings and monuments. Farmers from the vicinity were busy at their errands. Idlers sat outside the hotel; inside, lawyers, horse dealers, storekeepers, and "country squires" joined a member of Congress in "city style" dining. (84) Other villages showed a different kind of business. Near North Adams the coach passed several factories, with "the machinery whizzing, and girls looking out of the windows." Long two-storied boardinghouses stood nearby, "often with bean vines &c. running up round the doors; and altogether a domestic look." A "wild highland rivulet" was pressed into a "vast work of a civilized nature." (88)

Hawthorne stayed for a while, took a walk, and bathed in a secluded part of the stream. The "occasional wayfarers" he met were very different from those on the road: "country matrons," a doctor, an "underwitted," chatty old drunk. The old eccentric's wife was dead. His children were circus owners, "the gaze of multitudes," while he roamed and drank in the hills. While off the road, Hawthorne reflected on the curious way the "rough and untamed stream," still much as the Indians had known it, was harnessed to human purposes of making fabrics and sawing boards. He paused, in other words, to appreciate the sublime incongruity of what the literary historian Leo Marx has called "the machine in the garden," the juxtaposition of wild and tamed that made the economic transformation of America both acceptable and thrilling.[3] There was "a sort of picturesqueness in finding these factories, supremely artificial establishments, in the midst of such wild scenery." (88)

In the hotel in North Adams he found more men caught in the web of economic transition. One was a grimy, "disagreeable figure" with a maimed foot and amputated arm, a once-successful lawyer ruined by drink, and yet "something of a gentleman and a man of intellect." Rather than accept charity, he supported himself by making and selling soap. Another was a blacksmith who loved the tavern and hated a new liquor-license law. A man whose talk was "imbued with humor, as everybody's talk is, in New England," he owned a mill and was prospering. A third was a man of moderate habits, an elderly man in gray homespun who had come down from Vermont to learn about a "new mill-contrivance." He had sound information to give as well as receive; he seemed to expect and get a "plain and homely" deference. Hawthorne saw in him "a pattern character of the upper class of

New-England yeomen." Finally, a traveling, surgeon-dentist stopped at the hotel, put up advertising bills, and took some walks with Hawthorne. He was a man of "self-conceit" who attributed his good health to his stiff, upright posture. And he was inclined to brag about his "love affairs" and to rage against one or two girls who had "jilted" him. He was also a licensed Baptist preacher, "and is now on his way to the West, to seek a place of settlement in his spiritual vocation." (94–96)

From North Adams, Hawthorne took sidetrips to Williamstown and Shelburne Falls and then returned via Pittsfield, Stockbridge, and Litchfield. He visited caves and crags and other natural attractions, sometimes noting how previous tourists had carved their names and defaced the scenery. He toured a lime kiln and a marble factory. He attended funerals, a meeting between county commissioners and road builders, and commencement at Williams College. He heard the horns of stagecoaches in the mountains. With a novelist's eye he sketched rustic characters, business travelers, and some—like preachers, process servers, and nut sellers—in the warp between. Some of the Williams graduates were from the country, "half-bumpkin, half-scholar . . . their manners quite spoilt by what little of the gentleman there was in them." (113)[4] There is a sad portrait of a group of blacks in Williamstown, one discoursing on "the rights of his race," not so vociferously as to offend anyone, and the "advantages of living under laws." Another was intoxicated and shameful to the company. In a reformer collecting subscriptions for a religious and antislavery magazine, Hawthorne detected "a city and business air." (112, 136)

On August 18, a man came to North Adams to do advance work for a "Caravan of Animals." The logistics that he handled were like those needed to move an army. He would have been content with enough proceeds to cover expenses in this small village and then to "gather gain at larger places." But there was a problem: the selectmen had voted to prohibit "any public exhibition of the kind." They were concerned that the factory girls would squander their money and quit work for this entertainment. In a "mere farming town" the caravan would have posed a less threatening diversion. (117–8)

In a barroom in Shelburne Falls on August 31, Hawthorne crossed paths with another entertainer: "the Old Dutchman," a German, perhaps a Jew, who transported a diorama inside his wagon. He spoke with "considerable dramatic effect," but a glance through the glass windows of his "machine" was disappointing—"a succession of the very worst scratchings and daubings that can be imagined." The figures, including Napoleon, Nelson, and the Hand of Destiny, were old, dilapidated, and coated with tobacco smoke. More fun could be had from the magnified appearance of "a country boor" who was enticed to poke his head inside the glass and stick out his tongue. A dog added to merriment by biting its tail and racing around in circles. (129–30)

On September 4, Hawthorne finally had a chance to see the exhibition of animals under a canvas pavilion. The show was crowded, perhaps a thousand folk with "row after row of women" and "many men drunk, swearing and fighting outside." The caravan included a polar bear, an elephant, a monkey, a leopard, and a panther. Some animals were distressed by the heat; others were curiously quiet and domesticated. The hyena was ill-tempered. There was not much thrill when the showman pulled out four rather torpid anacondas. When his associate put his head and arm into a lion's mouth, however, the crowd was absolutely hushed. Hawthorne dined with the troupe and found it incongruous to see these "rough, ignorant" men, so recently engaged with snakes and lion, now "talking about their suppers, and blustering for hot meat, and calling for something to drink, without anything of the wild dignity of men familiar with the *nobility of nature*." (140–141)

Hawthorne was not insensitive to the spiritual and political stability symbolized by the New England village.[5] In the brief notes of his return home he complimented the neat appearance of the church and houses of Litchfield, a "remarkable instance" of the custom of situating villages on "the most elevated ground . . . so that they are visible for miles around." (149) As is well known, in many of his works of fiction, including *The Scarlet Letter,* he explored the subjection of individual personality to the communal law. But the familiarity of this theme is all the more reason to notice his equal and intense awareness of the histrionic and theatrical in American life.

Nor was that awareness restricted to this interlude in the Berkshires. Shortly before, he recorded extensive descriptions of Salem Common on the Fourth of July with its colorful profusion of booths, hawkers, and shows. (171–72) A few days later he attended a display of wax figures and was much taken with the showman, "a friendly, easy-mannered sort of a half-genteel character . . . [with] an air of superiority of information, a moral instructor, with a great deal of real knowledge of the world." (177) Similar observations crop up throughout his notebooks for other periods of his travels in the United States. They are less common in his English or European observations.[6] What fascinated him was the margin between the spontaneous and the routine, as in the contrast between the snappy spiel of the showman and the shabbiness of his displays, or between the breathless crowd and the banality of the lion tamer eating his dinner. This margin also cuts through his fiction. Consider the "rich and varied" menu of entertainment in the "many-purposed" village hall described in *Blithedale Romance* (1852)—lecturers, ventriloquists, thaumaturgists, wax mannequins, Ethiopian choirs, strolling players, spiritualists, and other experts in oral and visual "methods of addressing the public." There an audience expecting a demonstration of spiritualism and prophecy sees instead a triangular contest of powerful wills ending in a young woman's release from a mesmerist's thrall: "the true heart-throb of a woman's affection was too powerful for the jugglery that had hitherto environed her."[7]

To see Hawthorne's notebooks as a source of information to be converted into fiction is only one use of them. His fascination with theatrical scenes belongs also in the context of a traveler's experience among the peddlers, mountebanks, advocates, ministers, and men of affairs circling about even in the backwaters of New England. Here could be gained a sense of civilization as a succession of individuals trying to put on a face, show their stuff, and exert their influence. This sense could lead to a mocking distaste for others with their line of goods, as in this 1835 notebook entry:

> A sketch to be given of a modern reformer—a type of the extreme doctrines on the subject of slaves, cold-water, and all that. He goes about the streets haranguing most eloquently, and is on the point of making many converts, when his labors are suddenly interrupted by the appearance of a keeper of a mad-house, whence he has escaped.

Hawthorne added later: "Much may be made of this idea."[8]

The same awareness could turn one into a spectator at a drama featuring oneself:

> A perception, for a moment, of one's mental and moral self, as if it were another person—the observant faculty being separated, and looking intently at the qualities of the character. There is a surprise when this happens—this getting out of one's self, and then the observer sees how queer a fellow he is.[9]

Such perceptions may be available to a few persons in any period. But they were probably more easily available in a society in which distinctions of rank had dissolved and confidence was at a premium. The startling theatricality of America, as experienced on the road, was bound to accentuate these feelings. The kind of "surprise" Hawthorne describes can be supportive of social order, if the self-surveillance is carried out with a strict conscience. But it can also subvert morality by revealing its basis in artificial codes of conduct.[10] Both these possibilities are subjects of intense discussion in the modern era. Hawthorne's notebooks suggest how they may have arisen in America, not through links of intellectual influence, but through the circuitry of the road.

CHAPTER SIXTEEN

Specimens of Equivoke

Hawthorne observed that his children were "constantly personating some character or another," a servant, other children, "a mother, a peddler, a marketman." Gender and class did not appear to matter. "If their outward shapes corresponded with their imaginations, they would shift to and fro between one semblance and another, faster than ever Proteus did."[1]

Some travelers remarked that Americans in general were unusually gifted at imitating an entire *dramatis personae*. The Irish actor Tyrone Power, first of a theatrical family that eventually made a home in America, drew that conclusion from his extensive travels in the early 1830s. He was especially struck by "the great imitative powers" of American girls, many of whom could give a "quite remarkable" impression of "any actress or actor just then before the public."[2] Constance Rourke in her pioneering studies of American popular culture expanded Powers's insight: the "mimetic gift" was so "singularly common in all phases of American society" that one might think of antebellum America as "a strangely painted backdrop before which the American seemed constrained to perform."[3]

It should be noted that Power appreciated American manners and defended them against Dickens and other English critics. Americans adopted a "quiet formal strain of ceremony" in lieu of long-established codes of behavior. What was lost in polish and style was made up by the absence of pretension and discourtesy. Though he did not explicitly make the connection between mimicry and manners, one suspects that it was the imitative

167

skills of Americans that enabled them to assume habits of good behavior as a matter of individual achievement rather than as rules governing relations among social ranks.[4]

The mimetic American, not always quiet and formal, entered boisterously into American storytelling. In Augustus Longstreet's *Georgia Scenes* (1835), an educated traveler tells stories with a fine knack for recording rural speech. In a sketch entitled "Georgia Theatrics"[5] this traveler is riding up a slope when he overhears a barbaric exchange of taunts and whoops. One man threatens to leap down the other's throat and devour his chitterlings. The other boasts of taming wildcats. The grisly combat ends when one shrieks, "Enough! My Eye's Out!" and the other gloats over the torture he has meted out. When the traveler dashes up to intervene and help the poor maimed mortal, he finds only one strutting figure. "All that I had heard and seen was nothing more nor less than a Lincoln rehearsal; in which the youth who had just left me had played all the parts of all the characters in a Courthouse fight." Longstreet suggests some connection between this scene and the region's transition from "moral darkness" to religious awakening. It is interesting to compare these histrionics with those of Whittier's gypsies; both are examples of dramatic virtuosity that confuse benevolent intentions in a period of transition.

To interpret such reports, it will be useful to consider two sets of comparisons, one with studies of tricksters and "liminal" moments in all human societies, the second with studies of economic change in the twentieth century. The first approach is to follow influential theorists in several modern disciplines who focus on carnivalesque occasions of verbal and role-playing dexterity and on moments of transition and undefined structure when human beings find it possible, perhaps even mandatory, to shuffle through a succession of masks and try out an inventory of different voices.[6] Any comparison between an era of history and a ritual or festival in a traditional community must be tentative and limited, but the traveler in a region where transportation systems open up new influences—promoting trade, spreading religious light—may be acutely conscious of the different masks that people assume. The same insight may be available to those who stay in one place and watch an assortment of travelers—preachers, actors, peddlers, authors—who make their rounds carrying alternate versions of the outside world.

One characteristic of writers who aspired to speak for the new America of the antebellum era was their penchant for shifting from one voice to another, not in dialogue, but in speaking for themselves, as though they knew their audience to be conversant simultaneously with several modes of speech. The literary historian Lawrence Buell has detected this characteristic in Whitman, Melville, and Dickinson; and borrowing a term from M. M. Bakhtin's essays on Renaissance satire, he names it *polyglossia.*[7] In polyglossic American writings one sentence may ring with classical cadences, the next with verbal distinctions from law or philosophy; and the next, perhaps, abruptly swing into an urban or rural vernacular. A related strategy may be noticed in Whittier's mixing of classical mythology, Shakespearean allusions, and Burns's ballads as he sketches the folksiness of the Yankee gypsies. It may be advantageous for the writer-speaker to show awareness of refined culture, technical languages, and earthy patterns of speech: the first may "elevate" the others, the second lends expert authority, and the third introduces notes of spontaneity that otherwise elude American copiers of Old World manners. The result is a curious blend of earnestness and satire that takes with one voice what it gives in another.

This characteristic may be discovered in writers of other eras of transition. For example, the seventeenth-century poet John Donne may in a single stanza alternate between conversing and lecturing, between scientific and erotic terms, between contemplative, passionate, and cynical moods. These qualities were praised in the early twentieth century by "modern" admirers who wished to repudiate the constrained voice of Victorian politeness and the stultifying specializations of industrial society. They looked for a unity of mind and feeling, not for polyglossia. They may have overlooked the ravages of an earlier era of social change.[8] A more relevant example may be the Puritan minister Cotton Mather, who at the turn of the eighteenth century was adept at speaking in several vocabularies. He knew how to reach audiences in Massachusetts as well as in literary and scientific circles across the Atlantic. The difference between him and, let us say, Emerson is that he usually spoke in one voice at a time. His worlds were not overlapping and intersecting; and he did not assume his hearers were multiple linguists.[9] The writer who would speak for America a century later had a greater need to show audiences that he or she, like them, could speak and think as several persons in rapid succession.

Some kinds of role playing were required in hierarchical societies. The protagonist of Allen Tate's *The Fathers* remembered that his planter father spoke "with great ease at four levels": one kind of grammar and pronunciation for family and friends; a second, abounding in "archaisms," among the "plain people"; a third for the slaves; and "fourth, the Johnsonian diction appropriate to formal occasions, a style that he could wield in perfect sentences four hundred words long." Later conceptions of "correct English" would have meant nothing to him.[10] Historical studies of the Virginia aristocracy furnish many examples of a dramaturgy of speech and behavior that marked out relations of power and subservience.[11] The versatility of a

Mather or a planter differed, however, from that exhibited by "the people" in the mid–nineteenth-century economy of the road where proper roles were no longer fixed and well defined.[12]

When we come to a "specimen of equivoke" set down by theatrical manager Sol Smith, we know that lines are no longer clearly drawn. Two men named Caldwell find themselves hiring in the same Cincinnati hotel, one looking for an overseer for his Mississippi plantation, the other for a manager for his New Orleans theatrical company. The confusion begins when a man applying for the former position is shown to the latter employer. He is mystified to learn that he will be overseeing musicians and that his charges will board in hotels, resent being called slaves, and must never be whipped. "Where I have managed heretofore, it has been impossible to get on without whipping, I assure you." While this miscommunication winds toward its unhappy end, a would-be theatre manager applies to the planation owner and is astonished at the news that he must be prepared to use the lash. "I have never seen that system pursued where I have acted." But it would be impossible, he is told, to get along without it. Besides, the "slaves" don't object; "they are used to it"; and know they will be spared if they behave well. If they cannot be reformed they are sold, the planter tells the hurriedly departing man of the theatre.[13]

Here the fun depends on the idea that all businesses, including plantations, belong to a society where it is necessary to go north from year to year to hire footloose and ambitious employees. There is no commonly understood code; terms must be clarified and specified; mistakes occur. Impostors who lack the proper credentials are hard to detect.

Comparisons between the society observed by Power and Longstreet and past moments of carnival and poetic fusion are useful insofar as they highlight some features of antebellum America that may otherwise remain obscure. Contrasts between previous eras of hierarchical order and a new era of confusing transition also have explanatory uses but should not be wielded too rigidly. Though we may like to think of the times of the Renaissance satirists, Donne, antebellum Americans, and modernist critics as times of transition, and intervening eras as times of perfect order, it might not be hard to turn the tables and find order in the periods of flux and confusion where certainty supposedly prevailed. I raise the comparisons and contrasts, not to work out a schema for the oscillations of history, but as a means of investigating the reports on the mimetic propensities of antebellum Americans.

There is one more set of comparisons to employ, for the reports bring to mind one of the boldest, and sometimes most schematic, ventures in modern scholarship—the study of "modernization." Since World War II, at least, social scientists have sought to diagnose the differences between "modern" and "traditional" societies.[14] The motive has sometimes been to discover aids to poor nations who seek to escape colonialism and to enjoy the benefits of industrialized economies; sometimes to organize knowledge of all societies in a systematic, all-encompassing form; and even occasionally to identify some of the ills of modern living by contrast with "worlds we have lost." Until recently there has been a strong tendency to look for indices and causes of a "once-only" historical change in which the most private elements of life, such as procreation, and the most public aspects of the economy, such as the consumption of material goods, passed from one stage to the other.

Where scholarship has turned from economic development and social organization to the effects of "modernization" on the human personality, it had identified, not a single set of massive pressures that the individual must bend to, but a highly complex pattern of inconsistent roles through which the individual must negotiate from one portion of the day or year to the next. The individual's life responds to a kind of "multi-relationality" that requires "quick alertness to ever-changing constellations of phenomena." Fundamental aspects of feeling and behavior may have to be altered to suit the shifting impositions of different compartments of life. It is not easy to see the world as an integrated whole; "the threat of meaninglessness" is everywhere.[15] Things long treated as fixed become unstrung; things long regarded as essential appear only relative; and even to cling to a practice of ancient ritual is to change its meaning. Questions of sincerity, individual dignity, and authority must be thought of in dramatic terms. How does the individual actor develop a coherent sense of self amid a profusion of shifting roles? It may be tempting to see life as only a series of scripts; one may wish to regain faith in fundamental beliefs and to make war on the impure, the unholy, and the new.[16]

One essay on "protean man" in a world of "change and flux" admits that it has little to say of " 'character' and 'personality,' both of which suggest fixity and permanence." Contemporary historical forces oblige us, says the psychiatrist Robert J. Lifton, to think of self in the imagery of process. Nor is the process necessarily one of orderly development, as he finds in studies of young Asians who have veered from one passionate ideological conviction to another. "The protean style of self-process . . . is characterized by an interminable series of experiments and explorations—some shallow, some profound—each of which may be readily abandoned in favor of still new psychological quests." Lifton identifies this style among his patients, one of whom compared himself "to an actor on the stage who 'performs with a certain kind of polymorphous versatility,' " and in Saul Bellow's character Augie March ("I touched all sides, and nobody knew where I belonged"). He also finds it in Jean-Paul Sartre, Jack Kerouac, and Günter Grass; in Marcello Mastroianni and John Cage; wherever life and art are viewed as happening on the road, as con games perpetrated in the face of the absurd. The comical is sometimes enriched by feelings of disloyalty and guilt, for the protean man cherishes dreams of restored wholeness and conviction.[17]

These images of protean malleability may seem exaggerated for all but exceptional individuals in the late twentieth century. In America, moreover, where history begins with migration, adaptation of institutions, and conflict with Indians, and proceeds through revolution and civil war, it is hard to find a single drastic leap from tradition to modernity. "Multi-relationality" may have overtones of crisis when reasonably well understood walls are breaking down, but not when the "processes" are strikingly fluid and never-ending.

Nevertheless, we may see from the travelers' accounts that the dissolving power of a democratic revolution and a commercial economy had drawn Americans of the antebellum era toward a theatrical view of life. There may have been as much merriment and liberation as anxiety and distress in this discovery. The likelihood remains that some of the traits featured in the worldwide twentieth-century encounter with modernity were evident long before in the United States. Many accounts of antebellum culture emphasize the programs of reform and refinement that travelers promoted, and we have seen in Part Three how the travelers took the measure of what they saw according to standards of community and progress. But it is important not to neglect the other conclusion travelers had to weigh, the one that gave their programs added urgency: American life was unmasking the pretensions of history and disclosing a world of histrionic contrivance. Maybe this was a prelude to future progress; maybe it was simply the climax of a breakdown of traditional values. The meaning of the drama was not yet clear, but the fact of the contrivance was inescapable.

CHAPTER SEVENTEEN

On the Road

Improved roads, waterways, and, increasingly, railroads connected regions with other regions, cities with countryside, and cities with other cities in networks that travelers moved along as the shuttles of commerce and civilization. They passed the uprooted and dislocated, the casual and migratory workers. In the 1830s, Tyrone Power in the South saw dispossessed Indians wherever he went; he also saw coffles of slaves being moved onto lands the Indians had vacated.[1] Northern canals and lake towns teemed with semi-employed or casually employed laborers, often but not always Irish. In agricultural areas might be seen casual migrants and "raggedy men," economically indispensable but feared as Whittier feared the Barrington beggars. Meanwhile, tourists were making jaunts on their way to some grotto, spring, or peak. We have seen from Hawthorne's account of his companions on the road how a visit to Niagara might be fitted into the interstices of a busy life.[2]

To the traveler, each new locality resembled a stage where the residents—the courthouse brawler, the tavern storyteller, the factory girl at the circus—put on their acts. But certain travelers, as they walked on stage, gave performances that were central to their livelihoods. Their experiences seemed to define the conditions of intellectual life, especially for those getting started, and to raise troublesome issues for a society where old values and institutions were being traded away. In their own thoughts and in those of the audiences that received them, they evoked images of wonder and worry—wonder at bright new opportunities and exciting spectacles, worry at the approach of an age of materialism, novelty, uncertain authority, vice, and illusion.[3]

We have already encountered several peddlers in New England: stragglers barging into the Whittier farmhouse, the small-timer doing his circuit in western Massachusetts and laying plans to go west. Hawthorne saw others at the Williams commencement and elsewhere in the Berkshires. He was especially struck by an old peddler with a "nervous" and "half-frozen aspect" whom he saw selling nuts, apples, candy, and gingerbread at Salem's railroad station in January 1842. It was not just the cold that subdued this man; he seemed forlorn, "not as a man desperate, but only without hope." He sat there, his arms crossed, with a look of "patient despondency," and with "none of the cheerfulness and briskness in him, that made people talkers." Perhaps he was a mechanic or small trader accustomed to living in between "passably to do and poverty"; perhaps he had "lost a son" or had other reasons for unhappiness. In any event, he sat impassively "in the very midst of the bustle and movement of the world, where all our go-ahead stream of population rushes and roars along beside him. Travellers from afar, traders going up to Boston business, young men on a pleasure-jaunt— all sorts of various people sweep by him; and there he remains, nervous, chill, patient."[4]

This old man at the depot was a creature of the commerce that brought agricultural produce to the city and sent people scurrying in all directions. But he stayed at home. The normal peddler was not sedentary but itinerant, not speechless but voluble, not despairing but ambitious. In these and many other ways he became the prototype of the Yankee, a figure known for verbal cleverness, systematic journeying, and sharp trading. The term *peddler* was an old one: there are references to peddlers with packs in England at least as far back as the thirteenth century. For centuries it had been a term of reproach suggesting tricky dealings and loose morals. Even in the Puritan colonies, peddling had been one acknowledged way of acquiring some money before settling down, while it was also a synonym for unscrupulous vagrancy. By the early nineteenth century the peddler was a common figure everywhere. Timothy Dwight complained that peddling eradicated the moral feelings of Connecticut's young men, but he admitted that this method of selling tinware was extraordinary. Rip Van Winkle's termagant wife died from arguing with one—not very many men were her match with words. Enough peddlers were killed—it was dangerous to carry money on the road—to leave a luxuriant folklore of ghosts and curses. It was a poor, murdered peddler who first communicated with the Fox sisters at the celebrated "birth of spiritualism." But Whittier captured a more favorable memory in describing the schoolmaster in "Snow Bound," a jack-of-all-trades who wielded the birch briskly, excelled at winter sports, played a merry violin, told "mirth-provoking versions" of classical tales, and could "doff at ease the scholar's gown / To peddle wares from town to town."[5]

If the peddler could be a bearer of culture, he was primarily a vendor of material goods. "Tin, tin. Come in," in a home far from port or depot meant the availability of shining pans and kettles, china, finished cloth, and shoes—as well as amusing banter. Peddlers were indispensable middlemen between Eastern manufacturers such as Maine's tin makers; Lynn's shoemakers; and the makers of essences, hats, guns, locks, and clocks in Connecticut, and a scattered but covetous market for such goods.[6] They were legendary for their drive and ingenuity, their shrewd reading of the faces of those they dealt with, and the persistence with which they pursued their fortune. Power met a large number of these Yankees heading south by ship with their carts and horses, and he recognized the importance of this "hardy and enterprising class." They were "the mercantile pioneers of the continent, every corner of which they penetrate from the Atlantic to the Pacific, supplying . . . the frontiers with little luxuries that else would never find a way there for years to come. They thus keep the chain of civilization entire, binding the remotest settlers to the great Union by their necessities, to which it administers through these its adventurous agents, whose tempting '*notions*' constantly create new wants amongst the simple children of the forest and the prairie."[7]

Although Whittier set his descriptions of the peddlers in nostalgic looks back into New England childhood, the true charm of peddling was the chance to get a new start. It was a way off the farm, an alternative to the sea or the gold fields, that could lead to a mercantile business in a new inland city. Its appeal to farm families was the provision of luxuries and necessities. Peddlers were welcomed by Midwestern families, often ex–New Englanders setting out to reestablish civilization. These people were already open to novelty; for them the peddler was a familiar agent of change, a touch of the old as well as the new. Caroline Kirkland's semi-autobiographical heroine picked herself up from a spill in the Michigan mud to meet "a pedestrian traveller, a hard-featured, yellow-haired son of New England . . . with a tin trunk," and traded with him for "essences, pins, brass thimbles . . . balls of cotton . . . combs, suspenders and cotton handkerchiefs—an assortment which made us very popular on that road for some time after."[8]

A tinge of contempt and suspicion in some portrayals of the peddler captured misgivings about commercial progress in general. Some of this tinge later spread into American-style anti-Semitism (as more and more Jews entered peddling after mid-century). The peddler could be seen as threatening local ways and bringing in alien goods and habits. A Canadian writer, T. C. Haliburton, created the prototypical Yankee, Sam Slick, and revealed his devious tricks while urging farmers to resist their appetites and preserve their way of life, but to no avail—both the stories and goods were too enjoyable.[9] In the South, invaded annually from Connecticut, antipathy to the Yankee became central to regional loyalty. No one persuaded many Southerners not to buy the notions; with fewer towns, the region had many people who depended on such invaders. But the image of the Northerner as the unmarried, sharp-talking, money-grubbing, would-be destroyer of the South's peculiar way of life became a staple of regional antagonism. Yet Andrew Jackson was said to have been so much "the prince of hospitality" that "the poor, belated peddler was as welcome at the Hermitage as the President of the United States."[10]

The assault of the new was waged by those who peddled other kinds of goods, especially information. Medical knowledge is a good instance. There were "yarb and root" men, peddlers with an alleged specialty in old-time medicinal lore, sometimes with guidance from Indians. Others pulled teeth and set bones in a fashion well known for long years in rural America. But those who sold medical books and promoted "systems" of treatment tended to boast that their information was up-to-date; health questions were too serious to be left to family or communal tradition. Medical practice was subject to much choice. Whatever state controls had formerly existed were relaxed in antebellum America, and large regions had little access to urban physicians or even circuit-riding country doctors. Moreover, there were more than a dozen "systems" of treatment to choose from. To the centuries-old belief that doctors were charlatans were added new reasons for seeing them all as Connecticut Yankees, one part go-getter and one-part illusionist, sizing up their customers and vending their wares. "Regular" doctors regarded all the others as quacks, but for many people it was impossible to tell one from another or to judge the greater efficacy of old and new, the time-tested or the recondite. "Feel the pulse, smell the cane, look at the tongue, / Touch the gold, praise the old, flatter the young": so recites Samuel Woodworth's Dr. Stramonium, a boozy carpenter turned music teacher, then peddler, then schoolmaster, then preacher, "and now a physician . . . I pluck the poor *geese*, while the ducks exclaim *quack!*"[11]

Those who sold newspapers and magazines called themselves, not peddlers, but "agents." But they, too, through verbal performance conjured up images of a new way more excellent than the old. The *Northern Farmer* in 1855 carried a report, a kind of play-within-a-play, that captured the dramatic quality of the recurrent exchange. The magazine published news of better implements, improved stock, and more commodious houses that every farmer ought to know about. One of their agents in central New York is rebuffed by a stingy old man who drives him away with a cane. In time, however, this Farmer Slack asks his more prosperous neighbor Jones the secret of his success and learns, of course, that Jones has availed himself of "useful knowledge" in all his purchases and practices. Without the publications he subscribes to, Jones would be a poor man, too. "I now want *information*" says the converted Slack. He has lived sixty-five years "with my eyes shut to the 'improvements' going on, . . . having refused to admit a publication of any kind to enter my doors, except an almanac." His father taught him "to believe that '*book farming*' was a humbug," but now he must change his ways. He vows to subscribe immediately to some of the best publications, to replace his rickety buildings with new-model ones, and generally to avail himself of the blessings of the modern age. [12]

Was the traveling preacher much different from the peddler or agent? Some of them would have resented the question, since they conceived their mission as taming a wilderness all too open to materialistic appeals. So many kinds of preachers were on the road that generalization, in any case, is difficult. Some journeyed on their own hook; thousands more followed circuits for Methodists, Baptists, or other evangelical sects; others were home missionaries or agents for evangelical reform societies; some were professional revivalists on a small or grand scale. Some were well educated, others poorly, some not at all. In the Methodist regimen, circuit-riding was so routine and disciplined a role that its theatrical aspects were not disconcerting. (At least not to the preacher: there was an endlessly repeated story of an audience's refusing to give a comedian a single laugh; afterward, a local youth rushed up to say, "If it hadn't a been for the women, I should a snorted out right in meetin'."[13]) But the pressures of mounting a good performance day after day might impose too much strain on the soul of the revivalist. Such was the fear of Theodore Dwight Weld, at any rate, when he warned his beloved Charles Grandison Finney, "do you not find yourself running into *formality* . . . in the management of revivals? I mean of feeling. The machinery all moves on, every wheel and spring and chord in its place; but isn't the *main spring* waxing weaker?"[14]

Initially, the itinerant clergy were as likely to be portrayed as subverting the village ideal of the East as combatting sloth and ignorance in the woods or on the prairie. Only in the 1840s and 1850s did the longstanding opposition of parish minister to traveling revivalist begin to slacken; and as it did, the clergy tended to think of themselves as professionals on the move, more loyal to national networks of their fellows than to the communities they served in what seemed to be ever-briefer stints. [15] In the rural South and newly settled West, missionaries were sometimes resisted as alien and threatening. In some parts of the South, in particular, peddlers were more welcome than agents of the Sunday School society or any kind of missionary. [16] In the West, however, the traveling minister was often a valued contact with the world back east and a good sign of the spread, not only of churches, but also of schools and other civilizing influences. The novelist-historian Edward Eggleston in 1874 recalled from his Indiana childhood that the circuit riders were central to the process of settlement; they, "more than any one else, . . . brought order out of this chaos."[17]

As some contemporaries noted, reformers imitated the organization and methods of revivals. Frequently they were former clergy. In any case, they sought to deny the dimensions of their work that made them look like peddlers. They stressed their Christian earnestness and civilizing purpose. The liked to talk of acting on a global "stage" on which God viewed them and judged their deeds; or they viewed the barbaric West or benighted city as a "theatre" in which their concerted efforts might win approval from the better classes of citizens. They were reluctant to lay stress on the journeying itself or the tricks of seizing attention and making a sale. They spoke of themselves as "Christian reformers," alone in the universe, faithfully serving a divine commander.[18]

It is no disparagement of the intrinsic importance of many distinct reform movements to notice that all of them depended on the labors of a newly recognized class of colporteurs who traveled to speak in village halls, to attend conventions, to sell subscriptions and distribute printed goods. Every reformer's biography was likely to be organized, at least in part, around a series of journeys. Some of these, like Weld's antislavery orations in Ohio in the mid-1830s and Dorothea Dix's inspections of Massachusetts jails and madhouses in the early 1840s, took their place among the glorious legends of reform.[19] The letters and diaries of reformers usually commented on the travails of the road, the discomforts of hotels, the dangers of bad food, and the advantages of different modes of transit. Inevitably, some drew an analogy between the modern pace of travel and the progress of society in adopting new, holy ideas. Now that human speed in travel had progressed from three miles an hour to forty, wrote one reformer in 1835, it was time to go full steam ahead toward moral progress.[20] This was the impatience of reform that Hawthorne satirized in his report on the "Celestial Railroad" swooping across the Slough of Despond and all other obstacles once met by pilgrims on the journey of faith.[21]

With the image of the reformer as escaped madman, Hawthorne pointed out the sense in which reform was a sell. If you could convince someone you were a reformer and get them to "subscribe" to your society's publications, you were a reformer and a success. Otherwise, you might need to find more stationary, less risky, work. Executive boards of reform societies faced painful decisions when a good Christian was weak in the field. But someone who was poorly prepared, a bumbling speaker, or a troublemaker could not be trusted in an important territory. The pain might be concealed beneath discussions of having the right doctrines or the proper attitude, but there was always a submerged awareness that reform was serious business that required casting the right players in the parts.[22] So much was at stake for many of these new agents that it is small wonder they masked their vocational anxieties—did they have what it takes to get a purchase on life?—beneath solemn talk of a divine purpose.

The political world also featured travelers who traced the same circuits as peddlers, preachers, and reformers. In the first place, this was an era of expanding political parties, frequently run by professionals and claiming the loyalties of voters by the thousands in ever-wider circles of each state. A new style of campaigning, according to the leading authority, emphasized "dramatic spectacles," and politics as a whole assumed "a dramatic function," as it "enabled voters throughout the nation to experience the thrill of participating in what amounted to a great democratic festival that seemed to perceptive foreign observers to be remarkably akin to the religious festivals of Catholic Europe." The successes of the parties would have been impossible without a transportation network to carry letters and handbills, speakers and organizers. Not surprisingly, champions of older political styles deplored the cheapening and popularizing of public life, while others applauded large electoral turnouts and gaudy celebrations as the fruition of democracy.[23]

Secondly, at the center of politics moved men of the law—judges and attorneys making their circuits from one courthouse town to the next. Abraham Lincoln loved the circuit in Illinois that he traveled with Judge David Davis and a troupe of other lawyers. By night he regaled barroom audiences, sometimes as many as three hundred men, with his powers of mimicry and storytelling; and whenever possible, he went off to hear singers, actors, or Negro minstrels. By day he perfected skills in persuasion and negotiation in the courtrooms where he earned a reputation for "dramatic strokes." Through it all he maintained "the appearance of a rough, intelligent farmer," as he became seasoned in the American art of politics.[24] From road, to tavern, to courthouse, and back on the road to the next town—that was the course of the law.

From colonial times, courthouse days were inseparable from the excitement of the market square. The same thrills became identified with elections, too. With seemingly endless elections the absorption in political life became so intense that Finney saw ample justification for revivals. Without orchestrated religious fervor, those who drummed up political emotions would claim too much of the souls of Americans. Religionists needed to imitate all the devices of lawyers and stump speakers just to keep up with the pace of change.[25]

Actors and entertainers were also resigned to almost ceaseless travel. Alongside the peddlers, they were the constant traveling companions of the earnest men of religion and politics who sought to give the entire process a more solemn or redemptive purpose. Where the peddler accentuated the mercenary side of travel, the showman highlighted the necessity of style and presence. Both showed that life on the road, however wearing and grubby, could also be profitable and fun.

To some extent, the extension of theatre was a measure of the growth of cities.[26] Sometimes actors told stories of the seemingly miraculous appearance of a nighttime audience, particularly in the South, at a crossroads that by daylight was nearly deserted. But these were exceptions. It took concentrations of population to make possible profitable circuits for the stars to pass around. The extension of theatrical circuits, made up of a series of cities joined by rivers, canals, or good roads, is one of the basic achievements of American cultural history in the first half of the nineteenth century. At first only the cities of the Northeast—Boston, New York, Albany, and Philadelphia—could promise a profitable season for a performer. Then impresarios like Sol Smith and Noah Ludlow fastened together new strings of theatres in New Orleans, Mobile, Saint Louis, and points in between. Generally speaking, the lesser lights spent the season in one city where they played a sequence of monotonously similar roles behind stars who stayed for a week at a run. The lives of the stars, inevitably, consisted of as much travel as those of peddlers or revivalists, if not more.

Like actors in earlier eras, those of the antebellum era sought to deny suspicions of immorality that sullied theatrical reputations. Much was said of the refinement and good reputation of the best-known performers. Since this was one traveling business open to women, it was especially necessary to tout the purity of women of the stage. But in an age that put great emphasis on the home it was hard for the traveler to silence insinuations of vice. Rumors of lesbianism that pursued the great actress Charlotte Cushman, indicated deep misgivings current in society. Churchmen, self-conscious about their own itinerant tendencies, were zealous in drumming up suspicions of actors' morals. A series of tempestuous divorce proceedings, especially Fanny Kemble's in 1849 and Edwin Forrest's in 1851, did nothing to allay the doubts of those who hated the theatrical.[27]

The autobiographies of antebellum showmen tell us much about the economic development of inland cities and include many anecdotes about Indians, peddlers, and other wanderers. They tell stories concerning the rich and powerful of the United States and Europe. They expose moments of hilarity in mounting productions in rough spots and unpromising cities. They may depict a vision of American life in which the "operational" took precedence over the truthful or beautiful: what mattered was how things worked, how "effects" were achieved.[28] What they do not, for the most part, attempt or accomplish is extended analysis of theatrical productions. Such analysis would await the endeavors, decades later, of Edwin Booth and David Belasco. What the antebellum showmen gave in its place was a sense of the close connection between the humdrum and spontaneous, the preposterous and inspired improvisation. They tell of Forrest so carried away in Lear's mad scene that he tore off his wig and hurled it twenty feet across the stage; of a Philadelphia audience calling for the author of *Antigone* and the manager promising to bring him out in the future; of Sol Smith convincing theatregoers in Tuscaloosa that a fire in the last act of *Don Juan, or the Libertine Destroyed* had not really happened—including a burned stagehand, who declared, "I'll be d——d if that fire wasn't the best *imitation* I ever saw!"[29] These stories originate, of course, in less introspective minds than Whittier's or Hawthorne's, but they convey similar interest in a margin between the ordinary and unpredictable. It was a line drawn from life on the road.

There were important differences among the careers that required travel. Some were overtly mercenary or entertaining; others denied any such inference. Some sought to alter public taste by improving or taming it; others frankly pandered to the public. Some were bounded by the state lines hardened by federalism; some burst throughout the markets that crazily intersected state boundaries and encouraged regional and even national or international consciousness. There were, however, many points of convergence. Even those who wished to suppress the connections could seldom really do so, for the transportation revolution and the lives of travel it facilitated were of undeniable importance to them all.

Inevitably, the roles proved to be interchangeable. In the two decades after the Peace of Utrecht there were no well-defined professions with places ready for men to fill them. Instead, there were thousands of young men impatient for a different kind of career than the prevailing ones of the eighteenth century. They did not know exactly what they wanted, but like the peddler Hawthorne traveled with, they knew it was neither the confinement of the farm nor the torpor of the mills. Lucien Boynton, a young man from Vermont and a graduate of Middlebury College who tried schoolteaching, theological school at Andover, and superintending an academy before fixing on the law, dreamed of getting "a hold" on life. Training and connections were important, he realized, but he also wished to fit into a role, to find a "character" in which he would not feel awkward and uncomfortable. His career took him to Amoskeag in New Hampshire, Wilmington and Newark in Delaware, Richmond in Virginia, and Worcester and Uxbridge in Massachusetts, before he landed in Springfield, Illinois (home of a more illustrious farmboy-turned-attorney).[30]

The search was difficult, not only because professions were undefined, but also because there was so much competition. Whittier wrote in despair in 1828 that "the professions are already crowded full to overflowing." Prospects were dim even for a confident and talented youth. He might have to become a "tin peddler" or hawker of essences.[31] One social critic in the early 1830s thought too many farm boys were being educated: "There were more lawyers than could get an education honestly. . . . There were doctors to be found in every street of every village, with their little saddlebags; and they too must have a living out of the public. There were too many clergymen who, finding no places where they could be settled, went about the country begging for funds and getting up rag-bag and tag-rag societies."[32]

Ralph Waldo Emerson also commented on the young men who studied at college, tried to enter a profession in Boston or New York, and sank into depression if their initial ventures ended in failure. They were "timorous, desponding whimperers," no better than "parlour soldiers." How much more admirable was this young man: "A sturdy lad from New Hampshire or Vermont who in turn tries all the professions, who *teams* it,—*farms* it,— peddles, keeps a school, preaches, edits a newspaper, goes to Congress, and so forth, in successive years, and always, like a cat, falls on his feet, is worth a hundred of these city minions." He may be less educated but more resourceful; "he has not one chance but a hundred chances."[33] For such a man the place where he started out might have no influence on where he ended up. But the hops along the way were likely to be from one career on the road to another. They might in the end, however, lead to the city or back to the farm, as when a peddler—or even a fur trapper—used his stake to open a store or to buy some good farmland in the West.[34]

It is easy to find examples of every kind of hop. Best known, perhaps, are the ministers who moved on to agency and missionary life in the proliferating reform societies and the schoolteachers who deserted the classroom for almost every other kind of endeavor. Schoolteaching so rapidly became a female, and more stationary, occupation that scholars speak of the "feminization" of the schools.[35] Acting could also be a step toward better things, even the work of God. Adoniram Judson, for example, became one of the most beloved missionaries of the century because of his service in India and Burma. But he had suffered a bout of atheism as a student at Brown, left home and taught school for a while, changed his name, and traveled with a band of actors. Sobered by the death of a friend, he resumed his identity, entered Andover Seminary, joined with some classmates in founding the American Board of Commissioners for Foreign Missions, and went on to glory as a Baptist among the heathen.[36] Joseph T. Buckingham, a poor Connecticut boy who went on to be editor of the *Boston Courier* and a pillar of the Unitarian orthodoxy, had his stint in a theatrical company.[37] George J. Adams was a tragedian in Boston and, after his conversion to Mormonism, in

Nauvoo at the outset of an increasingly bizarre career that also included roles blending theatre with scripture in the renegade Kingdom of Saint James Colony in Wisconsin, an adventist church in Maine, and a colony in Jaffa, Palestine. He was always at the center of criticism for alcoholism, prostitution, and (in 1844) trying to introduce polygamy in Boston.[38]

Peddling, like acting, was less a "hold" than a temporary grip along life's climb. Many reformers tried it out when they first left home. The abolitionist Elizur Wright, who had an extremely frustrating search for a profitable vocation, experienced an embarrassing period as a peddler going from door to door with his carpetbag before he found the scheme that gave him claim to the title "the father of life insurance."[39] Bronson Alcott peddled notions in Virginia before moving on to experiments in education, enthusiastic participation in several reform movements, and a never-satisfied quest for literary distinction. His biographer aptly called his volume *Pedlar's Progress*.[40] The black abolitionist William Wells Brown exhibited a panorama and gave dramatic readings.[41] Even those who never actually peddled anything felt the resemblance between themselves and pitchmen in their efforts to sell their writings and hold onto listeners' attention. Opponents of reform reinforced this view. A Southern critic of William Lloyd Garrison spoke contemptuously of the fanatical "agents, who, having found peddling unprofitable, have taken to preaching."[42]

Actors, undoubtedly, were most likely to see all of American society as a drama. Sol Smith began one of his three autobiographical volumes with a dedication to the Georgia politician Mirabeau B. Lamar in which he recalled days of travel together, when "you as a candidate for Congress on your own hook, and I as leader of a chosen band of Thespians—when you, *in search of excitement*, delivered speeches on the then all absorbing subject of Nullification, and I, *in search of 'the dimes,'* acted plays in newly-built theatres." He concludes with a letter from Lamar: let us act our parts so well that we will have seats in the sublime theatre to be opened by the "GREAT MANAGER" hereafter.[43] Throughout Smith's volumes are evocations of days when theatrical conditions were so primitive that just to put the plays on was an accomplishment, of audiences so gullible that they mistook the most overdrawn performances before painted sets for reality, of incessant journeys in which all kinds of showmen and salesmen commingled in hilarious equality. He remembers actors turned preachers, reciting Shakespeare from the pulpit. He tells us that he was himself mistaken for a preacher by a hammy phrenologist who wound up making combs in Connecticut.[44] He captures the stylized posturing of countless business dealings. He has an endless stock of stories of ethnic confusion, of Creeks playing Peruvians, of blacks deceived by whites and whites by blacks. He introduces us to Okah Tubbee, a black loafer who named himself after an oak tub and played Indian roles—and who ended life as an actual representative of the Choctaws! Truly, for Smith all the world was, as he said, a stage.[45]

From his vantage point in Saint Louis, this transplanted New Englander furnishes independent corroboration of the sham and farce of lives on Mark Twain's Mississippi. If we are looking for an Ur-text in popular culture to help us discount the view of American civilization that traces its foundations to the New England village, if we wish to understand both corrosive and liberating consequences of travel, if we seek sources for Tom Sawyer's manipulation of Nigger Jim and the vulgar pretensions of the Duke and Dolphin, we could do worse than to acquaint ourselves with the world of actors and showmen that Smith depicts. As we try to understand American life as a masquerade, we may also notice that claims of being the Dauphin were not solely Twain's invention. A man named Eleazar Williams made such claims in New York literary circles; and so, on occasion, did the great traveler and artist John James Audubon.[46]

It remains to link the emergence of literary and intellectual vocations to the travesties and corruptions of the road. One way off the farm or out of a dreary apprenticeship for a young man who had gotten a little notice, perhaps, by writing some poems or essays for local newspapers was to become an editor. Sol Smith edited a Jacksonian paper in Cincinnati after leaving farm work and studying law. A list of prominent authors who started out as editors would be very long; behind them would be a longer list of those who never attained fame. Usually editorships were short-term stints, a few months during an election campaign, a year or two for a reform cause that ran out of funds, a year more for a literary magazine whose owners altered their tastes. Whittier alone went through nine before he was thirty. Nor were periodicals, which popped up and died like mushrooms, clustered in a few large cities. It was necessary to keep your bags packed and your obligations light.

The identification of intellectual opportunity with life on the road imposed severe limitations on women. It was not the case that women could not adapt to the rigors and uncertainties of travel. There were always some women who demonstrated otherwise: besides actresses, there were such examples as Ann Royall, who wrote travel books in the 1820s and edited a newspaper in the 1830s, and Frances Wright, who also wrote about travel and lectured on women's rights and other radical reforms in the same period. But Royall was attacked as an adulteress and dismissed as an eccentric, while Wright's frank discussions of birth control gained her notoriety as "the Great Red Harlot of Infidelity." Both were made to exemplify the dangers of women's overstepping the boundaries that ought to circumscribe their aspirations. Women could travel across the continent with their families, but when it came to setting forth on new careers, the road was a world where they did not belong. Versatility in performance, enjoyment of adventure, money-getting—these were considered to be male attributes. When Angelina Grimké began to lecture against slavery in the mid-1830s, New England clergymen rose in defense of the long-standing "biblical" separation of the sexes; and since church buildings often served as venues for antislavery addresses, many closed to her the halls under their control.[47] To prevent controversy, women who won fame as authors stressed that domestic hardships, not "male" ambition, drove them to write for a living, and in their works they emphasized the household duties and familial feelings of women. In her analysis of these women's cautious entrances on the public stage, Mary Kelley compares them to a *"lady singer"* who was escorted onto the stage by gentlemen and after each song returned to a seat among other ladies, one of whom draped her shoulders with a shawl.[48] The man who traveled was an entrepreneur, perhaps a culture bearer, at worst a scamp, but a woman who traveled was obliged to give reassurance that she was not a threat to morality. Frustrated by unequal access to public platforms, the novelist and reformer Lydia Maria Child exclaimed, "Oh, if I was a man, how I *would* lecture!"[49]

By the 1840s, a man might dream of going from the editor's desk to the arena in which intellectual distinction was most celebrated: the lecture circuit. Originally the creation of local educated elites who intended, largely through their own presentations, to uplift their communities, lyceums and lecture halls became by mid-century the stages for the greatest American celebrities. They were a proving ground where the provincial and shallow were sifted out from profound speakers who met the test of popularity. Highly paid lecturers like Bayard Taylor, Horace Greeley, Oliver Wendell Holmes, and Henry Ward Beecher gave useful knowledge in noble but accessible terms; they reached the top in the most democratic forum available. They were hailed as the worthiest heroes of a new era of civilization.[50]

Praise for these stars stressed the nobility of their attainments and the legitimacy of the test they had passed. They were not peddlers, not mountebanks; they were agents of national uplift. In fact, however, they paid for fame in ceaseless and exhausting travel that took a toll on health and tempers. While it was impossible not to enjoy wealth and honor, it is clear that at least some of the lecturers did get tired of giving the same lectures over and over away from their studies and their families. There is no need to feel sorry for the secure, prosperous, and adulated. What may be said, however, is that some of them saw in popular favor a legitimate halo, but others were well aware of the need to market themselves and dramatize their presence in order to reap the rewards of democratic culture.

For those who never won much fame, the itinerant life of editing and lecturing was even more clearly one of economic risk and vulnerability. They held on to visions of respectability and refinement, but the hold was precarious, always in danger of coming loose. The stars of the lecture circuits provided reassuring images of serenity and eloquence; they were free from huckstering and self-promotion (or so it seemed). They were not typical of the restless search for a grasp on life. They were "the first men of the country."[51]

In the end the lyceum star was celebrated for a kind of disinterestedness and nobility that was never available to peddler or showman and seldom to physician or preacher. He had a self-indulgence that the preacher or reformer must deny, a spiritual value that the salesman and actor could never reach. Though in celebrating him his countrymen denied certain troubling aspects of vocational pursuit in the American republic, it is instructive to see him in concert with all the others on the road. The point of looking at all the travelers together is to see how the circumstances of intellectual endeavor matched those in other fields. These circumstances not only affected those who searched for words to say and an audience to listen to them, they also furnished the content, the recurrent themes, of intellectual performance.

One of Hawthorne's tales, "The Seven Vagabonds" (1833), sums up the significance of the road for intellectual life with special luminosity. The scene is a crossroads, where routes diverge to Boston, Canada, and the sea. The narrator rambles up to a "huge covered wagon," which turns out to house "a wandering show man" with marvelous puppets and barrel organ and a "neat and trim" young book-peddler with an enticing stock of many kinds of literature. Both are praised elaborately. The first is like "Prospero, entertaining his guests with a masque of shadows"; the second is "a herald before the march of Mind." Soon they are joined by a "dark and handsome" foreigner and beautiful "damsel" carrying a fiddle, a show box exhibiting the wonders of the world, and other properties used in their shows at "brigade musters, ordinations, cattle shows, commencements, and other festal meetings in our sober land." Rain brings two others to join the company in the wagon. A beggar with a circular explaining his misfortune gets a donation from the narrator and then relates his past, with uncanny accuracy, and prophesies his future from a deck of greasy cards. A Penobscot Indian, who wanders about, living off "careless charity" and shooting his bow-and-arrow at fairs, turns out to be heading to the same destination as all the others: a camp meeting where there would be plenty of business for all six of this compatible "honest company."

A question faces the seventh. He wishes to accompany them to the camp meeting. "But in what capacity?" the showman asks, inverting normal standards of gentility. "All of us here can get our bread in some creditable way. Every honest man should have his livelihood. You, sir, as I take it, are a mere strolling gentleman." Although he believed that his "free mind" and "restless impulse" sufficed to equip him for the company, he now must go further:

> I proceeded to inform the company, that, when Nature gave me a propensity to their way of life, she had not left me altogether destitute of qualifications for it; though I could not deny that my talent was less respectable, and might be less profitable, than the meanest of theirs. My design, in short, was to imitate the story tellers of whom Oriental travellers have told us, and become an itinerant novelist, reciting my own extemporaneous fictions to such audiences as I could collect.

After some debate the others accept him, and the seven vagabonds go forth, with "marvellous jollity," toward the camp meeting. In the end they meet a dark figure riding with "rigid perpendicularity," a famous Methodist circuit rider, who tells them, "the camp meeting is broke up." So the "union" is "nullified," and the vagabonds disperse. But even the preacher had nearly smiled to see such "great diversity of character" together on the road.[52]

CHAPTER EIGHTEEN

Confidence and Sincerity

One way of thinking about the circuits of travel is to call them markets. When the freelance moved from Massachusetts to Illinois, he followed the same routes as other items in circulation: money, credit, grain, textiles, immigrant labor, purchasers of land, magazines, and even barn designs. When planter and impresario converged on Cincinnati for their seasonal hiring, they, too, were following routes of exchange. Today we adopt the convention of calling these extensive areas of exchange by the name of the booths and turnstiles of an ancient town: there is no single day or place of exchange; all the endeavors over widening areas constitute a "market."[1]

American scholars are increasingly alert to the consequences for cultural activity of the extension of these markets. Without ignoring such traditional subjects as patterns of intellectual influence and the succession of ideologies, we begin to learn how enhanced ability to sell foodstuffs in international markets affected cultural styles and allegiances in Jefferson's Virginia and how the shattering consequences of commercial and industrial change affected republican thought in Whitman's New York.[2] We no longer have the luxury of imagining that intellectual life is cloistered. Both context and substance are in some measure shaped by the transit of resources and the competition to enjoy them.

The effects of markets on intellectual life were experienced dramatically in the decades after the Peace of Utrecht. With mingled excitement and anxiety men and women tried to define life anew. Once-established patterns of existence no longer were available; new patterns were just within reach if one could get to them. This was one of the grand themes of Tocqueville's second set of volumes on democracy, which he took to be a kind of market for artists and philosophers. In his view, all forms of creative endeavor were affected, and probably damaged, by the need to sell cultural goods that once had received value and honor in a less risky, hierarchical world.[3] Despite Tocqueville's great prestige in America, and despite recurrent American protests against the inhospitality of America to the arts, few scholars until recently have inquired into economic conditions of the kind that he emphasized. Form and content, not royalties and publishers' costs, have been the staples of cultural history. Recent studies suggest that such neglect may now be receding.[4]

Though it is clear that only a few wealthy men could choose to write out of aristocratic detachment, it is uncertain whether most who aspired to artistic or literary eminence were able to see what they did as a market activity. They seldom spoke of the market at all. Some defined themselves by the lofty causes they represented; we think of Whittier and Whitman. Some promoted useful and uplifting messages to show the advantages of democracy or to tame its shabbier tendencies. The images of peddler and showman, Sam Slick and P. T. Barnum, were brought up from disturbing undercurrents in a debate about the effects of democracy. Did democratic culture bring heroes to prominence, or did it destroy frail but worthy talents?

Because the emerging intellectual classes spoke about it so reluctantly, it is difficult to be sure what, if anything, "the market" meant to them. One historian has offered a subtle and ingenious analysis of the "recession of causation" as a major consequence of the great "urban-industrial transformation" that is "symbolized by the image of a small, familiar, local market being absorbed into progressively larger market systems." In Thomas Haskell's account, "reflective individuals experienced a general recession of the perceived location of the important events, people, and institutions that influenced their lives." As they came to grips with large-scale "interdependence," those things which once seemed vital and spontaneous in the scene around them were reduced to secondary or incidental factors in much larger systems of consequence and responsibility. They were, as a result, less predisposed to discuss events in terms of "free choice" and more open to ideas of "determinants" beyond the control of the individual mind.[5]

Not until the 1890s, in Haskell's view, was this recognition, from which he dates the emergence of modern social science, elaborated by large numbers of thinkers. But he points to signs of crisis in the 1840s and 1850s in many fields, including law and medicine, where the "competent" resented the obstacles to social betterment and their personal preeminence posed by the fluid, disorganized conditions of democracy. "We are over-run in this country with charlatanism," wrote (in 1846) America's leading man of science, Joseph Henry of the Smithsonian Institution. "Our newspapers are filled with puffs of Quackery and every man who can burn phosphorous in oxygen and exhibit a few experiments to a class of young ladies is called a man of science."[6] We recognize in such complaints voices like those Tocqueville had been listening to. Here are the roots of the specialized disciplines and certified forms of expertise that competed more successfully with popular fashions in later decades. But in the antebellum era this was at most a minority report. While it is easy enough to see appeals for licensing and certification of competence as a strategy followed by selected groups with limited success in this era, it is hard to accept these complaints as the most typical or cogent early responses to what we think of as a market.[7]

In the antebellum United States the prevalent belief was that a man's talents and character had direct relation to his fortunes in life. There was little remoteness or abstraction in the most noticeable forms of thinking about causation. In fact, in the fading belief in original sin and in the absence of twentieth-century styles of social analysis, antebellum Americans seem to us to have singularly lacked any accepted view of psychological causation. When they did speak of causes, they often used lurid, personal terms. Today's economist may locate the causes of the panics of 1819 and 1837 in international market forces beyond the influence of America's policy makers, but in American politics of the era nothing was clearer than that the machinations of corrupt men (in the Jacksonian version) or the intrigues of the ignorant (in the Whig reply) were the guilty secret behind public distress. The political air reeked with cries of foul conspiracy. Examples could be drawn from every major political controversy of the age, from the "corrupt bargain" of 1824 to secession.[8]

Certainty that foul plots undermined the economy and threatened political freedom was one of the commonplaces of antebellum political thought, expressed not only in the fulminations of great leaders but also in some of the most successful popular movements and third parties in American history. The anti-Masonic movement was built on the conviction that a conniving fraternity of lawyers and politicians was twisting the processes of government to selfish ends. A series of anti-Catholic and anti-immigrant movements exposed nefarious schemes of the pope and his minions in America. Anti-Mormonism applied similar fears to new religious communities. These were not small movements: they mobilized thousands and called on the leadership of articulate and prominent men like Samuel F. B. Morse and Millard Fillmore. Some of the era's most popular fiction, particularly George Lippard's *The Empire City* and *New York: Its Upper Ten and Lower Million*, depicted Eastern cities as victimized by secret cabals of political, economic, and religious leaders convening to sate their lust and to grind the poor into ever-deeper degradation. Moreover, Lippard formed a secret brotherhood of his own to combat such conspiracies in real life. In many cities, street preachers peddled messages of hate, sometimes in obscurity, but often with much political influence.[9] From examining the crisscrossing suspicions, hyperbolic denunciations, and mushrooming popular movements, one historian detected a "paranoid style." Another points to "countersubversion" as a mode of thought and action that dealt with anxieties over the openness and assumed vulnerability of republican institutions and that set limits to the vaunted association-building tendencies of Americans. Everything depended on having citizens who thought on their own and, somewhat contradictorily, followed respectable *public* opinion. The man who subjected his will to a secret power might destroy the republic.[10]

Much of this rhetoric should be discounted. Democrats and Whigs denounced one another as dangerous conspirators seeking the spoils of office in the interests either of enriching the discredited "aristocratic" class or of shamefully manipulating the "mob." On occasion, however, they recognized that each needed the other for legitimacy, and tempered their actions accordingly.[11] The American penchant for immoderate suspicion of conspiracies was less innocuous (or so it will appear to those who esteem rational problem-solving) when it poisoned the slavery controversy, in Congress and in the press, with images of a "slave power" conspiracy and a "red abolitionist" conspiracy seeking to subvert a region's distinctive civilization. There was no more effective way of mobilizing the public than by ripping the masks off villains who were *causing* mischief and vice.

The "paranoid style" had precedents in European tradition from Cicero to Luther, and it has flourished in more recent periods of American history. What seems most remarkable about the anticonspiratorial mode of thought in the antebellum period is the way it was linked to issues of self-image and social success in a fluid economic and political situation. The upwardly mobile person, writes David Brion Davis, may experience "subjective frustration" at his continuing insecurity; he may find "that he had naïvely believed in the performances put on by his elders of the prestigious ranks, and that now he must stage a similar show." The disclosure of his own histrionic opportunity carried with it the unsettling realization that everyone else might be on stage, too. That is why, adds Michael Rogin, antebellum Americans were so preoccupied with "internal states." It was not deep knowledge of the self that they sought; rather, in their uncertainty about others' motives and their own as well, they looked for exemplars of "the authentic, spontaneous, natural man who wore no masks, played no roles, and never dissembled." The image of Andrew Jackson, for example, as a man of unfeigned wisdom and iron will provided his partisans with a counter-image to the omnipresent peril of corrupt masquerade.[12]

Lincoln recognized the dangers to the Whigs if the public formed a different impression of Zachary Taylor. He asked the Secretary of State to discuss with the Cabinet "the effect . . . on the public mind" of the President's decision to delegate responsibility for appointments to the separate departments. This decision was giving Taylor "the unjust and ruinous character of being a mere man of straw," an appearance that would hurt all the Whigs. It was worth remembering that Taylor had derived his greatest "popularity" out of stories that during the Mexican War he had gone into battle against the unanimous advice of his officers. The same impression must be created now. "He must occasionally say, or seem to say, 'by the Eternal,' 'I take the responsibility.' Those phrases were the 'Samson's locks' of Gen. Jackson, and we dare not disregard the lessons of experience."[13]

All commentators seem to agree that the expanding "markets" of modern capitalist economies depended on the emergence of a new kind of personality. Capitalism requires, according to a reflective summary of accounts that range from Marx and Weber to Foucault, "the energies of people who display a strongly self-monitoring disposition, people who routinely allow their behavior in the present to be shaped by obligations incurred in the distant past and by anticipations of consequences that lie far in the future."[14] Capitalism, by such accounts, has a hard time with peasants who lack self-conscious attention to their lives as careers, who do not understand the possibility of exerting themselves to make the present markedly different from the past and the future better than the present. It depends on a self-observing, dealing self.[15] In a sense, we have been observing the articulation of such a self in the midst of the confusion of antebellum America. We notice a heightened awareness of the dramatic and mercenary aspects of public careers. Out of this awareness springs a drive to set limits between histrionics in conspiratorial bad faith and the presentation of an authentic self, between unscrupulous peddling and professionally reliable self-expression.

It seems unlikely that many antebellum Americans could deploy the abstraction of the market or of a capitalist system to account for their experience. Most thought in traditional religious terms of a journey of life. They added Shakespearean terms about the stages of man. The more literate borrowed images from the legends of Jason, Orpheus, and Ulysses. Earnest and sober men on the road sought some way to separate the legitimate from the bogus. It was not usually possible to think of themselves as behaving naturally; it was necessary to be brought up well and to keep a close watch on themselves. What was needed was character.

Robert H. Wiebe has brilliantly delineated the pattern of young men's life-experience taken for granted in discussions of character. By their mid-twenties men were expected to have severed family ties, to have settled into a life's work, and to work with an energy that earlier generations might have found astonishing. Within ten years their success in life's voyage would be determined. Steady habits acquired in childhood would be a help, but each young man was irrevocably on his own. Temptations must be overcome: the world was filled with sharpsters and harlots. For those who failed, there was seldom a second chance. Flaws of character revealed in minor transgressions seeped through a man's entire being and explained his inevitable lack of direction and success. The equation could be read backward as well: in him who did not fare well, faults could surely be observed. To the exhilarating feeling of openness and choice, then, was added a strong sense of the perils of a defective character.[16]

Perhaps it was a consolation that character could be read easily. Gone were most of the old subtleties about the insidious work of sin. Though there was much tongue-clucking about imposture, few maintained the old Puritan insistence that hypocrisy was nearly everyone's fate. Blessed with a good upbringing and aided, perhaps, by the confirmation of a revival conversion, the young man could watch over his own habits and appearance and measure them against approved standards of behavior. Advice was available on every hand. Men like Francis Wayland, William Alcott, and Henry Ward Beecher set themselves up as explicators of community standards that young men could bear in mind as they investigated their conduct for signs of good character. These were frequently standards of abstinence—from masturbation, from alcohol, from gambling, from rich foods. They carried with them exhortations to industriousness, concentration, pious thoughts, and benevolent deeds. All would show up in appearance, the telltale marks of clothing, posture, and physiognomy that distinguished the hard-working from the shiftless, the reliable from the dishonest, the profligate from the pious, the healthy from the sick, the steady sailor from the bobbing cork on rough seas.[17]

Whom was this stream of advice directed to? The "young men" might be in any trade, but a favorite audience was the host of clerks working in trading firms, from Henry Ward Beecher's Indianapolis to Lewis Tappan's New York. Clearly the advice served the interests of merchant employers who needed to turn young men from the country into employees who could work long hours in good humor and good health, without carelessness or cheating. It spoke even more tellingly of the anxieties of these young men, beyond parental discipline, not yet steadied by marriage, keen to follow the rules of a new and frightening game. Some of the merchants had made the same journey and knew the perils: Lewis Tappan had wrestled with temptations in his clerking days; his mother had feared that he had frequented the theater, fallen in with "lewd women, and had contracted a disease that was preying upon your constitution." There was a widely circulating strain of worry that the new conditions of American life drove men insane.[18] The fact that some men rose from clerk's bench to Tappan's benevolent preeminence was a source of hope, but all but a few must be disappointed. All were expected to internalize controls, and their success would be exhibited in the manners they succeeded in adopting.

Throughout this period Americans sought to make sense of manners, and every foreign visitor weighed their success in doing so. By common agreement, America had no use for the "artificial" manners of Europe's upper classes. Not only were these an undemocratic way of distinguishing one group from the rest of society, but an immoral aspect of flattery and dissimulation was also associated with them. Lord Chesterfield's *Letters to His Son* (1779) had included advice on the seduction of ladies, and the post-revolutionary play *The Contrast* (1787) had shown how pretentious Americans might turn Chesterfield to vicious purposes. Despite these warnings, we learn from Arthur M. Schlesinger's study of American etiquette, Americans could not resist abridging and reorganizing Chesterfield's work to make it less offensive; "the adjective 'Chesterfieldian' passed into the language, shedding its offensive implications and bestowing the accolade of exceptional courtliness of bearing."[19]

There was much support for the idea that Americans needed to develop their own "distinctively American school of good manners" trimmed of European irrelevancy and promoting pleasant "exchanges."[20] Beside the conduct books that instructed young men on the standards of good character might be placed others that laid out Americanized rules for handling social situations. Irwin P. Beadle's *Dime Book of Etiquette* (1859) may be seen as forerunner to Emily Post's *Etiquette* (1922) and the syndicated columns in today's newspapers. At the same time, there was persistent belief in the identification of sincerity with simplicity. Anna Cora Mowatt's *Fashion* (1845) warned against the vanities of the nouveaux riches and the chicaneries of upstart clerks. Park Benjamin instructed lyceum audiences on the dangers of "Fashion."[21] An aspiring young lawyer in Springfield, Illinois, in 1842, spoke earnestly to the local temperance society about "the influence of fashion," which made drinking acceptable. It ought to be just as "unfashionable" for men to resist the temperance pledge as "to wear their wives' bonnets to church."[22] Manners were never a substitute for character.

Nevertheless, appearances were important. The word *character* was used to refer to a core of inner worth, but it had a histrionic double meaning. No one could succeed without looking the part, without being seen "in character." Even clergymen, who held forth against sham and mummery, were obliged to codify a set of visible signs of their role in society. In a world of greed they must present themselves as indifferent to "worldly enjoyments"; in a world of restless ambition they must visually demonstrate detachment and inner peace. The closest student of these matters sees in this advice and its acceptance the trappings of expertise appropriate to a redefined profession, trappings quite different from those of the aristocratic bearing of the colonial clergy.[23] The professional purpose of the minister was not only to preach Christianity but also to provide a model of living successfully in a Christian manner. The detachment, therefore, was modified by an awareness of social function in a complex, interrelated economy.

Americans were vulnerable to dissemblers. This was true in isolated regions, according to William Gilmore Simms, because folk were so delighted to have company that they failed to "scrutinize" a stranger's face. "A pleasant deportment, a specious [i.e., nice-looking] outside, a gentle and attractive manner," were all too winning among planters and country folk; and "the poor silly country girl"—the farmer's daughter who was frequently the victim—became the most familiar symbol of the guilelessness of backwater folk as the prey of unscrupulous visitors.[24] On the other hand, the frontier adventurer, as Susan Kuhlmann pointed out in an illuminating study of the figure of the confidence man in nineteenth-century fiction, often was credited with skills in reading character, self-dramatization, and manipulating others that were highly adaptive in an expanding society and economy. "IT IS GOOD TO BE SHIFTY IN A NEW COUNTRY": this was the favorite motto of Captain Simon Suggs, and it might have suited a succession of other exploiters of the weaknesses of their fellow human beings on the frontier. The resemblances between grifters, on one hand, and peddlers, evangelists, and politicians, on the other, were not left to later scholarly inference. They were central to the fun of the tales told of the tricksters.[25]

In some treatments, the confidence man became the great villain of the age. As Karen Halttunen reports from her study of advice manuals, he supposedly lurked in every passageway where an innocent youth could enter the city. He took various forms as he led the youth, through expressions of friendship and concern, into the pits of self-degradation.[26] He also infested the roads and waterways, as Herman Melville disclosed in the bleakest novel of the age, *The Confidence Man*. Part Satan, part Proteus, on a Mississippi River ship of fools, he changes shape from black beggar to white mendicant, from quack doctor to philosopher-scientist and cosmopolitan philanthropist. Along the way he encounters dupes and knaves in about equal measure. Melville had traveled the river; his description of the territory is accurate enough. But his professed aim was "for more reality, than real life can show." He refers to "that multiform pilgrim species, man," but it is clear that gullible and vicious forms outnumber all the rest. In a decidedly theatrical world, all are actors, the minister no less than the negro minstrel, and the sour hatred of the Indian-hater is no more imbalanced than the milky idealism of the Transcendentalist.[27] In some ways this vision is closer to the world of Samuel Beckett (or perhaps Gertrude Stein's Oakland: "there is no there there") than to that of Beecher, Tappan, or Emerson.

No one who believed in anything could derive much cheer from this novel. More typically, in the post-revolutionary American imagination, the figure of the confidence man stood in distinction to those who believed in and practiced virtue. It drew a line rather than erasing one. Yet in repeated, passionate reminders that temptation was everywhere, that seducers kept up fair appearances, and that one mistake would irretrievably cast you into a life of shame was ample suggestion that the boundary between vice and virtue was soft and permeable. Life easily could be reduced to a show or game. False and true, illegitimate and socially approved, public and private—all such distinctions might break down. They might easily be reversed, with suckers adhering to them while crafty go-ahead types took advantage of the rules. These were, as Michael Rogin says, "the themes of antebellum literature," and they were not fanciful but "derived from Jacksonian life."[28]

CHAPTER NINETEEN

Emerson on the World of Shows

"The ways of trade are grown selfish to the borders of theft, and supple to the borders (if not beyond the borders) of fraud," wrote Ralph Waldo Emerson.[1] But where were these borders? It would have been difficult to answer with precision. Emerson's lectures and essays are Mozartean in richness and complexity; there is no single correct way of approaching them. While putting Americans in contact with the European avant-garde and keeping them in contact with a Puritan heritage, he was also keenly aware of the ambiguities of the new economic era. Most of his written thoughts, as they passed from private notebook, to public lecture, to printed essay, probe these ambiguities and offer guidance for living in their midst.

Though I claim for him significant elements of modernity, he did not fall into Beckett-like gloom amid absurdity. Though none of his contemporaries thought more searchingly about the dilemmas of self and society, he was a public moralist who furnished "solutions" as well as disturbing statements of the puzzles and mysteries. In the end, he had less to say about the ethics of economic competition than about the psychology of vocational pursuit. That may be because he wrote for the young man who wishes to be "placed where he belongs."[2] Emerson spoke, for example, of the lawyer whose "own merits" are on trial "as well as his client's," and who must be convinced of the rightness of his case in order to win the verdict. "If he does not believe it, his unbelief will appear to the jury . . . and become their unbelief."[3] Emerson offered hints of a world in which everyone is properly located, a world in

199

which truth conquers deceit and tawdriness. Here was an alternative to "this mendicant America, this curious, peering, itinerant, imitative America," to this world of "trade, entertainment, and gossip," to "our masquerade" with its "tambourines, laughter, and shouting." In these times as in others, he wrote, "we owe to genius always the same debt, of lifting the curtain from the common, and showing us that divinities are sitting disguised in the seeming gang of gypsies and pedlars."[4]

These initial quotations suggest Emerson's awareness of the mimicry, theatricality, and vagabondage of the new professional culture forming in his times. Other writers traveled further, perhaps, but none read more acutely the ways that the road was both the extender of civilization and its subverter. None was more deeply aware of how travelers in this new world—ministers, lecturers, colporteurs—were all showmen and hucksters as well. This was an issue that could be played with in great fun. But it raised serious anxieties about what kind of civilization was being built and what confidence might be placed in the respectability, the moral worth, of those who traveled through it.

Emerson's mature essays show a finely balanced recognition of both interdependence and limitation. Our movements are impeded by "the sheaths and clogs of organization," he wrote, and by "the web of relation." We are limited also by family history and by a "physiology" of politics, both as individuals and as peoples; and this destiny can be read in appearances. It is hopeless to try to reform away the "limitation," or "Fate," that separates the humble toiler from the prince or poet, that drives the imperial nations to plant themselves "on every shore and market of America and Australia," and that permits us all to look at faces and figures in order to decipher the character of those we meet. One criticism of America was that it substituted "superficialness" for the submission to Fate that gave depth to great religious systems from Hinduism to Calvinism. Yet scientific intellect could penetrate nature's causes, and energetic men could build cities and play "a part in colossal systems." The genuinely liberating stance was neither to succumb meekly to limitation nor sentimentally to ignore it. One might acknowledge "the cunning co-presence of two elements" and accept the reality of a "double consciousness." "A man may ride alternately on the horses of his private and public nature, as the equestrians in the circus throw themselves nimbly from horse to horse, or plant one foot on the back of one and the other foot on the back of the other."[5]

Emerson liked to play with polarities. His own life hinged on a tension between privacy and public commitments that has left his reputation in controversy. He can be read, and celebrated, as progenitor of a long tradition of campaigns for reform and civic improvement.[6] He can also be criticized for shrinking from the fray. By his own account, he had a stay-at-home disposition, which was justified and reinforced by his views of the limitations of fate.[7]

His public career virtually began with a famous act of resignation. After leaving Harvard College he had made an unpromising beginning as a teacher in a school for young women. Then he turned to divinity school in search of a suitable field for his inherited eloquence. He held an aborted missionary assignment to western Massachusetts before landing a position as a settled minister. Fortified by an inheritance and insurance payments from the death of his first wife, he resigned from his parish with a protest over the perpetuation of the rite of communion and with exciting dreams of establishing a magazine and launching a career in literature and philosophy.[8]

In his new life he became the best-known analyst of the great reform movements of his age. But his public writings frequently stressed his lack of obligation to act in concert with others; and his private conversation and journals underscored the feelings of isolation and reserve with which he declined to join the community at Brook Farm and similar ventures. Sometimes he berated the reformers' superficiality; sometimes he admitted he was simply not disposed to make a commitment. "Do not ask me to your philanthropies, charities, and duties, as you term them . . . ; I sit at home with the cause, grim or glad."[9]

There was a note of domestic seclusion even in his best-remembered theme of "self-reliance." In the great essay by that title, he criticized traveling as "a fool's paradise" of imitation and distraction, and therefore an impediment to self-culture.[10] As his fame grew, Emerson contrived what might be called a myth of Concord, the aptly named town where he made his home. He thought of it as a hermitage, his *petit hameau,* though it was convenient to Boston by railroad. In Concord he enjoyed a revolutionary heritage (he is the poet of "the shot heard round the world"). He was also a modern Prospero in a half-pastoral world with farmer neighbors, half-manor with wooded grounds (including Walden's shoreland) and intellectual companions to walk and talk and spar with. "The ornament of the place," he told Carlyle, "is the occasional presence of some ten or twelve persons, good and wise, who visit us in the course of the year."[11]

Yet he was also, in the terms we are exploring, a man of the road. Not only had he passed through the characteristically restless stages of a search for a hold on life; during that same period he had tried to reconcile Shakespearean drama with his Puritan heritage. Numerous notebook entries affirmed the familiar view that theatre corrupted morals; yet he continued to wonder whether drama could be refined so as to promote good morals. Why should Christian influence be restricted to "the silence of a book, or the cold soliloquy of an orator," when dramatic communication was so much more gripping? Theatre could be turned to good purposes when "the higher circles of the community" exercised leadership by withdrawing support from violent and prurient elements on the stage. But surely a personal ambition rested in the thought that "the only chance which America has for a truly national literature is to be found in the *Drama*." Here was a new "field of exertion" that would purify what had formerly been vicious, and at the same time, as he put it, "wake a note from the wild."[12]

Emerson experimented in his notebook with soliloquies and dialogue, though writing plays did not turn out to be his métier. He became one of the great lyceum stars of his era, and he inevitably viewed his art as at worst a kind of peddling and at best a form of theatre. On visits to Eastern lecture halls and long circuits through the Midwest he saw himself as peddling "intellectual notions" and the experience of trying to hold an audience as a good "test of the wares of a man of letters."[13] While deeply suspicious of "public opinion" (which supported Andrew Jackson as president and tolerated "the obscenities of the Boston theatre"), he was professionally obliged to bow to the view that "the people are always right (in a sense) . . . the man of letters is to say, these are the new conditions to which I must conform."[14]

For many decades the American theatre had combatted religious hostility by presenting Shakespearean tragedies in the guise of "lectures," thus laying claim to a respectable literary middle ground between vulgar entertainment and moral instruction.[15] That same territory Emerson found himself striving to occupy. He insisted on the lecturer's instructional purpose. The lecturer must not cater to the public by saying what they expected to hear but must ask instead "what discoveries or stimulating thoughts have I to impart to a thousand persons?" Thus he recast a lucrative pursuit, not as commercial theatre, but as "a new literature." Better still: "I look upon the Lecture room as the true church of today & as the home of a richer eloquence than Faneuil Hall or the Capitol ever knew." Part of the thrill of the lecture was democratic: it "addresses an assembly as mere human beings, no more"; it satisfied their needs and depended on their patronage.[16] The larger part stemmed from the originality and instructiveness of the speaker, who fixed on a point between the belletristic and the moral similar to that which had been anticipated in Emerson's youthful program to reform drama.

Emerson's most familiar message had to do with the importance of being self-reliant, a nonconformist, unafraid of solitude. The instructed listener should finally stand in the same relation to society as did the lecturer to the dictates of public opinion. To this day Emerson's invocations of an authentic inner strength remain inspiring to those worried about the restrictions that conventions may impose on their integrity (or, as we now say, identity). But what did Emerson's audiences hear him to be saying? There were frequent jokes about his big words and misty abstractions; some suggested that he succeeded by being incomprehensible and thereby convincing audiences that they were being exposed to something profound, if slightly beyond them. At least some of his audiences in the Ohio Valley, ambitious young clerks, commercial representatives, and other professionals, systematically misunderstood what he said. When he borrowed figures of speech from technology and commerce in order to convey the superiority of self-discovering and idealistic pursuits, they failed to hear anything that might call into question materialistic goals or singleminded professional aspirations. Whatever Emerson thought he was telling them, they heard a gospel of success. [17]

Whether Emerson was aware of this kind of misunderstanding is an interesting question. I know of no place where he discussed it, no example of his commenting on an inaccurate review. [18] Though he did not court misunderstanding, it is hard to see how such an incisive reader of character could have been unaware of it. What seems incontrovertible is Emerson's comfort in his status as a celebrity in America's republican culture. He affected no pose of unworthiness. He did not conceal his fame beneath Christian purpose or reformatory zeal. He did not play the rustic farmer surprised that a market existed for his words. He shunned roles affected by contemporaries who dealt awkwardly with their entrances on the stage of democratic competition. Instead, he found parallels between his own search for means of stating his truest insights before the public and the nation's need to reconcile economic progress and social fluidity with higher moral purpose. Self-drama merged into national drama, and in both instances the middle ground between new literature and old religion was the region of greatest promise.

Celebrity demanded travel, but he never forsook his garden and woods in Concord. Celebrity involved show, but always a show of hard thought and ethical struggle that meant there was something to be *shown*. Moreover, what made Emerson the most influential public moralist of the nineteenth century was his exploration of the burdens of travel and, even more crucial, of show as the great problem of the new era. In a modern world we inevitably read appearances to see what may be trusted behind them. Either there will be nothing there, as Melville intimated, or strong, inward, reliable, progressive tendencies might be on exhibit. The lecturer was both the means of posing the question of what was worthwhile in a calculating age and an emblem of the best imaginable answer. [19]

We find in serious thinkers of the nineteenth century many statements of the alienating consequences of the division of labor. The extension of markets seemed to contract the scope (though not the significance) of each person's work. We usually go to Fourier and to Marx and Engels for this analysis, but it is embedded in the writings of Tocqueville, whose hopes and fears differed so widely from the socialists'. [20] It also runs throughout Emerson's best-known essays like "The American Scholar" (1837), which began with the "old fable" that "the gods, in the beginning, divided Man into men." By the modern period of economic complexity, human capacity was "so minutely subdivided and peddled out" that the "members have suffered amputation from the trunk, and strut about so many walking monsters—a good finger, a neck, a stomach, an elbow, but never a man." Emerson continued in language reminiscent of the abolitionists' definition of slavery: "Man is thus metamorphosed into a thing, into many things." People became their parts and routines; *the whole* was forgotten. The obligation of the scholar was to reintegrate human nature and reanimate the Soul. The scholar must be a prophet of "self-trust," the attitude tying the individual to "eternal law" rather than narrow convention.[21]

This analysis was elaborated in many lectures of the late 1830s, just as Emerson was learning to profit from managing his own lecture series and as the financial panic gave him a bitter measure of the shortcomings of the so-called "higher circles" that conducted America's business.[22] Specialization and interdependence seemed inevitable and potentially beneficial, but without the cultivation of ennobling qualities in sufficiently large numbers of citizens there would be much to tremble at and not much to admire. While published essays like "American Scholar" showed a polished optimism, some unpublished lectures were disturbing jeremiads. "The Present Age," for example, took a dark view of society's capacity to adjust to change. "External freedom" (that is, emancipation of individuals and classes from economic and political restraints) had fostered commerce and opened markets.

> The age may be well characterized as the era of Trade. . . . It perforates the world with roads. The old bonds of language, country, and king give way to the new connexions of trade. It destroys patriotism and substitutes cosmopolitanism. . . . It mingles all nations in its marts. . . . We have the beautiful costume of the Hindoo, the Chinese, and the Turk in our streets. Our domestic labor is done by the African. Our trench dug by the Irish. . . . The Indian squaw sells mats at our doors. And all contrasts which commerce so fast abolishes are brought within a holiday excursion of more softness and refinement than was in Syria or Rome. . . .

A fair enough vision for most listeners, if that were all Emerson chose to say (and if you were not the African or Irishman whom he glides over so quickly). What he proceeded to emphasize, however, was "the bribe of wealth" accompanying this revolution. The prospect of getting rich led to singlemindedness, unscrupulousness, even "insanity and suicide." It tempted "men of genius" to be faithless to the duty of "imparting their own word" and lowered them to "gratifying the public taste."[23]

Meditating on the manners and goals of the most advantaged classes in a democratic society, Emerson returned again and again to the need for great men. When he spoke of the larger needs of society as a whole, the keyword was *culture*. In order to understand his response to the posturings of the "era of trade," we must look closely at his views of decorum and self-trust, of greatness, and of culture. These are the topics to which I now turn.[24]

His views were often ambiguous. "We are dealing with a mind," according to one of his most discerning interpreters, "that makes any assertion of belief against the felt pull of its lurking opposite."[25] He asserted, in some respects, the superiority of the life of the civilized American "with a watch, a pencil, and a bill of exchange in his pocket" to that of the primitive hunter of New Zealand.[26] Yet Plato's philosophy and Plutarch's biographies remained a lasting rebuke to any confidence in human progress. With respect to health and faith, the primitive's condition might be preferable. The man of the market had lost all spontaneity. He trusted neither himself nor others.

The most telling comparison was not with the ancients or savages but with aristocratic classes of the pre-revolutionary era. Consider his troubled words on modern manners: "The congregation of men into large masses and the universal facility of communication with metropolitan refinement and opinion has had the effect of grinding off the asperities of individual character, introducing the dominion of fashion"; these forces had substituted "an universal regard to decorum for the sinews of virtue and intellect." He conceded that decorum had some good results: there was more widespread temperance in speech and behavior. But did the democratization of manners have any depth?

> Decorum is the undress of virtue. Decorum is a shadow or imitation of virtue and where virtue is not, this pantomime can very well be performed by every ordinary person. . . . decorum answers to the eye of the public the purpose of virtue or wisdom. . . . This is productive of much comfort. . . . It is a great convenience, like a good road or a steamboat.

Decorum was superficial when compared to the virtue that smaller numbers of gentlemen adhered to in an earlier era. "Everybody has enough breeding to entitle him to reap the benefit" of the "general convention" of decorum. "Go where you will there is hardly a churl in society." But in this "general levelling" there were no more "heroic manners."[27]

In reading Beaumont and Fletcher's tragedies, Emerson was struck by "the constant recognition of gentility, as if a noble behavior were as easily marked in the society of their age, as color in our American population." No introduction or proof was required: "When any Rodrigo, Pedro, or Valerio enters, though he be a stranger, the duke or governor exclaims, This is a gentleman,—and proffers civilities without end."[28] In linking high birth with noble behavior, Emerson overlooked much duplicity and intrigue in these plays. He also failed to see that the codes of dress and behavior once identifying gentlemen were as artificial as those signaling decorum in his day. For what he preferred to emphasize about a gentleman was unselfconscious honor: "You cannot persuade yourself that he would act differently if there were no spectators of his conduct." He appeared to have "no root" in the world, no selfish interest to promote, only a deeply ingrained attachment to certain forms of action and "disrelish" for certain others.[29] If Emerson had stopped with these observations, we might dismiss him as another illusion-ridden Federalist living in pre-revolutionary fantasy and thrashing against the direction of his times. But he did not settle for facile resolutions of his search for a truer basis of behavior to supersede the pantomime of manners in an "era of trade."

His calls for self-trust inspired his countrymen for generations to come. They may be read for premonitions of twentieth-century praise of "good faith" in ethical relations.[30] To locate Emerson in the conversation of his times, however, notice what he did *not* say. He did not have much to say about the family, and he put no hope in voluntary institutions and social pressures. He was not interested in learned behavior and "habits of the heart." He was unimpressed by shows of decorum, no matter how deeply ingrained were the habits that sustained these shows. What distinguished Emerson was the severity of his invocations to the self to place trust and reliance in itself. His famous calls to earnestness and sincerity can lead off into self-canceling circles of negation. He commends the reformer's original-ity, for example, but warns his listener that there is no virtue in bowing to a reform society's guilt-mongering influence at the cost of one's own priori-ties.[31] Emerson is not a moralist, then, who offers help in deciding what to do. For him, motive is all.

His lectures and essays on the individual suggest one respect in which the primitive hunter is better off than the civilized trader—proximity to instinct and nature. It would be a mistake, however, to exaggerate Emer-son's interest in the wild man.[32] For the most part, these contrasts under-scored a critique of the dramatized aspects of behavior in a commercial society. At much greater length he took up the language of Platonic philoso-phy, Eastern religions, and Romantic literature—the source was not cru-cial, and his audiences did not always follow him—in order to reveal a sense of authentic life growing up in the midst of what he termed a "world of shows."[33]

At one level, he recognized, "spectacles" and exhibitions may have socially convenient results. The individual imitates and learns. Love of the theatrical may also spark dissatisfaction with routine and a thirst for examples of bolder self-expression. It may even, at a deeper level, incite a wish to penetrate the façade of society and nature to glimpses of eternal truth. The existence of such truth was a given; whether it could really be attained might be an open question. In an age of "reflection" and "introversion," people were so conscious of history, sect, and movement that it might be impossible to do more than approximate the direct experience of the savage. "We take no leaps in the dark," he said. "We have intention in action; intention in manners; intention in discourse; intention even in thought." Far more than most moral critics of routine, Emerson makes it difficult to see how one could break out of the circles of learning and imitation. The "otherism" that besets society may be ineradicable.[34]

At times Emerson was willing to enumerate aids to escape. One was the famous walk in the woods celebrated in *Nature* (1836). "The tradesman, the attorney comes out of the din and craft of the street and sees the sky and the woods, and is a man again." Though we may think of the woods as only semi-natural and the walk itself as at least as "intentional" as those behaviors he discounted, the important points for him were the direct experience ("I become a transparent eyeball") and unconfined thoughts ("Man is conscious of a universal soul within or behind his individual life").[35] More generally, there were uses in any solitude, as gained by "two expedients" he recommended—to sit alone in a chamber reserved for yourself at whatever cost, and to keep a journal in order to render "account to yourself of yourself" on a rigorous and regular basis.[36] Literature, especially poetry, was another help. A repeated theme in Emerson's journal is the need for "a genuine poet of our time, no parrot and no child."[37] Some forms of influence are less self-defeating than others: "Literature," he explained, "is a point outside of our hodiernal circle through which a new one may be described. The use of literature is to afford us a platform whence we may command a view of our present life, a purchase by which we may move it."[38] Reading books is self-improving so long as we do not consume them to make others think more highly of us or use them as surrogates for experience.

The poet was only a special instance of a class of nonsolitary expedients: we must be open to recognition of great men. Here was the outcome of Emerson's meditation on democratic pantomime and the demise of heroic action. It was a commonplace of advice manuals that in building a good character the young man should emulate models of successful living.[39] Such was *not* the influence of the great on the tentative that Emerson had in mind. The need for great men was not to aid a life in its ordinary passages, but to encourage self-trust. The Great were "sincere" in much the same way as gentlemen once were noble. To them, "all circumstances" are "indifferent."[40] They confront the deepest questions of an age without calculation of profit or popularity. Their eloquent words and deeds pierce "the superficial crusts of condition which discriminate man from man." They are "representative," not in some sense of averageness or clientship, but because in a world where most people "resemble their contemporaries" they embody an idea and come to stand for an expanded awareness of human powers. Goethe and Napoleon, the major recent examples, were "both representatives of the impatience and reaction of nature against the *morgue* of conventions"; they "set the axe at the root of the tree of cant and seeming, for this time, and for all time."[41] Their admirable effect was not to create slavish followings but rather to inspire others to break the crust and rely on themselves.

The subject of heroes raised many unanswered questions. The distinction between servile and inspired patterns of emulation may not be tenable.[42] When Emerson imagines the emergence of "a great salesman; then a road-contractor," as well as great scientists and generals, we may wonder whether great men really could have the effect of controlling materialistic excesses and undercutting oppressive public opinion. For Emerson, however, the critical issue was to improve the goals and character of the upper middle classes, and the influence of great men was serviceable as part of a wider campaign for what he called culture.

That may be Emerson's greatest historical importance: he was the decisive advocate of notions of culture that gained luster in the late nineteenth century because of their relevance to concerns about materialism, class conflict, and national purpose.[43] In old age, he became a representative man in this ideology, celebrated for his advocacy of literature, his cosmopolitan learning, his appreciation of nature, and his calls for self-reliance. In his own thought in the antebellum years when he flourished as a lecturer and essayist, culture was the "lurking opposite" that pulled against his assertions concerning nature and self-reliance. I speak of opposition where Emerson apparently saw no inconsistency: "His own culture,—the unfolding of his nature, is the chief end of man."[44] It was nevertheless his view of culture that kept his critique of decorum and trade from turning to primitivism or atomistic individualism. It turned what otherwise might have been a strain of cranky Augustan complaint into an engaging corpus of moral criticism.

His exposition of "the Doctrine of Culture" began with concern over the "quackery" and discontent of the times. In his ideal economy, all citizens will find their proper individual callings, without going into debt, without pretension, without envy. Ultimately, "the entire working people of the earth" will see honor in their distinctive "arts" and will regard themselves as interdependent votaries of nature. "A truth which flows directly from the ideal view of the vocations is the honorableness of labor"; truly admirable societies do not promote "the fatal pride of idleness." But Emerson stopped short of idealizing manual labor, and his most telling sentences referred to insecurities of the young professional classes: "although young men whose friends are in a situation to set them up in business may do well, yet a young man without capital cannot honestly get a livelihood by tràde in our cities. Integrity would be a disqualification." The argument that "the highest culture comes from what we do" is not really a call to working with the hands; it is more a cry that a reasonable vocational order is a preliminary requirement for culture.[45]

Culture, viewed in relation to work, is a matter of hierarchy. Each craftsman's mind assigns the most "dignity and beauty" to the tasks "in which Culture is an end." "Hence the professions are more esteemed than the mechanic trades," and those who pursue "the especial purpose of getting laws and general results, as the chemist," enjoy even greater honor. In such a view, eventually the scientist or business executive who grasps a trade at a deeper or more general level will rank more highly in terms of culture than the person who carries out a specialized subdivision of the world's work.[46]

We cannot follow Emerson much further in these speculations joining work and culture, because in other writings, culture opposes the American preoccupation with work. If the 1837–1838 "Human Culture" lectures were concerned with quackery and opportunity, in an 1841 lecture, "The Method of Nature," he took an extreme position against all "routine." He professed respect for technology and industry, but only in the initial "act of invention" was there an "intellectual step" consistent with human potential. All the rest was "mere repetition," forms of role-playing that dehumanized everyone: laborers, clerks, managers, and scholars. Though this lecture hinted at the strongest of social criticisms—"Let there be worse cotton and better men"—a rejection of all forms of repetition left little to admire.[47] And in "Culture" (1851), he nearly dropped the language of craftsmanship, and his critique now applied directly to a business civilization in which the individual was defined by the skill that made him successful. The individual harped on only one string of personality, losing sight of many capabilities and, at the same time, exaggerating his own "weight in the system." It was an instance of "*chorea*": the person "turns round and continues to spin slowly on one spot." Alternatively it was a case of the "goitre of egotism," a characteristic disease of the modern economy.[48]

The individual, watching himself in a private mirror, limited the topics he thought about, the identities he assumed, and the townsmen he met in conversation. He was trapped by vanity. The use of culture was therapeutic: "The antidotes against this organic egotism are the range and variety of attractions, as gained by acquaintance with the world, with men of merit, with classes of society, with travel, with eminent persons, and with the high resources of philosophy, art and religion; books, travel, society, solitude." In addition to the medical metaphor, this man with a poor ear adopted one from music:

> Culture is the suggestion, from certain best thoughts, that a man has a range of affinities through which he can modulate the violence of any master-tones that have a droning preponderance in his scale, and succor him against himself. Culture redresses his balance, puts him among his equals and superiors, revives the delicious sense of sympathy and warns him of the dangers of solitude and repulsion.[49]

Emerson may seem to contradict earlier assertions about travel and solitude. Perhaps he does. Travel now seems beneficial; solitude, less so. But he still criticized Americans who toured Europe for the wrong reasons, and he continued to value solitude as an aid to a more highly developed moral nature. Nevertheless, we can understand how some business-minded listeners heard this lecture as unthreatening to their social aspirations. The essay may contain the outlines of a "culture industry" that furnished the acquisitions with which the professional classes could play roles as people of greater worth than others, not because they made more money, but because of their taste in reading, art, and, yes, travel. It is a far cry from an ideology for a world at work; it even approaches an ideology of conspicuous consumption, not of garish material things, but of refined thoughts. "I like people who like Plato," he says without apparent irony, because "this love does not consist with self-conceit."[50]

Emerson's conception of culture remained ambiguous on one point: he persistently discussed culture as an issue of individual growth, yet he clearly was concerned with its benefits to an interdependent society. "A reference to society is part of the idea of culture," he wrote in "Aristocracy" (1848). We may feel that he was willing in the later essays to compromise earlier goals and settle for mixed blessings—that is, for displays of etiquette and knowledge. The person who is well read and well traveled, who can discuss art and philosophy, may be more complete than the one whose vision is circumscribed by shop or office, but we may doubt that he will have all the qualities associated with rigorous journal-keeping and transparent encounters with nature. Perhaps the point to be stressed, however, is Emerson's rigorous effort to interpret the popular interest in gentlemanly manners as a hopeful sign for the future of democracy. He continued to deplore "fashion" and puppetlike decorum. He tried to reformulate the vision of an aristocracy based on merit; indeed, he had carefully chosen words of favor for Hindu castes, European chivalry, and other systems of inequality, even chattel slavery. There was hierarchy in nature, and society wished to honor it and to believe in its hereditary transmission. Yet in the nineteenth century, greatness must rely on "the good sense of the people." Sorely lacking was a "grand style of culture" that would delineate for "the feeling of the most ingenious and excellent youth in America" the steps by which they might pursue nonmaterialistic, nonutilitarian distinction. To be sure, he hinted at the existence of an invisible coterie of "the few" who seek "for their own sake . . . universal beauty and worth." Almost inevitably in the lecture format, however, Emerson listed what we admire in *all* those who aspire to culture: talent, imagination, elevated sentiment, self-reliance. Those who lacked these signs of distinction would defer to those who exhibited them. Those who merited preeminence, for their part, would maintain "some access to the heart of common humanity."[51]

We may wish to emphasize more open-ended and less hierarchical qualities of his later remarks on culture. It is a question of balance. Although he had less to say on the "honorableness" of manual labor, he offered a more elastic definition of culture for many who endeavored to improve themselves. He knew that the emergence of the best requires large numbers of the good; it takes "a great many cultivated women," for example, "in order that you should have one Madame de Stael." For all his praise of solitude, he was critical of American selfishness: "it is the secret of culture to interest the man more in his public than in his private quality."[52]

In the end, culture defined a circle in which several classes of Americans could join together. It pointed beyond the social conflicts of the past when "furious democracy" rejected "men of mark,"[53] and when the privileged classes decried upstarts, by giving to all the goal of cultivating their faculties and creating a more admirable America. The scope of American life was enlarged by the late 1840s; young men like those who once peddled in Virginia were now settling in Oregon or California. Emerson worried that the scope of the imagination might be narrowing as business became all-consuming. So his notion of culture became less individualistic, more harmonious and organic. It encouraged successful, mobile Americans to devote more time to programs of refinement. In place of hierarchy, Emerson envisioned an America given a new sense of purpose by the cultivated classes.

Some of Emerson's dicta on culture foreshadowed themes in late—nineteenth-century glorification of literature and the fine arts. Contrast with the walk in the woods this description of the walk amid works of art: "The mere passing through a gallery opens and educates the eye. The comparison of many forms drawn from the best thought and highest imagination of many cultivated painters enriches us by teaching the power of form. We have in sculpture and in painting now in the world more noble form than the eye ever saw in actual nature."[54] Passages like this one permitted a truncation of meaning similar to that which occurred to Matthew Arnold's famous definition of culture as "getting to know . . . the best that has been thought and said in the world." As Raymond Williams pointed out, Arnold actually called for "the re-examination of 'stock notions and habits' " and the pursuit of perfection in the individual and society. But his remarks are still usually abbreviated to suggest that acquaintance is sufficient; thus, culture equals exposure to art or the acquisition and display of good taste.[55] A similar truncation sometimes occurred in the reception of Emerson's views, and indeed I contend that he partly invited it. But only partly. Emerson's thinking about "the world of shows" was tense and ambiguous, but even in his most optimistic and democratic public statements he expected culture to undermine the individual's self-conscious calculations and to exert a reformatory influence on society.

As Emerson traveled from pulpit to lecture hall, he had sought a middle ground where self-drama merged with national drama. The ambiguities of culture show that this middle ground was always elusive. Emerson once complained that his audiences were pleased to think of his lectures as literary but were "shocked" by his insistence that his true subject was religion.[56] We are left, then, with the ironic futility of the lecturer's profession: he had to speak in many voices, and his performance was encircled by an audience who heard what they paid to hear. While he peddled inspiration, the result may have been the entrenchment of social convention.

PART FIVE

Modernity

People in a very large country, . . . people whose
communication is shared work, not shared speech, in
fact so self-conscious about their speech they needed
persuading (by Mencken, in the 1920s) that they *had* a
spoken idiom; people inheriting the possibility that one
might spend six months in one's cabin without sighting
anyone fit to be spoken to; people who find nothing
strange in the life style of Thoreau, who throve on the
self-containment that drove Robinson Crusoe nearly
mad; people whose sages almost within living memory
shuttled from lecture platform to lecture platform, and
who spend more of their lives listening to
schoolteachers than any other people in the world, and
who are addressed all their lives as *audiences* by the
politician, the columnist, the barber; people who did
not grow up anywhere near the neighbors they have at
present, and approach them (when necessary, about a
dog or a lawnmower) with embarrassed colloquial
ceremony: such people find it easier on the whole to
shape their emotions to the abstract or the inanimate.

—HUGH KENNER, *A Homemade World*

CHAPTER TWENTY

Against the Current

All Americans had "a lively faith in human perfectibility," according to Alexis de Tocqueville. "They think that the spread of enlightenment must necessarily produce useful results and that ignorance must have fatal effects; all think of society as a body progressing; they see humanity as a changing picture in which nothing either is or ought to be fixed forever; and they admit that what seems good to them today may be replaced tomorrow by something better that is still hidden." We might disagree with Tocqueville that *all* Americans shared any single faith. But if we modify his statement appropriately, so that it refers to civic-minded Americans like those he and Fredrika Bremer conversed with or those who attended Ralph Waldo Emerson's lectures, it is an excellent description of an outlook among Americans that was strikingly modern.[1] This outlook was unhampered by tradition, flexible, and progressive. It was confident of the powers of education and intellect and looked forward to continuous social improvement as the great benefit of democracy. But very little was required to turn flexibility into doubt and to turn faith in the flow of progress into a picture of humanity drifting forever in a sea of uncertainty.

To the pastlessness, mobility, and masquerade of the post-revolutionary decades I would like to add elements of modernity, defined in terms of both progressive improvement and uncertainty of conviction. To offer any argument about what is "modern" is to venture onto treacherous ground. The word has no precise meaning, and over time its connotations have changed.

Once it simply meant "currently existing," and at times it has signified being "up-to-date" or even "modish."² Many uses of the word refer to a sense of history in which recent times differ qualitatively from all that went before. This qualitative difference might be good or bad: in the nineteenth century to call something "modern" was usually to confer praise, but in the twentieth century the term conveys more awareness of loss and ambiguity. In the past few decades writers have become increasingly alert to the fleeting-ness of meanings of all words, and definitions of the word *modern*, and such cognates as "modernization" and "modernism," have figured prominently in controversies in almost every corner of intellectual life. It has gotten harder, not easier, to find a core meaning of modernity as these controversies swirl.³

Frequently it is assumed that the onset of modernity, whatever it means, came in the early twentieth century. December 1911 is a favorite date because that is when Virginia Woolf said that "human character changed,"⁴ but other dates—1905, 1913, 1922—also have their advocates. It will occur to many readers that this kind of specificity is most defensible with regard to literary and artistic movements such as those known as "modern-ism." It is much more difficult to assign dates to broad tendencies in American culture; nevertheless, Americans have shown recurrent and unde-niable interest in searching for a watershed in their history and demarcating when the modern era began. In the most famous scholarly effort to locate the "dividing line" between "a completely vanished world" and "our own time," Henry F. May selected the pre–World War I years, 1912 to 1917.⁵ Other scholars favor earlier dates: George Cotkin, for example, has uncovered in the last two decades of the nineteenth century signs of the challenges to past authority and acceptance of ceaseless change that are associated with moder-nity.⁶ My contention is that we can undertake this kind of expedition earlier in time: we will find signposts leading to modernity in American culture from Tocqueville's day onward.

Before proceeding, we must delineate some of the characteristics that have been called "modern." The task is difficult because competing intellec-tual and political movements have offered their own definitions. So many purposes crisscross in the contest to define modernity—how to improve society; how to appreciate art; how to justify faith; how to study the United States, Europe, the world—that a core definition is bound to be elusive. Since every definition includes elements of criticism and programs of recon-struction, none can be used without skepticism as a description of historical reality. Perhaps the most influential definition, at least until recently, was a historical one introduced by the Enlightenment and still familiar in college curricula and daily parlance. By dividing the past into three parts—ancient, medieval, and modern—Enlightenment savants were able to celebrate the release of human reason after centuries of tyranny and superstition. The

Enlightenment itself was complex: many prophets of progress found virtues in ancient times that they sought to revive after ages of suppression.[7] Today, most scholars recognize that this tripartite system, even in its most complex versions, skews the history of the Mediterranean world and Europe and ignores the past of most of the world's peoples; still, many retain it as a system of values that upholds human rationality and social progress. But in contemporary polemics, some critics of modernity repudiate the Enlightenment, assail "the new dark ages" we live in, and seek in their own way to recover and fortify vestiges of classical truth or religious tradition.

Several of the most important uses of the word *modern* in today's intellectual life substitute a two-stage understanding of history for the Enlightenment's drama in three acts. Planners and politicians, artists and intellectuals, have announced that the really decisive divergence from the past took place, not in the Enlightenment, but in much more recent times. They may build on a widely held popular feeling, described by David Lowenthal as "the notion of a timeless past until recently devoid of change, save for trivial or cyclic operations."[8] In any event, specialists on "modernization" tell us that, after a long, undifferentiated past, society experienced a radical break, and nothing has been the same ever since. Both society and the individual may have benefited; from this viewpoint, it still makes sense to speak of secular progress. But the severing of connections with the past has undermined common beliefs and fixed convictions. Specialists in "modernity" may exemplify the latter point by arguing that the three-part schema reflected nothing more than a human penchant for making up narratives with a beginning, middle, and end. History possesses no meaningful pattern; there are only human constructions made of words. This claim is itself often presented self-consciously as characteristic of a new, modern understanding of the human condition. After an almost endless past defined by contrived movements and ideologies, the human race has now set forth on a new adventure, one that may perhaps lead nowhere.[9]

As a first step toward unraveling these complexities, let us return to one of the key words of post–World War II social science: *modernization*. As we noticed in Chapter Sixteen, in an endeavor to understand and then eradicate differences between poor, "third-world" nations and those with more "advanced" economies in Europe and North America, economists popularized the idea of a once-only transformation that all nations could—and perhaps must—pass through. Economic "growth" took place in stages and spurts, in rocketlike "take-offs" rather than in slow accretions over centuries. Modernization was a process related to urbanization, industrialization, and several other *-ization* words that signify how historical change can reorganize people's lives. It usually meant thrift and planning, lower birthrates, faster transportation, time-discipline in the workplace, restrictions on the claims of tradition and community, acceptance of variation and change. Although changes in work, sex, play, and every other aspect of life might require painful adjustments, the process marked the route to the supposed good things of complex, advanced societies. [10]

The term *modernization* also proved attractive in historical study of Western societies, where it prompted keener and more systematic interest in sexual and economic behavior. A survey of family history, taking most of its examples from French history, observes that throughout the nineteenth century, antiquarians in every town and village meticulously recorded local manners, lore, and customs. (We took note of their American counterparts in Chapter Six.) These accounts assumed "a historical changelessness from the days of the Druids until the days of their fathers, whereupon 'the great decline of folklore' began." In fact, says the historian Edward Shorter, the early folklorists were right: "The machinery of modernization was grinding traditional society into piecemeal" by the end of the nineteenth century. "Modernization meant the dissolution" of a familiar "structured, changeless, compact traditional order," and while the process took place at different times in different places, "sooner or later the Great Transformation would take hold everywhere." [11]

The concept of modernization inspired landmark studies of transformation in Europe, the Middle East, and Asia, as well as brilliant scholarship on social change, often at the local level, in the United States. For a while it promised to reveal an entirely new synthesis of American history, one that embedded that history in universal human experience. [12] One talented historian told me that he showed his students that all the histories of all nations could be diagrammed in exactly the same way. If you ignored superficial changes of politics and disease, weather and war, and got down to the fundamental level of economics and demography, you could describe past centuries by one straight horizontal line across the chalkboard. Then you could draw an upward movement of the line, the "transition" from traditional to modern society; and then, another straight, unvarying line as modernized behavior stretches onward into the future. This was partly a joke. I don't think any historian ever really believed that the history of any society could be conveyed by three straight lines. But even the subtlest scholars, who went beyond economic indicators and studied the emergence of a modern personality, were apt to categorize almost all of human history as "traditional" and to assert that most people in the past resembled today's peasants, who "either do not think about the future or else feel that the future will be the same as the past." Then came, or will come, "the revolution in values" that makes change seem normal and rational planning and behavioral change seem desirable or at least unavoidable. [13]

Even scholars who cling to the notion of traditional timelessness would have to recognize that the transition to modern times in Europe and North America had stages peculiarly its own. In the twentieth century it is increasingly obvious that modernized societies will go through further transitions, some of them dramatic and disturbing. At some point an emphasis on thrift may give way to a thirst for consumption. Birthrates may sink below the point where couples are planning for their offspring's welfare and are instead unwilling to sacrifice their own pleasures. Economic growth may give way to stagnation compounded of lack of thrift, lack of foresight, and lack of risk. I haven't yet seen the term "post-modernization," but "post-industrialism" has already been around for a long time. [14]

"Modernization" may be one of those faddish terms whose day is past. It had obvious virtues for social and economic planners, who attempted to apply lessons learned from the history of affluent societies to poorer ones. But poverty too often resisted planning, and the free economic market now fires the imaginations of post–Cold War dreamers. Among historians, the term's limitations have drawn increasing attention: too much historical change escapes our attention if we lump together so much of the human past as "traditional." In any case, the notion of a once-only change really does not make much sense in American history, in which modernization has been playing itself out ever since the first migrations from Europe. Historians need critical detachment from the tendency of each generation of Americans to regard their age as one in which the old ways were lost. Historians should have second thoughts about treating any of the periods of American history, incredibly short periods by standards of historical enterprise elsewhere, as the one in which traditional forms of community life disintegrated and modern forms of social organization made their appearance. [15]

So let us retain the term *modernization* only in a very broad sense as "a process of social and economic development, involving the rise of industry, technology, urbanization, and bureaucratic institutions," with some attendant changes in personal character and social relations, "that can be traced back as far as the seventeenth century." [16] That means that modernization encompasses all of American history. Although it suggests analogies that help explain some attitudes that travelers observed in post-revolutionary America, such as the protean facility with roles, belief in progressive improvement, or feelings that the past was receding and convictions were temporary, it is of only the most general use in interpreting the events of a particular era.

Let us look more closely at another term: *modernism*. [17] This word has been made to ring throughout the academies by literary critics who apply it to Kafka, Joyce, Proust, Pound, and other major authors of the early twentieth century. Art historians use the same name for avant-garde artists of the same era. The name that fits Pablo Picasso, Kazimir Malevich, and Henry

Moore is used, in music, for Igor Stravinsky, Béla Bartók, and Charles Ives. It has similar uses in other arts, from architecture to pottery; whether it can be used intelligibly for science and other "cognitive" fields is an open question.[18] Interest in modernism has intensified in recent years with the claim that the modernist age is over, passé, and that we have entered the era of "postmodernism."

Although modernism can be defined formally, with reference to stylistic characteristics in the various arts, it can also be defined historically as an endeavor to break decisively with the past. While recognizing the existence of previous revolutions in art, the critic Herbert Read championed modern art on the basis that it was not simply a "turning point" or "turning over" but was instead "a break-up . . . some would say a dissolution. . . . the aim of five centuries of European effort is openly abandoned." No historical parallel was pertinent to this "abrupt break with all tradition." A more cautious critic, Lionel Trilling, called attention to "the bitter line of hostility to civilization" that ran through "modern" literature.[19] A similar observation will apply in any field where we hope to detect "modernism": severe condemnation and subversion of the efforts of centuries, if not all time.

In spite of the defiantly experimental and futuristic outlook of many modernists, there was a past for which they were often advocates: the past of folk-memory or traditional consciousness that the contemporary world threatened to eradicate. Impulses to revolt against regnant cultural standards and to regenerate society created a fascination with the primitive, exotic, and repressed.[20] In this respect, "modernism" was a repudiation of modernization; it called for a return to a timeless past that modernization supposedly had shattered. "The modern is acutely conscious of the contemporary scene," Stephen Spender wrote, "but he does not accept its values."[21] Trilling also situated modern literature in opposition to "the culture of democratic-capitalist industrialism and to that culture's dissolution of certain traditional roles, modes of life, personnels, qualities of art."[22]

Perhaps because the modernist stance is so contradictory—hostile to certain aspects of past and future, embracing others; fiercely individualistic, nostalgically communal; anti-industrial, yet fascinated by technology—it is difficult for scholars to use the term without confusion. The writer Malcolm Bradbury warns us that we must accept the existence of "many Modernisms."[23] In literary studies, there are debates over whether modernism was only a late version of Romanticism and whether the various versions of postmodernism have really broken free of the modernist aesthetic. "The old culture is wobbling," writes Daniel Singal, "but its successor is still not here."[24]

Even if it could be used clearly in other contexts, the label *modernist* is problematical in American studies. Singal has demonstrated how useful the term can be in analyses of early—twentieth-century American writers who deplored the middle-class social attitudes that we today often describe as "Victorian" and the attitudes toward literary and artistic refinement that had come to be associated with "culture." But their essential spirit may be found in the 1855 preface to Whitman's *Leaves of Grass*, which condemns lives of excessive prudence as "the great fraud upon modern civilization."[25] Do we, then, call Whitman a modernist? (Gertrude Stein gave the opinion that "the United States had the first instance of what I call Twentieth Century writing. You see it first in Walt Whitman."[26]) And what do we make of the Transcendentalists, in whose poetry the literary historian Perry Miller found "prognostications of a revolution, if not indeed the first victories of modernism"?[27] The most fascinating interpretation of American modernist writers, Hugh Kenner's *A Homemade World*, suggests that the modernist outlook is nearly traditional in America, with all its transiency, its dramatic talk, its recognition that "language may be less a heritage than a code."[28] It is possible that "modernism" includes so much that it gives no more help than "modernization" in understanding social change and intellectual expression over the past two centuries in the United States.

Now consider *modernity,* a term currently fashionable to designate where modern society and especially intellectual life have gone wrong, how they left secure moorings, in some versions, in Hellenic philosophy and, in others, in the neo-Hellenic past of the Founding Fathers. When Nietzsche described *Beyond Good and Evil* (1885) as "in all essential points . . . a criticism of *modernity,*" he repudiated Christian morality as well as scientific objectivity; he sought to destroy "quite simply everything that has hitherto been called truth."[29] Yet when Allan Bloom's *The Closing of the American Mind,* the astonishing bestseller of 1987, assailed "modernity," Nietzsche was the chief culprit, because he toppled the foundations of philosophical certitude, loosened the moorings of language, and challenged all traditional modes of authority. Bloom professed considerable respect for Nietzsche, who tried to face the consequences of "the decay of culture" with resolution, at least, and courage; America's professors and students in the 1980s—who were Bloom's real targets—coped all too comfortably without philosophic truth, religious faith, or firm respect for constitutional principles. They spoke glibly of "values" derived from the "self," while, as Bloom portrayed them, tuning into the mindless eroticism of rock music and drifting exhaustedly from fad to fad, victims of the loss of tradition and the disrespect for authority endemic in "democratic relativism."[30]

Alasdair MacIntyre's *After Virtue* was not a bestseller, but it is more soundly reasoned and more impressive to students of history and philosophy. It, too, indicts "modernity" as an agent of deplorable changes, corrosive of traditions. It speaks, for example, of "the way in which modernity partitions each human life into a variety of segments" and of "the relegation of art by modernity to the status of an essentially minority activity and interest." *After Virtue* shares some things with *Closing of the American Mind*, including recurrent references to Nietzsche as "*the* moral philosopher of the present age" and a more general view that failures of philosophy were the "key episodes" in the fragmentation and displacement of morality in social life.[31] But the differences are major: MacIntyre, for example, shows no sign of Bloom's devotion to timeless Platonic verities or of Bloom's belief that American intellectual life was thrown off course by emigrating German academics of the 1930s or by university radicals of the 1960s. His argument is not narrowly about America, and for the most part it takes no stand on recent issues in national or university politics. He certainly leaves no doubt that he dislikes many aspects of contemporary life—among them, the manipulativeness of social science and the managerial style of modern institutions, the therapeutic emphasis on the individual self, the severance of politics from shared tradition, the profusion of viewpoints that makes the resolution of moral discussion impossible, the absence of "community" and "moral consensus"—and he concludes with a bleak picture of withdrawal from the general society and the construction of "local forms of community" that may be sustained through "the new dark ages."[32] Most of his complaint, however, centers on wrong turns in moral philosophy taken during the Enlightenment.

At the core of his argument, MacIntyre contends that early modern thinkers wrongly repudiated the "moral tradition" that extended from Aristotle to Aquinas. This tradition recognized a "true end" for human beings— an essence, a *telos*—that it was the purpose of community institutions, including the science of ethics, to foster and bring to realization. With this tradition in ruins, the philosophers of the Enlightenment (especially Kant) had to undertake their project of trying to discover "new rational secular foundations for morality." That project, in MacIntyre's view, failed; all attempts to ground morality in human needs and intuitions were exposed by Nietzsche and a host of "existentialist and emotivist successors" as shams and delusions, as faulty attempts to drape statements about human wishes ("I *want* to do this" or "I *want* you to do that") with trappings of ethical obligation ("I *ought* to do this" or "it is your *duty* to do that"). Thus we are left with no alternative to the moral chaos of "modernity" unless a "premodern view of morality and politics is . . . vindicated . . . in *something like* Aristotelian terms."[33]

I do not mean to imply that the importance of *After Virtue* is merely illustrative. Throughout this book I have been influenced by its analysis. Clearly, MacIntyre has elevated discussion of issues both of substance and of method that are of burning importance to many moderns.[34] But I do take him as representing at its most serious a contemporary tendency to define "modernity" by repudiation and with the purpose of recovering something that modernity left behind.

Not all works that represent this tendency join Bloom and MacIntyre in resorting to classical philosophy for alternatives to modern failings, although there is today a strain of conservative complaint that classical and biblical elements in traditional American republicanism have been eroded by "modern individualism." Sometimes the complaint assumes an idealized nineteenth-century community where moral truths were clearer and moral living was easier. According to the widely read *Habits of the Heart* by Robert Bellah and associates: "Perhaps the crucial change in American life has been that we have moved from the local life of the nineteenth century— in which economic and social relationships were visible and, however imperfectly, morally interpreted as parts of a larger common life—to a society vastly more interrelated and integrated economically, technically, and functionally."[35]

The critique of modernity is not the exclusive property of conservatism. *The Communist Manifesto* called attention to the "everlasting uncertainty and agitation [that] distinguish the bourgeois epoch from all earlier ones." In modern times, "all fixed, fast-frozen relations, with their train of ancient and venerable prejudices and opinion, are swept away, all new-formed ones become antiquated before they can ossify."[36] In fact, complaints about "the crisis of modernity" transcend conventional political labels. The left as well as the right may attack Nietzsche, exalt community, and deplore any suggestion that language is inexact or that truth changes. Both left and right will have to accept limits to "the belief in progress that has dominated Anglo-American politics for the last two centuries," wrote historian Christopher Lasch as he explained how his critiques of modern social policy had originated in an endeavor to raise his children in a type of "extended family" that was easier to find in earlier times.[37]

Some of those who linger over praise of the nineteenth century are engaged in the necessary intellectual task of trying to understand the distinctive features of society that have emerged in our lifetime. Others may be indulging in nostalgia for the past-just-beyond-recall that is a recurrent feature of modern times. And even those who call for drastic change need some evidence from previous human history that the changes they seek are feasible. Nevertheless, it is important, in a book on the transitions and transformations of the post-revolutionary era, to recognize how modernity has been defined in recent times. Not only will this point to some "modern" traits that help in interpreting what went before, but it also indicates that periodizing American cultural history has come to serve contemporary purposes of identity and commitment. When I contend that some definitions have distorted the periods of the past and concealed continuities from the mid–nineteenth century to the present, it is not just historical accuracy that is at stake. Any discussion of modernity raises questions about what is of value from our past and whether our historical experience prepares us to face the future with purpose and conviction.

We cannot isolate the concept of modernity from a polemical debate about values and tradition that has been going on for several decades and that is currently at a peak. It is important to note, however, that it is possible to use "modernity" as a term expressing an inescapable awareness of uncertainties in the language we use and the universe we inhabit without deploring this predicament or seeking to overturn it. Though we have no hope of closure or resolution, the conditions of modernity may spur creativity in art, philosophy, or theology. We should note, in addition, that historians and critics have begun to trace instances of "modernity" in the past without asserting that the "modernity" of this figure makes him deplorably subversive of traditional values or the "modernity" of that figure makes her attractively free of the chains of the past. To mention just one recent example, George Cotkin has interpreted William James as a philosopher who confronted "essential problems of modernity"—from personal feelings of despair to scientific questions about the world's indeterminacy—without seeking thereby either to raise or to lower James's importance. I take Cotkin's purpose, somewhat akin to my own, to be that of arguing that we fail to understand James fully if we neglect to see that some issues of modernity have a longer history than ordinarily suspected.[38]

It is impossible to date when the "modern" era began. There are arguments for the sixteenth century, the seventeenth, the eighteenth. A new book attributes "the birth of the modern" to the fifteen years after Wellington's victory over the French and Jackson's over the English in 1815; and a reviewer who is an expert on modernization calls this argument "as strong (or as weak) as any other."[39] Similarly, it might be hard to decide whether the chaos of moral uncertainty in Western culture, deplored by Bloom and MacIntyre, set in with the Renaissance, the Reformation, the Enlightenment, Darwin, Nietzsche, Freud, or the diaspora of Continental intellectuals. It is almost equally impossible to agree when "modernism" entered intellectual life. Cotkin argues for the last decade or two of the nineteenth century; and many other scholars would agree that the turn of the century marked widespread awareness of irreversible and accelerating change.[40] Let us note, because it is of particular relevance to the present argument, that Gertrude Stein called the United States "the oldest country in the world" for the reason that "it has been living in the twentieth century longer than any other country"—that is, says Kenner, since the Civil War.[41] Without taking dates too seriously, may I add Tocqueville's corollary to Stein's theorem by saying that it was evident several decades before the Civil War that the United States was passing through historical changes that other nations were bound to experience?

Despite the elusiveness of dates and the polemical turbulence that cloaks the subject, we can enumerate some characteristics of modernity in intellectual culture. We can do so, moreover, without choosing a two-, three-, or thousand-stage scheme of history. These characteristics begin with the plurality of moral perspectives and inability to fix any of them as true or false (or even as traditional and unassailable) that has been the target of so many well-known books in recent years. We should add a feeling that, as knowledge in many fields advances, fragmentation occurs; it is impossible to connect and unify all knowledge in systems that command assent. Along with a sense of progress and recognition of fragmentation goes enhanced interest in psychology, human nature, and perhaps especially the intense emotions experienced in the nuclear family and small circles of friendship.[42] Each of these characteristics appears on both sides of most controversies. The modern intellectual may despise culture or seek to improve it, for example; may deplore or celebrate the tense coils of the nuclear family; or may see the shattering of previous orthodoxies as a liberation or a source of anxiety.

In the end, what may best characterize the modern intellect is a metaphor used to describe both shared history and private consciousness, the metaphor of a river or stream that flows in ways we cannot control, that overcomes our best-laid plans, that rushes through our subjective life, that obliges us to navigate with the utmost flexibility and sometimes causes us to drift.[43] This metaphor is recurrent in famous works of the last decades of the nineteenth century and the first decades of our own. But we also encountered it in Tocqueville, and it was a metaphor that helped in making sense of reality in an era when the past was receding and problems of sincerity and confidence were ever-present. We may think of this river repeatedly as we examine two lives of men who tried to hold on to as much as they could of their religious and patriotic heritage while virtually personifying the faith, which Tocqueville detected throughout America, in human perfectibility and the picture of humanity as a changing one "in which nothing either is or ought to be fixed forever."

CHAPTER TWENTY-ONE

A Step toward Modernity

Nearly a century before Virginia Woolf announced the birth of modern character, some thoughtful men and women recognized that familiar landmarks were being swept away, and there was no certainty about what might replace them. Addressing his European contemporaries in the introduction to *Democracy in America* (1835), Alexis de Tocqueville wrote: "Carried away by a rapid current, we obstinately keep our eyes fixed on the ruins still in sight on the bank, while the stream whirls us backward—facing toward the abyss." Ahead lay the dreadful prospect of a world "where nothing any longer seems either forbidden or permitted, honest or dishonorable, true or false." In an 1841 lecture, Ralph Waldo Emerson described the unsettling consequences of the testing, inquiring spirit that favorite doctrines and opinions could no longer escape. "Nothing solid is secure; everything tilts and rocks."[1]

In struggles to clutch at fragments of the past or to face the insecurities of the present, we may notice affinities between an earlier era and our own time. In fact, some of the tendencies that characterize "modern" intellectual life have important parallels in antebellum America. These tendencies include: attacks on privileged forms of discourse and attempts to develop new experimental ones, views of artists and intellectuals as solitary fugitives and prophets, acceptance of ceaseless change in society and religious doubt in the individual as unavoidable facts of life, a fascination with "inner" psychological states as compensation for political and professional frustration, intense clusters of intellectual friendship as the central focus of living. At least some of our nineteenth-century predecessors who were most fascinated by "interior life" and most inclined to see themselves as fugitives in a world of bustle and doubt were also believers in the essential goodness of human nature, the benefits of science, and the reliability of human progress. Perhaps we can see in their lives a rehearsal for later moments of tension, crisis, and inconsistency en route to modernity.

In this chapter and the next, I will explore these parallels by analyzing the lives of two antislavery leaders. The American antislavery movement may seem an odd place for such explorations. When we look for the origins of modern intellectual searching and experimentation, we tend to think of more recent periods. Nineteenth-century abolitionists, who pledged their unswerving allegiance to higher laws and held the nation to judgment in the light of universal truths, appear to have been paragons of a kind of intellectual certainty no longer available to the modern character. One highly influential study of abolitionism, Gilbert Hobbs Barnes's *The Anti-Slavery Impulse* (1933), stressed the inspiration of evangelical religion in the lives of antislavery leaders. The book was written, in part, to answer the form of skepticism and relativism that was popular in intellectual circles.[2] In the 1960s, when antislavery scholarship flourished, young champions of civil rights and social justice, no matter how secularized and ambiguous their own beliefs might be, continued to admire the stalwart moral resolution of the abolitionists who had braved the wind and tide of public opinion.

The crucial question faced by the abolitionists—what makes slavery evil?—was an especially difficult one because, up until then, most human societies had tolerated slavery. When the abolitionists sometimes asserted that their commitments were exclusively religious, they were indicating how hard it was to fix belief and identity in a world undergoing destructions and reconstructions. They tended to blend secular beliefs with religious convictions, though they frequently stood in opposition to religious authorities. They were eclectics and innovators, not traditionalists. In this chapter I will consider their actions as an episode on the way to a drifting, unmoored intellectual world. I choose the word *episode* to indicate that I deal with a small part of a long story. Let me also eschew the historian's overworked device of pretending the world was tidy before breaking down in the period under review. One important function of antislavery was as an effort to establish meaning in a world already at sea.

To explore this interpretation, I will attempt a fresh look at the life of one abolitionist, Henry Clarke Wright.[3] In writing his biography, I was struck by the turmoil and conflict in his youthful experience. His family trekked to the frontier when he was four; both his mother and a stepmother died during his youth; his father was frequently away from the family farm; his father and a grown-up brother argued vehemently over the rise and fall of Napoleon; his conversion during a revival combined painful meditation with community conflict; and his first career, as a hatmaker, was wrecked by the chaotic economy. Not all of this turmoil was unique to his life; some of it epitomizes an era of mobility and reversals.

When he made his way to Andover Seminary in 1819, Wright's sense of instability was intensified. Some of his confusion was simply that of a rural youth entering an institution of higher learning; he was also the only member of his class lacking previous college experience. Thus he had the outsider's sensitivity to vague and inconsistent formulations that veteran students memorized unflinchingly. United in despising Unitarianism, his orthodox professors were nevertheless plagued by controversial images of God, man, and history—matters on which they could barely agree. After the political antagonism of the 1790s and in the midst of New England's continuing religious feuds, it was no easy business to be orthodox. In order to allay suspicion in the churches that supported the seminary, the professors gave periodic (and sometimes contradictory) assent to specified creeds. Although boards of visitors kept watch over what was being taught, Leonard Woods, whose career was synonymous with Andover's growth for fifty years, regretted that they had not forced him to retract careless passages in his writings. Moses Stuart, illustrious professor of Bible studies, was praised both for upholding "unlimited latitude of inquiry" and for expressing "the most childlike and humble deference to the authority of Scripture." Andover was, in sum, a world where doctrines were ambiguous, where intellectual missteps were easy, and where suspicion and rancor lurked just below the surface. Wright's years there were racked with tension and doubt.[4]

The seminary made a stalwart effort to acquaint would-be ministers with the most advanced philosophical and critical methods while endeavoring not to alter doctrines or disturb faith. These efforts foundered on untenable distinctions between means and ends, techniques and content. Wright found himself learning languages and subjecting the Bible to German critical methods—the Bible that his father had read aloud daily, in English, as God's word. It was nonsense to expect that his faith would not be changed. A committee appointed to investigate the Andover curriculum reported that in these relativistic studies "the most matured and informed minds have sometimes been shaken, not to say contaminated and poisoned"; therefore it was no surprise that immature students, their religious ardor chilled, sank into "universal skepticism." Nor were language studies the worst of it. Wright also had his proofs of God's existence destroyed by his professors' impeccable logic, but got nothing in their stead. After two lectures by Woods he wrote in his diary:

> So far as his arguments go, as addressed to my intellect, he has made an atheist of me. My Head is an atheist; my Heart cannot be. God is Love, not Logic; is a Heart & not a Head—experience.

Orthodox Andover, a product of deep rifts in American culture, showed this young man that his only certainties were bound to be internal ones—internal and precarious: God is "a law of life," he wrote, "to each one what he conceives him to be."[5]

When leaving Andover and entering the ministry in 1823, Wright reflected, like many theology students in the years since, on the blessing that "speculative notions & doubts do not have much influence on our conduct; & that difficulties, started in the cloister, vanish in active life."[6] For almost a decade the routine life of a small-town minister did, as far as we can tell, silence his anxieties. But both rural revivalism and extracurricular activities at Andover had fanned a burning faith in the worldwide millennium, a faith that the humdrum tasks of a local pastorate were threatening to extinguish. More and more impatient for an important mission, Wright ultimately abandoned the ministry for a lifetime in reform—or, as he thought at first, traded a narrow ministry for a broader one. Similar shifts were typical of an entire generation of Andoverites: Wright was acting out, without knowing it, basic changes in the meanings of locality and professionalism in America.[7] In addition, when he moved from the ministry to service as traveling agent of Sunday School, Home Mission, and Peace societies, Wright discovered that his interests collided with those of local ministers who resented the time, energy, and publicity monopolized by national and international causes. To the intellectual and spiritual puzzles of his school days, in other words, were joined jolting perceptions of antagonism over the disposition of fame and influence in a democratic society.

Similarly, the antislavery movement brought to the surface rivalries that were scarcely yet defined and that signaled basic alterations in the organization of society. (The same point could be made about temperance movements, which stirred up numerous controversies over whether organization outside the churches caused infidelism.[8]) Living in Boston as an up-and-coming evangelical reformer in 1835, Wright initially sided with conservative ministers and laymen who detested William Lloyd Garrison's immoderate antislavery measures. At the same time, his own livelihood embittered him toward ministers who gave lip-service to the millennium while insisting that each reform society "benefit the people of the place where it meets."

These sluggards wallowed in vague attacks on sin but were unwilling to assail specific problems like drunkenness and slavery. They feared that if one specified a sin too closely, then Christianity would lose its essence. As Wright learned in arguing with one Boston leader:

> Brother Blagden thinks the whole tendency of the Anti Slavery movement & of the Temperance & Moral Reform & Peace movement—is to lead men to make all religion consist in breaking off from external sins. Seems to think it wrong to urge men to break off from external sins till their hearts are changed & the fountain is purified. He forgets that one of the best ways to conquer an evil propensity is—to cease to indulge it outwardly.[9]

Wright emphasized the narrow outlook of men who resented what they took to be the reform societies' insistence that local communities should give priority to national issues over their own spiritual welfare. The slave was becoming the symbolic focus of some complex arguments among ministers, arguments in which Wright increasingly found comfort in the company of translocal professional communities instead of old-time hierarchies, arguments in which a narrow emphasis on external behavior replaced traditional Christian views of the soul.

When he finally chose to switch allegiances, Wright noted in his diary that he actually ran down the street to sign his name in the antislavery membership book.[10] He had arrived at a decision after years of conflict and was reaching out—dramatically—for certainty in a universe where the foundations of faith seemed unstable and where power was flowing from local to national communities. It was a reaching out, however, that seemed virtually to negate its own intentions. As late as 1844, defending himself against the attacks of Scottish churchmen, Wright protested that his religious opinions were "in substance—in all essential particulars—like unto those held by John Calvin." But even while insisting on his orthodoxy, he admitted the need of no other guide "than my own experience and observation."[11] The Scots would surely have retorted that these were fickle guides, turning Christianity against itself, casting it loose from traditional moorings.

It is appropriate at this point to add two observations concerning Wright's years as an abolitionist. First, his strong commitment enabled him to speak with a moral certainty verging on priggishness; it is for highminded denunciations of opponents that he and other Garrisonians are best remembered. Second, despite this illusion of certainty, he actually passed through a succession of changing opinions on every conceivable subject, eventually becoming a freelance lecturer whose business required a stock of new radicalisms to peddle each year. Try as he might, he never could articulate the principle uniting his shifting stands, though he came closest by reiterating a capitalized slogan, "CHANGE—REVOLUTION," which called for the continuous remodeling of institutions to fit human needs.[12]

Perhaps because of its response to uncertainty, antislavery was a movement unusually concerned with boundaries. We cannot fully understand abolitionists—particularly the radical "new breed" who emerged in the 1830s—if we fail to appreciate their earnest philosophical endeavor to distinguish the places that God had assigned to different parts of the created universe. Human rights were proved and asserted out of a system of limits, rules, and submissions. This point may be illustrated by following notes that Wright kept at the 1836 training sessions for agents of the American Anti-Slavery Society. These notes are by far the fullest account of one of the high points in antislavery history, coming at a time when the movement had built up a good base of adherents, when it was pretty clear that abolition was not going to receive the support of mainstream institutions, and when the movement was shifting tactics from distribution of tracts and pamphlets to agitation by speakers and organizers. The spirit of 1836 was one of heady, collegial examination of every "branch" of the subject of slavery in order to determine the unambiguous truth and equip speakers like Wright to face any exigency.

The sessions were animated by a fundamental dispute over the nature of slavery—and therefore over the logic of immediate abolition. The principles at stake were a moral definition of slavery, offered by Theodore Dwight Weld, and an economic or "English definition," advocated by Weld's beloved patron, Charles Stuart. Stuart favored an economic definition of slavery as involuntary, uncompensated labor, while the Americans at the sessions insisted on a religious definition based on a divinely ordained, hierarchical scheme: slavery was, in effect, a sinful rearrangement of God's disposition of persons and things. According to Wright's notes, Weld defined slavery as "Holding & Treating persons as Things":

> In other words—Making men means, mere means, to an end in which they
> have no interest, no part. As I use my pen to write, the pen having no
> interest or concern in the writing. As the using of an ax to cut with, the
> interest of the ax not being taken into account. As the using of a Lamb for
> food, the interest of the Lamb not being consulted, but all sacrificed, his
> very life taken. As the use of a Horse to travel, the interests of the horse not
> only not being consulted, but all sacrificed. In this Weld maintains consists
> the essential sin of slavery. It takes man out of the sphere in which God
> placed him & puts him in a sphere designed to be occupied by others.[13]

The problem with Stuart's view (that slavery was simply involuntary, uncompensated labor), as the agents picked it apart, was that it failed to address the case in which the slave accepted his alienation and was willing to be a slave. It made "the degree of unwillingness on the part of the slave the measure of the sin of slavery." But the slave had no right to accept the condition of servitude:

> God placed man in a certain state. Gave him a nature adapted to that state & to no other. If a man goes out of it he wages war against God; he denaturalizes himself, makes himself a different being from what God made him. God made him above the Brute & but little lower than the Angels. Man has no right to place himself in a condition below the brutes & with himself a thing.[14]

One could scarcely wish for a sharper statement of the way in which abolitionism required freedom and imposed obligations on all individuals, including the slaves. Weld made it emphatic, in any event, that: "No matter what the slave may think of the condition—whether he came into it voluntarily or involuntarily—the Master sins in claiming a right to hold & use . . . a man as a thing." Even if a slave were "so degraded, so ignorant, so insensible to his relation to God, so lost to a sense of accountability as to be willing to be a thing," this would not exculpate the master, but only magnify his guilt. "If I place myself in . . . a passive condition, I sin. If another holds me in that condition, or connives at my remaining in it, or sees me in it & does not try to get me out of it he sins against God."[15]

Furthermore, it was of no avail for the master to claim that he was benefiting or assisting the slave: "the motives which lead the Master in thus holding him can never save him from guilt, cannot increase or diminish the essential sinfulness of the act." In the question-and-answer dialectic of the training sessions, the agents were confronted with the case of a master who worried that by setting an individual free he might consign him to a worse fate.

> If you set him free he will be taken up & sold to a hard & cruel master in N. Orleans. He is at once put into a condition where he is lashed, fettered, crushed and ground down, shut out from all good & comfort. Can you love him and let him go to such certain perdition?

The answer was absolutely clear:

> Yes. I can. I do that individual a greater injury by transgressing for one moment that eternal principle which gives a man a right to himself, under God, than I should by letting him go free. Every violation, for a moment, of that holy principle which makes a distinction between a person, a man & a thing is a greater crime against that neighbour than the giving it up at once though by doing so he suffers death & worse than death.[16]

As the agents explored it, "the philosophy of slavery" focused attention on the development of the individual self, in terms similar to those with which Orlando Patterson has described "social death" and David Brion Davis has identified "the inherent contradiction of slavery."[17] Wright's expression is again representative:

> To say I myself am a slave—I am a thing, a contradiction in terms. . . . The very language expresses the wickedness of slavery. . . .
>
>   Most certainly oppression is involved in slavery. . . . But cruelty & oppression are not the essential sin of slavery.
>
>   . . . The nearer slavery comes to the very center of existence—to *I myself*, to that which constitutes me as one being, my individuality, my personality—the more horrid it appears. It claims my body. It is of little account. But when it comes to my mind, my will, to the *I am*, the *I myself*, it takes away my all.[18]

More than simply the free moral agency of the slave was at issue in this struggle. In denouncing slavery, the abolitionists admitted the necessity of living in a world in which each person had to find his or her own place. At the same time they asserted, not always convincingly, that it would not be a place of their own making, but would conform to an ordained system of boundaries. The abolitionists themselves were facing the challenge of building new careers in an exhilarating world of free, fluid economic activity, and that world was deeply disconcerting to them. For young men and women attracted to careers as reformers, it was difficult to accept the proposition that self-assertion has no limits, a proposition that not only violated still-familiar warnings against the sin of pride but also implied that professional failure is a sign of a defective self. And yet the necessity of self-assertion became nearly inescapable as the central meaning of individual endeavor in the post-revolutionary world. Thus, although the pattern that we see in numerous antislavery and reform biographies begins strongly—with youthful excitement over the breakdown of prerogatives and the unfolding of opportunities in a world transformed by the revolutions of the previous half-century—it often leads to uncertainty, false starts, and an anxious hopping from profession to profession.

As he took notes at the New York meetings, Wright, like Weld and others there, agonized over the rightfulness of his assertion of self. He had already given up two old-fashioned careers, as a hatmaker and minister, each preceded by years of training; and as he ventured toward the freer life of a public lecturer he tried diligently to find some divine sanction for his efforts. At the training sessions he recorded his feelings after a "solemn & interesting" prayer meeting:

Have seldom felt my soul more bowed down before God & I seemed to get near to God. To feel deeply the responsibility of my present work. I felt that it was a great & awful thing to live in this world. In the cause of Abolition felt that I am a Coworker with God. I am going down into the dark, deep caverns of sin & degradation to look after the image of God, which slavery has seized & cast down & turned into an article of merchandise to be bought and sold for gold & silver. God help me in this holy work.[19]

Here was a contradictory situation. It was supposedly the slave, not the abolitionist, whose life was determined and transformed by the marketplace. The abolitionist wished to regard himself as operating in a system of boundaries secure against forces of flux and disorder. The abolitionist was, to be sure, living out a career of professional mobility and efforts to change opinion, and yet he spoke as though slavery was the realm of the marketplace and thus the anomaly in God's plan.

Despite its supposed fixity, its emphasis on boundaries, its denunciation of the conjunction of man and thing, there was something provisional and ambiguous about the "philosophy of slavery." It harked back to a traditional view in which persons were born into and stayed in a sphere or station in life. Its depiction of the chaos of the slave system sounded like medieval horror at the anarchy that would inevitably follow the unsettling of authority, or like the seventeenth-century Puritan John Winthrop's aspersions on the state of "natural" liberty.[20] But Winthrop and his forerunners believed that there was a system of submissions and protections entailed in the divine plan that assigned each person his or her station. The immediatist "philosophy of slavery" indicted such submission and protection. The abolitionists painted slavery as anarchic; yet so was freedom. But even if freedom were "ruinous," neither slave nor master could avoid it. Abolition may be said to have called for the anarchic, boundless world that it simultaneously deplored. In this paradox, together with the shifting religious and professional context in which it was embraced, lies much of the explanation of antislavery as a step toward modernity.

Through his strong inclination to split and compartmentalize his personality, Wright illustrates yet another, more psychological presentiment of modernity. We see this most clearly in the existence of the "other self"— "H.C.W."—who supervised his morals and guided him through each stage of his physiological growth. This better self carried echoes of his mother (who died when he was six); their communings sometimes took the form of bizarre assignations. In his book entitled *The Living Present and the Dead Past* (1865), Wright described a night on a steamer from New York to Boston when he took this self to bed and enjoyed "the most intimate and ennobling of all relations," a phrase with clear sexual meaning in his other writings. "I feel that my destiny is entirely in thy hands," he told himself. "As the steamer glides over the waters . . . lying in my berth with thee, I am passing the night in most intimate communion with thee, and with that loving, anxious one that hovers around thee or nestles in thy heart to shelter thee from harm. Full of hallowed beauty and glory is the night, and never to be forgotten; because of the vitalizing and ennobling intimacy I enjoy with the loving, gentle, and just one, who is ever present in thy [the other self's] bosom to *welcome me to my home in Heaven*." Similar specters hover over a multivolume dialogue with an ideal wife that he was composing at his death.[21]

This habit may reflect some measure of confusion regarding sex, death, and the body. To meet a version of oneself in a dream is not unusual, however; it is only Wright's inflated language as he reports the intercourse that distances him from a modern sensibility. He allows us to view him in the process of internalizing (if with only partial success) a moral conscience. Like many contemporaries, he favored a rather superficial view of personality development, in which children would acquire good character solely through their mothers' kind moral instruction. He was deaf to the importance of paternal discipline, or other vestiges of a passing order, in the installation of conscience. It was hard for him to see that a revolt against his father or any other authority influenced the positions he took or directions he chose. In his 1835 argument with George Washington Blagden, we may recall, he advocated "external" reform rather than a deep psychological definition of sin. Throughout his life he insisted that good behavior consisted of obeying easily identified laws—a viewpoint that he eventually called "Anthropology" in order to distinguish it from the worthless arcana of "Theology."[22]

Although Wright's view of character was shallow, he still exhibited introspective traits that place him among the generation described by Emerson as "young men [who] were born with knives in their brains, a tendency to introversion, self-dissection, anatomizing of motives." His curiosity with respect to his own family past, moreover, marks him as a distant precursor of Freud.[23] Calling his autobiography *Human Life* (1849), he made it clear that he assigned greater significance to *la petite histoire* of parents and children than to *la grande histoire* of generals and potentates. In a popular book for children, *A Kiss for a Blow* (1842), and numerous other works, he expanded on the analogy between sibling rivalry and the wars of nations; he hoped that wiser child-rearing would yield an harmonious world. *Human Life* contains impressive passages of self-analysis intended to recover the feelings of childhood and to find connections between his father's violence and his own adult pacifism.[24] Although his view of character has a Victorian superficiality, in short, there are ways in which he anticipated the twentieth century's psychological understanding of human nature. It is not surprising that sickness and health are dominant themes in his writings, and those of many other reformers, from the 1840s onward. Feelings of well-being were supplanting morality (or wisdom) as the desired outcome of self-knowledge.

As previously indicated, Wright also celebrated "CHANGE," and his works pleaded the virtues of a booming era of commerce and liberty. In addition to the coincidence of superficial morality with introspective habits, we face one more paradox: this herald of a new era was deeply absorbed in backward-looking memories of childhood. He reverted to childhood for lessons about "human life," salted with occasional sketches of a bygone era—the sugar camp, men drinking at work, old women's spook stories, taciturn Indians on wooded trails.[25] The nostalgic tone of antebellum writing could serve as a cover for far-reaching redefinitions of time and society. What Wright found in childhood were not the particulars of power and affection in one environment, but a generalized myth of universal human psychology. In a sense he certified the *past-ness* of one type of society and located the durable stuff of human life within the guilt and sorrow of what we today would term an Oedipal family. Lost mother, vengeful father, conflicted children, independence and career—this drama comfortably endured throughout the dislocations and adjustments in society at large.

In a brilliant essay in his *Fin-de-Siècle Vienna*, Carl E. Schorske has traced "counterpolitical" implications in Freud's exploration of the unconscious.[26] At the risk of oversimplifying Schorske's subtle argument, let me distinguish two senses in which psychoanalysis originated counterpolitically. First, it arose from the frustrations of an ambitious, talented son of a liberal Jewish family, a man working his way through a collapsing political order in which others of his class had previously experienced reasonable rewards and protection. In tracking his dreams back to infantile erotic sources, Freud bypassed immediate professional setbacks and downplayed political feelings that must have been bitter and rankling. The invention of psychoanalysis exemplifies the way great intellectual breakthroughs of the modern era have resulted from evasive responses to the disintegration of privileged arrangements and the suspension of long-held convictions about the public good. As Schorske eloquently concludes: "By reducing his own political past and present to an epiphenomenal status in relation to the primal conflict between father and son, Freud gave his fellow liberals an ahistorical theory of man that could make bearable a political world spun out of orbit and beyond control."

The second sense in which psychoanalysis was counterpolitical is that Freud created and presided over an apparatus that parodied politics, complete with congresses and manifestos, alliances and factions, triumphs and apostasies. Schorske quotes Freud's revealing joke that one of his professional advances—an academic promotion, no less—came "as if the role of sexuality had been suddenly recognized by His Majesty, the interpretation of dreams confirmed by the Council of Ministers, and the necessity of the psychoanalytic therapy of hysteria carried by a two-thirds majority in Parliament." As we follow the contests for loyalty and assent within "the psychoanalytic movement"—not only in Freud's lifetime but as continually reenacted[27]—we may conclude that Freud personified, on a majestic level, follies that we ordinarily dismiss as "academic politics," strategies that reflect unfortunate confusion about the role of intellectuals in a competitive, bureaucratic society.

I comment on Schorske's essay at such length in order to identify the compensatory uses of "self-knowledge" in an era like our own, one that shares only the most provisional and confused understanding of the public welfare. And the compensatory quality of much modern thought goes a long way toward explaining its fragmentation and its fluctuating gestures toward intimacy, moral certainty, and political relevance. It is this aspect of modernity that seems currently most disturbing to many critics of American culture.[28]

But such instances of compensation are not limited to Freud's time or our own. As an interpreter of the remembered family past, Wright stands as an American exemplar of the transition to modernity that Schorske illuminates. Developments marked by struggle in Europe often have American counterparts with the deceptive appearance of being natural consequences of free choice. Wright experienced nothing comparable to the frustrations of Austria's Jews; indeed, he rose from obscure origins to financial security and professional prominence in a uniquely American manner. This champion of radical visions of free labor was, nevertheless, the son of a Federalist veteran, and he had married into the elite of the seaport city of Newburyport. Thus he came by birth and marriage to hold the view that politics was shabby, that society was in decline, that merit in a democracy went unrewarded. He trained for an office, the clergy, that was expected to usher in the millennium and that gave him the status of gentleman, wearing silk gloves and dining with fine silver. But in fact this office was losing allure and authority in the eyes of well-trained seminarians, who deserted it for more prestigious callings. Wright protested unceasingly against a vocational life drained of sacred meaning, against a society of fraudulent play-acting. The introverted, ahistorical side of his thought compensated less for frustrated ambition, as in Freud's case, than for feelings of being cast adrift. He could never endure in the belief that he was secure or prominent. Ambition was set loose; society was purposeless, and anxiety was a fact of existence.[29]

Certainly Wright's antislavery world was counterpolitical in Schorske's second sense: it parodied politics. He enjoyed a micro-universe of factions and maneuvers, resolutions and battles, as his enemies, ranging from political abolitionists to Scottish churchmen, learned to their chagrin. (I sometimes think the internal history of abolitionism has fascinated historians

because of its resemblance to events in academic departments and professional organizations.) As a cosmopolitan antinationalist, Wright was free to
indulge triumphantly political fantasies, as when he imagined himself presid-
ing over multitudes in a world's convention to be held in the Highlands: "I
should like to congregate all of human kind on these mountains around and
speak to them of human brotherhood."[30] In actual life he shared with other
reformers a canny way of going outside politics and discovering new forms of
access to "the people." On his circuits as a lecturer and reformer, as a
liberator of humankind from the dismal captivities of the past, he caught the
rising importance of conjugal intimacy and of bearing successful children.
He discovered everywhere those humble versions of politics—who rules the
home? when are children entitled to independence?—that demanded a
remedial science of the family to replace the public contest of ideas.

One outcome of this style of thinking was the impoverishment of political
dialogue and the magnification of sentimental references to home and family.
Of course, Wright did not by himself make these things happen, but his life
may nonetheless denote a turning-point in the now oft-lamented "fall of
public man." In addition, he virtually personifies the "feminization of American culture" in which Ann Douglas has detected collusion between clergymen, who were losing out in the public arena, and talented women, who were
inching their way inside.[31] From the dismissal of Calvinist theories of atonement to denials of personal ambition, from the creation of a depoliticized,
unheroic history to the exploitation of new cultural marketplaces—all of
Douglas's themes are salient in Wright's life. Let me emphasize one positive
result of the confusion and drift that I have been outlining: it opened the way
for middle-class men to empathize with those who were previously off-stage
in Western history. The splitting of selves could take the form of projection
into another's place. Introspection could bring forth new interest in the
civilizing mission of wives and mothers, once considered the carnal under-
side of human society, but accorded new standing as purifying and stabilizing
forces in a society where social roles became more fluid. Douglas emphasizes
the manipulative, Madison Avenue–side of this apolitical process, but
Wright and other male contemporaries showed great curiosity regarding
women, considerable success in learning how they felt, and an unmistakable
wish to support their public aspirations. He had turned his own back on
politics, however, and lacked a theory whereby political victories were possible or desirable. And so he glorified women's maternity instead—an ironic
instance of the lack of moorings that I have been describing!

A similar irony pertained to blacks. Racked by uncertainty in his own
career, Wright broke through in 1835 to the persona of "the Genius of
Africa": "I would feel, think and speak as one whose body has felt the
lacerating scourge—whose heart has been torn and into whose soul the iron

has entered," he announced. He asked conservative churchmen to imagine themselves the victims of uncompensated work (this was before the Weld–Stuart debate), to imagine their wives the casualties of unprotected chastity.[32] Throughout his life similar feats of projection moderated his own vocational anxieties and freed him to speak for distant underclasses. Yet he spent almost no time among Northern blacks and felt no call to visit the South. And when the suffrage became a lively issue, he opposed the enfranchisement of the ignorant and uneducated, black or white.[33] He was still enough of a child of Federalism for that! Lacking a coherent theory of political community, he showed diminishing interest in slaves once their chains were broken.

As an aging reformer, he withdrew farther from politics than ever and gave little thought to conflicts of power or social class. His religious views were barely coherent except that he kept faith in "*Progression.*" There were "but two classes: i.e. the progressive party and the stationary party"; one was forever "holding back, and trying to back the wheels and put the brakes to the car of progress, and pointing the world to the dead past," while the other cried, "put on the steam, ease the brakes, and rush on to the final station; with the sublime watchword, 'Nearer to man, nearer to God!' " Here, too, his views were in tune with those of his contemporaries.[34]

Looking inward, looking backward, Wright simultaneously promoted a positive outlook on changes in collective life. In his initial antislavery stage, he liked to denounce bondage as inconsistent with eternal truth, thus repudiating the relativism and impermanence that his own experience seemed to dictate. But once he was fully immersed in a career of itinerant lecturing, it was clear that truth must be verified according to the currents of the present age. Through a kind of trick he sometimes asserted that there were self-evident laws governing body and soul, nature and morals. Thus he brought together two strains—progressivism and scientism—that became prominent features of religious modernism. Only in his case the scientism meant little more than that audiences should have a compliant attitude toward expositors of new truth, and his progressivism showed remarkably little clarity concerning the improved society of the future.

To illustrate this direction of Wright's thinking, consider a passage on spiritualism from his *The Errors of the Bible.* Like many of his contemporaries, Wright never doubted, despite the charlatans who passed themselves off as mediums, that many genuine communications were being received. His emphasis was less on the messages of consolation and enlightenment that departed souls were sending than on the promise of continuing human growth that the existence of the spirits seemed to promise. While faulting the Bible's conception of "the superior state"—that is, the life of the spirit after the body's death—Wright carefully refrained from specifying his own too closely. Jesus alluded to "a fixed state . . . holding out no hope that the mistakes and sins of this state can be remedied there," but Wright felt it "more natural" to suppose a state of continuing self-examination and correction. It was "more rational," too, to believe human beings were "free agents" in the superior state "as they are here; that they progress in knowledge and goodness there as they do here. . . . The social relations and sympathies will exist there as they do here, only in a higher and purer form." His inferences were "natural" and "rational" because they suited human needs. Even after death, it seemed, history would be a fluid process without a given end, carrying on the best and worst of nineteenth-century life, only in a vaguely heightened fashion.[35] Some sought guidance from communication with the spirits; some looked for outlines of a better world that was bound to come. But the assurance Wright found was murky and tenuous. After a long, mobile lifetime the one thing certain was that life would constantly evolve in a progressive direction.

Antislavery was, then, grasped in the quest for certainty, and in retrospect it has presented some scholars and activists with a model of certainty in public life. But it also gave voice to an introverted view of human nature and gave welcome to vast changes in the social order. Setting out to fix his life to moral imperatives, Wright moved as well toward a shifting, uncertain modernity. The question may be addressed: how many abolitionists followed the same course? In fact, others come to mind who had rather similar careers, and the movement as a whole may be said to have harnessed religion to politics in the hope of executing part of God's design—only to find that it was the uncontrollable drift of politics that carried religion along with it or that religion was relegated to a private sphere of uncertain meaning. If they had been willing to withdraw from the mainstream of society and live out the years together as a secluded sect, they might have protected convictions of moral truth from the ravages of historical experience in a society where shared traditions were tenuous. But this was never their intent. They were supremely interested in public issues and in the nation's progress. Much the same may be said of proslavery intellectuals and of others who were slow to take a forceful stand for or against human bondage.[36] In staking a claim to absolute certainty and then shifting the grounds of their convictions, abolitionists and some of their contemporaries remind us of Tocqueville's Americans who put up houses to shelter them throughout their lives and sold these houses before the roofs were erected, who changed professions endlessly, and who pursued a perfection that was forever fugitive. In the end, all they could hope to hold on to, as they accepted the reality of ceaseless change, was compensatory self-knowledge amid the flow of time.

Do we lose anything by discovering in an abolitionist's experience uncertainties that we recognize as distant cousins to our own? If we admire his commitment to combatting the great evil of slavery and the dedication with which he and his associates persevered in that fight for several decades, there is no reason to slacken our admiration. All we must give up is the feeling that commitment was easier for abolitionists because moral truth was more easily determined then than now. It is always tempting to look back beyond current memory for a time when decisions were less confusing and faith was not as hard to maintain. Perhaps all moderns have something in common with those whom Tocqueville depicted as fixing their eyes on a receding shore and drifting toward an unknown future at their backs. What we may gain from a look at Wright and his contemporaries is an appreciation that the dilemmas of modern living are not of recent origin. In their time, no less than in our own, everything tilted and rocked.

CHAPTER TWENTY-TWO

The Experience of Change

The emergence of characteristics of modernity is so clearly visible in the careers of antislavery intellectuals because of their endeavor to anchor a steadfast moral commitment in a historical situation where everything was shifting. As religious denominations divided and proliferated, as political parties rose and fell with competing visions of progress, as old trades vanished and new professions defined themselves, as the countryside from Jackson's Cumberland to the Berkshires entered a new era of economic competition, as immigrants poured off ships and settlers crossed the prairies and mountains, the abolitionists asserted a view of morality that was true beyond compromise. Even as they made this assertion, they were aware that no historical tradition sustained it. For a time they clung to a belief that a sovereign God gave laws that were unaffected by decisions of the democratic public, and their best recourse was to appeal to private conscience. But they could not count on conscience. Having taken an uncompromising stand on a public issue on which popular opinion ebbed and flowed and political options alternated between inaction and compromise, they were bound to hope that the consciences of American citizens could be instructed and changed. Perhaps the lesson was that neither private consciousness nor historical experience offered much certainty, but that, somehow, taken together, they might make it possible to face the future with confidence and conviction. Theodore Parker cherished such a hope in the confluence of the private and the historical. Parker, who enjoyed great popularity in his career as lecturer

243

and preacher, was a less individualistic thinker than Henry Wright, and he grappled more openly with the direction of American democracy.

Like Wright, Parker journeyed into theological training as a poor boy without a bachelor's degree. He came from a bookish home, however, and when he started out at Harvard Divinity School in 1834 he already boasted the capacity for disciplined study that eventually enabled him to claim some facility in seventeen languages.[1] After leaving home, he had worked and saved, while sending money to his father to replace him as a laborer on the family farm in Lexington, Massachusetts, until he could afford divinity school. While there, he made ends meet by teaching a class and tutoring students in Hebrew. His academic success was signaled by his selection as an editor of the *Scriptural Interpreter* and publication of several of his articles in this new Unitarian journal. But in the midst of this success he passed through what he called "the great spiritual trial of my life." He kept this crisis to himself. As he wrote his fiancée after feeling "*blue*, terribly blue," all one week, "I never speculate on the causes of such chilling damps that come over the soul, like a frost in July. . . . It is enough to *bear* them without going about to analyze the nature of the complaint." The conclusion was much like the one Wright had reached at Andover: religion was a matter of consciousness and experience.[2]

In his dark night at the divinity school Parker found solace in psychology and history. "Religious consciousness was universal in human history"—this was his discovery from self-examination and from poring over books in all his languages. The Enlightenment had cut people off from the traditional authorities that justified faith: from historical communities and sacred texts. All that remained was human nature, and on that subject the conventional texts were too narrow, too restricted to external sensations and stimuli, to explain the religious "instincts" he felt in his own consciousness and recognized in the histories of all peoples. Among the "primal intuitions of human nature," three stood out: belief in the existence of the divine, or God; belief in the existence of a moral law that ought to be obeyed; and an intuition of immortality ("a consciousness that the essential element of man, the principle of individuality, never dies").[3] Obviously, the third was least well-defined; it amounted less to assurance of immortality than to a vague assumption that human nature is both private and continuous. Parker never treated immortality with the clarity and system that he brought to theism and morality. Few of his contemporaries were more lucid on the nineteenth century's most perplexing issue: the finality of death. But on the other conclusions of his student days—the need to rely on human nature, the universality of religious instincts, the certainty of God and moral law—he rested his life's work.

Although interior consciousness may seem a rather insecure basis for proving the external existence of God or morality, controversies over theism and over moral law were central to the two grand campaigns in which he won his reputation as a heroic, creative figure in the epic of American liberalism. First came the controversy within Unitarianism, which he stepped into almost as soon as he left divinity school, the controversy usually associated with the term *transcendentalism* (though Parker himself seldom embraced the term). To an older generation of Unitarian ministers, who had achieved impressive victories over Calvinistic adversaries in the ecclesiastical warfare of the early nineteenth century, several of Parker's sermons—especially those known as *The Transient and Permanent in Christianity* (1841) and *A Discourse of Religion* (1842)—went too far toward severing Unitarianism from the historically continuous Christian movement. They ostracized him from collegial exchanges of pulpits and schemed to censure him and force his resignation from their fellowship. Their attacks on his works, as well as the works of Emerson and a few other young enthusiasts, culminated in bitter argument over the authenticity of the miracles related in the gospels. These miracles, in the opinion of older ministers, retained for the Bible and Christianity a sacred status safe from critical methods that men and women applied to other books and movements. To a new generation, Unitarianism in this controversy tainted itself with old-fashioned sectarian exclusiveness, while Parker gained stature as a victim of bigotry and champion of human ability and human liberty. But for Parker himself, the central issue was theism. In human nature, particularly human consciousness, flourished an instinctive reverence that posed the surest modern alternative to atheism. The weak arguments of ancient authoritarianism, which Unitarians clung to, gave to atheism its specious plausibility.

Second came the national controversy over slavery, which dominated Parker's life from the mid-1840s to his death in 1860. To trace his activities during these years would be nearly equivalent, wrote his first biographer, "to writing the history of the anti-slavery movement."[4] He participated avidly in scores of conventions. Because of his leadership role in Boston's opposition to the Fugitive Slave Law, he expected to go to jail, and he was in fact tried, but acquitted, for obstructing legal processes. He was one of the "secret six" who kept in close touch with the plans and actions of John Brown from Kansas to Harper's Ferry, Virginia. In a celebrated moment, Parker married the fugitives William and Ellen Craft and gave the husband a Bible and a knife so that he would hold in one hand "the noblest truths in the possession of the human race" and in the other the instrument to protect his wife's liberty. Most of all, however, he served antislavery as preacher and lecturer on the supremacy of the moral law. "*I must reverence the laws of God, come of that what will come,*" he wrote President Fillmore in explaining his defiance of federal laws. "*I must be true to my religion.*"[5] To a friend he wrote: "if there is a God who is the Author of Men and of the Universe, then man owes

Allegiance to that God, to the Laws of his own Nature and to the Constitution of the Universe. This allegiance must override all claims of any human legislation, all claims of King Monarch, or of King Many."[6]

Add to Parker's roles in Transcendentalism and antislavery his prophetic sermons on women's rights, the problem of poverty, and the excessive influence of the business classes in the nation's politics, and it is easy to see why he has often been hailed as a crucial figure in the emergence of liberal Americanism. He was "the link," wrote Daniel Aaron, "between Emerson and the postwar reformers," one of the first "to recognize and protest against the signs of the coming business age."[7] To Henry Steele Commager he was a crusader for American liberalism and, simply, "the Great American Preacher."[8] Describing Parker in such terms is irresistible, for that is how his first biographer presented him and, indeed, how he saw his own life. He is "now perceived to have been bone of the bone and flesh of the flesh of America," wrote John Weiss in the midst of the Civil War. He was "a representative man," "a genuine American," "a pioneer of this America which has been sending her dreadful columns over roads of his surveying and which he helped to clear." "The spirit of the American idea pervaded" all his speeches, and his audiences counted on him to "encourage and instruct the awakening conscience."[9]

His writings take his revolutionary heritage so seriously that he might count as an exception to the erosion of historical memory in this period. He praised George Bancroft's "thoroughly *democratic*" history of the Revolution for departing from "the life of kings, priests, nobles, soldiers, and the like" and turning instead to the "*Life of the Million.*" He shared with Bancroft a story, passed down through "family tradition," about his grandfather John Parker who told his men at Lexington: "Don't fire unless fired upon; but if they mean to have a war, *let it begin here.*" He also advised Bancroft to take more notice of the role of blacks in revolutionary battles. Engravings of Bunker Hill once showed a black soldier firing arms, for example, "but now-a-days a white man is put in his place."[10] Revolutionary heritage and democratic principles converged in the antislavery struggle and defined "the American idea" that government must defend and expand the "rights of man."[11]

Yet it was not historical memory that energized Parker's orations on America; it was a biting awareness of changes in American life. He was very much a man of the road, a model of the peddling and play-acting dimensions of professional life. As a boy he traveled to Boston to sell fruit. Though his search for a vocation was less protracted than some others', he had a stint as a schoolteacher and thought earnestly about the law before deciding that he could not plead a cause for hire if he knew it was not right. Friends warned him that the ministry was a lusterless field, but he felt drawn to it.[12] After divinity school he was, as his biographer called him, "an itinerant vendor of the gospel" looking for a settled position. Then, after eight years in a small parish, in 1845 he became preacher to a huge congregation that met in Boston theatres—first the Melodeon, and later the Music Hall, where a huge bronze Beethoven loomed behind him as he talked. Thus the man who condemned theological disputation as a masquerade stood proudly every Sunday on a stage built for other forms of entertainment. He also won success on the lecture circuit, giving forty to eighty lectures a year and loving this "original contrivance for educating the people," especially in rural areas where "the lions" of culture would otherwise have gone unheard. "The world has nothing like it," he wrote in 1857. "In it are combined the best things of the Church, *i.e.*, the preaching, and of the College, *i.e.*, the *informing thought,* with some of the fun of the Theatre." But to his travails on the lecture circuit he attributed the consumption that cut short his life.[13]

He had the traits as speaker and writer that the masquerade of American life brought to the fore. From childhood he revealed "overwhelming powers of mimicry; the gait, gesture, tone of voice and pet phrases, even the habit of thinking, and the average opinions of a person, were all faithfully reproduced by him." This talent continued to delight acquaintances throughout his life.[14] To attacks on his enemies in which he unmasked them—"stealing the clothes away from skeleton doctrine, or the rouge and false teeth from some mediaeval spinster of the orthodox churches"—he often lent "a touch or two of mimicry, just enough to let a person here or there appear to color the bigotry or the foolishness." Some admirers thought this knack genial and harmless: he was "like an improvisatore," and his sincerity kept him from really directing ridicule at any individual.[15] Emerson praised his "masterly sarcasm—now naked, now veiled." But the target never enjoys satire, and resentment of his debunking mimicry plagued him throughout his career. Many friends regretted his style of argument, and Parker was at constant pains to explain that he intended no offense. "I never wrote a line with any ill-will, or *sarcastic* humour, toward man or maid," he protested to one friend. To another he insisted, "I call sarcasm *malicious irony—a stripping-off the flesh* in wantonness," a defense unconvincing to those who failed to see Parker as simply the innocent victim of bigoted persecution.[16]

Parker wished to be seen as the native Yankee peeling off the sophistries of obfuscators in theology and politics. He had left home, he remembered in 1860, as "a raw boy, with clothes made by country tailors, coarse shoes, great hands, red lips, and blue eyes."[17] He ventured into the miracles controversy under the pseudonym of the rustic "Levi Blodgett"; to an untutored person it was clear that faith in Christ could not rely on the occurrence of miracles (though in this voice he was willing to believe that the miracles really happened).[18] He always prided himself on the choice of simple images: "If I were to speak of birds in a sermon, I should not mention the

nightingale and the skylark, but the brown thrasher and the blackbird."
Through lectures and correspondence he tried to circumvent his critics and
reach a vast public of honest, unpretentious Americans.[19] In fact, the story
of his life, as he reviewed it, showed that "the scholarly class" was more
hostile to truth than was the multitude. Thus he had learned to redirect his
energies, to prefer "homely speech," and had found "my sentiments and
ideas visibly passing into the opinions and literature of the people."[20]

Shortly before his death, Parker rested in the Alps among a group of
scholars, men who savored irony and boasted of modern intellectual attitudes. He astonished them by his skill in felling trees with an ax. This story
captures the ambiguous relationship between his intellectual tastes and his
identification with American humility and manliness.[21] His simplicity was
not merely a pose, but its limited significance is apparent if we remember
that Parker had few peers as a collector of languages, books, and new ideas.
He denounced the American ideal of the self-made man when it was used to
excuse shallow education. Americans knew too little of classical literature
and scientific principles; they assumed too readily that a bright person could
"extemporize" his way to success in the pulpit, bar, or laboratory.[22] He who
wrote as "Levi Blodgett" also studied Hegel, dropped allusions to Pierre
Bayle, and translated Wilhelm DeWette's *Introduction to the Old Testament.*
If he was a genuine American, he was also inveterately cosmopolitan. While
expressing his preference for plain talk and down-home images, he acknowledged to his congregation that "in philosophic terms, and in all which
describes the inner consciousness, our Saxon speech is rather poor, and so I
have been compelled to gather from the Greek or Roman stock forms of
expressions which do not grow on our homely and familiar tree, and hence,
perhaps, have sometimes scared you with 'words of learned length.' " This is
not the best sentence he ever wrote, but its insecure alternation between
demonstrations of folksiness and of sophistication is characteristic of his
thought.[23] Even when his subject was language itself, he exemplified the
mutually interrupting vocabularies the most American of writers resorted to.
Even the disintegratedness of his cosmopolitanism was typically American.

His definition of Americanness was surprisingly parochial. Though he
enjoyed his "welcome in most of the lecture halls between the Mississippi
and the Penobscot,"[24] traveled in Europe, dabbled in Coptic and Swedish,
and generalized about universal human consciousness, he saw America as
New England writ large. Moreover, a tint of nineteenth-century racism colored many of his writings. The Anglo-Saxon race, with a "natural instinct for
progress" and a love of freedom, with blood "not long before inoculated with
Christianity which yet took most kindly in all Teutonic veins," had settled
Massachusetts Bay. This race was distinct from the Irish whose *"bad nature"*
Parker regularly denounced in terms that can be described as bigoted, from

Southerners whom he viewed with hatred as degenerates from Anglo-Saxon purity, and even from blacks, whom he classed among "inferior races which have always borne the same ignoble relation to the rest of men, and always will."[25] In Parker's inconsistent thinking were other strains that mitigated such racism, including his belief in transcendent law and his interest in historical idealism and relativism. Still, the antislavery vision that he evoked in the North resembled a form of sectionalism permeated with ethnic hatred. Certainly, this vision was highly localized. His love of "good old Boston," "the noblest of cities," grew as his hatred of the slave power intensified, and he feared its destruction at the hands of Southerners, of Irish, of blacks.[26]

He was acutely sensitive to the signs of social change. He gave his audiences statistics showing that Massachusetts's population more than doubled between 1820 and 1855, while the percentage of males working on farms declined. Life expectancy had increased, as had the value of taxable property and the products of industry, the number of schools, and the thousands of young persons receiving instruction. While revealing undeniable progress, these statistics concealed, as Parker interpreted them, a hidden toll of physical and moral decline. Factory workers and urban ladies had less physical strength and health than their ancestors who worked in the open air. "The industrial, like other battles, is won with a loss." Suicide was on the increase; abortions were so common that statisticians feared to study them; "in Massachusetts in 1854 one man out of each 302 was either a crazy man or a natural fool." Crime, drunkenness, prostitution, and poverty were public disgraces.[27]

Parker's antislavery orations charted the vectors of moral decline.[28] Side by side with paeans to America's "Democratic idea" appeared stark meditations on the aggressive proclivities of the nation's people. The pervasive love of money, the corruptions of party politics, the despotism of the plantation, and the expansion of Roman Catholicism—all threatened to turn America into one more example of the fall of iniquitous empires. Society had deviated from religious values: schools failed to cultivate moral feelings, and political leaders ignored the supremacy of the Higher Law.[29] As a result, the slave power won repeated victories, which Parker recited, like a rosary of doom, in speech after speech.

Jeremiads of old predicted the demise of Babylons, but the American jeremiad served to identify a sacred mission, castigate anomalous evil tendencies, and prepare for greater things to come. Parker vaulted from images of doom to predictions of limitless glory. "Our institutions will correct most of the ills we complain of—our industry, our schools, newspapers, books, and freedom of thought," he said of Massachusetts. "One day we shall have also a community without idleness, want, ignorance, drunkenness, prostitution, or crime. . . . the future will be brighter than the past." America would indeed eradicate slavery:

> The South will be as the North—active, intelligent. . . . Then by peaceful purchase, the Anglo-Saxon may acquire the rest of this North American continent. . . . Nay, we may honourably go further South, and possess the Atlantic and Pacific slopes of the Southern continent, extending the area of freedom at every step. We may carry thither the Anglo-Saxon vigour and enterprise, the old love of liberty, the love also of law; the best institutions of the present age—ecclesiastical, political, social, domestic.

"What a spectacle," he told an audience who a moment before were stunned by the horrors of the fugitive slave law, "the Anglo-Saxon family occupying a whole hemisphere, with industry, freedom, religion!"[30]

In order to understand the personal sense of history underlying his prophecies, we are fortunate to have the long letter to his congregation he wrote while seeking convalescence from tuberculosis in the West Indies in 1859. Usually known as *Theodore Parker's Experience as a Minister*, it is a rich blend of spiritual autobiography and analysis of public affairs. Naturally, much of it consists of self-justification for his conduct in the controversy among Unitarians and self-congratulation for his role in the antislavery conflict. What may be surprising, because of his denunciation of the evils of America, is his sense of good fortune in living when he did. It was not just that he could boast of rising from humble origins to great influence, though that was certainly part of the story. But he also appreciated that it was "a piece of good fortune" to be a young man "in the most interesting period of New England's spiritual history, when a great revolution went on—so silent that few knew it was taking place, and none then understood its whither or its whence."[31]

Parker did not see himself as born too late, like some European Romantics of his era; he did not regret coming after the generation of revolutionaries who fought the good fight against ancient hierarchies. Instead, he celebrated the more immediate past in which significant heroism occurred. The rise of Unitarianism, despite his quarrels with its leaders, was one evidence of an inspiriting assault on tradition. The rise of Universalism, which rejected the foul doctrine of eternal damnation, was another. Antislavery, public education, temperance, and other reform movements added to the evidence. Great men abounded in the historical era he defined, intellectuals like William Ellery Channing and Emerson, as well as the brave reformers. There were inquisitions and martyrs. It was thrilling to be young in such a time, when "great questions were discussed, and the public had not yet taken sides."[32]

In the dispute between tradition and progress that had commenced during his youth, the key issue was human nature. From various European sources had come writings that prompted new investigations of the physical "constitution of man" and untapped emotional reservoirs. Movements for communitarian labor reform and women's rights sought to make social institutions more consonant with human needs and abilities. In religion, the "theologic despisers of mankind" were challenged by new movements that rejected old notions of sin. Men and women could no longer be commanded to believe any doctrine without persuasion that it conformed with human observation, conscience, and reason. Parker himself had come to see that a perfect God meant that human nature was "adequate," not defective. More than adequate, in fact: "Human life in all its forms, individual and aggregate," was "a perpetual wonder." He not only placed his trust in human consciousness but also repudiated Pauline prudery. He celebrated the human body and its impulses—"God put no bad thing there."[33]

"The Kosmos of immortal and progressive man," he asserted, "is my continual study, discipline, and delight"; and he hoped, "Oh, that some young genius would devise the 'novum organum' of humanity, determine the 'principia' thereof, and with deeper than mathematic science, write out the formulas of the human universe, the celestial mechanics of mankind!" In spite of his curiosity about the "faunas and floras" of the "inner soul," to call Parker a precursor of Freud would strain the evidence. Human consciousness, as he explored it, was a benign source of law.[34] Like Henry Wright, he went beyond the ersatz folklore that contemporaries relished and sought in fragments of autobiography both the elements of instinctive human life and the particular influences that shaped his personal conduct. But his memories look, to a reader of the succeeding century, censored, incomplete, and uninterpreted.

Before turning to his family he devoted pages to Brontë-like description of his childhood's "Material Surroundings": giant boulders, a monstrous tree, "huge, corky fungi," and some lovely flowers growing even in "ill-formed ditches whence peat had been cut for fuel or for manure." The house, "a cheerless shelter" on infertile land, infected him with the consumptive poison that children of this territory bore with them and transmitted to their children.[35] When he got to his mother and father, his memory was expurgated. The "earliest fact of consciousness I ever felt pained at" had occurred when his father would not kill a calf and had a neighbor do it for him. This neighbor, a deacon of the church who had lost all his children, catechized four-year-old Theodore. Whom did he love best in the world? "Papa." Better than himself? "Yes, sir." Papa interjected: would he prefer to take a whipping, if one of them must, instead of his father? "I *said* nothing," but the plain fact of preferring his father to take the pain "tormented me for weeks in my long clothes."[36]

His father was both a skilled workman and a reader of history whose education had been cut short by the Revolution. He was sturdy and healthy, unlike "men brought up in the effeminate ways" of modern civilization.[37] But Parker did not link this observation to any thought that forsaking his father's way of life explained his own ill-health. Instead, he insisted his father had supported his intellectual precocity and drive. He associated the satisfaction he felt in maturity when a black minister praised him as "a *friend of mankind*" with his "deep joy" as a child when a school examiner praised his intelligence to his father. Clearly, he rehearsed memories of the sort that depth psychologies later classified and interpreted, but he could not unravel the connections between youthful emulation and mature altruism.

Memories of his mother allowed even fewer traces of conflict. Domestic and industrious, she was eminently religious: "To her the Deity was an Omnipotent Father, filling every point of space with His beautiful and loving presence." Theodore thanked her for "the nice and delicate care she took of my moral culture." Of all the events of his life, the one that left the deepest impression, he recalled, took place when he was four. He nearly killed a little tortoise but was checked by "a voice within me" announcing, "It is wrong!" When he told his mother, she "wiped a tear from her eye with her apron" and explained that he had experienced "the voice of God in the soul of man." If he listened, it would always guide him along the right path.

He was the youngest of his family's first nine children, and the tenth did not arrive till five years later. He was "mother's darling," according to his biographer; she "never weaned him." It must have been hard to leave such a childhood: he recalled humiliation when he was forced to change from infancy's "long clothes" to the tight-fitting garb of a boy. Perhaps he connected his early privilege with his abiding religious consciousness. Most of his incoherent effusions about immortality show a deep wish to disbelieve the possibility of loss. "Some parents have a strange way of educating their children; they take the breast from them spiritually as well as corporeally," he later wrote; "they do not train them up in love but in fear."

He recorded no memories of sibling rivalry, of violence, of unchaste thoughts. Childhood memories indicated how he wished to see himself as a man. He insisted both that he had no envy of others who bested him in childhood wrestling and that no personal animosity, despite the sarcasm, contaminated the antagonisms of his adult years.[38] In the serene evasions of his recollections of transitions in childhood we are prepared for some of the denials carried on in the name of the higher law. The sanitized naïveté of these recollections of childhood is congruent with the incompleteness of his commentary on the great battles in which he won fame.

First, he battled against Unitarianism; not as external critic, but from within as a voice of true and legitimate religion. He epitomizes the way one of the great generational conflicts in American cultural history was waged without direct examination of the agendas of father and son, parricide and youthful assertion.[39] Second, modern scholars observe that "the emotional core of Parker's great orations against slavery was constructed out of calls to violence and appeals to racial, tribal consciousness," that he was able to express feelings of "absolute hatred" associated with feelings of stifled manliness.[40] But Parker did not see this at all. In his own view, he was a man of peace; bloodshed would be avoided when New England manhood rose up in moral force against external aggressors (the kidnappers) and weak betrayers of the sacred hearth (Daniel Webster and other compromising politicians).

Third, he was quicker than most males to embrace the women's rights movement of his time. He shocked the orthodox by praying to God as Mother and showed unusual willingness to discuss sexual impulses, even female sexuality, as natural and necessary. But he tended to pity women who had no husbands or too few children; he criticized ladylike education that neglected housekeeping; and he believed that even when given equal rights women would generally prefer domestic to public functions. He called God Mother, "not by this figure implying that the Divine Being has the limitations of the female figure . . . but to express more sensibility, the quality of tender and unselfish love, which mankind associates with Mother than aught else besides."[41] He was a feminist who had remarkably little to say about women's public self-assertion. The emancipation of women was subsumed in their idealization. And in praising American practicality he showed hostility toward women's concerns with beauty.[42]

There is no point in faulting Parker for not holding views of psychology that flourished a half-century later. His focus on human nature belonged to an early stage of liberal progressivism, long before it learned to doubt the universality of moral law or to credit the universality of destructiveness and repression. However bland they may look to us, his ruminations on parents, childhood, and sexuality help to locate him in an era letting go of traditional verities and reaching optimistically for emerging certainties in the future. They are related to a drifting sense of sea-tossed change and subterranean currents that reduced life to experience. In such a period of adjustment, it was useful to maintain a view of the personal past from which unwelcome strains of antagonism had been erased.

The public past, in contrast, was shaped by conflict. Parker defined four great estates—"the organized trading power," "the organized political power," "the organized ecclesiastical power," and "the organized literary power"—in each of which a timid, respectable element was all too willing to let humanity down. They made him "the best hated man in America" until he learned to spread his ideas directly among the people without their aid.

"These four great social forces" were not, however, traditional, legitimate powers that forced opponents into un-American, iconoclastic recklessness. To the contrary, the inheritance of liberty, from Anglo-Saxon and Revolutionary roots, belonged to Parker and the movements to which he affiliated. The lesson of history, furthermore, was not that what the past had created should be undisturbed; it was a lesson of progressive development and inevitable change (which Parker considered to be the same). "The American people are making one of the most important experiments ever attempted on earth, endeavoring to establish an industrial democracy" based on principles of equal rights and popular sovereignty. "Certainly, we have human history against us," because the experiment had never before been tried on such a scale, "but I think human nature is on our side, and find no reason to doubt the triumph of the American idea."[43]

There were telling omissions from Parker's rendition of the historical moment through which he lived. His account of America's grand experiment excluded Jackson and the democracy. He did not heap scorn on them; apparently, they were too contemptible even to mention. America's political leadership, generally disappointing, showed occasional greatness. Washington was preeminent; his like would not appear again soon. Jefferson received passing praise for "his ideas." John Quincy Adams transcended the claims of section or party; his true greatness emerged not in his presidency but in his unpopular stance as an antislavery congressman voicing the claim of "the eternal right." The disgraced Webster possessed "greatness, even nobleness." Sumner and Seward were men "of great mark." But there is no reference to Jackson, by name, in *Theodore Parker's Experience*, and remarkably few in his other writings.[44] Parker probably had Jackson in mind when he commented: "In America there are few objects of conventional respect— no permanent classes who are born to be reverenced; and as men love to look up and do homage to what seems superior, a man of vulgar greatness, who has more of the sort of talent all have much of, is sure to become an idol if he will but serve the passions of his worshippers."[45] Parker's liberalism clearly did not oblige him to praise the decisions of *vox populi*. The "people" whom he praised were not the electorate but that circle of progressive, aspiring Easterners and Midwesterners who thronged to hear him in the lecture halls.

In religion as in politics, Parker contrived a popular-democratic view of history devoid of the people's most cherished creations. Writing thirty years later, after extensive research, another New England Unitarian noted throughout American life, by the end of the second decade of the nineteenth century, a marked "disposition to relax severity." Among evangelicals as well as religious liberals, Henry Adams detected a turning away from orthodox dogmas simply because they were "inconsistent with human self-esteem."[46] Parker, however, found evidence of religious progress only among Unitarians, Universalists, and freethinkers. Other American religious movements either belonged to the ecclesiastical estate that he disparaged or reflected, like the Democrats in politics, the conventional passions of the multitude. He failed to notice the rout of traditional systems of thought that emphasized human sinfulness and the precariousness of the social order. His account of the promise of the historical moment is weakened by overlooking the decline of Calvinism and dismissing revivalism as "hateful" and backward-looking.[47] Only briefly did he note: "Everywhere in the American churches there are signs of a tendency to drop all that rests merely on tradition and hearsay, to cling only to such facts as bide the test of critical search, and such doctrines as can be verified in human consciousness here and today."[48] This observation appears in "The Political Destination of America and the Signs of the Times," a major early assessment of American character written during the year of revolution in 1848, and even there it is undeveloped and passes over evangelicalism.

A look at recent scholarship on this period may suggest that it was just as well that Parker pushed his interpretation of history no further. We may wonder, indeed, how such a discerning public figure could have been so wrong in saying as much as he did. No one denies, of course, the extension of the franchise, the orchestrated frenzy of politics, the irreverence for the past, the emotional campaigns of revivalism. But scholars regularly present a portrait of the age as one of rampant consolidation in which the turmoil of the years immediately following the Revolution subsided. In this portrait, parties, led by wealthy men, prevented the people from making real choices. Conceptions of polite culture expanded to include many who formerly were left out of genteel, respectable lives. At the same time, scholars tell us, class lines were hardening around this polite society: there are many references to racism, social control, repression, middle-class social order. Strikingly, studies of evangelicalism depict the transformation of revivalism from the defiant enthusiasm of the 1750s or 1790s to respectable social control in the mid–nineteenth century. The ebullient reform movements that once seemed the hallmarks of an era of liberation now seem to indicate bourgeois moralizing forces that caged the implicit dangers of democracy.[49]

Was an intelligent participant in his times like Parker oblivious to changes that historians find so important? In part, perhaps. Although he had wrestled his way into Bostonian eminence and maintained antagonism toward the great estates, he was always a spokesman for progressive refinement and social order. Thus, if repressive cage doors clanked down while he hymned the opening of America, he may well have failed to see them. He was also well aware that other people were much less hospitable than he to "the great forward movements of mankind."[50] Progress was not inevitable; it came through struggle. In sermons against the fetishes of wealth and in advice to accept sexuality as natural to the human body—to cite just two examples—he was no servant of repressive conventions.

The larger truth is that consolidations and boundaries had ambiguous meanings: they left many people out but brought many others in. Revivals and temperance campaigns may indeed have erected barriers that separated a polite, respectable middle class from a rootless, casual work force. They enabled some people to express their difference from others.[51] The lyceums may have singled out the forms of curiosity and ambition that separated moral and earnest folk from the brutal and ignorant. The idea that New England was the epicenter of civilizing forces in a rough, wild continent plainly had the effect of drawing lines between regions where good work was under way and others where nothing was yet done. From certain perspectives, the lines being drawn in the reordering of the post-revolutionary world may appear imprisoning and unjust. But as Parker viewed them, these lines were elastic and could be stretched in accordance with new definitions of equality. The society they demarcated showed substantial gains over previous centuries: would its critics really prefer eighteenth-century attitudes toward women's rights, sexuality, or education?[52] And Parker was not merely celebrating the newest status quo. Some of his great sermons laid the basis for subsequent cries for more widespread distribution of privilege and respectability.

Besides, critics of Parker and the liberal vision he articulated ought to be careful not to adopt a view of evangelicalism as narrow as Parker's own. The major evangelical denominations did indeed furnish new institutions of middle-class respectability as the anti-hierarchical defiance of an earlier day's revivalism diminished. This revaluation of religious emotion is one of the great changes in American culture from the mid–eighteenth to the mid–nineteenth century, and it was related to a major reorganization of society. Evangelicalism encouraged feelings of appreciation and commitment in a transforming universe. It gave to the dictates of the heart priority over logic and theological abstraction. It was fully consistent with the programs of educational progress, emotional release, and literary refinement celebrated on the lecture circuits. Evangelical ministers were commonly on the local boards of lyceums as well as historical societies, libraries, and other cultural institutions. Evangelical denominations set up scores of new colleges and seminaries. Some of the lions of the lecture circuits were evangelical clergymen and professors. Moreover, evangelicalism was critically important to the reform movements that Parker hailed as hopeful indicators of America's moral progress. To the extent that Parker's version of history arrayed liberal reform and revivalistic religion as conflicting forces, it was a distortion.

Although there was indeed a mean-spirited element in revivalism that called for God to smite Parker and cheered his fatal illness, it would be more accurate to see Parker as reconciling what previously had been separated—

liberal Unitarian theology and evangelical reform impulses—in a new historical synthesis.[53] A case could be made for Parker himself as a great revivalist by noting his jeremiads on America's rampant problems, denunciation of the segregation of political expediency from divine law, castigations of the heartless rich, appeals to the intuition and emotion of the people, and repeated expressions of the need for "a real revival" including major changes in values and habits.[54] Where the line was drawn between Parker and the revivalists was, not over the importance of extending and strengthening religious belief in a secular democracy, but over the authority of the Bible.

By and large, American evangelicals had replied to decades of criticism of their innovations by claiming fidelity to scripture. God chose to work through "new measures" in altered stages of history, and it sometimes came to light that what had previously passed for properly Christian rituals and creeds were actually barriers to true Christian feeling and action. But there was one infallible source of guidance: the Bible. The fact of so much diversity and innovation, in a nation without an establishment to absorb and legitimize change, made the necessity of a bedrock source of authority in matters of faith all the more urgent. There was no arbiter that could determine what precisely constituted scriptural doctrine, but Americans commonly assumed, in good Protestant fashion, that any individual could see for himself or herself what the Bible said, and in revivals, owning up to the truth of the Bible became a key rite of passage for young people. American revivalism, oscillating between the pressure of collective emotion and the duty of private judgment, assumed that to all honest judgments the Bible would look and be the same.

It made this assumption despite the regularity with which new movements to end sectarianism by reducing issues of faith to the incontrovertible doctrines of scripture produced new sects and additional controversy. Whether new sects relied wholly on the revelation of the Bible, as with the so-called Christians; or on fresh modern revelations, as with the Mormons, the result was equally paradoxical. All evangelicals—and that means the majority of American Christians—sought to place absolute reliance on a text and thus, in turn, on a view of the human mind as unchangingly able to read texts in the same way and to draw the same conclusions. Parker's deviation from this orthodoxy and his insistence on raising troublesome issues about texts and human psychology made him detestable to the evangelicals. In this same deviation we recognize his modernity.

Parker's role in American theological conflict at mid-century is puzzling, however, in that he, like other revivalists, professed to revere the Bible and to take an ahistorical approach to human psychology. At least, he did most of the time, for it is impossible to state without ambiguity the positions on revelation, human nature, and history that Parker preached throughout his experience on earth. This does not mean that he was insincere or uncertain, only that he seems not to have felt any need to probe issues that a twentieth-century reader might have urged him to face. For better or worse, he was the preacher who put the Bible in William Craft's hand so that the ex-slave would hold the source of the world's greatest truth, and he was also the man accused of demolishing the Bible's sacred status in modern civilization. He revered Jesus as the exemplar of perfection, greater than all other prophets and teachers; yet he was vilified for eliminating the basis of Christianity as true religion.

In part, the problem was one of temperament and intellectual method. Even though he took radical positions that alienated him from conventional opinion, and even though he presented himself as an interpreter of the most advanced scholarship, he always spoke as a tribune of the people's common sense. In his own mind, he modified evolving tradition without subverting it. Despite his bravado, he exemplifies William James's later account of the manner in which people accept new ideas: "New truth is always a go-between, a smoother-over of transitions. It marries old opinion to new fact so as to show a minimum of jolt, a maximum of continuity."[55]

This characteristic stance may be seen in his critique of David Strauss and other myth critics of the Bible. He saw three choices. We may agree with Strauss that the Bible rests on "no historical ground which is firm and undeniably certain, but only a little historical matter, around which tradition has wrapped legends and myths." Or instead, "we may believe every word is historically true, . . . that there is neither myth nor fable," as did some scholars and many evangelical believers. Or we can see "that the Bible, and in particular the New Testament, always rests on historical ground, though it is not common historical ground, *nor is it so rigidly historical that no legendary or mythical elements have entered it.*" The first two "theories" were simple and attractive, but untenable, "while the *third is natural, easy, and offends neither the cultivated understanding nor the pious heart.*"[56] The point is important because Parker rose to prominence as a linguist and biblical scholar who recognized that there was too much in German higher criticism for Americans to ignore it. As a student he quickly learned "that the Bible is a collection of quite heterogeneous books, most of them anonymous, or bearing names of doubtful authors, collected none knows how, or when, or by whom; united more by caprice than any philosophic or historic method, so that it is not easy to see why one ancient book is kept in the Canon and another kept out."[57] Yet he persisted in defining a natural and easy way for believing the Bible was a holy work and as rooted in history as possible.

Similarly, he worked his way out of familiar distinctions between inductive and intuitive approaches to knowledge, between a psychological sensationalism based on observation of the facts of the universe and a transcendentalism based on *a priori* promptings of the human spirit. His radical reputation placed him in the latter camp, and his account of his student crisis leads us to expect that that was where he belonged. Nevertheless, he criticized other Transcendentalists for placing too little emphasis on scientific and historical fact. Knowledge of God, in particular, arose spontaneously from intuitive perception, but it was "beautifully confirmed" by observations made in the material world. No doubt, he said, the religious sentiment came first, but this belief did not quell Parker's lifelong inquiries into biblical and ecclesiastical history and comparative ethnology for confirming evidence of that persistent human feeling of dependence on the infinite.[58] In his own view, he endeavored to rescue historic Christianity from being dragged down by misguided champions who attached it to abhorrent views of divine caprice and human sin and implausible stories of miracles. He protected historic Christianity, equally, from the absurdities of pantheists who regarded God as nothing "but the sum-total of the existing universe" and of atheists who took the further step of dismissing God altogether.[59] Only the universal religious consciousness, recognizable in "the deep words of Jesus,"[60] beneath the wash of unlikely narratives and beyond the shifting claims of churchmen throughout the centuries, could confidently sustain the "Theism" or "Absolute Religion" that he cherished.

This seeker for the *via media* was hated and admired because of the complex, unresolved quality of his ruminations on history that seemed destructive to both church and sacred text. He wanted to believe both that the truth emerged from the process of history and that truth was changeless and absolute. He was sure that history supported religion. "The history of the world shows clearly that Religion is the highest of all human concerns." History recorded the stages of cultural development, from animal wildness, to fetichism, to polytheism, to monotheism; in Christian civilization, furthermore, it recorded the progress through dark ages of Catholic error to the increasingly humane triumphs of the Reformation and Unitarianism. Ascent was not uniform: there were savage saints and modern idolators, and everywhere was evidence "that no two men can exhibit their Religion in just the same way." However "subjective conceptions" varied, the common instinctive element was always visible; the direction of progress was never in doubt.[61] Parker's uncompleted magnum opus was to have shown in the history of religion, and specifically Christianity, that "the development of man's spirit, of his soul as well as mind," was no more "arbitrary" than developments in science and politics.[62] This masterwork was unfinished. The explanation was not deficiency of scholarship, nor was it simply the pressing call of antislavery and the intercession of disease. Parker could not make the facts of history race forward as progressively as they were supposed to do. He was too anxious to cling to ancient truth and too impressed by the destructiveness of time.

The slavery controversy forced some rethinking. It made him reluctant to take seriously the corollary to a view of progressive development that made ethical pronouncements relative to the time and place where they were framed. At one point in his career, abolitionists scolded him for seeming to hold that slavery had been permissible in ancient civilizations. In time he found that laws verified by human intuition indicted the same crimes in all ages.[63] More fundamental was his mounting appreciation of the influence of Jesus and the power of words to transcend history. Impressed as he was by evidence that both Old and New Testaments were flawed by errors stemming from the historical circumstances of their composition—even Jesus acquired "the erroneous notions" of his times—there was something awe-inspiring in the continuing influence across the centuries of this "collection of books," which was "woven into the literature of the scholar," gave strength to the "affianced maiden" and shipwrecked mariner, and accompanied "the peddler, in his crowded pack." The plain words of "a young man full of genius for Religion," "the companion of the rudest men," repudiated by the mighty but welcomed in the hovels of the poor and weak, had lit a ray of light shining for all times. This record of truth prevailing throughout the chaos of history was too precious for the scholar-reformer of the mid–nineteenth century to discard.[64]

Truth everlasting was one of the major themes—Parker surely would have said *the* major theme—of *The Transient and Permanent in Christianity*. This ordination sermon incited rebukes from orthodox churchmen, embarrassed Unitarian colleagues, and alienated Parker from his own sect. He later distanced himself from it as too hastily written. Perhaps so, though he was never more eloquent, passionate, and compelling. It is hard not to think that here we see his deepest feelings unobscured by the poses of scholar or reformer. The sermon's excitement springs from its appreciation of the unabated vitality and pertinence of words uttered many centuries ago.

The text was from Luke: "Heaven and earth shall pass away: but my words shall not pass away" (21:33). Christ stated his redemptive truth in words. Nothing seems more fleeting than a word, "an evanescent impulse of the most fickle element." Christ did not even write them down; he "scattered them broadcast" and "trusted them to the uncertain air." Yet all over the world they proved to be imperishable, still as "distinct as when first warm from his lips," their influence deepening and widening wherever men and women lived. The text in which they occurred was like a river "that springs up in the heart of a sandy continent, having its father in the skies, and its birthplace in distant, unknown mountains; as the stream rolls on, enlarging itself, making in that arid waste a belt of verdure wherever it turns its way;

creating palm groves and fertile plains, where the smoke of the cottages curls up at eventide, and marble cities send the gleam of their splendour far into the sky; such has been the course of the Bible on earth." All this melioration—not a boy or girl in Christendom whose lot was not improved by "that great book"—because a rather simple young man "told what he saw—the truth"—and "lived what he felt—a life of love."[65]

· This river of Christian influence and social progress was only one image in Parker's treatment of a "topic that seems not inappropriate to the times in which we live." There was also "the stream of time" that "has already beat down philosophies and theologies" and laid bare "a perishing element in what we call Christianity." Jesus' word may have been forever, but "who tells us that *our* word shall never pass away? that *our* notion of his Word shall stand forever?"[66] The theme that appalled critics in Parker's day and seizes the attention of modern readers is the fallibility of texts and the textuality of all forms and institutions. By far the majority of the pages of this sermon take up the variability of doctrines and institutions from one era to the next. The difference between the Christianities of different eras is "greater than the difference between Mahomet and the Messiah"; and "the difference at this day between opposing sects of Christians," and between some of those sects and "that of Christ himself, is deeper and more vital than that between Jesus and Plato, pagan as we call him." Almost all the doctrines and institutions that had been made to pass for Christianity were inessential and transient, and so they remained in the present. Doctrines were based on opinion; "like the clouds of the sky, they are here to-day; tomorrow all swept off and vanished." Forms and institutions were based on temporary fashion; they were "rubbish" piled against "the temple of Truth."[67]

Mostly Parker rehearsed these observations without explaining why they were so, but he did offer an important analogy between the histories of religion and of science. Though there could be only one "system of nature," there were inevitably many theories of nature because of the varying observations human beings made, the limitations of their vision, changes in the instruments they used, faults in the deductions they made, and the "second-hand" quality of many premises they accepted. For similar reasons, he maintained, there could be only one absolutely true religion, but philosophies of religion were numerous and subject to change. In both cases truth was unvarying, but doctrines were "transitory."[68]

One ostensible conclusion was that Jesus avoided the pitfalls of observation and opinion that corrupted so much of the religion that took his name. Those who respond to the truth he preached do the same, and the lesson is that all people, like Jesus, must "worship with nothing between us and God." Parker gave almost no attention to describing or analyzing the history-free, cultureless condition such worship must require. Since his purpose was to justify the adoption in his own time of views that others counted as dangerous heresies, his argument was ambiguous. It was bound to be heard, not as praising immutable texts and absolute religion, but as authorizing the widest range of private searches for truth.

The analogy between science and religion raised disturbing questions, though Parker could not have understood the vulnerability of American liberalism to changes in the procedures and findings of science. There were enough problems in his contention that Jesus in religion, like Euclid in science, articulated fundamental laws, each of which "is true . . . because it is true," not because of the personal authority of the one who expressed it.[69] This was to ignore important issues of scientific demonstration and verification, even if one believed the universe to be a hard object that yielded everlasting knowledge. But Parker entertained the insight that what counted as scientific and religious knowledge was subject to changing conventions and resources, and we are entitled to wonder what might happen to his own "system" if the scientific conception of the universe enlarged and scientific theories came to seem more provisional and competitive. It was very important to Parker to retain the glimmer of permanence even if culture and history yelled *transience*. And he was able to do so primarily by appealing to a faith in the universality of human nature and the invariability of science and ethics.

Even though key issues about the historical relativism of scientific truth did not emerge clearly for several decades after his lifetime, Parker, in his deeply contradictory and often ambivalent expressions, had already shown an unsettling awareness of the degree to which social institutions and personal motivations were shaped by cultural conventions. How to reconcile this awareness with some of his cherished convictions, including his belief in progressive development and timeless truth, is a problem he scarcely explored. It is better to read his "discourse," a word chosen to indicate something of the provisional and unsystematic quality of his own utterance, as we might read a poem expressing strong emotions and troubling insights, rather than as we might read a philosophical investigation. Life was a matter of "experience," in which cultural tradition felt the pressure of new challenges, no matter how directly the individual sought to communicate with God.

On the Bible, as on other subjects, Parker sought to navigate along a middle course. On one hand, his thoughts contrast with Thoreau's in the "Sunday" chapter of *A Week on the Concord and Merrimack Rivers*, which uses the same text from Luke. Coasting along his rivers, feeling holier than churchgoers scurrying over a bridge, musing on the insubstantiality of history and artificiality of civilization, Thoreau meditated on the power of each myth "to express a variety of truths." To view a myth dogmatically was "like striving to make the sun, or the wind, or the sea symbols to signify exclusively the particular thoughts of the day. But what signifies it? In the mythus a superhuman intelligence uses the unconscious thoughts and dreams of men as its hieroglyphics to address men unborn." While praising the life of Jesus (comparable to that of "my Buddha"), Thoreau questioned whether ordinary Christians—followers of custom, slaves of conscience—could ever really see the "beauty and significance" of the New Testament. As the freedom of the river journey contrasted with the conventionality of the churches, Thoreau offered thoughts on genius and poetry. He was less dogmatic about human nature than Parker, more open-ended in his understanding of the meanings of words and things, more skeptical of material and intellectual progress, more uncompromising in his opposition to authority. "Even Christ, we fear, had his scheme, his conformity to tradition, which slightly vitiates his teaching."[70] On the other hand, of course, there were Christians, inside and outside Unitarian New England, for whom the slightest doubts about scriptural authority were blasphemy, and for whom attacks on the historical succession of Christian institutions and doctrines invited anarchy. The most innovative, democratic sects were likely to be the most intolerant of anyone who dwelt on errors in the Bible.

Parker's *via media* needs emphasis because it calls attention to essential compromises in the liberal progressive temper as it took shape in the United States. He illustrates most of the traits of modernity uncovered in the life of Henry Wright—attacks on old privileges, receptiveness to new methods, fascination with human needs and emotions. He was an influential celebrant of the progress of culture and human intelligence, but there was an unmoored quality to his statements on present experience and social goals. Much more than Wright (though less than Thoreau), he recognized that deserting the shore of the past meant a disturbing voyage on the stream of the constantly shifting present. Yet he also tried, rather poignantly, to attach as much significance as possible to the progressive development of civilization and the permanence of truth, two reassuring thoughts even if it was somewhat illogical to hold them simultaneously. He became increasingly a hero to subsequent generations, and well he should, for he had articulated the liberal progressive view of history better than any other American of his era. He also had explored the language of discourse, experience, and transiency that expressed the doubts and reservations of later generations as they confronted modernity.

EPILOGUE

Retelling the Story

As our physiognomic expressions vary, each face
bearing upon it as a signboard, the idiosyncrasies which
characterize the soul within, so may we learn the
impossibility of every mind seeing truth with the *same
eye*, or accepting it on the *same plane*. We *must* differ in
our opinions, just as certainly as travellers differ in
their descriptions, who view a landscape from various
eminences of the same hill, or from different standpoints on the top, or under varying conditions of the
atmosphere—clouds or sunshine, fog or rain, storms or
snow. When this great principle is realized interiorly—
as applicable to the mental vision as well as to the
bodily eye, then will the golden rule be *lived*—not
talked.

> —HARRIOT K. HUNT, *Glances and Glimpses; or, Fifty
> Years Social, Including Twenty Years Professional Life*

No single story that survives from the Age of Jackson can impose unity on all
the themes of America's early transition from a new nation, bearing a revolutionary legacy, to a modern nation, trying to chart a course down the stream
of time. There is no single story that could dislodge Manny Schwartz's
feelings that only the past, symbolized by the Hermitage, is nourishing and
protective and that we have strayed too far from lost ideals and traditions. No
story can cure popular nostalgia or disprove contentions that only in the past

265

century has America passed through its great transformation. Since then, as Cecelia Brady learned, all we can do is collect information without any certainty about what we ought to do. "You can't test the best way—except by doing it. So you just do it."[1] That's better than suicide in a world of fakery, but didn't America promise something better than that?

Some stories we have heard and retold promise almost nothing better. We may pause beside Alexis de Tocqueville at Frenchman's Island, muse on nature as retreating paradise, observe the cottage abandoned by greedy man, and repeat sadly, "What! Ruins so soon!" Mostly, however, we have heard stories containing glimpses of something better in the very process of change, in thoughts of "natural grandeur" coming to an end and anticipation of civilization's "triumphant march." In such "consciousness of destruction, this *arrière pensée* of quick and inevitable change," Tocqueville found the source of the American continent's "touching beauty."[2] Often these stories wish to freeze forever some midpoint in the process of change—the suburban villas designed by Andrew Jackson Downing and admired by Fredrika Bremer, the landscaped parks promoted by Frederick Law Olmsted as alternatives to the barbarism of city and frontier, the "partially cultivated country" surrounding New England villages that Henry David Thoreau called "the natural consequence of what art and refinement we as a people have."[3] But the wish cannot be satisfied. The city edges out into the suburbs; parks become barbaric; the pastoral village is deserted.

In some versions, the American story features theatrical illusions, not very sophisticated ones at that, and games of confidence testing the mettle of young men who leave their country homes to seek their fortunes. Similar tales come down from other times and places, but Nathaniel Hawthorne gave us versions located exactly among post-revolutionary Americans who rushed to discard relics of the past and to embrace the comforts of the present. In his versions, Americans too readily deceived themselves and embraced the pretensions of others. They were too eager to accept the madman as a reformer. Hawthorne reminds us more clearly than any other post-revolutionary storyteller that it was not the destruction of nature alone, but the destruction of the past as well, that awakened misgivings and regrets; yet he also evokes the wonder of a new world in which storytelling itself is the foremost intellectual activity. His tale "The Seven Vagabonds" deserves frequent retelling,[4] and the mood of the American audience may change from one occasion to the next. "How perfect!" the audience may exclaim one day after hearing the narrative of the young man who goes off with gypsies and resolves to make his living as a wandering reciter of fictions. "Is that all there is?" we hear the day after. This is one story that Hawthorne never quite finished: from a later rendition we discover that the young man goes back to life under the oppressive care of an old-school parson. But the young man cannot forget his adventure with the vagabonds and returns to a life of itinerancy and fiction.[5]

Yet it is only a single story, and it may leave out much. Perhaps it omits those who were never offered or accepted the New England minister's guardianship and thus could not leave it. Except for a beautiful carnival entertainer, it leaves out women. Men may have sometimes complained about the restless masquerade of professional life, but the road was open to them as it was usually not to respectable women.

We see some of the meanings of the road in the private diaries of Elizabeth Steele, a bright New Jerseyan who married a traveling lecturer named Wright in 1846. She set off with him immediately on his travels through the South, where he lectured at colleges and public halls on electromagnetism, astronomy, and other scientific subjects, and examined heads and effected cures on the side. The incessant travel was arduous and occasionally dangerous, but as her diary makes plain, enjoyable, too. The roads were filled with travelers. She saw a minstrel show and courthouses packed with lawyers. Never was life more fun than in the winter of 1849 when the Wrights traveled in Florida with a couple named Schaffer, who exhibited a menagerie. One evening Mrs. Wright watched Mrs. Schaffer, "the lion queen," perform.

> She astonishes the natives with her daring. There are a great many bets that she is a man, passing off for a woman. Some remark, if a woman can do that they are capable of anything.

Seven weeks later the two couples rendezvoused in an Alabama town "thronged with country people come to see the managerie." According to Mrs. Wright's diary:

> Mrs. Schaffer performed splendidly today. The pavilion was filled to overflowing. This is an exciting way to live so that sometimes I almost fear a quiet life will not be agreeable.[6]

Elizabeth Wright was pregnant and soon settled down in Prairie du Sac, Wisconsin, where she managed a home built out of profits from the scientific lectures while her husband continued his traveling ways alone.*

---

*Some male residents of her town disapproved of women's attending to business, as Elizabeth Wright was obliged to do while her husband was on tour. One response to men's incessant traveling may have been adamancy about women's domestic sphere, but no doubt new roles for women were easily imagined. A young woman in Boston, Mary Dow, wrote to her husband, an auctioneer trying to make a go of it in California, that she was

Of course, it is not just the story of the seven vagabonds that ignored women's professional aspirations. The side of American culture that was associated with images of the road, with its peddlers and entertainers, constricted intellectual opportunity for some, at least in the short run, while expanding it for others. As we have seen, however, American culture had another side, preoccupied with the improvement of manners and intelligence and the perfection of civilization. Here women had many roles to play. Although Bremer, for example, rhapsodized on the beautiful homes built for sheltered wives by traveling husbands, she also described how networks of women supported educational and cultural initiatives across the length and breadth of the continent. Without such women, Henry Wright would not have received a scholarship to go to Andover Seminary, and Theodore Parker would have found the lecture halls, in which he won fame, half-empty and perhaps unbuilt. In the long run, women's support of reform and progress proved to be a first step toward new endeavors of their own. "A few years ago," reported a black participant in a New York antislavery meeting, "Men in this City hissed at the mere idea of Women's speaking in public in promiscuous assemblies." But times were changing: men began to flock to conventions, "attracted by the announcement that Women are to take part in the deliberations, and they are often more desirous of hearing Women, than Men."[7]

As it stands, the story of the vagabonds recovers only part of what Tocqueville said all Americans believed, the half that presented humanity as a constantly changing picture.[8] Can we recite the story in a different way, revising it to include the other half? Can we turn it into a story about education and progress as well as mummery and huckstering; can we make it reflect the visions of Ralph Waldo Emerson and Parker as well as those of Sol Smith and P. T. Barnum? Can we transpose Elizabeth Steele Wright back beside her husband and the lion queen? Suppose the young man who leaves home is female, or suppose that a brother and sister, or husband and wife, escape the parson's oppressive domicile. Or suppose that some of the collegial vagabonds are reformers, including women, who hold strong convictions about what is morally right and that together they make speeches, collect funds, and fill petitions with the names of Americans who aim to end injustice and to spread enlightenment. They journey along the same roads as

---

learning to stand up for herself in public. A friend had teasingly compared her to Abigail Folsom, an eccentric reformer notorious for haranguing conventions. "Do you think I shall do to turn *lecture*[r] and advocate 'Womans rights'[?]" she asked her husband. "I am get[t]ing very independent and am assured if I have my way much longer you will find it harder to tighten the rein than in the first place." To J. Gilman Dow, June 16, 1850, Papers of John Russell Young (Library of Congress).

vendors and mountebanks whose purposes are less uplifting, and in moments of worry they view their own activities as no different from their companions'. Sometimes they themselves enjoy, or shudder at, stories in which the most high-minded performances are reduced to meaningless claptrap, stories in which life is indistinguishable from a masquerade.

Through it all, they grope for ways to defend moral earnestness amid a world of shows. Some turn to new reforms; others see in literature and lecture halls a means of elevating the democratic populace. They know, more and more each year, that life is an uncharted stream, but they never go so far as to doubt the existence of fundamental truth. They accept the modern world but are reluctant to turn their backs on the past. Sometimes they go back to take a look at the protective homes they departed from. When nothing about the future appears secure, some of them turn to spiritualism and hope for guidance from the dead, while others find reassurance in the survival of Jesus' simple words or the prevalence of religious emotions throughout the centuries in spite of the demise of orthodoxies and the crumbling of conventions. Of the bad, they say, "this too shall pass"; of the good, "the signs of the times point ahead to perfection."

No one wrote this story. Those who were most committed to promoting the advance of civilization did not indulge much in fiction. As a story that we are inventing, this one may not have much action, though no less than Hawthorne's, and we might need to pay more attention to the vagabonds' encounters with love and death.[9] Even so, it has other defects when compared with Hawthorne's. It lacks the "self-referential" intricacy prized by the modern intellect: it does not turn back into itself as a story told about storytelling. It is hard to frame a story around people who felt the significance of their actions lay outside their own lives. If our goal is to capture a sense of connectedness between post-revolutionary encounters with modernity and those of later times, we could not tell a traditional story, and we would have to experiment with language and form in order to show our recognition of the fragmentation of public experience and the illogical flow of private consciousness. We might not be able to do so in a historical narrative that rests on empirical facts. We could never do so in a book conveniently structured so that it reaches an end.

Notes

Notes to Prologue

1. F. Scott Fitzgerald, *The Last Tycoon: An Unfinished Novel*, ed. Edmund Wilson (New York: Scribner's, 1986), 3–20, 33, 131, 135.

2. *Ibid.*, 129.

3. Robert Sklar, *F. Scott Fitzgerald: The Last Laocoön* (New York: Oxford, 1967), 335–41.

4. See George Dangerfield, *The Awakening of American Nationalism, 1815–1828* (New York: Harper, 1965); and *idem, The Era of Good Feelings* (New York: Harcourt, Brace, 1952). The portrait of Monroe is in *ibid.*, 97. On Madison, see Drew R. McCoy, *The Last of the Fathers: James Madison and the Republican Legacy* (Cambridge, England: Cambridge Univ., 1989). For Jefferson and Adams, see Lester J. Cappon, ed., *The Adams–Jefferson Letters*, 2 vols. (Chapel Hill: Univ. of North Carolina, 1959), II, 456.

5. See Arthur Schlesinger, Jr.'s, great work, *The Age of Jackson* (Boston: Little, Brown, 1945). On the common man, see Carl Russell Fish, *The Rise of the Common Man* (New York: MacMillan, 1927); and on the ubiquity of reform, see Alice Felt Tyler, *Freedom's Ferment: Phases of American Social History to 1860* (New York: Harper & Row, 1965); and Henry Steele Commager, ed., *The Era of Reform, 1830–1860* (Malabar, Fla.: Robert E. Kreiger, 1978). For the most recent view of this era as "a remarkable and life-enhancing age," in which Jacksonianism and reforms were interconnected, see Robert V. Remini, *The Jacksonian Era* (Arlington Heights, Ill.: Harlan Davidson, 1989), 98.

6. For a comprehensive summary of criticisms of received views, see Edward Pessen, *Jacksonian America: Society, Personality, and Politics* (Urbana: Univ. of Illinois, 1985).

7. Harry L. Watson, *Liberty and Power: The Politics of Jacksonian America* (New York: Noonday, 1990), 28–29. I received Charles Sellers's *The Market Revolution, 1815–1848* (New York: Oxford, 1991), a more extensive work with the same theme, too late to consult in completing this book.

8. Robert H. Wiebe, *The Opening of American Society: From the Adoption of the Constitution to the Eve of Disunion* (New York: Vintage, 1985), 143–67.

9. Lee Benson, *The Concept of Jacksonian Democracy: New York as a Test Case* (Princeton: Princeton Univ., 1961), 12, 336; Gordon S. Wood, "Ideology and the Origins of Liberal America," *William and Mary Quarterly* 44 (July 1987): 640.

10. The excitement is recaptured in Lionel Trilling, "On the Teaching of Modern Literature," *Beyond Culture: Essays on Literature and Learning* (New York: Viking, 1965), 3–30.

11. It may be only in contemporary controversy that this claim needs to be made. Note that Trilling (in *op. cit.*) went well back in time—to Diderot's *Rameau's Nephew*, for example. Note also that in American Studies, Perry Miller saw precursors of modernist formal experiments in works like Amos Bronson Alcott's orphic utterances and in Transcendentalist poetry. *The American Transcendentalists: Their Prose and Poetry*, ed. Perry Miller (Garden City, N.Y.: Anchor, 1957), 217.

12. I follow other historians in using this term to indicate my awareness that I am not discussing all aspects of life that anthropologists include when they study "culture." See, for example, Thomas Bender, *New York Intellect: A History of Intellectual Life in New York City from 1750 to the Beginnings of Our Own Time* (Baltimore: Johns Hopkins, 1987), xv.

Notes to Chapter One

1. *Diary of My Travels in America*, trans. Stephen Becker (New York: Delacorte, 1976), 13, 41, 60–61, 71, 116–7, 119.

2. Ann Erwin, typescript, April 1818, Yeatman-Polk Collection, Tennessee State Library and Archives. I owe this reference to the kindness of Harold Moser.

3. *The Works of Philip Lindsley, D.D.*, ed. Le Roy J. Halsey, 3 vols. (Philadelphia: Lippincott, 1859–1866), I, 439, and III, 607–12; F. Garvin Davenport, *Cultural Life in Nashville on the Eve of the Civil War* (Chapel Hill: Univ. of North Carolina, 1941), 1–31.

4. Davenport, *Cultural Life, passim*; Henry Ruffner, "Notes on a Tour from Virginia to Tennessee in the Months of July and August 1838," *Travels in the Old South: Selected from the Periodicals of the Times*, ed. Eugene L. Schwaab, 2 vols. (Lexington: Univ. of Kentucky, 1973), II, 351.

5. Anita Shafer Goodstein, *Nashville, 1780–1860: From Frontier to City* (Gainesville: Florida Univ., 1989), chaps. 3, 9. "Good Village" is Goodstein's term.

6. There are two excellent interpretative studies of this tour: Fred Somkin, *Unquiet Eagle: Memory and Desire in the Idea of American Freedom, 1815–1860* (Ithaca: Cornell Univ., 1967), 131–74; Anne C. Loveland, *Emblem of Liberty: The Image of Lafayette in the American Mind* (Baton Rouge: Louisiana State Univ., 1971). The latter notes the differences between the reactions of "upper-class"

Americans and those of "the majority" (129–30) and discusses the issue of "relativism" (89–92, 126). Somkin raises searching questions about alienation from the past.

7. A. Levasseur, *Lafayette in America in 1824 and 1825; or, Journal of a Voyage to the United States*, 2 vols. (Philadelphia: Carey & Lea, 1829), II, 152. In the account that follows, I rely on this work and, in greater detail, Edgar Ewing Brandon, *A Pilgrimage of Liberty: A Contemporary Account of the Triumphal Tour of General Lafayette through the Southern and Western States in 1825, as Reported by the Local Newspapers* (Athens, Ohio: Lawhead Press, 1944), 229–55.

8. Like other European visitors, Lafayette's secretary commented on the "entirely American" manners of women: "that is, they devote almost their whole existence to the management of the household, and the education of their children." Though many were good conversationalists, they lived in relative retirement. "Young ladies," on the other hand, were well educated and enjoyed "unlimited liberty," which gave them a "grace and frankness" that contrasted with the reserve of Europe's sequestered young ladies. Once they were engaged, they began to put aside their "thoughtless gaiety." After marriage, they were remarkable for their "severe conjugal fidelity"—and for their retirement. Levasseur, *Lafayette*, I, 126–27. *Cf.* Tocqueville's more famous description of the same pattern, below pp. 118–19.

9. Levasseur, *Lafayette*, II, 165.

Notes to Chapter Two

1. George Wilson Pierson, *Tocqueville in America* (Garden City, N.Y.: Doubleday, 1959), 366–8.

2. *Ibid.*, 368, 372; Alexis de Toqueville, *Journey to America*, ed. J. P. Mayer, trans. George Lawrence (Garden City, N.Y.: Anchor, 1971), 280–85.

3. Tocqueville, *Journey*, 283.

4. *Ibid.*, 285.

5. *Ibid.*, 268.

6. Tocqueville, *Democracy in America*, ed. J. P. Mayer, trans. George Lawrence (Garden City, N.Y.: Anchor, 1969), 278. Unless otherwise noted, all references are to this edition.

Notes to Chapter Three

1. This is one theme of Harriette Simpson Arnow's *Seedtime on the Cumberland* (New York: MacMillan, 1960).

2. In these pages I generally follow Robert V. Remini, *Andrew Jackson and the Course of American Empire, 1767–1821* (New York: Harper & Row, 1977); *Andrew Jackson and the Course of American Freedom, 1822–1832* (New York: Harper & Row, 1981); and *Andrew Jackson and the Course of American Democracy, 1833–1845* (New York: Harper & Row, 1984), which I cite hereafter as Remini, *Jackson*, I, II, and III. I also rely on *The Papers of Andrew Jackson*, vol. I, ed. Sam B. Smith and Harriet Chappell Owsley (Knoxville: Univ. of Tennessee, 1980); and vol. II, ed.

Harold D. Moser and Sharon MacPherson (Knoxville: Univ. of Tennessee, 1984), hereafter cited as *Papers of Jackson.*

   3. Michael Paul Rogin, *Fathers and Children: Andrew Jackson and the Subjugation of the American Indian* (New York: Knopf, 1975). See also my review essay, *History and Theory* 16 (1977): 175–95.

   4. Remini, *Jackson,* I, 38–39; *Papers of Jackson,* I, 12.

   5. W. J. Cash, *The Mind of the South* (New York: Vintage, 1960 [1941]), 20, 22.

   6. Goodstein, *Nashville,* 1–18.

   7. See Remini, *Jackson,* I, 54–5, 87. Documentation is "incomplete," but he was "a willing participant in any land scheme that seemed promising."

   8. Rogin, *Fathers,* 165–205.

   9. On the general pattern, see Goodstein, *Nashville,* 20–21.

   10. *Ibid.,* 11. On tertium quids (unaligned political operators) and quiddery, see Robert Wiebe, *Opening,* 196–99.

   11. *Papers of Jackson,* I, 72, 74, 103, 111, 117, 147, 183, 230.

   12. See the story that Remini takes from James Parton, in Remini, *Jackson,* I, 40. Jackson has been placed in a populist tradition mainly on the basis of appeals to "the humble members of society" in his Bank Veto message and other presidential addresses. He had nothing in common with late–nineteenth-century populist calls for soft currency, and in the Depression of 1819 he opposed debtor relief. And many scholars have pointed out that the Bank Veto benefited people who were far from humble.

   13. See John William Ward, *Andrew Jackson—Symbol for an Age* (New York: Oxford, 1962), 13–29. This is still the best analysis of the Jackson legend.

   14. Remini, *Jacksonian Era,* 21–22; Watson, *Liberty and Power,* 96–97. The story is irresistible.

   15. A good approach to the changing portraits may be found in Charles Sellers, ed., *Andrew Jackson: A Profile* (New York: Hill & Wang, 1971).

   16. To John Coffee, June 18, 1824, *The Correspondence of Andrew Jackson,* ed. John S. Bassett, 6 vols. (Washington: Carnegie Institution, 1926–1935), III, 256. This work is cited hereafter as *Correspondence of Jackson. Cf.* Jackson's letter to George W. Martin, Jan. 2, 1824, *ibid.,* II, 222: "I am told the opinion of those [in Washington] whose minds were prepared to see me with a Tomahawk in one hand, and a scalping knife in the other has greatly changed and I am getting on very smoothly."

   17. To Coffee, Feb. 5, 1824, *ibid.,* 229.

   18. See the letters, 1817 and 1822, to A. J. Donelson, *ibid.,* II, 275–76, 440–42; III, 156–57, 159, 162, 178–79; the letters, 1829–1832, to and concerning his ward A. J. Hutchings in *ibid.,* IV, 54–57, 76, 348–49, 376–77, 405–6; and to Andrew Jackson, Jr., *ibid.,* V, 335–36. In 1822 he imagined Donelson's election to the presidency (III, 162); in other words, the decorum he recommended was allied with dynastic dreams.

   19. See chap. 6, "The Decline of the Gentleman," in Hofstadter, *Anti-intellectualism in American Life* (New York: Vintage, 1966), 145–71; and chap. 3,

"Andrew Jackson and the Rise of Liberal Capitalism," in *idem, The American Political Tradition* (New York: Vintage, 1954), 45–67.

20. Robert Gray Gunderson, *The Log-Cabin Campaign* (Lexington: Univ. of Kentucky, 1957); Ward, *Andrew Jackson—Symbol*, 79–97.

21. Ralph Ketcham, *Presidents above Party: The First American Presidency, 1789–1829* (Chapel Hill, Univ. of North Carolina, 1984). Actually Ketcham, who makes subtle distinctions throughout, focuses more on Martin Van Buren than on Jackson as the architect of a new order. In general, however, historians have been too anxious to demarcate the end of republicanism and its replacement by democratic liberalism, when in fact several traditions, some of them contradictory, blended in nineteenth-century thinking. See Dorothy Ross, *The Origins of American Social Science* (Cambridge, England: Cambridge Univ., 1991), 22–30.

22. James Parton, *Life of Andrew Jackson*, 3 vols. (New York: Mason Brothers, 1860), III, 684–85, is quoted, without the irony, at the outset of Remini, *Jackson*, I, 1–2. On the "mistake," see Parton, *op. cit.*, III, 694. On the Whig view of Jackson, see Charles Grier Sellers, Jr., "Andrew Jackson versus the Historians," *Mississippi Valley Historical Review* 44 (1958): 615–19.

23. In 1887, Bancroft came to Nashville and told black students at Fisk University that Jackson ranked second only to Washington among America's presidents. Lilian Handlin, *George Bancroft: The Intellectual as Democrat* (New York: Harper & Row, 1984), 340.

24. Garry Wills, *Cincinnatus: George Washington and the Enlightenment* (Garden City, N.Y.: Doubleday, 1984). For advice to Jackson to cultivate the Cincinnatus analogy, see Arthur P. Hayne to Jackson, Dec. 27, 1827, *Correspondence of Jackson*, III, 386.

25. Of his view of himself as shunning electioneering, a view that he expressed to family and intimates as well as political associates, there are numerous examples. See *Correspondence of Jackson*, III, 46, 141, 170, 173–74, 190, 210, 269–70, 280, 297, 309–10. On this anti-political style of republicanism, see (generally) Ketcham, *Presidents above Party*; on classical images of the farm-retreat, see Howard Mumford Jones, *O Strange New World: American Culture, The Formative Years* (New York: Viking, 1964), 226–72.

26. To Mrs. Jackson, Jan. 10, 1824, *Correspondence of Jackson*, III, 223; to James Mease, Jan. 8, 1825, roll 10, Papers of Andrew Jackson (microfilm supplement). I am grateful to David Hoth for the latter reference.

27. To George Kremer in *National Intelligencer*, May 7, 1824, roll 10, Papers of Andrew Jackson (microfilm supplement).

28. *Correspondence of Jackson*, II, 219–20. The phrase comes from Jackson's aide, John Reid, and is mistakenly attributed to Jackson by Bassett.

29. Remini, *Jackson*, I, 144, 379–80; II, 7–8, 354; III, 189, 332. See also Stanley F. Horn, *The Hermitage: Home of Old Hickory* (Richmond: Garrett & Massie, 1938).

30. Dangerfield, *Era of Good Feelings*, 123.

31. *Papers of Jackson*, I, 91–92, 101, 152. *Cf.* 1799 example in *ibid.*, 223.

32. *Correspondence of Jackson*, III, 249.

33. *Ibid.*, III, 274. This was in 1825.

34. *Ibid.*, IV, 36. "The list of Jackson's wards is almost endless. . . . New names turn up with fresh examination." Remini, *Jackson*, I, 474, n. 6. Like many women whose husbands traveled, Rachel Jackson had significant responsibilities for managing the plantation. But this contradiction was not atypical of republican motherhood.

35. *Correspondence of Jackson*, IV, 42.

36. Remini, *Jackson*, I, 60, 316, 403. For similar disdain of her appearance in Washington, see *ibid.*, II, 85.

37. *Ibid.*, II, 331–32.

38. *Nashville Union*, June 12, 1845.

39. Parton, *Life*, III, 641–48.

40. James Smith to Finis Ewing, Sept. 4, 1838, Finis Ewing Papers, Tennessee Historical Society. *Cf.* Remini, *Jackson*, III, 444–47, which gives Edgar's version but follows Smith's.

41. There is no pattern to his references to divinity. While Providence in various versions (such as "the all ruling power") may be most common, he also refers to angelic hosts and to the God of Isaac. In a single letter to Rachel he refers to both the "Goddess of slumber" and "the great 'I Am.' " *Papers of Jackson*, I, 91–92.

42. To William B. Conway, April 4, 1831, *Correspondence of Jackson*, IV, 256. A similar statement appears in his letter to Ellen M. Hanson, March 25, 1835, *ibid.*, IV, 333.

43. See Nathan O. Hatch, *The Democratization of American Christianity* (New Haven: Yale, 1989). Andrew Jackson was not a "Christian" in the radical nondenominational sense. He offered no comments, so far as I can discover, on the Second Great Awakening. On his views, see Arda Walker, "The Religious Views of Andrew Jackson," East Tennessee State Historical Society, *Publications* 17 (1945): 61–70.

44. Ezra Stiles Ely, "The Duty of Christian Freemen to Elect Christian Rulers," in *American Philosophic Addresses, 1700–1900*, ed. Joseph L. Blau (New York: Columbia Univ., 1946), 548–62. *Cf.* Daniel T. Rodgers, *Contested Truths: Keywords in American Politics Since Independence* (New York: Basic, 1987), 117–18.

45. Ezra Stiles Ely to Jackson, July 3, 1829, *Correspondence of Jackson*, IV, 49.

46. To William P. Lawrence, *ibid.*, IV, 565.

47. See the account from *American Presbyterian* in *Nashville Whig*, July 20, 1838.

48. Parton, *Life*, I, vii.

Notes to Chapter Four

1. Charles Capen McLaughlin *et al.*, *The Papers of Frederick Law Olmsted*, vol. II, *Slavery and the South, 1852–1857* (Baltimore: Johns Hopkins, 1981), 247–54. Hereafter: Olmsted, *Papers*.

2. Laura Wood Roper, *FLO: A Biography of Frederick Law Olmsted* (Baltimore: Johns Hopkins, 1973), 53, 63; "Passages in the Life of an Unpractical Man," in

Olmsted, *Papers*, vol. I, *The Formative Years, 1822–1852* (Baltimore: Johns Hopkins, 1977), 98–113.

3. These details are summarized and interpreted in Charles E. Beveridge, "Introduction," Olmsted, *Papers*, II, 1–41. See also Arthur M. Schlesinger's introduction to *The Cotton Kingdom* (New York: Knopf, 1953).

4. Olmsted, *Papers*, I, 304.

5. See notes in *ibid.*, II, 84–85.

6. Quoted in Roper, *FLO*, 47.

7. To Frederick Kingsbury, Oct. 17, 1852, in Olmsted, *Papers*, II, 82.

8. Olmsted, *Papers*, II, 131–32.

9. See *Cotton Kingdom*, 394–95, 557.

10. The phrase is from Beveridge, "Introduction," II, 16. See also Elizabeth Stevenson, *Park Maker: A Life of Frederick Law Olmsted* (New York: MacMillan, 1977), 97–100. The significance of the event is overlooked in Roper, *FLO*, 93–94.

11. See *Papers*, II, 232–36. There is little evidence of other activities in Nashville except for references to a visit to an iron works. *Ibid.*, II, 258, 267. Stevenson refers to visiting a bookshop and other sights, but her source is not clear. *Park Maker*, 98. Olmsted said nothing about Nashville in his books on the South.

12. See Olmsted, *Papers*, II, 238–45, 256–70.

13. *Cotton Kingdom*, 518–19, 522, 554–55, 560–61. These passages all come from the *Journey through the Back Country*. See also the "Letter to a Southern Friend" at the start of *Journey through Texas; or, A Saddle-Trip on the Southwestern Frontier* (New York: Dix, Edwards, 1857), vii–xxix.

14. *Cotton Kingdom*, 555.

Notes to Chapter Five

1. *Papers of Jackson*, II, 291–92.

2. James Renwick, *Life of DeWitt Clinton*, as quoted in Roger H. Brown, *The Republic in Peril: 1812* (New York: Columbia Univ., 1964), 182. For an example of party rhetoric soaked in memory, see the "Communication to the Readers of *The Old Soldier*," signed by Abraham Lincoln and four other Whigs in 1840. "The old soldiers" of the War of 1812 had learned the necessity of organization to repulse a foe. "We, your sons and younger brothers," banded together to disperse General Harrison's enemies "and place him in the chair, now disgraced by their effeminate and luxury-loving chief." Roy P. Basler, ed., *The Collected Works of Abraham Lincoln*, 9 vols. (New Brunswick: Rutgers Univ., 1953–1955), I, 205.

3. Allan Nevins, ed., *The Diary of Philip Hone, 1828–1851*, 2 vols. (New York: Dodd, Mead, 1927), II, 729–30. In excavating a cellar, workmen had found and removed two pieces of cannon from the Revolution.

4. *Historic Notes of Life and Letters in New England*, as excerpted in Perry Miller, ed., *The Transcendentalists* (Cambridge: Harvard, 1950), 494. On the declining status of the aged and the emerging "cult of youth," see David Hackett Fischer, *Growing Old in America* (New York: Oxford, 1977).

5. Bernard Bailyn, *The Ideological Origins of the American Revolution* (Cam-

bridge: Harvard, 1967), 301–19; Jay Fliegelman, *Prodigals and Pilgrims: The American revolution against patriarchal authority, 1750–1800* (Cambridge, England: Cambridge Univ., 1982); Robert H. Bremner *et al.*, *Children and Youth in America: A Documentary History*, vol. I, *1600–1865* (Cambridge: Harvard, 1970), 131–32, 343–44.

6. "Social Reform," as quoted in Walter Hugins, ed., *The Reform Impulse, 1825–1850* (New York: Harper & Row, 1972), 249–54.

7. For a brilliant study of the fraying ties of the past, see Somkin, *Unquiet Eagle.* For an argument that tradition is "problematical" in America, despite the abundant materials on the Revolution, see Michael Kammen, *A Season of Youth: The American Revolution and the Historical Imagination* (New York: Knopf, 1978). For careful analysis of the effects of popular sovereignty on historical reasoning, see Martyn P. Thompson, "The History of Fundamental Law in Political Thought from the French Wars of Religion to the American Revolution," *American Historical Review* 91 (1986): 1,103–28; and James T. Kloppenberg, "The Virtues of Liberalism: Christianity, Republicanism, and Ethics in Early American Political Discourse," *Journal of American History* 74 (1987): 9–33.

8. My inquiry is inspired by David Lowenthal, *The Past Is a Foreign Country* (Cambridge, England: Cambridge Univ., 1985).

9. All quotations are taken from George H. Callcott, *History in the United States, 1800–1860: Its Practice and Purpose* (Baltimore: Johns Hopkins, 1970), 25–26.

10. *Ibid.*, 33–34, 71. Percentages were derived from Frank Luther Mott's *Golden Multitudes: The Story of the Best Seller in the United States* (New York: MacMillan, 1947). The figures are heavily influenced by fashions in literary taste. Eighteen of the twenty historical best-sellers of the 1820s were novels, including works by Scott, Cooper, and Irving. Only two were nonfiction.

11. Callcott, *History*, 35–45; David D. Van Tassel, *Recording America's Past: An Interpretation of the Development of Historical Societies in America, 1607–1884* (Chicago: Univ. of Chicago, 1960), 95–102, 181–90.

12. Herbert B. Adams, *The Study of History in American Colleges and Universities* (Washington: Government Printing Office, 1887), 47.

13. *Proceedings of the Essex Institute*, I (Salem, Mass.: Essex Institute, 1856).

14. *Historical Collections of the Essex Institute*, I (Salem, Mass.: Essex Institute, 1859).

15. James R. Newhall, *The Essex Memorial, for 1836: Embracing a Register of the County* (Salem, Mass.: Henry Whipple, 1836).

16. *A Week on the Concord and Merrimack Rivers* (New York: Library of America, 1985), 207.

17. See Donald M. Scott, "Print and the Public Lecture System, 1840–1860," in William L. Joyce *et al.*, *Printing and Society in Early America* (Worcester, Mass.: American Antiquarian Society, 1983), 294. Scott is excellent on the conveying of knowledge as a public commodity. See his "The Popular Lecture and the Creation of a Public in Mid-Nineteenth-Century America," *Journal of American History* 66 (1980): 801–2.

18. See Blake Nevius, "Chronology," in James Fenimore Cooper, *The Leatherstocking Tales*, I (New York: Library of America, 1985), 1,327–28.

19. C. Peter Ripley *et al.*, eds., *The Black Abolitionist Papers*, 5 vols. (Chapel Hill: Univ. of North Carolina, 1985–1992), IV: 298; Elizabeth F. Ellet, *The Women of the American Revolution*, 3 vols., 4th ed. (New York: Baker & Scribner, 1850), ix–x. See also Linda Kerber, " 'History Can Do It No Justice': Women and the Reinterpretation of the American Revolution," *Women in the Age of the American Revolution*, ed. Ronald Hoffman and Peter J. Albert (Charlottesville: Univ. of Virginia, 1989), 3–42.

20. Russell E. Miller, *The Larger Hope: The First Century of the Universalist Church in America, 1770–1870* (Boston: Unitarian Universalist Association, 1979), 346–48.

21. Davis Bitton and Leonard Arrington, *Mormons and Their Historians* (Salt Lake City: Univ. of Utah, 1988), 3–28; Joseph Conforti, "Edwardsians, Unitarians, and the Memory of the Great Awakening, 1800–1840," *American Unitarianism, 1805–1865*, ed. Conrad Edick Wright (Boston: Massachusetts Historical Society and Northeastern Univ., 1989), 31–50.

22. George F. Willison, *Saints and Strangers* (New York: Reynal & Hitchcock, 1945), 427–30; Sacvan Bercovitch, *The Puritan Origins of the American Self* (New Haven: Yale, 1975), 87.

23. George Forgie, *Patricide in the House Divided: A Psychological Interpretation of Lincoln and His Age* (New York: Norton, 1979).

24. Basler, *Collected Works*, I, 108, 112 (emphasis in original). The classic text of the Romantic sense of having been born too late is Alfred de Musset, *Confession of a Child of the Century* (New York: Fertig, 1977).

25. Basler, *Collected Works*, I, 278–79. A series of orations and manifestoes imitated the Declaration of Independence as they called for reform of American habits or institutions. It is possible to treat them as evidence of ties to the Revolution, but I think they show ties that were so weak that it was possible to justify almost any new departure in a parody of the Declaration. For the evidence, see Philip Foner, ed., *We, the Other People: Alternative Declarations of Independence by Labor Groups, Farmers, Woman's Rights Advocates, Socialists, and Blacks, 1829–1975* (Urbana: Univ. of Illinois, 1976). For an incisive analysis of the way the grounds of argument shifted to "timeless good" rather than "the good shaped and determined in time," see Major L. Wilson, *Space, Time, and Freedom: The Quest for Nationality and the Irrepressible Conflict, 1815–1861* (Westport, Conn.: Greenwood, 1974), 102–3.

26. Whittier, *The Stranger in Lowell* (Boston: Waite, Peirce, 1845), 152–54.

27. George Bancroft, *History of the United States of America*, rev. ed. (1882–1885), as excerpted in *A Library of American Literature from the Earliest Settlement to the Present Times*, ed. Edmund Clarence Stedman and Ellen MacKay Hutchinson, 11 vols. (New York: Charles L. Webster, 1889–1890), VI, 3–6.

28. Wilbur R. Jacobs, "Francis Parkman's Oration 'Romance in America,' " *American Historical Review* 68 (1963): 692–97.

29. Stephen Fender, "American Landscape and the Figure of Anticipation:

Paradox and Recourse," in *Views of American Landscapes*, ed. Mick Gidley and Robert Lawson-Peebles (Cambridge, England: Cambridge Univ., 1989), 53, 62. See also John F. Sears, *Sacred Places: American Tourist Attractions in the Nineteenth Century* (New York: Oxford, 1989), 61.

Notes to Chapter Six

1. Callcott, *History*, 94.

2. Ward, *Andrew Jackson—Symbol*, 83–86.

3. That is to say, the favorite roles written for him, since he also excelled in distinctive American performances as Lear, Hamlet, and Richard III. See Richard Moody, *Edwin Forrest: First Star of the American Stage* (New York: Knopf, 1960).

4. William Winter, quoted in Arthur Hornblow, *A History of the Theatre in America from Its Beginnings to the Present Time*, 2 vols. (New York: Benjamin Blom, 1965), II, 45.

5. David Grimsted, *Melodrama Unveiled: American Theatre and Culture, 1800–1850* (Chicago: Univ. of Chicago, 1968), 185–95; Robert C. Toll, *Blacking Up: The Minstrel Show in Nineteenth-Century America* (New York: Oxford, 1974), 37; Anna Cora Mowatt, "Fashion," in Richard Moody, ed., *Dramas from the American Theatre, 1762–1909* (Boston: Houghton Mifflin, 1969), 309–49; Francis Hodge, *Yankee Theatre: The Image of America on the Stage, 1825–1850* (Austin: Univ. of Texas, 1964).

6. Basler, *Collected Works*, I, 367–70, 379.

7. *The Writings and Speeches of Daniel Webster*, ed. James W. McIntyre, 18 vols. (Boston: Little, Brown, 1903), III, 30. See also Ward, *Andrew Jackson—Symbol*, 94–95; Maurice Baxter, *One and Inseparable: Daniel Webster and the Union* (Cambridge: Harvard, 1984), 271–72.

8. They appeared in *The Sketch Book* (1819–1820).

9. Simms, *The Wigwam and the Cabin* (*Life in America*) (Ridgewood, N.J.: Gregg, 1968 [1845]), 190; Simms, *The Yemassee: A Romance of Carolina* (Boston: Houghton Mifflin, 1961 [1853]), 4.

10. Alonzo Lewis, *History of Lynn* (1829) was his acknowledged source for the long poem *Moll Pitcher*. He elsewhere consulted Charles W. Upham, *Lectures on Witchcraft* (1832); Samuel G. Drake, *Book of the Indians* (1833); and Samuel G. Drake, *Antiquities of Boston* (1856). On the influence of Burns and others, see Edward Wagenknecht, "Editor's Introduction," in Whittier, *The Supernaturalism of New England* (Norman: Univ. of Oklahoma, 1969 [1847]).

11. The use of the term *folklore* in English to signify "the Lore of the People"— including "manners, customs, observances, superstitions, ballads, proverbs"—and its systematic study dates from an 1846 letter to the British *Athenaeum*. In Swedish, *folklif,* or "folklife," dates from 1847, and the similar German terms *Volksleben* and *Volkskunde* were in regular use after 1806. See Simon I. Bronner, *American Folklore Studies: An Intellectual History* (Lawrence: Univ. of Kansas, 1986), 12–13.

12. Both quotations are in Bronner, *American Folklore Studies*, 6.

13. In a 1973 address on "the contemporaneity, as opposed to the antiquity, of

folklore," Richard Dorson wrote: "The unofficial culture can be contrasted with the high, the visible, the institutional culture of church, state, the universities, the professions, the corporations, the fine arts, the sciences. This unofficial culture finds its own modes of expression in folk religion, folk medicine, folk literature, the folk arts, and folk philosophy. Yet the unofficial culture reflects the mood of its times fully as much as does the official culture, for both are anchored in the same historical period" (quoted in Bronner, *American Folklore Studies*, 126). Bronner defines the professional middle class's interest in a usable past at p. 2.

14. Whittier, *Supernaturalism*, 29–30.

15. Harriet Beecher Stowe, *Oldtown Folks*, ed. Henry F. May (Cambridge: Harvard, 1966), 49.

16. Samuel Griswold Goodrich, *Recollections of a Lifetime* (1857), on "the meeting-house of 1830" in Stedman and Hutchinson, *Library*, V, 288–89; Alice Cary, *Clovernook; or, Recollections of Our Neighborhood in the West* (1851–1853), in *ibid.*, VII, 530–39.

17. "Song of Myself," stanza 44, *Leaves of Grass* (Philadelphia: McKay, 1891), 72.

18. Hawthorne, "Time's Portraiture," *Tales and Sketches* (New York: Library of America, 1982), 585–92.

19. See Sean Wilentz, *Chants Democratic: New York City and the Rise of the American Working Class* (New York: Oxford, 1984).

20. Rollin G. Osterweis, *Romanticism and Nationalism in the Old South* (New Haven: Yale, 1949), 3–5, 98–99; Allen Tate, *The Fathers* (Denver: Alan Swallow, 1960), 62–71.

21. John Esten Cooke, *The Virginia Comedians; or, Old Days in the Old Dominion* (Ridgewood, N.J.: Gregg, 1968 [1854]), 14.

Notes to Chapter Seven

1. D. H. Meyer, *The Instructed Conscience: The Shaping of the American National Ethic* (Philadelphia: Univ. of Pennsylvania, 1972), 23–25, 43–50, 84.

2. These paragraphs follow Lowenthal, *The Past*, chap. 4.

3. Hawthorne, "Fire-Worship," *Tales and Sketches*, 841–48; Lucy Larcom, *A New England Girlhood* (New York: Corinth, 1968 [1889]), 23. The shutting-up of fireplaces, said Larcom, "marks an era."

4. Hawthorne, "Sir William Phips," *Tales and Sketches*, 12.

5. *Cf.* Lowenthal, *The Past*, 191.

6. Catherine Maria Sedgwick, *Hope Leslie*, ed. Mary Kelley (New Brunswick: Rutgers, 1987), 5.

7. Hawthorne, *The Blithedale Romance* (New York: Dell, 1960), 21–23.

8. Sedgwick, *Hope Leslie*, 5–6.

9. *Virginia Historical Register* 3 (Jan. 1850): ii, as quoted in Callcott, *History*, 48.

10. Van Tassel, *Recording America's Past*, 103–10.

11. Among them, Peter Force's nine volumes of colonial archives, Jared

Sparks's twelve volumes of Washington's writings, Francis P. Blair's seven volumes of diplomatic correspondence, the collections of the Massachusetts Historical Society, and the particularly important work of Lyman Draper at the Wisconsin Historical Society. See Callcott, *History*, 110–12.

12. See Michael Kammen, *A Machine That Would Go of Itself: The Constitution in American Culture* (New York: Knopf, 1987), 86–90, 97, 100. Hints that the documentary past was incomplete and concealed terrible secrets were explored by a few novelists. See, *e.g.*, George Lippard's introduction to the sensational disclosures in the best-selling *The Monks of Monk Hall* (New York: Odyssey, 1970 [1844]), 3.

13. Letter to F. H. Underwood, March 4, 1859, in Oliver Wendell Holmes, *John Lothrop Motley: A Memoir* (1879), as excerpted in Stedman and Hutchinson, *Library*, VII, 253–55.

14. See Callcott, *History*, 215–21; Peter Novick, *That Noble Dream: The 'Objectivity Question' and the American Historical Profession* (Cambridge, England: Cambridge Univ., 1988), 44–46.

15. See Charles B. Hosmer, Jr., *Presence of the Past: A History of the Preservation Movement before Williamsburg* (New York: Putnam's, 1865), 29–40.

16. Tocqueville, *Democracy in America*, 38; Willison, *Saints and Strangers*, *passim;* John McPhee, "Travels of the Rock," *New Yorker* (Feb. 26, 1990), 108–17. The era's fascination with Plymouth Rock was first suggested to me in a 1986 talk at Vanderbilt University by John Seelye.

17. Lyman Beecher, "The New England Fathers," in Stedman and Hutchinson, *Library*, IV, 349.

18. Bacon, "What and Who Were the Puritans," in *ibid.*, VI, 88–91.

19. Prentiss, "The Sons of New England," in *ibid.*, 408.

20. Sedgwick, *Hope Leslie;* Dixon Wecter, "The Pilgrim Fathers and the American Way," in Michael McGiffert, ed., *Puritanism and the American Experience* (Reading, Mass.: Addison-Wesley, 1969), 246.

21. See, for example, David Grayson Allen, *In English Ways: The Movement of Societies and the Transferal of English Local Law and Custom to Massachusetts Bay in the Seventeenth Century* (Chapel Hill: Univ. of North Carolina, 1981); Philip F. Gura, *A Glimpse of Sion's Glory: Puritan Radicalism in New England* (Middletown, Conn.: Wesleyan Univ., 1984).

22. On the "legend" of a shared Puritan tradition in the past, see Rush Welter, *The Mind of America, 1820–1860* (New York: Columbia Univ., 1975), 282. In general, Whigs praised the discipline of New England progenitors rather than joining Democrats like Bancroft in imputing to them a love of liberty. To make their point, Whigs were willing to scale down the significance of the Revolution. For thoughtful analysis of Whig reactions to American forgetfulness of ancestral claims, see Jean Matthews, " 'Whig History': The New England Whigs and a Usable Past," *New England Quarterly* 51 (June 1978): 193–208.

23. *The English Notebooks*, ed. Randall Stewart (New York: Modern Language Association, 1941), 294. In *The Marble Faun* (New York: Penguin, 1990), Hawthorne counts it as America's advantage not to have the past "piled upon the back of

the Present" (302). On the other hand, the "brief duration of American families" and the brevity of memory are described as frightening (119).

Notes to Chapter Eight

1. Morton J. Horwitz, *The Transformation of American Law, 1780–1860* (Cambridge: Harvard, 1977), 34–40.

2. *Ibid.*, 130–39. On vested rights, see Alfred H. Kelly, Winfred A. Harbison, and Herman Belz, *The American Constitution: Its Origins and Development*, 7th ed. (New York: Norton, 1991), 186–90, 227.

3. "Unitarian Christianity," *The Works of William E. Channing, D.D.* (Boston: American Unitarian Association, 1886), 367–84. Ironically, Unitarians may have been more sensitive to problems in the historical continuation of Christianity than other movements that admitted to less "interpretation" in their sectarian innovations.

4. Hatch, *Democratization*, 182.

5. Finney, *Lectures on Revivals of Religion*, ed. William G. McLoughlin (Cambridge: Harvard, 1960), 272, 276. For a dramatic account of the issues raised by revivalism, see Perry Miller, *The Life of the Mind in America from the Revolution to the Civil War* (New York: Harcourt Brace, 1965), 3–95.

6. *White–jacket*, as quoted in David Brion Davis, ed., *Antebellum American Culture* (Lexington, Mass.: Heath, 1979), 458.

7. *Letters of Theodore Dwight Weld, Angelina Grimké Weld, and Sarah Grimké*, ed. Gilbert Hobbs Barnes and Dwight Lowell Dumond, 2 vols. (Gloucester, Mass.: Peter Smith, 1965), I, 296. *Cf.* Major Wilson's analysis of the way the Free Soilers turned slavery's participation in the historical process into a sign of its defectiveness when contrasted with timeless, universal liberty. See his *Space, Time, and Freedom*, 162–63.

8. Norman Ware, *The Industrial Worker, 1840–1860* (Chicago: Quadrangle, 1964), xvi; Alan Dawley, *Class and Community: The Industrial Revolution in Lynn* (Cambridge: Harvard, 1976), 60.

9. Francis Paul Prucha, *Indian Policy in the United States* (Lincoln: Univ. of Nebraska, 1981), 153–79; Wilcomb E. Washburn, *The Indian in America* (New York: Harper & Row, 1975), 167–68.

10. See John Todd, "Old-Fashioned Talk on the Woman Question," in Stedman and Hutchinson, *Library*, VI, 32–34, as a transitional statement in a long train of thought that can be traced in Cynthia D. Kinnard, *Antifeminism in American Thought: An Annotated Bibliography* (Boston: G.K. Hall, 1986); and Cynthia Eagle Russett, *Sexual Science: The Victorian Construction of Womanhood* (Cambridge: Harvard, 1989). See also Josiah Nott, "Two Lectures on the Natural History of the Caucasian and Negro Races," in Drew Gilpin Faust, ed., *The Ideology of Slavery* (Baton Rouge: Louisiana State Univ., 1981), 206–38; Robert F. Berkhofer, *The White Man's Indian: Images of the American Indian from Columbus to the Present* (New York: Vintage, 1978), 55–62.

11. "History" (1836), *The Selected Writings of Ralph Waldo Emerson*, ed. Brooks Atkinson (New York: Modern Library, 1950), 123–44.

12. Stephen E. Whicher, ed., *Selections from Ralph Waldo Emerson* (Boston: Houghton Mifflin, 1960), 369; *The Early Lectures of Ralph Waldo Emerson*, ed. Stephen E. Whicher, Robert E. Spiller, and Wallace E. Williams (Cambridge: Harvard, 1959–1972), III, 231. "The whole trend of his thought," his modern editors summarize, "was to cut loose from the past as the past in order to emphasize the timeless present" (*ibid.*, II, 2). See also A. Robert Caponigri, "Brownson and Emerson: Nature and History," *New England Quarterly* 18 (1945): 370, 378.

13. "I am not aware that any man has ever built on the spot which I occupy. Deliver me from a city built on the site of a more ancient city, whose materials are ruins, whose gardens cemeteries." *Walden and Civil Disobedience* (New York: Penguin, 1983), 211, 311.

14. See Robert Gross, "Culture and Cultivation: Agriculture and Society in Thoreau's Concord," *Journal of American History* 69 (1982): 42–61, for an incisive treatment of the local agricultural context of Thoreau's thought.

15. Thoreau, *Walden*, 53.

16. *Ibid.*, 374. Here he echoed Ecclesiastes 9:4 on the hope that subsists to the living.

17. Henry David Thoreau, *The Maine Woods* (New York: Crowell, 1961), 103.

18. *Ibid.*, 83, 310.

19. Thoreau, *A Week*, 198–99.

20. *Ibid.*, 48–50, 109–10.

21. Review of E. G. Squier and E. H. Davis, *Ancient Monuments of the Mississippi Valley*, in *Literary World* (1848), as quoted in William Stanton, *The Leopard's Spots: Scientific Attitudes toward Race in America, 1815–1859* (Chicago: Univ. of Chicago, 1960), 85.

22. *Ibid.* See also Lowenthal, *The Past*, 337–39.

23. Wesley Frank Craven, *The Legend of the Founding Fathers* (New York: New York Univ., 1956), 1.

24. This was clear in the debate aroused by Robert Bork's and Edwin Meese's proposed jurisprudence of "original intent" at the bicentennial celebration of the Constitution. Although justices William Brennan's and Thurgood Marshall's version of constitutional law was equally "historical" in its reference to the long line of amendment and reinterpretation of the Constitution, their view was dismissed as radical and "unprincipled." Even those who disagreed with the Bork-Meese position sometimes failed to see any historical position between literal adherence to the vision of the Founders and simply adapting to the needs of an ever-changing present.

25. J. R. Lowell, "Self-Possession *vs.* Prepossession," *Atlantic Monthly* 8 (1861): 761–69, as quoted in Lowenthal, *The Past*, 118.

26. On the importance of such stories, see Alasdair MacIntyre, *After Virtue: A Study in Moral Theory*, 2d ed. (Notre Dame: Notre Dame Univ., 1984), 216.

27. *Stranger in Lowell*, 14. For a brief account of the Oxford movement and its polemical *Tracts for the Times*, see R. K. Webb, *Modern England: From the Eighteenth Century to the Present* (New York: Dodd, Mead, 1971), 229–33. Webb does not support the judgment that in English ecclesiastical life they called in vain.

Notes to Chapter Nine

1. Tocqueville, *Democracy in America*, 283–84.

2. *Journey to America*, 127–28.

3. *Ibid.*, 343–49.

4. That is also the emotion in which he said *Democracy in America* was composed. See *Democracy in America*, 12, where George Lawrence translates the term as "dread." But "terror" was used in the earlier Henry Reeve translation, available in many editions. The displacement of religious emotion from religion to nature and history may be taken as characteristic of Tocqueville.

5. Actually La Croix de Watines came to America before the French Revolution, squandered his wealth, and eventually returned to France. Thus he did not at all exemplify the points that Tocqueville used him to make. But there were fictional tearjerkers that converted him to a victim and exile. See André Jardin, *Tocqueville: A Biography*, trans. Lydia Davis (London: Peter Halban, 1988), 123–24.

6. Exile was a key theme in all of Tocqueville's work. A recent study traces the origin of his insight into the importance of the heart in politics to musings about banishment while watching a Sicilian family doting on a young boy. Bruce James Smith, *Politics and Remembrance: Republican Themes in Machiavelli, Burke, and Tocqueville* (Princeton: Princeton Univ., 1985), 157–58.

7. Harriet Martineau, for example, was "not really interested in America at all. She was interested in certain abstract propositions which America could prove." R. K. Webb, *Harriet Martineau: A Radical Victorian* (London: Heinemann, 1960), 172.

8. On cultural independence, see John Allen Krout and Dixon Ryan Fox, *The Completion of Independence, 1790–1830* (New York: MacMillan, 1944); Larzer Ziff, *Literary Democracy: The Declaration of Cultural Independence in America* (New York: Penguin, 1982).

9. Henry Adams, *History of the United States During the Administration of Thomas Jefferson and James Madison*, 2 vols. (New York: Library of America, 1986 [1889–1891]), I, 31–47. For a sharp critique, see Noble E. Cunningham, Jr., *The United States in 1800: Henry Adams Revisited* (Charlottesville: Univ. of Virginia, 1988), 4. The use of travelers' reports as a guide to social history of the early republic continued long after Adams. See, for example, Allan Nevins, ed., *American Social History as Recorded by British Travellers* (New York: Henry Holt, 1923); and Oscar Handlin, ed., *This was America: True Accounts of People and Places, Manners and Customs, as Recorded by European Travelers to the Western Shore in the Eighteenth, Nineteenth, and Twentieth Centuries* (Cambridge: Harvard, 1949). For sensible comments on the uses of travel reports, see Richard L. Rapson, *Britons View America: Travel Commentary, 1860–1935* (Seattle: Univ. of Washington, 1971), 195–213, 262–65.

10. Michael Chevalier, *Society, Manners, and Politics in the United States*, ed. John William Ward (Garden City, N.Y.: Anchor, 1961). Not until George Rogers Taylor's authoritative *The Transportation Revolution, 1815–1860* (New York: Rinehart, 1951) did American scholarship carry this inquiry much further.

11. Webb, *Harriet Martineau*, 158.

12. Frances Trollope, *Domestic Manners of the Americans* (London: Century, 1984 [1839]), 313–23, 72, 142, 268, 134.

13. *Ibid.*, 39.

14. Charles Dickens, *American Notes and Pictures from Italy* (London: Oxford, 1957), 64, 245.

15. Trollope, *Domestic Manners*, 321–22.

Notes to Chapter Ten

1. Frank Kermode, *The Classic* (London: Faber & Faber, 1975), 134. There were great differences between the meanings of *Democracy in America* in antebellum classrooms and in the interpretations of the Cold War era, and current readings are different still. Yet there is something that prevails through time.

2. See James T. Schleifer, *The Making of Tocqueville's* Democracy in America (Chapel Hill: Univ. of North Carolina, 1980).

3. See Pierson, *Tocqueville in America*, 1–22; R. R. Palmer, ed., *The Two Tocquevilles, Father and Son: Hervé and Alexis de Tocqueville on the Coming of the French Revolution* (Princeton: Princeton Univ., 1987).

4. On details of writing and publication, see Schleifer, *Making*, 3–34; Jardin, *Tocqueville*, 194–276. On events of 1848–1851, see *ibid.*, 407–72.

5. Smith, *Politics and Remembrance*, 182–84.

6. Jerrold Seigel, *Bohemian Paris: Culture, Politics, and the Boundaries of Bourgeois Life, 1830–1930* (New York: Viking, 1986), 7–8. *Cf.* Tocqueville's 1848 remarks on the restiveness of the masses and selfishness of the ruling class, Appendix III, *Democracy in America*, 749–58.

7. Karl Marx and Friedrich Engels, *Basic Writings on Politics and Philosophy*, ed. Lewis S. Feuer (Garden City, N.Y.: Anchor Press, 1959), 9–10. For sustained comparisons, see Irving M. Zeitlein, *Liberty, Equality, and Revolution in Alexis de Tocqueville* (Boston: Little, Brown, 1971). See also Robert Nisbet, "Tocqueville's Ideal Types," in Abraham S. Eisenstadt, ed., *Reconsidering Tocqueville's* Democracy in America (New Brunswick: Rutgers, 1988), 190–91.

8. *Democracy in America*, 18. On his personal tendency to depression, see Jardin, *Tocqueville*, 61, 373–74, 384, 452, 528–32.

9. *Democracy in America*, 444, 483–84.

10. *Ibid.*, 13–14.

11. *Ibid.*, 14–15.

12. *Ibid.*, 18–19.

13. This contrast between their views of utopia follows, I think, from other key differences between Tocqueville and Marx. The former cherishes class cooperation, the taming influence of religion, and the conserving influence of the law; the latter, class solidarity and ripping away the illusions of religion and traditional institutions. Nonetheless, they share much: the sense of ongoing revolution, the analysis of intellectual confusion, and even a low regard for the bourgeoisie's fantasy that it can brake the revolution. In addition, despite a few prescient passages on wealth and

alienation, Tocqueville offered nothing approaching Marx's understanding of the significance of industrial change. But see Seymour Drescher, ed., *Tocqueville and Beaumont on Social Reform* (New York: Harper & Row, 1968).

14. *Democracy in America*, 18.

15. Letter to Henry Reeve, Nov. 19, 1839, quoted in *Democracy in America*, xi.

16. See George W. Pierson, foreword to Schleifer, *Making*, xv; Appendix III to Tocqueville's *Democracy in America*, 2 vols., ed. Phillips Bradley (New York: Knopf, 1963), II, 385–91.

17. *Democracy in America*, 20.

18. *Journey*, 76. *Cf.* the competition of kings and nobles in Tocqueville's analysis of the decline of European feudalism (*Democracy in America*, 10).

19. *Journey*, 47. But Sparks later felt that Tocqueville misconstrued the point. See Schleifer, *Making*, 192–93, 217.

20. For a selection of early American laments as well as observations on the continuities between these laments and those of later eras, see Lewis P. Simpson, ed., *The Federalist Literary Mind: Selections from the* Monthly Anthology and Boston Review, *1803–1811* (Baton Rouge: Louisiana State Univ., 1962), 47–74.

21. *Democracy in America*, 251; *Journey*, 55, 162, 369.

22. *Journey*, 185–87.

23. *Ibid.*, 134, 285.

24. *Democracy in America*, 280.

25. *Ibid.*, 282.

26. *Ibid.*, 285–86.

27. *Ibid.*, 278, as well as 62, 65, 104, 110, 161, 169.

28. Note that "energy" was a key term for what he admired in America. Not only was the North superior to the South in energy, but America excelled Europe, and republican government excelled monarchy, in infusing "throughout the body social an activity, a force and an energy." *Journey*, 155; see also 183. There was a price to be paid in irregularity of administration and restlessness of the population, but this was acceptable.

29. Charles A. Beard and Mary R. Beard, *The American Spirit: The Idea of Civilization in the United States* (New York: Collier, 1962), 158.

30. *Journey*, 155, 183.

31. *Democracy in America*, 507–8.

32. *Ibid.*, 35.

33. See *ibid.*, Appendix I, 714–21, where he provides a bibliography for historians who wish to follow up what he admits is a brief and tentative historical sketch.

34. For references to Kent, see notes in *Journey*, 237–44.

35. On the expansion of New England, see Charles E. Clark, *The Eastern Frontier: The Settlement of Northern New England* (New York: Knopf, 1970). On Americans' sense of mission, see Ernest Lee Tuveson, *Redeemer Nation: The Idea of America's Millennial Role* (Chicago: Univ. of Chicago, 1968). On New England influences in the South, see E. Brooks Holifield, *The Gentlemen Theologians: American Theology in Southern Culture, 1795–1860* (Durham, N.C.: Duke Univ., 1978), 26–27; and Fletcher M. Green, *The Role of the Yankee in the Old South* (Athens:

Univ. of Georgia, 1972). But see Jack P. Greene's critique of the view that attributes so much weight to New England in *Pursuits of Happiness: The Social Development of Early Modern British Colonies and the Formation of American Culture* (Chapel Hill: Univ. of North Carolina, 1988).

36. *Democracy in America*, 48.

37. *Journey*, 119–20.

38. *Ibid.*, 350, 360.

39. *Ibid.*, 350–403.

40. *Ibid.*, 143, 147, 364, 395. In the end, however, even as all these "exiled members of the great human family" meet in the wilds, they are unable to cooperate. They cling to "indestructible classifications" built on prejudices about skin color, material condition, and degree of education.

41. *Ibid.*, 399.

42. *Ibid.*, 133, 355. As Thomas Bender stresses after reviewing important community studies: "The mere fact of moving does not necessarily imply an atomized society. In fact, nineteenth-century Americans moved from *community* to *community*. That these communities were constructed, so to speak, on the spot does not make them any less communal." See his *Community and Social Change in America* (Baltimore: Johns Hopkins, 1982), 92.

43. *Ibid.*, 143, 391, 403.

44. *Ibid.*, 383.

45. *Ibid.*, 356, 362.

46. *Democracy in America*, 471. Lawrence Levine uses this observation as part of his argument that the line between highbrow and lowbrow culture was relatively unimportant in America before recent times. See his "William Shakespeare and the American People," *American Historical Review* 89 (Feb. 1984): 34–66.

47. William H. Gilman *et al.*, eds., *The Journals and Miscellaneous Notebooks of Ralph Waldo Emerson*, 16 vols. (Cambridge: Harvard, 1960–1982), VII, 433. Hereafter: *JMN*.

Notes to Chapter Eleven

1. Nina Baym, "Melodramas of Beset Manhood: How Theories of American Fiction Exclude Women Authors," *American Quarterly* 33 (1981): 123–39. See also Adelaide Morris, "Dick, Jane, and American Literature: Fighting with Canons," *College English* 47 (Sept. 1985): 467–81.

2. *Homes of the New World* consists of letters to a sister in Sweden (who died before she returned home), giving virtually a day-by-day account of her experiences and impressions. A few letters to prominent Swedes—the Queen Dowager, a minister, a scientist, a theologian—repeat and summarize reflections previously offered *en passant*. The epistolary format, used also in her novels, results in a long, unindexed, sprawling work of a kind admired by her contemporaries. It lacks the argumentative coherence of Tocqueville's political science. The translation, though by a kindred spirit in the international world of reform, is horrible. In large part, the work's neglect is owing to its inaccessibility to modern readers. See *The Homes of the*

New World; Impressions of America, trans. Mary Howitt, 2 vols. (New York: Harper, 1853).

3. Quoted in *Life, Letters, and Posthumous Works of Fredrika Bremer*, ed. Charlotte Bremer (New York: Hurd & Houghton, 1868), 79. Doris R. Asmundsson, "Fredrika Bremer: Sweden's First Feminist," *Woman as Mediatrix: Essays on Nineteenth-Century European Women Writers*, ed. Avriel H. Goldberger (Westport, Conn.: Greenwood, 1987), 99–109, is appreciative and too uncritical. Donald Meyer, *Sex and Power: The Rise of Women in America, Russia, Sweden, and Italy* (Middletown, Conn.: Wesleyan Univ., 1987), 163–68, is more analytical, but much about Bremer's feminism remains elusive.

4. Bremer, *Life*, 82.

5. Fredrika Bremer, *Hertha*, trans. Mary Howitt, 2 vols. (New York: G.P. Putnam, 1856), iv.

6. Having read *Home* and *Neighbors*, Lucy Larcom recalled, "some of us must not be blamed for feeling as if no tales of domestic life half so charming have ever been written since." *New England Girlhood*, 244.

7. Bremer, *Homes*, I, 20.

8. *Ibid.*, 122.

9. *Ibid.*, 53, 72. The only informant she shared with Tocqueville was Joel Poinsett.

10. *Ibid.*, 22, 72.

11. *Ibid.*, 31–32.

12. *Ibid.*, 246.

13. *Ibid.*, 15; II, 567.

14. *Ibid.*, I, 200.

15. *Ibid.*, 246.

16. *Ibid.*, 144. For the inspiration Harriot Hunt derived from meeting and traveling with Bremer, see her *Glances and Glimpses; or, Fifty Years Social, Including Twenty Years Professional Life* (Boston: John P. Jewett, 1856), 235–38, 276, 289.

17. Bremer, *Homes*, I, 195.

18. *Ibid.*, 434; II, 555–56.

19. *Ibid.*, I, 169, 528.

20. *Ibid.*, 501.

21. *Ibid.*, 432.

22. *Ibid.*, 529.

23. *Ibid.*, 489. These comments may bring to mind Thomas Jefferson's division of women into "Angels" and "Amazons," a distinction showing a preference for thoroughly domestic women. See Fawn Brodie, *Thomas Jefferson: An Intimate History* (New York: Norton, 1974), 238.

24. *Homes*, II, 220.

25. *Ibid.*, 559–60. *Cf.* Carroll Smith-Rosenberg, "The Female World of Love and Ritual: Relations Between Women in Nineteenth-Century America," *Disorderly Conduct: Visions of Gender in Victorian America* (New York: Oxford, 1985), 53–76. The "pet" is identified as Kemble's daughter Sally in Margaret Armstrong, *Fanny Kemble: A Passionate Victorian* (New York: MacMillan, 1938), 323.

26. *Homes*, I, 53; II, 560.

27. *Ibid.*, I, 53.

28. *Ibid.*, I, 391; II, 504.

29. *Ibid.*, II, 121.

30. *Ibid.*, 150.

31. *Ibid.*, I, 499.

32. *Ibid.*, 455–83; II, 129.

33. *Ibid.*, I, 543; II, 521.

34. *Ibid.*, I, 258, 374; II, 492, 275, 654.

35. *Ibid.*, I, 277–78; II, 221. See also II, 541.

36. *Ibid.*, I, 492–93; II, 203–8, 246, 533–35.

37. *Ibid.*, I, 290–93.

38. *Ibid.*, 306–15, 352–54, 392–93, 490–92; II, 157–60, 234–38, 410–12.

39. *Ibid.*, II, 128.

40. *Ibid.*, 159–60. She had caught exactly the themes emphasized in modern studies of slave religion. See Lawrence W. Levine, "Slave Songs and Slave Consciousness: An Exploration in Neglected Sources," *Anonymous Americans: Explorations in Nineteenth-Century Social History*, ed. Tamara Hareven (Englewood Cliffs, N.J.: Prentice-Hall, 1971), 99–130; Albert Raboteau, *Slave Religion: The "Invisible Institution" in the Antebellum South* (New York: Oxford, 1978), 311–12. The blacks, like the whites, compared themselves to Israelites, but for them America was Egypt, not the promised land. The time to cross the River Jordan was nigh, and it would provide both material and spiritual fulfillment.

41. See the conversation with a man who wished to go back to Africa in Bremer, *Homes*, II, 484–85.

42. *Ibid.*, 542.

43. *Ibid.*, I, 365–67; II, 601–11.

44. *Ibid.*, II, 23, 96, 172.

45. *Ibid.*, 220, 173.

46. *Ibid.*, 108–70, quotation at 169.

47. Egotism, according to Bremer, also tempted autobiographical writers: *ibid.*, I, iii–iv. Worry about a lack of self-restraint is an important theme, the other side of American individualism, which connects writings about women and writings about America.

48. *Ibid.*, II, 121.

49. *Ibid.*, 137, 145.

50. *Ibid.*, I, 45.

51. *Ibid.*, 382–3, 524; II, 127, 382–83.

52. *Ibid.*, I, 39–40.

53. *Ibid.*, 28–30, 41, 118, 153, 175, 221, 233; II, 563. John McAleer, *Ralph Waldo Emerson: Days of Encounter* (Boston: Little, Brown, 1984), 478–85, discounts the criticism and exaggerates her love of Emerson.

54. Bremer, *Homes*, I, 233.

55. *Ibid.*, 45, 474–75.

56. *Ibid.*, 19, 46; II, 628.

57. *Ibid.*, II, 629–31. For the appeal of this article to Olmsted, see Olmsted, *Papers*, I, 75.

58. Bremer, *Homes*, I, 539, 488; II, 90.

59. *Ibid.*, II, 135.

60. *Ibid.*, 143–45.

61. *Ibid.*, 136.

62. *Ibid.*, 19. The contrast between Tocqueville's and Bremer's accounts of the West conforms very well to Annette Kolodny's account of male fantasies of erotic conquest of nature versus female fantasies of tending a garden. See her *The Land Before Her: Fantasy and Experience of the American Frontiers, 1630–1860* (Chapel Hill: Univ. of North Carolina, 1984), xii–xiii.

63. Bremer, *Homes*, II, 25.

64. *Ibid.*, 141. Though pointing out that many immigrants, including Swedes, came to the West, a point that Tocqueville missed, she still found "the formative spirit" to be "Anglo-Norman" (II, 136).

65. *Ibid.*, I, 490.

66. *Democracy in America*, 584–603.

67. Tocqueville, *Journey*, 43, 109, 230. *Democracy in America*, note U, pp. 731–33, offered by Tocqueville in support of his chapters on women, describes the "physiognomy" of a pioneer woman, not her views or conversation.

68. See Linda Kerber's account of "republican motherhood" in her *Women of the Republic: Intellect and Ideology in Revolutionary America* (Chapel Hill: Univ. of North Carolina, 1980), 189–231, 269–88.

69. See the discussion of Catharine Beecher's *Treatise on Domestic Economy* (1843) in Kathryn Kish Sklar, *Catharine Beecher: A Study in American Domesticity* (New York: Norton, 1976), 156–61.

70. An instructive review of relevant studies is Linda K. Kerber's "Separate Spheres, Female Worlds, Woman's Place: The Rhetoric of Women's History," *Journal of American History* 75 (1988): 9–39.

71. Tocqueville, *Democracy in America*, 596n. On women as popular authors, see Mary Kelley, *Private Woman, Public Stage: Literary Domesticity in Nineteenth-Century America* (New York: Oxford, 1984). Tocqueville's comment is disproved by male writers, too, as any reader of Hawthorne's *Scarlet Letter* will agree.

72. Bremer, *Homes*, I, 489–90.

73. *Ibid.*, II, 103–4.

74. *Ibid.*, 555–56.

75. *Ibid.*, I, 91, 191.

76. *Ibid.*, 435, 490.

77. *Ibid.*, 189.

78. *Ibid.*, 190.

79. *Ibid.*, II, 141–42, 453–54. *Cf.* II, 104, on women glad to get away from their children. The contradiction between what mothers were supposed to feel about pregnancy, delivery, and child care and what they said to one another and to their

diaries is clarified in Sylvia Hoffert, *Private Matters: American Attitudes toward Childbearing and Infant Nurture in the Urban North, 1800–1860* (Urbana: Univ. of Illinois, 1989).

80. Bremer, *Homes*, II, 569–70.

81. *Ibid.*, 141, 454, 569, 617.

82. See *ibid.*, 616, where she remembers a conversation with her correspondent who scorned the rule of the "wrong-headed." But see also Asmundsson, "Fredrika Bremer," 103–4, for evidence that after her return from America she was strongly drawn toward Christian socialism and that she was influential in the struggle to win civil rights for Swedish women.

83. Tocqueville, *Democracy in America*, 601.

84. Bremer, *Homes*, II, 141.

Notes to Chapter Twelve

1. See Cushing Strout, *The American Image of the Old World* (New York: Harper & Row, 1963).

2. Mark Twain's *The Innocents Abroad* (1869) is the great satire on the pilgrimages of Americans to the Old World. It is easy enough, following Twain's lead, to ridicule the aspirations of Americans to cultural polish and the inappropriateness of their attempts to comprehend sights seen too briefly and not really within their ken. Twain had his own agenda, leading toward a late–nineteenth-century assault on the quest for gentility. But his points struck home.

3. Sculley Bradley in Robert E. Spiller *et al.*, *Literary History of the United States* (New York: MacMillan, 1963), 834.

4. Cooper, *Gleanings in Europe*, 2 vols. (New York: Oxford, 1928, 1930), I, 296.

5. I have discussed these writings in *Childhood, Marriage, and Reform: Henry Clarke Wright, 1797–1870* (Chicago: Univ. of Chicago, 1980), 264–80.

6. *English Traits*, in Emerson, *Selected Writings*, 676. Carlyle had already pronounced in the first of the *Latter-day Pamphlets* (1850) on the absence of greatness and originality in America. All the Americans had done was to produce "eighteen millions of the greatest *bores* ever seen in this world before." Olmsted seeks to answer Carlyle in his essay on American civilization, discussed below.

7. Olmsted, *Walks and Talks of an American Farmer in England* (Ann Arbor: Univ. of Michigan, 1967 [1852, 1859]), 41–42.

8. *English Traits*, 676–77. *Cf.* Ziff, *Literary Democracy*, 26–30.

9. R. W. B. Lewis, *The American Adam: Innocence, Tragedy, and Tradition in the Nineteenth Century* (Chicago: Univ. of Chicago, 1958); Charles L. Sanford, *The Quest for Paradise: Europe and the American Moral Imagination* (Urbana: Univ. of Illinois, 1961).

10. Wayne Franklin, *Discoverers, Explorers, Settlers: The Diligent Writers of Early America* (Chicago: Univ. of Chicago, 1979).

11. Bayard Taylor, *Eldorado; or, Adventures in the Path of Empire* (New York: George P. Putnam, 1855), 257.

12. *Ibid.*, 8.

13. Fuller, *Summer on the Lakes*, in *The Writings of Margaret Fuller*, ed. Mason Wade (New York: Viking, 1941), 50; Emerson, *English Traits*, 547.

14. *Liberator*, May 26, 1848, p. 1. See Perry, *Childhood, Marriage, and Reform*, 286–87. *Cf.* Jacob Abbott, *New England and Her Institutions* (Boston: J. Allan, 1835): "You can hardly find a dwelling in New England . . . in which some periodical print is not taken. The newspapers of the day are scattered far beyond the route of the mails, and the region of passable roads. The lonely settler will weekly emerge from his distant home in the woods, to get his newspaper" (25).

15. *The Portable Thoreau*, ed. Carl Bode (New York: Viking, 1964), 592–630.

16. An important exception is Fanny Fern's *Ruth Hall* (1855), in which a poor widow makes her way to literary fame. See *Ruth Hall and Other writings*, ed. Joyce W. Warren (New Brunswick, N.J.: Rutgers Univ., 1986). Further exceptions would appear in the 1860s and 1870s.

17. *Life and Letters of Bayard Taylor*, ed. Marie Hansen-Taylor and Horace E. Scudder (Boston: Houghton Mifflin, 1895), 98–153. He was fortunate to come to New York just as it was establishing literary preeminence over Philadelphia. Albert H. Smyth, *Bayard Taylor* (Boston: Houghton Mifflin, 1896), 61–64. But the advantages of big city over country town would have obtained elsewhere besides New York.

18. One biographer points to "the close-knit, almost incestuous nature of the literary world in Taylor's time. He knew personally nearly everyone of importance, or someone who knew the people he didn't know." Paul C. Wermuth, *Bayard Taylor* (New York: Twayne, 1977), 177. *Cf.* Bender, *New York Intellect*, 157–58. This is one of the most valuable studies of intellectual history in many years. On the many movements and coalitions in the city's intellectual life in the mid–nineteenth century, see pp. 119–205.

19. *At Home and Abroad*, second series (1862), 205, 118, as quoted in Wermuth, *Bayard Taylor*, 62, 64.

20. Josiah Royce, *California from the Conquest in 1846 to the Second Vigilance Committee in San Francisco (1856): A Study of American Character* (Boston: Houghton Mifflin, 1886), 304.

21. Fuller, *Summer*, 28, 46–47.

22. Langley Carleton Keyes, "Kirkland, Caroline Matilda Stansbury," *Notable American Women, 1607–1950: A Biographical Dictionary*, 3 vols, ed. Edward T. James *et al.* (Cambridge: Harvard, 1971). II, 337–39.

23. Kirkland, *A New Home—Who'll Follow? Glimpses of Western Life*, ed. William S. Osborne (New Haven: New College and Univ. Press, 1965), 31, 35, 221, 226–27.

24. Stilgoe, *Common Landscape of America, 1580 to 1845* (New Haven: Yale, 1982), 77. The great proslavery thinker George Fitzhugh twitted travel writers that they really could not see Southern life from the roads. Eric McKitrick, ed., *Slavery Defended: The Views of the Old South* (Englewood Cliffs, N.J.: Prentice-Hall, 1963), 40.

25. Stilgoe, *Common Landscape*, 1–29, 43–58; Beveridge, "Introduction," in Olmsted, *Papers*, II, 7.

26. Louis S. Gerteis, *Morality and Utility in American Antislavery Reform* (Chapel Hill: Univ. of North Carolina, 1987), 157–63.

27. Olmsted, *Papers*, II, 234.

28. *Ibid.*, 239.

29. *Ibid.*, 198.

30. *Ibid.*, 89, 138.

31. *Ibid.*, 278, 300. See also Beveridge, "Introduction," Olmsted, *Papers*, vol. III, *Creating Central Park, 1857–1861*, ed. Charles E. Beveridge and David Schuyler (Baltimore: Johns Hopkins, 1983), 5.

32. Olmsted, *Papers*, II, 146. Stilgoe speaks of "substitute towns": "Friends met friends on the way to isolated churches or courthouses or on the way to crossroads stores, and local residents encountered the infrequent long-distance traveler. Even in regions dotted with stores, the peddler . . . brought news and novel merchandise and attracted swarms of people in every hollow. On the better stretches of road young men held informal horse races, and friends stopped everywhere to sit under trees and conduct business. Southerners treated their roads as extensions of church, courthouse and store, seeing in them the potential for excitement that northern city dwellers found in streets" (*Common Landscape*, 71, 74).

33. Olmsted, *Papers*, II, 157, 311–12.

34. *Ibid.*, 307–9.

35. Stilgoe calls them "half-landschaft and half-wilderness" (*Common Landscape*, 22–23).

36. On the village as "fantasy contrast" allowing the emigrant to "believe in the existence of a constant reference point" back home, see Lawrence Buell, *New England Literary Culture: From Revolution through Renaissance* (Cambridge, England: Cambridge Univ., 1986), 310.

37. Bushnell, *Work and Play* (New York: Charles Scribner, 1866), 77–78.

38. *Ibid.*, 111.

39. *Ibid.*, 110.

40. *Register of Debates, 21st Cong., 1st sess.*, as quoted in Schlesinger, *Age of Jackson*, 62.

41. *The Education of Henry Adams* (Boston: Houghton Mifflin, 1930), 43–45. But there was a lurking attraction, too, to a boy's eyes, in the climate and foliage; "the want of barriers, of pavements, of forms; the looseness, the laziness; the indolent Southern drawl; the pigs in the streets; the negro babies and their mothers with bandannas; the freedom, openness, swagger, of nature and man."

42. *The Letters of John Greenleaf Whittier*, 3 vols., ed. John B. Pickard (Cambridge: Harvard, 1975), I, 355.

43. Frank Owsley, *Plain Folk of the Old South* (Baton Rouge: Louisiana State Univ., 1949) is the classic statement. For a restatement emphasizing Celtic derivations, see Grady McWhiney, *Cracker Culture: Celtic Ways in the Old South* (Tuscaloosa: Univ. of Alabama, 1988).

44. Larry E. Tise, *Proslavery: A History of the Defense of Slavery in America, 1701–1840* (Athens: Univ. of Georgia, 1987), 124–79. See also Donald G. Mathews, *Religion in the Old South* (Chicago: Univ. of Chicago, 1977), 166–67.

45. See, for example, Drew Gilpin Faust, *A Sacred Circle: The Dilemma of the Intellectual in the Old South, 1840–1860* (Philadelphia: Univ. of Pennsylvania, 1986); David F. Allmendinger, *Ruffin: Family and Reform in the Old South* (New York: Oxford, 1990), 106–25.

46. Holifield, *Gentleman Theologians*, 3–23; Clement Eaton, *The Growth of Southern Civilization, 1790–1860* (New York: Harper & Row, 1961), 247–94; Jane H. Pease and William H. Pease, "Intellectual Life in the 1830s: The Institutional Framework and the Charleston Style," *Intellectual Life in Antebellum Charleston*, ed. Michael O'Brien and David Moltke-Hansen (Knoxville: Univ. of Tennessee, 1986), 233–54.

47. "Notes on the Pioneer Condition," in Olmsted, *Papers*, vol. V, *The California Frontier, 1863–1865*, ed. Victoria Post Ranney (Baltimore: Johns Hopkins, 1990), 575–63, quotation at 706. I have also consulted the manuscript version at the Library of Congress, Manuscript Division, under the title "History of Civilization in the United States" (Olmsted Papers microfilm, rolls 41–43), a title bestowed by someone who evidently tried to prepare the manuscript for posthumous publication. Some portions are dated 1856, some 1862–1864, some after the war.

48. Olmsted, *Papers*, V, 593–612, 757–63.

49. *Ibid.*, 597.

50. *Ibid.*, 741–46. Many of the travelers, including Dickens, had written more valuable works, in Olmsted's view, when they were not reporting on America.

51. *Ibid.*, 669–79.

52. *Ibid.*, 682–700, 733–34, 751 (quotation), 754.

53. *Ibid.*, 707–20, 759.

54. *Ibid.*, 727–33.

55. *Ibid.*, 723, 728.

56. *Ibid.*, 608, 746.

57. *Ibid.*, 736–40, 742 (quotation).

58. *Ibid.*, 724–25.

59. For an illuminating discussion of the belief in "democratic excellence" shared by Olmsted and other New York professionals in the 1860s and 1870s, see Bender, *New York Intellect*, 175–76.

Notes to Chapter Thirteen

1. Gross, "Culture and Cultivation," 54–55.

2. *Collected Poems of Henry Thoreau*, ed. Carl Bode (Baltimore: Johns Hopkins, 1964), 17–19.

3. *Ibid.*, 25.

4. He went to Minnesota in May 1861 and died a year later.

5. Thoreau, *Walden*, 371.

6. *Poems*, 141.

7. *Walden*, 378.

8. See Davis, *Antebellum American Culture*, for an interpretation based on this theme.

9. *Walden*, 51, 114, 255.

10. *Ibid.*, 136.

11. *Ibid.*, 277.

12. *Ibid.*, 116, 121.

13. *Ibid.*, 286.

14. He did advocate moral and intellectual improvement, but through a program of self-discovery, closeness to nature, and experiment that readers often miss.

15. He was working on *A Week* while living at Walden Pond from 1845 to 1847. *Maine Woods* reports on journeys in 1846, 1853, and 1857; *Cape Cod*, in 1849, 1850, and 1855. Excerpts from *Walden*, *Cape Cod*, and *Maine Woods* appeared intermittently in magazines in the mid-1850s.

16. Stilgoe, *Common Landscape*, 51; Stevens, *The Collected Poems of Wallace Stevens* (New York: Vintage, 1982), 76.

17. *Walden*, 125, 203.

18. *Maine Woods*, 199.

19. *Ibid.*, 4.

20. *A Week*, 9.

21. *Maine Woods*, 362.

22. *Cape Cod*, 893.

23. *Maine Woods*, 91–92.

24. *Ibid.*, 107.

25. *Ibid.*, 201.

26. *A Week*, 138.

27. *Ibid.*, 161. The railroads had also made the locks uneconomical; they were wearing out and becoming impassable so that boating on the river would soon be at an end. Thus one form of civilization conflicted with another.

28. *Maine Woods*, 167.

29. *Ibid.*, 156.

30. *Ibid.*, 65–66.

31. *Ibid.*, 302.

32. *Ibid.*, 112, 260.

33. *Ibid.*, 32, 44.

34. *Ibid.*, 23.

35. *Ibid.*, 22.

36. *Ibid.*, 214.

37. *A Week*, 160.

38. See the fascinating article by Alan Taylor, "The Early Republic's Supernatural Economy: Treasure Seeking in the American Northeast, 1780–1830," *American Quarterly* 38 (Spring 1986): 6–34.

39. *Poems*, 17, 141, 219.

40. Michael T. Gilmore, *American Romanticism and the Marketplace* (Chicago: Univ. of Chicago, 1985), 49–50.

41. *Maine Woods*, 132.

42. *Cape Cod*, 1,039.

43. *A Week*, 288.

44. *Ibid.*, 163.

45. *Ibid.*, 163–68.

46. *Ibid.*, 45.

47. *Maine Woods*, 29.

48. *Ibid.*, 301.

49. *A Week*, 44–45.

50. *Ibid.*, 38, 51, 158, 190, 197, 260.

51. *Maine Woods*, 11.

52. *Ibid.*, 19.

53. *Ibid.*, 203–4.

54. See the stimulating essay by Nikolai Cikovsky, Jr., " 'The Ravages of the Axe': The Meaning of the Tree Stump in Nineteenth-Century American Art," *Art Bulletin* 61 (1979): 611–26.

55. *Maine Woods*, 291. *Cf.* 300.

Notes to Chapter Fourteen

1. Olmsted, *Papers*, V, 584.

2. Whittier, *Stranger in Lowell*, 116–17. For "A Yankee Zincali," see 61–74.

3. The alternate title was used in *The Boston Book, Specimens of Metropolitan Literature* (1849). For memories of similar "odd estrays," see Larcom, *New England Childhood*, 34–36, 119, 165. For brief but valuable leads to many related subjects, see Richardson Wright, *Hawkers and Walkers in Early America: Strolling Peddlers, Preachers, Lawyers, Doctors, Players, and Others, from the Beginning to the Civil War* (Philadelphia: J.B. Lippincott, 1927). It is also worth recalling Philip Lindsley's discussion of Nashville beggars in chap. 1 above, p. 14.

4. For common ground in Islamic and Christian ideas of conscience, see David Little, John Kelsay, and Abdulasiz A. Schedina, *Human Rights and the Conflict of Cultures: Western and Islamic Perspectives on Religious Liberty* (Columbia: Univ. of South Carolina, 1988). The most famous American expression of the inner dialogue over acts of charity is Thomas Jefferson's "Head and Heart" letter to Maria Cosway, Oct. 12, 1786, in *The Life and Selected Writings of Thomas Jefferson*, ed. Adrienne Koch and William Peden (New York: Modern Library, 1944), 395–407. Commentaries are more likely to discuss the view of psychology and its philosophical origins than the issue of alms giving.

5. Stephen Foster, *Their Solitary Way: The Puritan Social Ethic in the First Century of Settlement in New England* (New Haven: Yale, 1971), 124–27; Walter I. Trattner, *From Poor Law to Welfare State: A History of Social Welfare in America* (New York: Free Press, 1989), 18–21.

6. Robert F. Berkhofer, Jr., *The White Man's Indian: Images of the American Indian from Columbus to the Present* (New York: Vintage, 1979), 90. I have not found the source of the quoted lines.

Notes to Chapter Fifteen

1. The friend was Mary Peabody. Nathaniel Hawthorne, *The American Notebooks*, ed. Claude M. Simpson (Columbus: Ohio State Univ., 1972), 585, 682–98.

In the pages that follow, references to this volume appear in parentheses in the text.

2. Mary Gordon's comments on a writer's journal are apt in this instance: "they are the place where he or she is not performing, not showing off. In his or her journals, the writer is unprofessional, unbuttoned, unguarded. A writer uses a journal to try out the new step in front of the mirror. He or she can abandon constraints of narrative form and allow the luxury of verbal spontaneity." See her review of the *Journals of John Cheever*, in the *New York Times Book Review*, Oct. 6, 1991, p. 1.

3. Leo Marx, *The Machine in the Garden: Technology and the Pastoral Idea in America* (New York: Oxford, 1967), 267–68. For other interpretations, see John F. Sears, *Sacred Places: American Tourist Attractions in the Nineteenth Century* (New York: Oxford, 1989), 196–98; John F. Kasson, *Civilizing the Machine: Technology and Republican Values in America* (New York: Grossman, 1976). For another reference of this kind in the *American Notebooks*, see p. 100.

4. For similar expressions, see pp. 115, 135. Hawthorne took a dim view of the ineffectual "cultivation" taking place in America's academies and colleges.

5. On the icon of the New England village, see Buell, *New England Literary Culture*, 304–18.

6. See Cushing Strout, ed., *Hawthorne in England: Selections from* Our Old Home *and* The English Notebooks (Ithaca: Cornell, 1965). He commented on street life, fairs, and festivals in England without finding the same theatrical characters. He repeatedly mentioned one group Americans were unfamiliar with and easily fell prey to. Beggars and "peripatetic tricksters" were a well-established feature of English cities (214–17, 269). By far the most colorful characters he described, however, were the American travelers who entered the consul's office; they were stricken with illusions and fantasies, in contrast with the "stolidity" and "weight" of the English (17, 59, 174). Emerson was even more impressed by the "veracity" of the English, "who do not easily learn to make a show." With the English, he wrote, "We will not have to do with a man in a mask." *English Traits*, in Emerson, *Selected Writings*, 585.

7. *Blithedale Romance*, 232–40. For an interpretation of this work that stresses veils, masks, and the stage, see Terence Martin, *Nathaniel Hawthorne* (Boston: Twayne, 1983), 147–62.

8. *Hawthorne's Lost Notebook, 1835–1841*, ed. Barbara S. Mouffe (University Park: Pennsylvania State Univ., 1978), 12.

9. *Ibid.*, 78.

10. Important and relevant studies include Peter L. Berger, "Sociological Perspective—Society as Drama," *Invitation to Sociology: A Humanistic Perspective* (Garden City, N.Y.: Anchor, 1963), 122–50; Elizabeth Burns, *Theatricality: A Study of Convention in the Theatre and in Social Life* (New York: Harper & Row, 1972); Erving Goffman, *The Presentation of Self in Everyday Life* (Garden City, N.Y.: Anchor, 1959). A list of other discussions of roles and theatricality would be endless and would include Nietzsche, Sartre, Foucault, and all "modern" reexaminations of moral conviction. There are important suggestions in Richard Sennett, "Two on the

Aisle," *New York Review of Books*, Nov. 1, 1973, pp. 29–31, which criticizes Goffman's view as limited to "a world without time."

Notes to Chapter Sixteen

1. *American Notebooks*, 410–11, 427.

2. Tyrone Power, *Impressions of America, during the Years 1833, 1834, and 1835*, 2 vols. (London: Richard Bentley, 1836), I, 211.

3. Constance Rourke, *American Humor: A Study of the National Character* (New York: Harcourt Brace, 1959), 106.

4. Power, *Impressions*, I, 240–42. Thomas Mann has a young marquis explain: "it is nice of the English to have spread the word 'gentleman' around the world. Thanks to them, we have a designation for a man who is not a nobleman, to be sure, but deserves to be, deserves it more than many a one who is styled '*Hochgeboren*' " (*Confessions of Felix Krull, Confidence Man* [New York: Vintage, 1969], 228). This is said to a confidence man who is intrigued by "the idea of *interchangeability*" (218) and who will, in fact, exchange places with the marquis. The Americans, it might be said, carried the principle of interchangeability further, made it possible for larger numbers to adopt the manners of gentlemen and ladies, and expanded the danger of confidence tricks. Goffman uses an 1839 American guide to gentlemanly manners to illustrate his analysis of "impression management." See his *Presentation*, 50–51.

5. Augustus Longstreet, "Georgia Theatrics," *Georgia Scenes* (New York: Harper & Bros., 1851)), 9–11. The book also includes the practical joker Ned Brace; see "The Character of a Native Georgian," 32–52. Longstreet, a Methodist clergyman with literary ambitions, shortly afterward became president of Emory College and later of the universities of Mississippi and South Carolina. He wrote no more in this line, yet his book is recognized as an early instance of what came to be called Southwestern humor. *Cf.* Bernard De Voto, *Mark Twain's America* (Boston: Little, Brown, 1932), 96; Kenneth Lynn, *Mark Twain and Southwestern Humor* (Boston: Little, Brown, 1959), 66–68.

6. Most studies of "liminality" are inspired by the anthropologist Victor Turner. For illuminating applications of the concept to Jacksonian America, see Carroll Smith-Rosenberg, "Davy Crockett as Trickster: Pornography, Liminality, and Symbolic Inversion in Victorian America," *Disorderly Conduct*, 90–108; Lawrence Foster, *Religion and Sexuality: Three American Communal Experiments of the Nineteenth Century* (New York: Oxford, 1981), 8–9.

7. Buell, *New England Literary Culture*, 157–60. An important study of conflict between "civil language" and popular speech appeared when this book was nearly completed: Kenneth Cmiel, *Democratic Eloquence: The Fight over Popular Speech in Nineteenth-Century America* (New York: William Morrow, 1990).

8. See, for example, T. S. Eliot, "The Metaphysical Poets," *Selected Essays* (New York: Harcourt Brace, 1960), 247–48; Charles Monroe Coffin, *John Donne and the New Philosophy* (New York: Humanities, 1958), 6. On the "muddle" of historical discussions of "dissociation of sensibility," see Frank Kermode, *History and Value* (Oxford: Clarendon, 1988), 124, 128.

9. David D. Hall, "The World of Print and Collective Mentality in Seventeenth-Century New England," *New Directions in American Intellectual History,* ed. John Higham and Paul K. Conkin (Baltimore: Johns Hopkins, 1979), 166–80.

10. Tate, *Fathers,* 17. *Cf.* Cleanth Brooks, *The Language of the American South* (Athens: Univ. of Georgia, 1985), 16–33.

11. See Rhys Isaac, *The Transformation of Virginia, 1740–1790* (Chapel Hill: Univ. of North Carolina, 1982), esp. 323–57.

12. See, for example, Olmsted's attempt to come to terms with the speech and behavior of Alabamians who often showed contradictory features of gentlemanliness, boorishness, and violence, all "united in the same man." Olmsted took this as evidence of "a new phase and style of civilization" as well as "a remarkably frontier character." Olmsted, *Papers,* II, 207.

13. Solomon Smith, *Theatrical Management in the West and South for Thirty Years* (New York: Harper, 1868), 53–54.

14. Key works include Karl Polanyi, *The Great Transformation* (New York: Rinehart, 1944); and Alex Inkeles and David H. Smith, *Becoming Modern: Individual Change in Six Developing Countries* (Cambridge: Harvard, 1974). Influential historical studies start with C. E. Black, *The Dynamics of Modernization* (New York: Harper & Row, 1966); and include on the United States, Richard D. Brown, *Modernization: The Transformation of American Life* (New York: Hill & Wang, 1976). See also works cited below in chap. 20, n. 10.

15. Peter Berger, Brigitte Berger, and Hansfried Kellner, *The Homeless Mind: Modernization and Consciousness* (New York: Vintage, 1974), 37–38.

16. See Stanford M. Lyman and Marvin B. Scott, *The Drama of Social Reality* (New York: Oxford, 1975), for a social-scientific adoption of the idea that "reality is a drama, life is theatre, and the social world is inherently dramatic" (3). For an insightful critique, see Liam Hudson, "Living theatre," *Times Literary Supplement,* March 19, 1976, p. 312.

17. Robert Jay Lifton, "Protean Man," in *The Psychoanalytic Interpretation of History,* ed. Benjamin B. Wolmon (New York: Basic, 1971), 33–49. I do not mean to suggest that the Bergers, Lifton, and others provide a unified body of interpretation. They do not. But the images found in their writings are strikingly reminiscent of some in the antebellum era.

Notes to Chapter Seventeen

1. Power, *Impressions,* II, 123–25, 194, 255.

2. On American tourism, which gathered steam in the 1820s and 1830s, see Sears, *Sacred Places.*

3. A useful symposium on the varieties of itinerancy is *Annual Proceedings of the Dublin Seminar for New England Folklife,* vol. 9, *Itinerancy in New York and New England,* ed. Peter Benes (Boston: Boston Univ., 1986). Also of great importance for understanding the social context of itinerancy is Steven Hahn and Jonathan Prude, eds., *The Countryside in the Age of Capitalist Transformation: Essays in the Social History of Rural America* (Chapel Hill: Univ. of North Carolina, 1985).

4. *American Notes*, 222–26. Hawthorne said he would like to follow him home and see the "domestic life" behind this "outward image as shown to the world." He was the basis for "The Apple Dealer" in *Tales and Sketches*. For descriptions of other peddlers, see *American Notes*, 110, 136, 172.

5. *The Poetic Works of John Greenleaf Whittier* (Boston: Houghton Mifflin, 1892), 212. Other sources for this paragraph include: *Oxford English Dictionary*, s.v. "pedlar"; Wright, *Hawkers*; Timothy Dwight, *Travels in New England and New York*, 4 vols. (Cambridge: Harvard, 1969), II, 33–34; Slater Brown, *The Heyday of Spiritualism* (New York: Hawthorn, 1970), 100–107.

6. R. Carlyle Buley, *The Old Northwest: Pioneer Period, 1815–1840*, 2 vols. (Bloomington: Indiana Univ., 1962), I, 559–61; Margaret Coffin, *The History and Folklore of American Country Tinware, 1700–1900* (New York: Galahad, 1968), 46–48, 68–76, 98–103, 185–201; R. Malcolm Keir, "The Tin Peddler," *Journal of Political Economy* 21 (1913): 255–58; David Jaffee, "Peddlers of Progress and the Transformation of the Rural North, 1760–1860," *Journal of American History* 78 (1991): 511–35.

7. Power, *Impressions*, II, 43–44. On the Industrial Revolution as "the apotheosis of the peddler," *cf.* Ware, *Industrial Worker*, xi–xii.

8. Kirkland, *New Home*, 54–55.

9. Thomas Chandler Haliburton, *The Clockmaker: Sayings and Doings of Samuel Slick of Slickville* (Boston: Houghton Mifflin, 1871 [1837]). V. L. O. Chittick, *Thomas Chandler Haliburton (Sam Slick): A Study in Provincial Toryism* (New York: Columbia Univ., 1924), contains much information on the history and reputation of peddling.

10. Horn, *Hermitage*, 1. *Cf.* McWhiney, *Cracker Culture*, 260–61.

11. David Grimsted, ed., *Notions of the Americans, 1820–1860* (New York: George Braziller, 1970), 35–37. For a good example of an attack on "quacks" and the public credulity that sustained them, see Dr. D. McCauley's 1846 article, "Humbugiana," in Paul F. Paskoff and Daniel J. Wilson, eds., *The Cause of the South: Selections from* De Bow's Review, *1846–1867* (Baton Rouge: Louisiana State Univ., 1982), 142–47.

12. T. B. Miner, "Progress of the Age," *The Northern Farmer* (1855), as quoted in Henry Glassie, *Pattern in the Material Folk Culture of the Eastern United States* (Philadelphia: Univ. of Pennsylvania, 1968), 189–92. For the increasingly hardened stereotypes of old and new farmers, see Clarence H. Danhof, *Change in Agriculture: The Northern United States, 1820–1870* (Cambridge: Harvard, 1969), 22–24.

13. Richard M. Dorson, *American Folklore* (Chicago: Univ. of Chicago, 1959), 66; Mark Twain, *A Connecticut Yankee in King Arthur's Court* (New York: Hill & Wang, 1970), 49–50.

14. Barnes and Dumond, *Letters of Theodore Dwight Weld*, I, 15.

15. Donald Scott, *From Office to Profession: The New England Ministry, 1750–1850* (Philadelphia: Univ. of Pennsylvania, 1978).

16. Bertram Wyatt-Brown, "The Antimission Movement in the Jacksonian South: A Study in Regional Folk Culture," *Journal of Southern History* 36 (1970): 501–29. For examples of colorful anti-missionary rhetoric, see B. F. Riley, *A History*

of the Baptists in the Southern States East of the Mississippi (Philadelphia: American Baptist Publishing Society, 1898), 170.

17. Edward Eggleston, *The Circuit Rider* (Lexington: Univ. of Kentucky, 1970), 6.

18. Beriah Green in *Quarterly Anti-Slavery Magazine*, I (1835–1836), 34–67, ˙160; Perry, *Childhood, Marriage, and Reform*, 2. Some contemporaries noted the reformers' reliance on the example of the revivals. See, for example, Calvin Colton, *Abolition a Sedition* (Philadelphia: George W. Donahue, 1839), 66–70.

19. Robert Abzug, *Passionate Liberator: Theodore Dwight Weld and the Dilemma of Reform* (New York: Oxford, 1980), 25–27, 52–58, 123–63. Weld had traveled previously as a lecturer on mnemonics and a member of Weld's "holy band." On Dix, see *Notable American Women*, I, 486–89. Her father was an itinerant minister who wrote and sold his own tracts. Her life was made of journeys, first in insecurity and distress, later as a paragon of philanthropic motives.

20. Henry C. Wright, Journal (Harvard College Library), XX, 11–16 (June 20, 1835).

21. *Tales and Sketches*, 808–24.

22. Clifford S. Griffin, *Their Brothers' Keepers: Moral Stewardship in the United States, 1800–1865* (New Brunswick, N.J.: Rutgers, 1960), 90–98; John L. Myers, "The Early Antislavery Agency System in Pennsylvania, 1833–1837," *Pennsylvania History* 31 (1964): 62–86.

23. Richard P. McCormick, *The Second American Party System: Party Formation in the Jacksonian Era* (New York: Norton, 1973), 349–50. For Michel Chevalier's comparison of a procession with European religious festivals, see Watson, *Liberty and Power*, 3–4. See also Jean H. Baker, "The Ceremonies of Politics: Nineteenth-Century Rituals of National Affirmation," in *A Master's Due: Essays in Honor of David Herbert Donald*, ed. William J. Cooper *et al.* (Baton Rouge: Louisiana State Univ., 1985), 161–78.

24. David Freeman Hawke, ed., *Herndon's Lincoln* (Indianapolis: Bobbs-Merrill, 1970), 38, 109–43. According to Herndon, "a portion of the bar in every county seat, if not a majority of lawyers everywhere, were politicians" (141).

25. Finney, *Lectures on Revivals*, 11, 196, 208, 211, 214, 217–18.

. 26. Neil Harris, *Humbug: The Art of P. T. Barnum* (Boston: Little, Brown, 1973), 37–8; James H. Dormon, *Theater in the Ante Bellum South, 1815–1861* (Chapel Hill: Univ. of North Carolina, 1967), viii–x, 30–101, 173–202.

27. Joseph Leach, *Bright Particular Star: The Life and Times of Charlotte Cushman* (New Haven: Yale, 1970), 165–66, 169–74, 179, 196, 210, 218, 234; Edward Wagenknecht, *Merely Players* (Norman: Univ. of Oklahoma, 1966), 93, 107–17; J. C. Furnas, *Fanny Kemble* (New York: Dial, 1982), 340–47.

28. See, for example, Noah Ludlow, *Dramatic Life as I Found It: A Record of Personal Experiences* (St. Louis: G.I. Jones, 1880); Smith, *Theatrical Management; idem, Theatrical Journey-Work and Anecdotal Recollections of Sol. Smith, Comedian* (Philadelphia: B. Peterson, 1854); and *idem, Theatrical Apprenticeship and Anecdotal Recollections* (Philadelphia: Carey & Hart, 1846). On the "operational aesthetic," see Harris, *Humbug*, 61–89.

29. Garff B. Wilson, *A History of American Acting* (Bloomington: Indiana Univ., 1966), 25; *The Autobiography of Joseph Jefferson*, ed. Alan S. Downer (Cambridge: Harvard, 1964), 80; Smith, *Theatrical Management*, 62.

30. Scott, "Popular Lecture," 795–96; Solon J. Buck, ed., "Selections from the Journal of Lucien C. Boynton, 1835–1853," *Proceedings of American Antiquarian Society*, n.s. 43 (Oct. 1933), 329–80.

31. Pickard, *Letters*, I, 17.

32. William Seymour Tyler, *History of Amherst College during Its First Half-Century, 1821–1871* (Springfield, Mass.: C.W. Bryan, 1873), 183.

33. "Reforms," *Early Lectures*, III, 264–65. *Cf.* "Self-Reliance," in Emerson, *Selected Writings*, 162. The pattern persisted for several decades. Eggleston, for example, was a Methodist minister, Bible salesman, soap manufacturer, insurance salesman, librarian, and exhibitor of photographic transparencies in the late 1850s and 1860s before his writing career took hold. Holman Hamilton, "Introduction," *Circuit Rider*, vi–vii.

34. See William H. Goetzmann's pioneering article, "The Mountain Man as Jacksonian Man," *American Quarterly* 15 (1963): 402–15.

35. Scott, *From Office to Profession*; Michael B. Katz, *The Irony of Early School Reform: Educational Innovation in Mid–Nineteenth Century Massachusetts* (Cambridge: Harvard, 1968), 56–59; Sklar, *Catherine Beecher*, 180–82.

36. Francis Wayland, *A Memoir of the Life and Labors of the Rev. Adoniram Judson, D.D.*, 2 vols. (Boston: Phillips, Sampson, 1853), I, 22–25.

37. Joseph Tinker Buckingham, *Personal Memoirs and Recollections of Editorial Life* (New York: Arno, 1970 [1852]), 51–52.

38. Robert S. Fogarty, *Dictionary of American Communal and Utopian History* (Westport, Conn.: Greenwood, 1980), 4–5; Foster, *Religion and Sexuality*, 188–89.

39. Lawrence B. Goodheart, *Abolitionist, Actuary, Atheist: Elizur Wright and the Reform Impulse* (Kent, Ohio: Kent State Univ., 1990), 119–22.

40. Odell Shepard, *Pedlar's Progress* (Boston: Little, Brown, 1937). See also the January 1820 letter to his parents in *The Letters of A. Bronson Alcott*, ed. Richard L. Herrnstadt (Ames: Iowa State Univ., 1969), 1–2.

41. Clare Taylor, ed., *British and American Abolitionists* (Chicago: Aldine, 1974), 358; William E. Farrison, *William Wells Brown: Author and Reformer* (Chicago: Univ. of Chicago, 1969), 173–76, 296–305.

42. Hotspur, as quoted in George Fredrickson, ed., *William Lloyd Garrison* (Englewood Cliffs, N.J.: Prentice-Hall, 1968), 105.

43. *Theatrical Apprenticeship*, 7, 254. Smith was an upstate New Yorker, son of a military tract farmer from Massachusetts. He had tried farming, storekeeping, and printing. He had been connected with the Swedenborgian church in Cincinnati and knew that theatres and churches were alike part of the institutional apparatus of the next world.

44. *Ibid.*, 269–70.

45. *Ibid.*, 77–82, 268–69; Smith, *Theatrical Apprenticeship*, 15, 30, 117, 190; *idem*, *Theatrical Journey-Work*, 53, 63–66, 85, 142, 241–43. See also Daniel F. Littlefield, Jr., ed., *The Life of Okah Tubbee* (Lincoln: Univ. of Nebraska, 1988).

46. George Haven Putnam, *Memories of My Youth, 1844–1865* (New York: G.P. Putnam's, 1914), 45–46; Adam Gopnik, "Audubon's Passion," *New Yorker* (Feb. 25, 1991), 97.

47. See Betty L. Fladeland's sketch of Angelina Grimké, Russell B. Nye's of Ann Royall, and Paul S. Boyer's of Frances Wright, in *Notable American Women*, II, 97–99, III, 204–5, 680–81. The judge in the treason trial after racial violence in Christiana, Pennsylvania, charged that female "vagrant lecturers" poisoned the "moral atmosphere" of communities (as did male agitators, too). See W. U. Hensel, *The Christiana Riot and Treason Trials of 1851* (Lancaster, Pa.: New Era, 1911), 87. On criticisms of Mary Lyon's "masculine style" of traveling and raising funds for Mount Holyoke College, see Carol Ruth Berkin and Mary Beth Norton, *Women of America: A History* (Boston: Houghton Mifflin, 1979), 195–98.

48. Kelley, *Private Woman*, vii.

49. To Louisa Loring, March 1837, as quoted in Wiebe, *Opening*, 166.

50. See Scott, "Popular Lecture," and "Print and the Public Lecture System"; Carl Bode, *The American Lyceum: Town Meeting of the Mind* (New York: Oxford, 1956).

51. *Hampshire Gazette* (1852), as quoted in Scott, "Print and the Public Lecture System," 282.

52. *Tales and Sketches*, 139–55. Hawthorne returned to this idea in "Passages from a Relinquished Work" (1834), in which the narrator, dissatisfied with life under the puritanical guardianship of a village parson, recalls his encounter with the vagabonds and his plan to become "a wandering story teller" as a way of spiting the parson "who would rather have laid me in my father's tomb, than see me either a novelist or an actor; two characters which I thus hit upon a method of uniting." He runs off, travels with a religious exhorter, and enjoys success by performing his act in a theatre. The story that he tells, "Mr. Higginbotham's Catastrophe," concerns a tobacco peddler and rumors of murder heard from travelers on the road.

Notes to Chapter Eighteen

1. On the changing scope and definition of the market, see Jean-Christophe Agnew, *Worlds Apart: The Market and the Theatre in Anglo-American Thought, 1550–1750* (Cambridge, England: Cambridge Univ., 1986), 41–43. See this work generally on the interacting metaphors of market and stage.

2. Isaac, *Transformation of Virginia*; Wilentz, *Chants Democratic*.

3. See esp. Tocqueville, *Democracy in America*, 429–500.

4. I refer to such works as David F. Allmendinger, Jr., *Paupers and Scholars: The Transformation of Student Life in Nineteenth-Century New England* (New York: St. Martin's, 1975); *idem, Ruffin*; Buell, *New England Literary Culture*, 7; Kelley, *Private Woman*. The work of the scholar who did pioneer work on "the profession of authorship," William Charvat, has gained new readers.

5. Thomas L. Haskell, *The Emergence of Professional Social Science: The American Social Science Association and the Nineteenth-Century Crisis of Authority* (Urbana: Univ. of Illinois, 1977), 37, 39.

6. Henry, as quoted in Haskell, *op. cit.*, 66. On related themes, see Thomas Bender, "The Erosion of Public Culture: Cities, Discourses, and Professional Disciplines," in Thomas L. Haskell, ed., *The Authority of Experts* (Bloomington: Indiana Univ., 1984), 84–106.

7. We might notice that Haskell has also discovered in the market conditions that allowed the development of humanitarian outlooks, including those that opposed slavery in eighteenth- and nineteenth-century England and America. That is, the recognition of an extensive economic system may have weakened the view that misery and subjection were inevitable or naturally prescribed conditions, let alone that sufferers in those conditions were somehow personally to be blamed for their deficiencies. The same recognition may have compelled some individuals to see their lives as connected with those of slaves in remote lands. See Thomas L. Haskell, "Capitalism and the Origins of the Humanitarian Sensibility," *American Historical Review* 90 (1985): 339–61, 547–66; "Convention and Hegemonic Interest in the Debate over Antislavery," *ibid.* 92 (1987): 829–78. But since the image of a market and the idea of receding causality could be used to explain and justify the sad but inevitable casualties of competitive economic activity, it is hard to know what to make of these abstractions. A recession of causality may impede rather than encourage empathy, though it may oblige sensitive souls to reconsider traditional attitudes toward individual benevolence and municipal relief.

8. As I write, the poison gathers new public potency, with headline-grabbing investigations of the possibility of Zachary Taylor's assassination.

9. Roger Butterfield, "George Lippard and His Secret Brotherhood," *Pennsylvania Magazine of History and Biography* 79 (1955): 285–309; Wilentz, *Chants Democratic*, 77–87. Allan Whitmore of the University of Southern Maine, who is working on an important study of street preachers, has generously shown me some of his findings.

10. Richard Hofstadter, *The Paranoid Style in American Politics* (New York: Knopf, 1965); David B. Davis, "Some Themes of Counter-Subversion: An Analysis of Anti-Masonic, Anti-Catholic, and Anti-Mormon Literature," *Mississippi Valley Historical Review* 47 (1960): 205–24; Davis, *The Fear of Conspiracy: Images of Un-American Subversion from the Revolution to the Present* (Ithaca: Cornell Univ., 1971), 66–148.

11. Ketcham, *Presidents above Party*, 144; Michael F. Holt, *The Political Crisis of the 1850s* (New York: Norton, 1978), 12–13.

12. Davis, *The Slave Power Conspiracy and the Paranoid Style* (Baton Rouge: Louisiana State Univ., 1969), 26–27; Rogin, *Fathers and Children*, 258.

13. Basler, *Collected Works*, II, 60. For Lincoln's eulogy playing up this aspect of Taylor's character, see *ibid.*, II, 85.

14. Haskell, "Conventions and Hegemonic Interest," 853.

15. See Agnew, *Worlds Apart*, 152–88.

16. Wiebe, *Opening*, 265–90.

17. Clifford E. Clark, Jr., "The Changing Nature of Protestantism in Mid-Nineteenth Century America: Henry Ward Beecher's *Seven Lectures to Young Men*," *Journal of American History* 57 (1971): 835; Carroll Smith-Rosenberg, "Sex as Symbol in Victorian Purity: An Ethnohistorical Analysis of Jacksonian America,"

American Journal of Sociology 84, Supp. (1978): 212–47; Ronald G. Walters, *Primers for Purity: Sexual Advice to Victorian America* (Englewood Cliffs, N.J.: Prentice-Hall, 1974); Stephen Nissenbaum, *Sex, Diet, and Debility in Jacksonian America: Sylvester Graham and Health Reform* (Westport, Conn.: Greenwood, 1980); Meyer, *Instructed Conscience*. As an example of what Goffman calls "expression control," consider the virtuous Trueman's reaction when he first sees the dishonest clerk Snobson in Anna Cora Mowatt's *Fashion;* he is immediately repelled by Snobson's appearance and tells his merchant cousin that when he next hires a clerk he should "take one that carries his credentials in his face" (II, i).

18. Bertram Wyatt-Brown, *Lewis Tappan and the Evangelical War against Slavery* (Cleveland: Case Western Reserve, 1969), 17; James B. Stewart, *Holy Warriors: The Abolitionists and American Slavery* (New York: Hill and Wang, 1976), 39; David J. Rothman, *The Discovery of the Asylum: Social Order and Disorder in the New Republic* (Boston: Little, Brown, 1971), 116.

19. Arthur M. Schlesinger, *Learning How to Behave: A Historical Study of American Etiquette Books* (New York: MacMillan, 1946) 12. An illuminating study of etiquette is Karen Halttunen, *Confidence Men and Painted Women: A Study of Middle-Class Culture in America, 1830–1870* (New Haven: Yale, 1982), 153–90.

20. These terms were Nathaniel Willis's, as quoted in Schlesinger, *Learning*, 21. For a satirical look at Willis's own pretensions and coldheartedness by his sister, see Fanny Fern, "Apollo Hyacinth," *Ruth Hall*, 259–60.

21. For an account of Benjamin's address, see Buck, "Selections from Journal of Lucien C. Boynton," 371.

22. Abraham Lincoln, as quoted in Walter Hugins, ed., *The Reform Impulse, 1825–1850* (New York: Harper & Row, 1972), 205.

23. Scott, *From Office to Profession*, 64, 131–32.

24. Simms, *Wigwam and Cabin*, 160. These remarks are preface to a tale, not only of heartbreak and deceit, but also of (thwarted) slave stealing.

25. David Crockett's *Narrative* (1834) introduces the peddler Slim, for example; and in Johnson Jones Hooper's *Adventures of Captain Simon Suggs* (1845), the confidence man takes on both vote-seekers and revivalist as rivals. See Susan Kuhlmann, *Knave, Fool, and Genius: The Confidence Man as He Appears in Nineteenth-Century American Fiction* (Chapel Hill: Univ. of North Carolina, 1973), 11–32.

26. Halttunen, *Confidence Men*, 2–8.

27. Melville, *The Confidence Man: His Masquerade* (New York: Holt, Rinehart and Winston, 1964), 7, 199. *Cf.* Donald M. Scott, "Itinerant Lecturers and Lecturing in New England, 1800–1850," in Benes, *Itinerancy*, 75.

28. Rogin, *Fathers and Children*, 258.

Notes to Chapter Nineteen

1. "Man the Reformer," in Hugins, *Reform Era*, 35.

2. His language would today be called sexist; his references to men in profes-

sions cannot be changed to more inclusive, less genderized terms without distortion. According to Quentin Anderson: "Emerson could not conceive of women except as bound to the reciprocal duties imposed by motherhood and the care of the household" and thus as "incapable of self-reliance." Emory Elliott *et al.*, *Columbia Literary History of the United States* (New York: Columbia Univ., 1988), 701.

3. "The Method of Nature," in Miller, *American Transcendentalists*, 298; *Early Lectures*, II, 300.

4. Whicher, *Selections*, 271, 368, 369, 371.

5. "Fate," in *ibid.*, 351.

6. See, for example, Daniel Aaron, *Men of Good Hope: A Story of American Progressives* (New York: Oxford, 1961).

7. Stephen E. Whicher, *Freedom and Fate: An Inner Life of Ralph Waldo Emerson* (Philadelphia: Univ. of Pennsylvania, 1953), is a work of continuing importance for all students of Emerson.

8. Ralph L. Rusk, *The Life of Ralph Waldo Emerson* (New York: Columbia Univ., 1949), 89–167. For comments on the "exaggerated antisocial mood" of Emerson's early verses, see *ibid.*, 99. On his inheritance, *cf.* McAleer, *Days of Encounter*, 108; and Kenneth Lynn, *The Air-Line to Seattle: Studies in Literary and Historical Writing about America* (Chicago: Univ. of Chicago, 1983), 23–32.

9. Whicher, *Selections*, 144. For the strongest case that can be made for Emerson as a reformer, see Len Gougeon, *Virtue's Hero: Emerson, Antislavery, and Reform* (Athens: Univ. of Georgia, 1990). It is clear that Emerson's commitment to reform grew sharply in the 1850s, but Gougeon concedes that even when he saw the usefulness of "totally public lives" like William Lloyd Garrison's and Wendell Phillips's, "he continued to see such an emphasis as extremely limiting to the development of the individual" (190).

10. "Self-Reliance," in Whicher, *Selections*, 164. He did acknowledge that "poor country boys of Vermont and Connecticut formerly owed what knowledge they had to their peddling trips to the Southern States." And he supported efforts to overcome local prejudice and "know the world." See "Culture," in Atkinson, *Selected Writings*, 725. But what you took with you was essential to what you got out of traveling.

11. Whicher, *Selections*, 124. Not all was peaceful. In 1840 he noted that during all the years that he was "entertaining and entertained by so many worthy and gifted friends . . . poor Nancy Barron, the mad-woman, has been screaming herself hoarse at the Poorhouse across the brook and I still hear her whenever I open my window" (*ibid.*, 134).

12. *JMN*, I, 139–41, 150, 260, 289, 298; II, 22–24. He had been fascinated by theatrical posters from his childhood days on, and he enjoyed theatre and opera when traveling. See Edward Wagenknecht, *Ralph Waldo Emerson: Portrait of a Balanced Soul* (New York: Oxford, 1974), 69–73. Also see Sanford E. Marovitz, "Emerson's Shakespeare: From Scorn to Apotheosis," *Emerson Centenary Essays*, ed. Joel Myerson (Carbondale: Southern Illinois Univ., 1982), 122–55.

13. Whicher, *Selections*, 302; McAleer, *Days of Encounter*, 497.

14. *JMN*, III, 100; XIV, 27–28; McAleer, *Days of Encounter*, 497.

15. Kurt L. Garrett, "Palliative for Players: The Lecture on Heads," *Pennsylvania Magazine of History and Biography* 103 (1979): 166–76.

16. *JMN*, IV, 372; VII, 224, 278.

17. Mary Kupiec Cayton, "The Making of an American Prophet: Emerson, His Audiences, and the Rise of the Culture Industry in Nineteenth-Century America," *American Historical Review* 92 (1987): 597–620.

18. He did, of course, dismiss admiration and idolatry, and he was impatient with complaints about the remoteness of his lectures from "real life." Moreover, he noted that his audiences preferred him to describe his topic as literary, political, or domestic rather than call it religious. Whicher, *Selections*, 139, 171, 274.

19. On the "problem which belongs to us to solve" in "the age of calculation and criticism," see *Early Lectures*, III, 199.

20. Tocqueville, *Democracy in America*, 555. For Emerson's association of alienation with the masquerade of the cities, see Mary Kupiec Cayton, *Emerson's Emergence: Self and Society in the Transformation of New England, 1800–1845* (Chapel Hill: Univ. of North Carolina, 1989), 224. There are few studies of alienation and classic American writers, but see John Diggins, "Thoreau, Marx, and the Riddle of Alienation," *Social Research* 39 (1972): 571–98.

21. "The American Scholar," in Atkinson, *Selected Writings*, 46. *Cf.* "Address on Education," *Early Lectures*, II, 196, on the profusion of "parts," "but no whole." Regarding social roles as real and things as "absolute value," a man becomes "not their master but their slave."

22. *Early Lectures*, II, 207. See also William Charvat, "American Romanticism and the Depression of 1837," *The Profession of Authorship in America, 1800–1870*, ed. Matthew J. Bruccoli (Columbus: Ohio State Univ., 1968), 49–67.

23. *Early Lectures*, II, 160–61.

24. A related topic would be friendship, which Emerson discussed frequently (and practiced coldly) as an institution through which to avoid solitude, alienation, and mummery. See the brilliant discussion in Cayton, *Emerson's Emergence*, 201–17.

25. Whicher, *Freedom and Fate*, 58.

26. *Early Lectures*, II, 174.

27. *Ibid.*, 142, 162.

28. *JMN*, VII, 380; *Early Lectures*, II, 327.

29. *Early Lectures*, II, 140.

30. In spite of its Victorian earnestness, it bears some resemblance to Sartre on good faith.

31. "New England Reformers," in Atkinson, *Selected Writings*, on originality (451); *Early Lectures*, III, 209. *Cf.* the famous question in "Self-Reliance" (150)— "are they *my* poor?"—and *Early Lectures*, II, 107, 287, 293.

32. As so often, one can find contradictory assertions. At one point he says, "As the contemporaries of Columbus hungered to see the wild man, so undoubtedly we should have the liveliest interest in a wild man, but men in society do not interest us because they are tame." Whicher, *Selections*, 83. More typically, he speaks of a natural hierarchy in which people of insight and taste are superior to those who are "gross and thoughtless, the animal man."

33. *Early Lectures*, II, 297. Elsewhere he speaks of "this vertigo of shows and politics." Whicher, *Selections*, 262.

34. *Early Lectures*, II, 170, 226, 296–97; III, 351–54. In "Circles" and "Experience" he draws the net so tightly as to make direct experience virtually impossible. There is no permanence, no unmediated fact; only series opening into further series. See Whicher, *Selections*, 168–78, 254–74. These essays show Emerson at his most modern, and their importance in late–twentieth-century Emerson studies continues to grow. See the use of them in B. L. Packer, *Emerson's Fall: A New Interpretation of the Major Essays* (New York: Continuum, 1982).

35. *Nature*, in Atkinson, *Selected Writings*, 6, 10, 15.

36. *Early Lectures*, II, 261.

37. Whicher, *Selections*, 304.

38. "Circles," in *ibid.*, 173.

39. Wiebe, *Opening*, 273.

40. *Early Lectures*, III, 81, 242; "Self-Reliance," 154; "The Poet," in Whicher, *Selections*, 222–41.

41. Emerson, *Representative Men* (Garden City, N.Y.: Dolphin, n.d.), 249, 388 (emphasis in original); *Early Lectures*, II, 109.

42. Carlyle was probably on firmer ground in seeing modern heroes as standing above the herd and supplying objects of veneration and a respect for order in the aftermath of revolution. Carlyle, *On Heroes, Hero-Worship, and the Heroic in History* (Garden City, N.Y.: Dolphin, n.d.), 194–95.

43. I discuss the ideology of culture in *Intellectual Life in America* (Chicago: Univ. of Chicago, 1989), 263–81.

44. *Early Lectures*, II, 215. But one could find quotations where culture seems opposed to cultivation. Thus in his journal in October 1837: "Culture, in the high sense, does not consist in polishing or varnishing, but in so presenting the attractions of nature that the slumbering attributes of man may burst their iron sleep and rush, full grown, into day. Culture is not the trimming and turfing of gardens, but the showing the true harmony of the unshorn landscape with horrid thickets and bald mountains and the balance of land and sea." Whicher, *Selections*, 85.

45. *Early Lectures*, II, 233–46.

46. *Ibid.*, 234.

47. Miller, *American Transcendentalists*, 50.

48. "Culture," *Selected Writings*, 719.

49. *Ibid.*, 720, 721. On his poor ear, see McAleer, *Days of Encounter*, 556–60.

50. "Culture," 723. This is from the lecture series whose misunderstanding Cayton treats in "Making of an American Prophet, 611–14.

51. "Aristocracy," in Miller, *American Transcendentalists*, 286–307. It is interesting to compare Karen Halttunen's analysis of the sentimental goal of transparency in the 1830s and 1840s and its accommodation in the 1850s to the necessity of theatrical aspects of life. See *Confidence Men*, 157–90. While Emerson in this essay scorns "graceful manners" and "independence in trifles" and in many ways retains allegiance to the ideal of transparency, seeking a version of "that word Gentleman" that refers to "the deeps of man," he nonetheless seems to accept a cold view of "the

game of the world" and "the game of society" and to show new interest in a system of class loyalties checked by generally democratic sentiments (291, 297, 302, 307).

52. "Culture," 727, 731.

53. *Early Lectures*, II, 214, 53.

54. *Ibid.*, 265.

55. Raymond Williams, *Culture and Society, 1780–1850* (New York: Columbia Univ., 1983), 114–15; Alan Trachtenberg, "American Studies as a Cultural Program," *Ideology and Classic American Literature*, ed. Sacvan Bercovitch and Myra Jehlen (Cambridge: Cambridge Univ., 1986), 178. Examples of truncating Arnold's meaning appear almost weekly. While drafting this chapter, I saw it quoted in this way in American Airlines' advertisement of its sponsorship of performances by the Nashville Symphony Orchestra. See *Center Stage* (symphony program), Nov. 14, 1987.

56. Whicher, *Selections*, 139.

Notes to Chapter Twenty

1. *Democracy in America*, 374. This passage was called to my attention by Stanley Cavell, *Conditions Handsome and Unhandsome: The Constitution of Emersonian Perfectionism* (La Salle, Ill.: Open Court, 1990), 15. Cavell associates this description of Americans with the later "antimoralism" of John Dewey.

2. This distant association between modishness and modernity might be unsurprising in light of the sociologists' contention that identity in a modern society, where traditional hierarchy has broken down, entails a degree of role playing. Human beings have to learn the parts that society has fashioned for them. The emergence of this contention in America I have tried to treat historically in previous chapters. For a lucid account of major sociological writings, see Berger, *Invitation to Sociology*. "Role theory," he points out, "has been almost entirely an American development" (94).

3. See Raymond Williams, *Keywords: A Vocabulary of Culture and Society* (New York: Oxford, 1976), 174–75. In my first graduate course in history in 1963, Walter Simon gave me the assignment of writing an essay on how the word *modern* had changed in meaning over time. Using the *Oxford English Dictionary*, I constructed an account much like the one in this paragraph. This was well before intellectual history took what some scholars have called a "linguistic turn," and my fellow students (who were given other words) and I were more resistant to the exercise and more surprised by the results than graduate students would probably be today.

4. *Mr. Bennett and Mrs. Brown* (1924), as quoted in many places, including Irving Howe, ed., *Literary Modernism* (Greenwich, Conn.: Fawcett, 1967), 15; Malcolm Bradbury and James MacFarlane, *Modernism, 1890–1930* (Middlesex, England: Penguin, 1976), 33; Daniel Joseph Singal, "Towards a Definition of American Modernism," *American Quarterly* 39 (1987): 7; Daniel Bell, "Modernism Mummified," *ibid.* 39 (1987), 122.

5. *The End of American Innocence: A Study of the First Years of Our Own Time, 1912–1917* (Chicago: Quadrangle, 1964), vii.

6. George Cotkin, *Reluctant Modernism: American Thought and Culture, 1880–1900* (New York: Twayne, 1992), xii.

7. Peter Gay, *The Enlightenment: An Interpretation. The Rise of Modern Paganism* (New York: Knopf, 1967). For a recent statement that links modernity to similar values, see Stephen Toulmin, *Cosmopolis: The Hidden Agenda of Modernity* (New York: Free Press, 1989). In order to show how a new view of modernity contrasted with an earlier one, Lionel Trilling turned to Matthew Arnold's "On the Modern Element in Literature" (1857), which praised the reasonable judgment, critical spirit, and scientific inquiry in Periclean Athens. Arnold "seems to dismiss all temporal idea from the word [modern] and makes it signify certain timeless intellectual and civil virtues." Trilling, *Beyond Culture* (1961), as excerpted in Howe, *Literary Modernism*, 69–70.

8. David Lowenthal, "The Timeless Past: Anglo-American Historical Preconceptions," *Journal of American History* 75 (March 1989): 1,264.

9. For an intelligent, readable survey of this current, see Mark C. Taylor, "Descartes, Nietzsche and the Search for the Unsayable," *New York Times Book Review*, Feb. 1, 1987, pp. 3, 34.

10. For useful surveys and critiques of the literature on modernization, see Raymond Grew, "Modernization and Its Discontents," *American Behavioral Scientist* 21 (1977): 289–312; Raymond Grew, "More on Modernization," *Journal of Social History* 14 (1980): 179–87; and Peter N. Stearns, "Modernization and Social History: Some Suggestions, and a Muted Cheer," *Journal of Social History* 14 (1977): 189–209. See also works cited in Chapter 16, nn. 14–15. By emphasizing governmental policies and attitudinal changes, the literature on modernization sometimes avoided the issue of capitalism. In some cases it was meant as an alternative to Marxist analysis for the Third World. It was never clear whether social changes must precede economic growth or might come as a consequence of growth. A common formulation was that in America and Western Europe the social changes, as shown in the birth rate, came first; the Third World was seeking to reverse the order.

11. Edward Shorter, *The Making of the Modern Family* (New York: Basic, 1975), 13–14, 21.

12. For an interpretation of early national America as a developing country, see Seymour Martin Lipset, *The First New Nation: The United States in Historical and Comparative Perspective* (New York: Basic, 1963). Even the Civil War and Reconstruction were interpreted under the rubric of modernization—evidence of its high status in recent academic thought. See Eric Foner, "The Causes of the American Civil War: Recent Interpretations and New Directions," *Civil War History* 20 (1974): 197–214; James M. McPherson, *Ordeal by Fire: The Civil War and Reconstruction* (New York: Knopf, 1982).

13. Robert Wells, "Family Planning and Demographic Transition," *Journal of Social History* 9 (Fall 1975): 1–19. See also Richard D. Brown, "Modernization and the Modern Personality in Early America, 1600–1865: A Sketch of a Synthesis," *Journal of Interdisciplinary History* 2 (Winter 1972): 201–228. What makes these articles so useful is that they avoid a crude scheme breaking history into stages. Brown treats traditional and modern elements as coexisting.

14. See Seymour Martin Lipset, ed., *The Third Century: America as a Post-Industrial Society* (Stanford, Calif.: Hoover Institution, 1979).

15. See the shrewd comments of Robert F. Berkhofer, Jr., in "The New or the Old Social History?" *Reviews in American History* 1 (March 1973): 24–25.

16. Singal, "Towards a Definition," 7.

17. This term first arose in theology to signify tendencies in American Catholicism condemned by Rome and various "liberal" tendencies deplored by Protestant fundamentalists. See William Hutchison, *The Modernist Impulse in American Protestantism* (Cambridge: Harvard, 1976), 2–3. After 1910, all Catholic clerics were required to take an "oath against Modernism" attesting to their agreement that the existence of God can be proved; that miracles and prophecies were signs of divine revelation; that Christ founded the Church; that dogmas do not change their meanings over time; and that faith is not simply subconscious, heartfelt assent, but real intellectual acceptance of truth heard from an external source. See *New Catholic Encyclopedia*, 16 vols. (New York: McGraw-Hill, 1967), IX, 995. Sometimes "Americanism," reprobated in an 1899 encyclical, was used to refer to the idea, related to "Modernism," that the Church should modify doctrines to fit a new period of civilization. See *ibid.*, I, 443.

18. The starting point to discuss it is David A. Hollinger, "The Knower and the Artificer," *American Quarterly* 39 (Spring 1987): 37–55.

19. Read, *Art Now* (1933), quoted in Bradbury and MacFarlane, *Modernism,* 20; Trilling, "On the Modern Element in Modern Literature," in Howe, *Literary Modernism,* 60.

20. See Walter L. Adamson, "Modernism and Fascism: The Politics of Culture in Italy, 1903–1922," *American Historical Review* 95 (April 1990): 365–66.

21. Spender, *Struggle of the Modern* (1963), as excerpted in Howe, *Literary Modernism,* 49.

22. Trilling, "Our Hawthorne," *Hawthorne Centenary Essays*, ed. Roy Harvey Pearce (Columbus: Ohio State Univ., 1964), 437. On modernism as response to modernization, see Singal, "Towards a Definition," 7–8.

23. Bradbury, "The Nonhomemade World: European and American Modernism," *American Quarterly* 39 (1987): 36.

24. Singal, "Towards a Definition," 23.

25. *Complete Poetry and Collected Prose*, ed. Justin Kaplan (New York: Library of America, 1982), 21.

26. "How Writing Is Written" (1935), as quoted in *Gertrude Stein's America*, ed. Gilbert A. Harrison (Washington: Robert B. Luce, 1965), 93.

27. Miller, *American Transcendentalists*, 217.

28. *A Homemade World: The American Modernist Writers* (New York: Knopf, 1975), 83–84, 213–19.

29. *The Philosophy of Nietzsche* (New York: Modern Library, 1954), 908, 924.

30. Bloom, *The Closing of the American Mind: How Higher Education Has Failed Democracy and Impoverished the Souls of Today's Students* (New York: Simon & Schuster, 1987), 51, 67. Note that Bloom's teacher Leo Strauss coined the term "the modernity project" used by Bloom and others to describe, with disapproval,

most of philosophy and social thought of recent centuries. The best historical critique of Bloom's best-seller is Fred Matthews, "The Attack on 'Historicism': Allan Bloom's Indictment of Contemporary American Historical Scholarship," *American Historical Review* 95 (April 1990): 429–47.

31. *After Virtue: A Study in Moral Theory*, 2nd ed. (Notre Dame, Ind.: Notre Dame Univ., 1984), 114, 204, 227. It should be noted that the statement of the relationship between philosophy and social history (p. 36) is extremely elusive in terms of chronological or other priority.

32. *Ibid.*, 263. Note, as evidence of the conflicting definitions of *modern*, that some aspects of this indictment of bureaucratic institutions and praise of community would place MacIntyre among the modernists as defined by Trilling or Spender.

33. *Ibid.*, 117–18. One problem in MacIntyre's argument, as I understand it, is that he seeks in the premodern or, as he sometimes calls it, "the classical tradition" of morality, a method for removing moral assertions from their contemporary status as opinions or wishes and for giving them the status they once held under reason and revelation of being either "true or false." This was the status that early modern thinkers cast away, and hence came all our woe. (*Ibid.*, 52–53) Though he asserts that all philosophies of morality are related to either existing or ideal social conditions, he plainly has no use for the relativism of modern social science, which explains utterances in terms of their speakers' frames of reference, or of modern popular thought, with its easy talk of individual values. He is a philosopher with unusual respect for history. He recognizes that the Aristotelian tradition was "always in conflict with other standpoints." (*Ibid.*, 118) He is interested in traditions, in the telling of stories to pass on tradition, and in the well-established roles that defined heroism and virtue in traditional societies. It is hard to see how true-or-false statements could be made without reference to particular social circumstances (as he seems to accept in a postscript, *ibid.*, 268), how the travails of modern thought, however lamentable, can be liberated from the consequences of industrialization and other aspects of modern economic and social history, and how premodern conceptions and practices of virtue could be restored in nontraditional societies where roles are less fixed. The title of his next book may bring some of these problems concerning relativism to the fore: Alasdair MacIntyre, *Whose Justice? Which Rationality?* (Notre Dame: Notre Dame Univ., 1988). For a discussion similar to mine, see Thomas L. Haskell, "The Curious Persistence of Rights Talk in the 'Age of Interpretation,' " *Journal of American History* 74 (December 1987): 994–1,002.

34. During a year I lived in England, 1988–1989, one national newspaper, the *Independent*, featured for several months weekly columns starting with an excerpt from *After Virtue*, giving MacIntyre's description of the qualities of the post-Enlightenment individual, and with replies, criticism, and reflection from different quarters of religious thought.

35. Robert N. Bellah *et al.*, *Habits of the Heart: Individualism and Commitment in American Life* (New York: Harper & Row, 1986), 50, 143.

36. Marx and Engels, *Basic Writings*, 10; Marshall Berman, *All That Is Solid Melts Into Air: The Experience of Modernity* (New York: Simon & Schuster, 1981).

37. Christopher Lasch, "The Obsolescence of Left and Right," *New Oxford Review* (April 1989), 6, 11.

38. George Cotkin, *William James, Public Philosopher* (Baltimore: Johns Hopkins, 1990), 1, 88–91. His paper, "Modernity and Moralism: The Case of William James," given at the Canadian American Studies Association meeting in Montreal, Nov. 1987, made his engagement with pushing back the origins of "modernity" even clearer.

39. Eugen Weber, review of Paul Johnson, *The Birth of the Modern: World Society, 1815–1830*, in *New York Times Book Review*, June 23, 1991, p. 3.

40. Cotkin, *Reluctant Modernism*. For a brilliant study of the breakup of cultural continuities, see Carl E. Schorske, *Fin-de-Siècle Vienna: Politics and Culture* (New York: Knopf, 1980).

41. *Homemade World*, 121.

42. For a provocative discussion of this theme, see James Hoopes, *Consciousness in New England: From Puritanism and Ideas to Psychoanalysis and Semiotic* (Baltimore: Johns Hopkins, 1989).

43. This metaphor has a famous expression in William Graham Sumner's "The Absurd Effort to Make the World Over" (1894), as well as in important works of pragmatism and progressivism by William James, Walter Lippmann, and others.

Notes to Chapter Twenty-One

1. Tocqueville, *Democracy*, 13; Emerson, "Method of Nature," in Miller, *American Transcendentalists*, 51.

2. Gilbert Hobbs Barnes, *The Anti-Slavery Impulse, 1830–1844* (New York: Harcourt Brace, 1964). Barnes wrote to a friend, as William G. McLoughlin revealed in introducing a 1964 reissue of the book, of his intention to disprove the opinion that "no revival of religion had or could produce a social movement of intrinsic importance" (xxv).

3. Wright was born in 1797 in Sharon, Connecticut, and his family moved to Hartwick, New York, in the "Cooper Country" in 1801. Brought up on a farm, he was an apprentice and journeyman hatmaker before enrolling at Andover Seminary in 1819. He was ordained a minister in 1823 and served a parish in West Newbury, Massachusetts, from 1826 to 1833. During this time he married a wealthy Newburyport widow, and after she moved to Philadelphia in 1837 he gave that city as his address for the rest of his life. But he was almost always on the road. Determined to become a reformer, he found employment with Amherst College, the American Home Missionary Society, the American Sunday School Union, the American Peace Society, and a consortium of Boston churches, before signing on as an agent of the American Anti-Slavery Society in 1836. As an abolitionist, he was a Garrisonian; that is, he was a close associate of the controversial leader William Lloyd Garrison and promoted the view that antislavery principles called for other radical stands, including woman's rights and pacifism. In 1838, he became a founding member and traveling agent of the New England Non-Resistance Society. He spent much of the 1840s in Great Britain, where he wrote and lectured on pacifism and antislavery. For

the rest of his life he was a freelance author and lecturer on these subjects as well as marriage, child rearing, the Bible, health, and spiritualism. His dispatches from the field appeared almost weekly in Garrison's newspaper, *The Liberator.* During the Civil War years he spoke throughout the Midwest in support of Abraham Lincoln and the war against slavery. He died in 1870. There is a perceptive sketch of Wright in Peter Walker's *Moral Choices: Memory, Desire, and Imagination in American Abolitionism* (Baton Rouge: Louisiana State Univ., 1978). My full-length study of his life is entitled *Childhood, Marriage, and Reform.* In quoting him here, I have eliminated almost all of his excessive underlinings.

4. The chief sources for this discussion of Andover are Leonard Woods, *History of the Andover Theological Seminary* (Boston: James R. Osgood, 1885), 173–78; and *A Memorial of the Semi-Centennial Celebration of the Founding of the Theological Seminary at Andover* (Andover: Warren F. Draper, 1859), 169–78. To place Andover in broader contexts of American cultural history, see Bruce Kuklick, *Churchmen and Philosophers from Jonathan Edwards to John Dewey* (New Haven: Yale, 1985), 85–215.

5. Wright, Notes on Scriptural and Theological Studies, (Boston Public Library), Jan. 1, 1820, p. 37.

6. Wright, Miscellaneous Writings on Theology and Education (Harvard College Library), no. 6.

7. On these developments, see the valuable works of Donald M. Scott: *From Office to Profession;* "The Popular Lecture"; and "Print and the Public Lecture System." See also Cayton, "Making of an American Prophet," 600.

8. See, *e.g., Infidelity and Benevolence Societies: A Discussion between the Rev. William Watson, and the Editor of the Waterbury American* (Waterbury, Conn.: E.B. Cooke, 1848).

9. Wright, Journal (Harvard College Library), XIX, 7–15 (June 10, 1835). For a characterization of Blagden as a "proslavery clergyman" (which may distort the complex issues separating him from Wright), see Tise, *Proslavery,* 363.

10. Wright, Journal (Boston Public Library), XVII, 85–86 (May 16, 1835).

11. *Liberator,* Feb. 2, 1844, p. 4.

12. *Liberator,* May 8, 1846, p. 3.

13. For Wright's notes at the convention, see his journal (Harvard College Library), XXXII, 142–397 (Nov. 15–30, 1836). For another report of Weld's speech, see Angelina Grimké, Notebook kept at Agents Convention, Angelina Grimké to Jane Smith, Nov. _____, 1836, and Nov. 19, 1836, all in the Weld Papers (William L. Clements Library, University of Michigan). There is strong resemblance between these reports and Theodore Dwight Weld, *The Bible against Slavery; or, An Inquiry into the Genius of the Mosaic System, and the Teachings of the Old Testament on the Subject of Human Rights* (Detroit: Negro History Press, 1970 [1837]), 14–19.

14. Journal (Harvard College Library), XXXII, 196.

15. *Ibid.,* 197.

16. *Ibid.,* 213.

17. Orlando Patterson, *Slavery and Social Death: A Comparative Study* (Cam-

bridge: Harvard, 1982); Davis, *The Problem of Slavery in Western Culture* (Ithaca: Cornell, 1966), 62. Angelina Grimké (see note 13 above) praised Weld's remarks as revealing "the philosophy of slavery."

18. Wright, Journal (Harvard College Library), XXXII, 215.

19. *Ibid.*, 220.

20. Perry Miller and Thomas Johnson, eds., *The Puritans: A Sourcebook of Their Writings*, 2 vols. (New York: Harper Torchbooks, 1963), I, 205–7. *Cf.* David Brion Davis, *The Problem of Slaveryr in the Age of Revolution, 1770–1823* (Ithaca: Cornell Univ., 1975), 266.

21. Wright, *The Living Present and the Dead Past; or, God Made Manifest and Useful in Living Men and Women as He Was in Jesus* (Boston: Bela Marsh, 1865), 95–99; "Mine and Thine, in the Realm of Thought," 4 vols. (Boston Public Library).

22. Wright, *Anthropology; or the Science of Man: In Its Bearings on War and Slavery, and on Arguments from the Bible, Marriage, Death, Retribution, Atonement and Government, In Support of These and Other Social Wrongs* (Boston: Bela Marsh, 1850).

23. Emerson, "Historic Notes," in Miller, *Transcendentalists*, 496. For an analysis setting Freud in the context of the Victorian middle classes, see Peter Gay, *The Bourgeois Experience*, vol. I, *Education of the Senses* (New York: Oxford, 1984).

24. Wright, *A Kiss for a Blow; or, A Collection of Stories for Children Showing Them How to Prevent Quarrelling* (Boston: Bela Marsh, 1842); *Human Life: Illustrated in My Individual Experience as a Child, a Youth, and a Man* (Boston: Bela Marsh, 1849).

25. Excerpts from his autobiography are put to such folkloric use in Louis C. Jones, ed., *Growing Up in the Cooper Country: Boyhood Recollections of the New York Frontier* (Syracuse: Syracuse Univ., 1965), 93–187.

26. Schorske, "Politics and Patricide in Freud's *Interpretation of Dreams*," *Fin-de-Siècle Vienna*, 181–207.

27. See Janet Malcolm, *In the Freud Archives* (New York: Knopf, 1984).

28. I refer to the attack on "narcissism," "psychobabble," and indeed "modernity" itself that has come from so many quarters in recent years. See Christopher Lasch, *The Culture of Narcissism: American Life in an Age of Diminishing Expectations* (New York: Warner, 1979); Bellah *et al.*, *Habits of the Heart*; Bloom, *Closing of the American Mind*.

29. In literary studies the transition from Federalism to Romanticism is a well-defined subject. For an excellent recent study, see Buell, *New England Literary Culture*, 84–102. Historical studies would benefit from closer attention to literary scholarship on this subject.

30. Wright, *Human Life*, 116–18.

31. Richard Sennett, *The Fall of Public Man* (New York: Knopf, 1977); Richard John Neuhaus, *The Naked Public Square: Religion and Democracy in America* (Grand Rapids, Mich.: Eerdmans, 1984); Ann Douglas, *The Feminization of American Culture* (New York: Knopf, 1977). For important challenges to Douglas's argument, see Kelley, *Private Woman*.

32. *Liberator*, Dec. 19, 1835, p. 2. "I am a *Negro*," he declared in 1861. Wright

to Gerrit Smith, Jan. 15, 1861, Gerrit Smith Papers (George Arents Research Library, Syracuse University).

33. *The Ballot: What Does It Mean? Who Shall Use It?* (n.p., n.d. [1865]).

34. *Liberator*, July 14, 1865, p. 3. Similar views may be found throughout the writings of the period, as in Emerson's famous distinction between "movement" and "establishment." The same terms were brandished in France after the failed revolution of 1848. See Seigel, *Bohemian Paris*, 7–8.

35. *The Errors of the Bible, Demonstrated by the Truths of Nature; or Man's Only Infallible Rule of Faith and Practice* (Boston: Bela Marsh, 1857), 12–13.

36. See Lawrence Friedman, *Gregarious Saints: Self and Community in American Abolitionism, 1830–1870* (Cambridge, England: Cambridge Univ., 1982); Lewis Perry, " 'We Have Had Conversation in the World': The Abolitionists and Spontaneity," *Canadian Review of American Studies* 6 (1975): 3–26. For similarities in other movements, even proslavery, *cf.* Faust, *Sacred Circle*; Allmendinger, *Ruffin*; Bertram Wyatt-Brown, "Proslavery and Antislavery Intellectuals: Class Concepts and Polemical Struggle," in Lewis Perry and Michael Fellman, eds., *Antislavery Reconsidered: New Perspectives on the Abolitionists* (Baton Rouge: Louisiana State Univ., 1979), 308–36; Wyatt-Brown, "Modernizing Southern Slavery: The Proslavery Argument Revisited," *Region, Race, and Reconstruction: Essays in Honor of C. Vann Woodward*, ed. J. Morgan Kousser and James M. McPherson (New York: Oxford, 1982), 27–49.

Notes to Chapter Twenty-Two

1. He had in fact passed Harvard's undergraduate entrance examinations and, without attending classes, passed all other requirements for the A.B., though his inability to pay fees kept him from the degree.

2. John Weiss, *Life and Correspondence of Theodore Parker*, 2 vols. (New York: Appleton, 1864), I 85; II, 455.

3. I use the version of *Theodore Parker's Experience as a Minister* printed as an appendix in Weiss, *Life*, II, 447–513, quotation at p. 455. Cited hereafter as *Experience*.

4. Weiss, *Life*, II, 68.

5. *Ibid.*, 100–101. Just when violence was justified in a democracy was an issue that always vexed him, as Jeffrey Rossbach shows in *Ambivalent Conspirators: John Brown, The Secret Six, and a Theory of Slave Violence* (Philadelphia: Univ. of Pennsylvania, 1982).

6. Parker to S. J. May, Sept. 25, 1852, as quoted in Michael Fellman, "Theodore Parker and the Abolitionist Role in the 1850s," *Journal of American History* 61 (Dec. 1974): 670.

7. Aaron, *Men of Good Hope*, 22.

8. Henry Steele Commager, *Theodore Parker, Yankee Crusader* (Boston: Beacon, 1960), vii, 281. The phrase is from Parker's gravestone.

9. Weiss, *Life*, I, vii, viii, 178; II, 73. Weiss was an ardent disciple chosen by Parker's widow to compile his memoirs.

10. *Ibid.*, I, 11; II, 234–35.

11. *Ibid.*, II, 72.

12. *Experience*, II, 451.

13. Weiss, *Life*, I, 89 (the phrase about itinerancy is Weiss's); I, 304–5; II, 246–48.

14. *Ibid.*, I, 42.

15. *Ibid.*, 297. See, for example, the mimicry of Harvard faculty at *ibid.*, II, 336–37.

16. *Ibid.*, I, 45, 143, 273. See also I, 116, 174, 176, 182. *Cf.* William R. Hutchison, *The Transcendentalist Ministers: Church Reform in the New England Renaissance* (New Haven: Yale, 1959), 109, 116–17.

17. Weiss, *Life*, I, 50.

18. *The Previous Question between Mr. Andrews Norton and His Alumni, Moved and Handled in a Letter to all Those Gentlemen* (Boston: Weeks, Jordan, 1840).

19. Weiss, *Life*, I, 300; II, 43–44.

20. *Experience*, II, 507–8.

21. Weiss, *Life*, II, 300.

22. *Ibid.*, 13.

23. *Experience*, II, 505.

24. *Ibid.*, 508.

25. For quotations, see Fellman, "Theodore Parker," 676–81. On Parker's "romantic racialism," see Rossbach, *Ambivalent Conspirators*, 148–49.

26. See Fellmen, "Theodore Parker," 672, 677, 683–84; Weiss, *Life*, II, 381, 399.

27. "The Material Condition of the People of Massachusetts," in *The Collected Works of Theodore Parker*, 12 vols., ed. Frances Power Cobbe (London: Trubner, 1863–1865), VIII, 158–98, quotations at 161, 178, 191.

28. See, for example, "The Present Crisis in American Affairs," May 1856, in Cobbe, *Works*, VI, 261–65. See also "An Address Delivered before the New York City Anti-Slavery Society," May 1854, *ibid.*, 161; "Some Thoughts on the Progress of America," May 1854, *ibid.*, 12.

29. "Material Condition," 197. Other essays illustrating the antislavery jeremiad are collected in Cobbe, *Works*, V–VI. No Catholic paper opposed slavery, he maintained; Irish immigrants voted for proslavery Democrats, and the rulers of the Church inevitably befriended despotism. See "The Dangers Which Threaten the Rights of Man in America," July 1854, in Cobbe, *Works*, V, 127–29.

30. "An Address on the Condition of America," May 1854, in Cobbe, *Works*, V, 328.

31. *Experience*, II, 481–82, 457–58, 461.

32. *Ibid.*, 457–61.

33. *Ibid.*, 475, 503; Aaron, *Men of Good Hope*, 35.

34. *Experience*, II, 503.

35. Weiss, *Life*, I, 17–21.

36. *Ibid.*, 35, 40.

37. *Ibid.*, 22.

38. *Ibid.*, 23, 25–26, 29, 30–31, 34, 40–41.

39. For a famous account that retrieved these integenerational issues, see Miller, *Transcendentalists*.

40. Fellman, "Theodore Parker," 674–75.

41. *Experience*, II, 471, 491. See also Weiss, *Life*, I, 290–91, for his delight in women's looks and a memory of repressed attraction in childhood. See also *ibid*., I, 347, 422; II, 23–25, 265, 284, 333, 418, 429. He exemplified what Peter Gay calls "the tender passion," the enclosure of lustful appetite within the sentiment of marriage. *Cf. ibid*., I, 386–88; Gay, *Bourgeois Experience*, vol. II, *The Tender Passion* (New York: Oxford, 1986). Perhaps his view of the limitations of women's bodies does make him a precursor of Freud.

42. See his disparagement of Margaret Fuller's "twaddle" about the "absence of art" in the United States. Writing from Rome, he boasted of our "cattle-shows, and mechanics' fairs, and ploughs and harrows, and saw-mills; sowing machines, and reaping machines, thrashing machines, planing machines, etc." He doubted there was a single sawmill in all the Papal States. "When a nation runs after beauty to the neglect of use—alas! for that people." Weiss, *Life*, II, 377.

43. *Experience*, II, 475–78, 491; Weiss, *Life*, I, 52.

44. See, for example, Cobbe, *Works*, IV, 166, 170, 199, 205, 273, 276. It is not clear what sources Aaron relies on in saying that Parker agreed with Emerson that "the Whigs had the best men, the Democrats the best principles," and that he would have joined the Democrats if they had "weeded out" some elements from their ranks. See his *Men of Good Hope*, 33.

45. *Experience*, II, 492. Henry Adams later offered a similar conclusion about democracy's heroes. The United States had "scores of supposed leaders, whose only merit was their faculty of reflecting a popular trait" (*History*, 1,334). I suspect, though I cannot prove, the influence of Tocqueville on both Parker and Adams here and elsewhere.

46. Adams, *History*, 1,443–44. For a recent account of revivalism as part of a "revolution in choices," see Wiebe, *Opening*, 157–61. See also Miller, *Life of the Mind*, 3–95.

47. *Experience*, II, 452.

48. Cobbe, *Works*, IV, 89.

49. I intend this as a composite view evident in many recent works, though no single work may subscribe to all these points. The view was an important corrective to earlier and often exaggerated depictions of an "era of reform." Among the earliest works to emphasize repressive aspects of the era were Joseph R. Gusfield, *Symbolic Crusade: Status Politics and the American Temperance Movement* (Urbana: Univ. of Illinois, 1963); Rothman, *Discovery of the Asylum*; and Lawrence J. Friedman, *Inventors of the Promised Land* (New York: Knopf, 1975). Many of the strongest arguments for Jacksonian-era elitism and inequality are brought together in Edward Pessen, *Jacksonian America*. A study that emphasizes repression is Ronald T. Takaki, *Iron Cages: Race and Culture in Nineteenth-Century America* (New York: Knopf, 1979). For a critique of all this: James B. Stewart, "Young Turks and Old Turkeys: Abolitionists, Historians, and the Aging Processes," *Reviews in American History* XI (1983): 231–32.

50. *Experience*, II, 461.

51. Paul E. Johnson, *A Shopkeeper's Millennium: Society and Revivals in Rochester, New York, 1815–1837* (New York: Hill and Wang, 1978), 116–35, is the clearest statement. There are many examples and helpful analysis of the drawing of boundaries in Davis, *Antebellum American Culture*.

52. Perspicuous scholarship in women's history has already rejected the view of the colonial period as a golden age. See Mary Beth Norton, *Liberty's Daughters: The Revolutionary Experience of American Women* (Boston: Little, Brown, 1980), xiv.

53. For influential works recognizing the neglected role of revivalism in reform, see Barnes, *Anti-Slavery Impulse*; and Timothy L. Smith, *Revivalism and Social Reform: American Protestantism on the Eve of the Civil War* (Baltimore: Johns Hopkins, 1980). The more general connections between evangelicalism and progressive culture await their historian. On the grotesque calls for Parker's affliction, see Weiss, *Life*, II, 250.

54. "A False and True Revival of Religion," April 1854, and "The Revival of Religion Which We Need," April 1854, in Cobbe, *Works*, III, 211–56.

55. James, *Pragmatism*, ed. Bruce Kuklick (Indianapolis: Hackett, 1981), 31.

56. "Strauss's Life of Jesus," 1840, Cobbe, *Works*, IX, 66–67. He made a similar point about Emerson, whom he generally admired as the most advanced and useful thinker of the age, but who went too far in remarks about divinity in man. See Weiss, *Life*, I, 114. As I drafted this chapter, the Bishop of Durham stirred up controversy in the Church of England by taking a similar view of the Ascension: "There must be some historical truth behind it, but I think it's obviously a built-up story." *Independent* (London), May 1, 1989, p. 3.

57. *Experience*, II, 453.

58. See *Discourse of Religion*, in Cobbe, *Works*, I, esp. 1–23, on his epistemology. See also the excellent commentary on his inconsistencies in Hutchison, *Transcendentalist Ministers*, 102–4.

59. *Experience*, II, 498.

60. *Discourse*, in Cobbe, *Works*, I, 248.

61. *Ibid.*, I, v, 1, 14, 27–29.

62. Weiss, *Life*, II, 48–66.

63. See William Goodell in *Principia*, Dec. 3, 1859, p. 1; July 1, 1860, pp. 260–61. *Cf.* Weiss, *Life*, I, 79–80.

64. *Discourse*, in Cobbe, *Works*, I, quotations at 165, 192, 198, 211–12.

65. *The Transient and Permanent*, in Cobbe, *Works*, VIII, 2, 18–19, 24.

66. *Ibid.*, 1–2, 4–5.

67. *Ibid.*, 4, 9.

68. *Ibid.*, 6–7.

69. *Ibid.*, 17.

70. Thoreau, *A Week*, 50, 55, 57.

Notes to Epilogue

1. See above, p. 5.

2. See above, pp. 81, 101.

3. See above, p. 150.

4. See above, pp. 186–87.

5. See "Passages from a Relinquished Work," *Tales and Sketches*, 139–55.

6. Elizabeth Steele Wright, Diary, II, Feb. 2, 1849; March 23, 1849 (Library of Congress).

7. J. B. Sanderson, May 1845, in Ripley *et al.*, *Black Abolitionist Papers*, III, 464.

8. See above, p. 215.

9. In reading A. S. Byatt's clever novel *Possession* (London: Vintage, 1991), in which researchers piece together evidence of a love affair, death, and tragedy, in the Victorian literary world, I was reminded of my own attempts, in *Childhood, Marriage, and Reform,* to uncover the details of Henry Wright's relationships with three women—an Irish Quaker, an Ohio abolitionist, and a Massachusetts physician. In fiction, Byatt can go backward in time to reveal what researchers in the present may never find out.

Index